CW01103018

ALLIED DUNBAR

INVESTMENT AND SAVINGS GUIDE 1990–91

ALLIED DUNBAR

INVESTMENT
AND
SAVINGS GUIDE
1990–91

General Editor

Harry Littlefair, Investment Consultant and
Director of Persimmon plc

LONGMAN

© Allied Dunbar Financial Services Limited 1990

ISBN 0 85121 6420

Published by

Longman Law, Tax and Finance
Longman Group UK Limited
21–27 Lamb's Conduit Street, London WC1N 3NJ

Associated Offices

Australia, Hong Kong, Malaysia, Singapore, USA

All rights reserved. No part of this publication may be reproduced, stored in a retrieval system, or transmitted, in any form or by any means, electronic, mechanical, photocopying, recording, or otherwise, without either the prior written permission of the publishers, or a licence permitting restricted copying issued by the Copyright Licensing Agency Ltd, 33–34 Alfred Place, London WC1E 7DP.

No responsibility for loss occasioned to any person acting or refraining from action as a result of the material in this publication can be accepted by the author or publishers.

The views and opinions of Allied Dunbar may not necessarily coincide with some of the views and opinions expressed in this book which are solely those of the author and no endorsement of them by Allied Dunbar should be inferred.

A CIP catalogue record for this book is available from the British Library.

Printed and bound by Biddles of Guildford Ltd, Guildford, Surrey

Preface

The *Allied Dunbar Investment and Savings Guide* is now in its eleventh year of publication. This year the word 'Savings' has been added to the title to reflect more fully the book's contents. A new chapter (3) on the Financial Services Act 1986 has been added to help stress the importance of investor protection. A further new chapter (6) has been included to give prominence to the growing number of tax privileged investments which have become available in recent years.

The subjects covered in the first decade of this Guide have been presented to the reader in a precise and logical way with property being split into three chapters with separate chapters for investment trusts and unit trusts. Other chapters have also been split.

It is important to note that Scottish law varies from English law on many subjects, but in most aspects of tax, trusts and domicile, the two systems coincide.

The law is stated as at 31 March 1990 but the 1990 Finance Act has been included.

My grateful thanks are due to my predecessor as general editor, Christopher Robinson, whose work over several years has led to the Guide's popularity. My thanks are due also to the growing list of authors for their hard work and discipline, and to my friends Norman Railton and Graham Hadley for their valued assistance.

Harry Littlefair
August 1990

Contributors

David Ballance, MA (Oxon), is with Allied Dunbar Asset Management plc working as an Investment Manager specialising in UK equities.

Robert Brown is a Director of CS Investment Management Limited, a specialist UK-based investment management company which is part of the Union Bank of Switzerland Group. He is a former partner of Phillips & Drew, Vice President of Union Bank of Switzerland and has been involved in private client investments for 18 years.

Andrew Bull, ARICS, is a Partner at Jones Lang Wootton, the world's largest independent property consultants. He is a committee member in the fund management department, one of JLW's specialist activities providing investment and management services for clients' property portfolios.

Jeremy Burnett Rae, MA (Oxon), Barrister, is Investment Secretary for Allied Dunbar Asset Management plc which manages over £8,000,000,000 in international investments on behalf of unitholders.

Tony Foreman and **Andrew Grant** are with Pannell Kerr Forster, an international firm of Chartered Accountants specialising in large family companies and privately owned businesses; in addition, PKF owns a financial services company. The authors provide tax and financial planning advice to these firms and their proprietors.

David S Fuller is Chairman of Chart Analysis Ltd and Editor of *Fuller Money*. Chart Analysis is an independent research company providing advisory services and five chart libraries covering world stockmarkets, interest rates, bonds, currencies and commodities. The company also hosts the Chart Seminar at a number of international venues each year.

Peter Howe, LLB, Barrister, is a Divisional Director in the legal department of Allied Dunbar Assurance plc. The legal department provides complete legal and technical service to companies in the Allied Dunbar Group. Financial Services legislation is his principal area of specialisation.

Vince Jerrard, LLB, ACII, Solicitor, is also a Divisional Director in the legal department of Allied Dunbar Assurance plc. Mr Jerrard is head of the department's product development group and has contributed chapters to other Allied Dunbar publications, including the *Tax Guide*, *Capital Taxes Guide* and the *Business Law and Tax Guide*.

Harry Littlefair was, up to his retirement from full-time work in 1988, Vice Chairman of Allied Dunbar Unit Trusts plc and Allied Dunbar Asset Management plc having previously been Managing Director of both. During this time he saw periods of service on the Take-Over Panel, Pro-NED, and the Executive Committee of the Unit Trust Association. Today he is a member of the Financial Services Tribunal, an Investment Consultant to Allied Dunbar, an advisor to two pension funds, and a Director of Persimmon plc, a leading house builder.

John Myers and **Valerie Bennett** are from Solon Consultants, a specialised research firm that focuses on property and alternative investments, linking the use of computer databases with desk records and field interviews. John Myers is also a visiting professor at Strathclyde Business School and he has been a contributor to the *Allied Dunbar Investment and Savings Guide* since it was first published in 1980.

Catherine Paice, MA (Cantab), is a freelance journalist specialising in agricultural land tenure and property.

John W Shock, MA (Cantab), FCA of the Middle Temple and Gray's Inn, Barrister, is the author of *Capital Allowances* published by Longman and capital allowance editor of *British Tax Encyclopedia*.

John Smithard, a member of The Stock Exchange, is with Greenwell Montagu Stockbrokers, which specialises in private client stockbroking.

Contents

		Page
Preface		v
Contributors		vi

1 Introduction 1
1.1	Annual publication	1
1.2	The investment adviser	2
1.3	Types of investor	3
1.4	Ways of arranging and holding investments	4
1.5	The nature of an investment	5
1.6	Investment policy—general principles and special factors	7
1.6.1	Diversification	7
1.6.2	Balance	7
1.6.3	Advice of specialists	8
1.6.4	Taxation	8
1.6.5	Commission and expenses of buying and selling	10
1.6.6	Buying and selling prices	10
1.6.7	Investing for the future	10
1.6.8	Other benefits	11
1.6.9	Methods of investment	11
1.6.10	Gearing	11
1.7	UK investors	12
1.7.1	Introduction	12
1.7.2	The wealthy	13
1.7.3	The medium wealthy	14
1.7.4	The not-so-wealthy or small investor	15
1.7.5	Widows	16
1.7.6	Trustees	18
1.8	Overseas investors	20
1.8.1	Exchange control	20
1.8.2	Taxation	20
1.8.3	Other restrictions	22
1.9	Conclusion	22

x Contents

2 The Finance Act 1990 — 23
- 2.1 Income tax — 23
- 2.2 Capital taxes — 23
- 2.3 Indirect taxes — 24
- 2.4 Savings and investments — 24
- 2.5 Businesses — 26
- 2.6 Charities — 26
- 2.7 Implications for the investment and savings industry — 27

3 Investor protection — 29
- 3.1 Introduction and background — 29
- 3.2 Basic framework — 30
- 3.2.1 Authorisation — 30
- 3.2.2 Exemptions — 31
- 3.2.3 Authorisation criteria — 31
- 3.3 Rules and regulations — 31
- 3.3.1 Business conduct — 34
- 3.3.2 Seeking business — 34
- 3.3.3 Customer agreements — 35
- 3.3.4 Complaints and compensation — 35
- 3.4 Complaints and remedies — 35
- 3.4.1 Basic procedures — 35
- 3.5 Overseas aspects — 36
- 3.6 Conclusion and future developments — 37
- Sources of further information — 37

4 Unlisted investments — 39
- 4.1 Introduction — 39
- 4.1.1 Types of unlisted security — 39
- 4.2 Highlights of the previous year — 39
- 4.3 Types of unlisted investment — 42
- 4.3.1 National Savings Bank accounts — 42
- 4.3.2 National savings certificates — 43
- 4.3.3 National savings index-linked certificates — 44
- 4.3.4 National savings income bonds — 45
- 4.3.5 National savings capital bonds — 46
- 4.3.6 National savings yearly plan — 46
- 4.3.7 Premium savings bonds — 47
- 4.3.8 Local authority mortgage bonds — 48
- 4.3.9 Commercial banks—current accounts, deposit accounts, savings accounts and certificates of deposit — 48
- 4.3.10 National Girobank deposit accounts — 49
- 4.3.11 Building society accounts — 50

4.3.12	Tax exempt special savings accounts (TESSAs)	51
4.3.13	Certificates of tax deposit	52
4.3.14	Treasury bills	52
4.4	Comparing different types of security	53
4.4.1	Security against default	53
4.4.2	Rate of return	54
4.4.3	Tax advantages	54
4.4.4	Convenience and cost of dealing	54
4.4.5	Ability to realise the investment	54
4.4.6	Maintenance	55
4.5	Preview of 1991 and conclusion	55

5 Listed investments 57

5.1	Introduction	57
5.2	Highlights of the previous year	58
5.3	Comparing different types of security	62
5.3.1	Security against default	63
5.3.2	Rate of return	63
5.3.3	Tax advantages	63
5.3.4	Convenience and cost of dealing	64
5.4	The Stock Exchange	64
5.4.1	Constitution and regulatory role	64
5.4.2	The primary and secondary markets	65
5.4.3	The Unlisted Securities Market, the Third Market and other markets	65
5.4.4	Overseas securities	66
5.4.5	Dealing on The Stock Exchange	67
5.4.6	Stockbroker services and licensed dealers in securities	73
5.4.7	Sources of information	74
5.5	Listed public sector securities	75
5.5.1	British government stocks	75
5.5.2	Local authority negotiable bonds	82
5.5.3	Other public sector stocks	83
5.5.4	Eurobonds	84
5.6	Listed company fixed interest securities	84
5.6.1	Legal nature	84
5.6.2	Pre-conditions	86
5.6.3	Characteristics	86
5.6.4	Taxation	87
5.6.5	Suitability	88
5.6.6	Mechanics	88
5.6.7	Safe custody	88
5.7	Ordinary shares	88

5.7.1	General		88
5.7.2	Warrants and options		95
5.7.3	Offers from companies		97
5.8	Preview of the year ahead		100
5.9	Conclusion		101
	Sources of further information		102
	Useful addresses		103

6 Tax beneficial investments and savings — 105

6.1	Introduction	105
6.2	Tax privileged investments	105
6.2.1	TESSAs	106
6.2.2	National savings certificates	107
6.2.3	National savings yearly plan	108
6.2.4	National savings index-linked certificates	110
6.2.5	Premium bonds	111
6.2.6	Personal equity plans	111
6.2.7	Insurance policies	113
6.2.8	Friendly society investments	113
6.2.9	Pension policies	114
6.2.10	Enterprise zone property trusts	114
6.3	Conclusion	115

7 Investment trusts — 117

7.1	Introduction	117
7.2	Historical background	117
7.3	Highlights of the previous year	118
7.4	Legal nature	119
7.5	Conditions for purchase	120
7.6	Characteristics	120
7.6.1	Spread of risk and flexibility	120
7.6.2	Income and capital gains	121
7.6.3	Investment overseas and currency management	121
7.6.4	Stock market price and underlying net asset value	123
7.6.5	Gearing	125
7.7	Taxation	127
7.7.1	Approval of investment trusts	127
7.7.2	Approved investment trusts—capital gains	127
7.7.3	Approved investment trusts—income	128
7.8	Unapproved investment companies	128
7.9	Suitability	129

	7.10	Mechanics	130
	7.11	Maintenance	131
	7.12	Preview of the year ahead	131
	7.13	Conclusion	132

8 Unit trusts and offshore funds — 133
- 8.1 Introduction — 133
- 8.2 Historical background — 133
- 8.3 Authorisation — 134
- 8.4 Highlights of the previous year — 135
- 8.5 Pricing of units — 135
- 8.6 Legal nature — 136
- 8.7 Conditions for purchase — 138
- 8.8 Characteristics — 139
- 8.8.1 General characteristics — 140
- 8.8.2 Types of unit trust — 141
- 8.9 Taxation — 142
- 8.9.1 Introduction — 142
- 8.9.2 Taxation of approved and authorised unit trusts — 143
- 8.10 Suitability — 146
- 8.11 Mechanics and maintenance — 146
- 8.11.1 Mechanics — 146
- 8.11.2 Maintenance — 147
- 8.12 Unauthorised unit trusts — 148
- 8.13 Exempt unit trusts — 149
- 8.14 Preview of the year ahead — 149
- 8.15 Offshore funds — 150
- 8.16 Unauthorised property unit trusts — 151
- 8.17 Suitability — 151
- 8.18 Authorised property unit trusts — 152
- Sources of further information — 152

9 Residential property — 155
- 9.1 Introduction to real property — 155
- 9.2 Legal, taxation and cost factors of real property — 157
- 9.2.1 Legal — 157
- 9.2.2 Taxation — 159
- 9.2.3 Costs — 165
- Residential property
- 9.3 Highlights of the previous year — 170
- 9.4 Direct investment in residential property — 170
- 9.4.1 Personal homes — 170
- 9.4.2 Holiday homes and time sharing — 171

9.4.3	Let houses and flats	172
9.4.4	Blocks of flats	174
9.5	Preview of the year ahead	175
9.6	Conclusion	175

10 Commercial property 177

10.1	Introduction	177
10.1.1	Types of investors	177
10.1.2	Property valuation	178
10.2	Types of commercial property	178
10.2.1	Purchase of commercial property	178
10.2.2	Lease of commercial property	179
10.2.3	Rent reviews	179
10.2.4	Rental growth	179
10.3	Shops	182
10.3.1	General	182
10.3.2	Prime	183
10.3.3	Secondary	183
10.3.4	Tertiary	183
10.3.5	Out of town shopping	183
10.4	Offices	184
10.4.1	General	184
10.4.2	Conclusion	184
10.5	Industrial	185
10.5.1	General investment: factories and warehouses	185
10.5.2	Location criteria	185
10.5.3	Institutional criteria	185
10.5.4	Yields	186
10.6	Hi-tech	186
10.7	Agriculture	186
10.8	Leisure	187

11 Agricultural land, woodlands and miscellaneous 189

11.1	Introduction	189
11.2	Highlights of the previous year	189
11.3	Agricultural land	191
11.3.1	Vacant possession land	191
11.3.2	Tenanted land	196
11.3.3	Finance	200
11.4	Woodlands	202
11.5	Miscellaneous agricultural-linked investments	203

11.5.1	Mineral-bearing land	203
11.5.2	Farm shops and garden centres	204
11.5.3	Accommodation land	205
11.5.4	Sporting rights	206
11.6	Preview of the year ahead	208
11.7	Miscellaneous direct property investments	208
11.7.1	Wildlife parks, pleasure gardens, riding schools, golf courses and mansion houses	208
11.7.2	Stud farms and training establishments	209
11.7.3	Caravan and camping sites and mobile home parks	210
	Sources of further information	211

12 Business ventures (without participation in management) — 213

12.1	Introduction	213
12.2	Highlights of the previous year	215
12.3	Minority holdings in private companies	215
12.3.1	Introduction	215
12.3.2	Powers of the minority	216
12.3.3	Liability for uncalled capital	218
12.3.4	Transfer of shares	218
12.3.5	Loans	219
12.3.6	Taxation	220
12.3.7	Conclusion	222
12.4	Private investment companies	222
12.5	Business Expansion Scheme	224
12.5.1	Introduction	224
12.5.2	Tax relief available	225
12.5.3	Individuals eligible for relief	226
12.5.4	Qualifying companies	227
12.5.5	Qualifying trades	228
12.5.6	Assured tenancy schemes	230
12.5.7	Qualifying investments	230
12.5.8	Withdrawal of relief	231
12.6	Dormant partnerships	232
12.6.1	Introduction	232
12.6.2	Loan creditors	232
12.6.3	Rights and liabilities	233
12.6.4	Taxation	234
12.7	Membership of Lloyd's	234
12.7.1	Introduction	234
12.7.2	Application for membership	236
12.7.3	Conditions of membership	237

	12.7.4	Taxation	238
	12.8	Investment in another's expertise	239
	12.9	Racehorses	240
	12.9.1	Introduction	240
	12.9.2	Stallions	241
	12.9.3	Taxation	242
	12.10	Backing plays	242
	12.11	Options on books	244
	12.12	Preview of the year ahead	244
		Sources of further information	244

13 Life assurance — 247

	13.1	Introduction	247
	13.2	Highlights of the previous year	247
	13.2.1	Pensions and life assurance new business	247
	13.2.2	A new life office taxation regime	250
	13.2.3	Policy taxation charges	250
	13.3	Life assurance policies	250
	13.3.1	Legal nature of life assurance policies	250
	13.3.2	Pre-conditions of life assurance policies	251
	13.3.3	Divisions and types of life assurance policies	251
	13.3.4	Characteristics of regular premium policies	254
	13.3.5	Characteristics of single premium policies	255
	13.3.6	Taxation of life assurance policies	256
	13.3.7	Suitability of life assurance policies	261
	13.3.8	Charges	263
	13.3.9	Mechanics of life assurance policies	264
	13.3.10	Maintenance of life assurance policies	264
	13.4	Purchased life annuities	264
	13.4.1	Legal nature of purchased life annuities	264
	13.4.2	Pre-conditions of purchased life annuities	265
	13.4.3	Characteristics of purchased life annuities	265
	13.4.4	Taxation of purchased life annuities	266
	13.4.5	Suitability of purchased life annuities	267
	13.4.6	Mechanics of purchased life annuities	267
	13.4.7	Maintenance of purchased life annuities	267
	13.5	Preview of the year ahead	267
	13.6	Conclusion	268
		Sources of further information	269

14 Pension contracts — 271

	14.1	Introduction	271
	14.2	Highlights of the previous year	271
	14.3	The State pension scheme	272

14.4	Contracting-in and contracting-out	273
14.5	Types of pension contracts	274
14.6	Characteristics of pension contracts	274
14.7	Eligibility, taxation, contribution limits and benefits	275
14.7.1	The life company	275
14.7.2	Personal pension plans	275
14.7.3	Contracting-out via a PPP	278
14.7.4	Retirement annuity contracts (s 226 contracts)	279
14.7.5	Occupational schemes	280
14.7.6	Loans and self-investment	283
14.7.7	Contracting-out via an occupational scheme	284
14.7.8	Unapproved occupational schemes	285
14.7.9	Simplified occupational schemes	285
14.7.10	Free-standing AVC schemes	285
14.8	Suitability	286
14.9	Preview of the year ahead	286
14.10	Conclusion	287
	Sources of further information	287

15 Commodities 289

15.1	Introduction to the commodity markets	289
15.2	Highlights of the previous year	290
15.3	Nature and divisions of commodities	290
15.3.1	Softs and metals	290
15.3.2	Physicals and futures	291
15.3.3	Opportunities for investment	292
15.4	Pre-conditions for commodities	292
15.5	Characteristics of commodities	293
15.6	Taxation of commodities	294
15.6.1	Commodity transactions	294
15.6.2	Options	294
15.6.3	Managed funds	295
15.6.4	Suitability of commodities	295
15.7	Methods of participation	296
15.7.1	Cash metals and metal trusts	296
15.7.2	Cash and carry transactions	297
15.7.3	Managed funds	298
15.7.4	Options	300
15.7.5	Private trading accounts	301
15.7.6	How to participate	302
15.8	Preview of the year ahead	303
	Sources of further information	304

16 Gold and other valuables — 305
- 16.1 Introduction — 305
- 16.1.1 A long-term hedge in precious metals — 305
- 16.1.2 Gold coins — 306
- 16.1.3 Coins manufactured in other precious metals — 307
- 16.1.4 Other valuables — 308
- 16.1.5 Selected forms of investment in valuables — 309
- 16.2 Highlights of the previous year — 309
- 16.2.1 Hoarded gold — 309
- 16.2.2 Gold in manufacture — 310
- 16.2.3 Diamonds — 311
- 16.3 Current developments — 311
- 16.3.1 Gold internationally — 311
- 16.3.2 Japan's entry into the market — 313
- 16.3.3 Other precious metals — 315
- 16.4 Counterfeits and forgeries — 315
- 16.4.1 Counterfeit coins — 315
- 16.4.2 Gold mine frauds — 317
- 16.5 Opportunities and costs — 317
- 16.5.1 Suitability — 317
- 16.5.2 Recovering gold from wrecks — 318
- 16.5.3 Costs of ownership — 318
- 16.5.4 Advisers — 318
- 16.6 Taxation — 319
- 16.6.1 Tax planning — 319
- 16.6.2 VAT — 319
- 16.7 Preview of the year ahead — 320
- 16.7.1 Limiting factors — 320
- 16.7.2 Market fundamentals — 320
- 16.7.3 Behind the rusting curtain — 321
- 16.8 Conclusion — 322
- Sources of further information — 322

17 Art and antiques — 323
- 17.1 Introduction — 323
- 17.1.1 A form of alternative investment — 323
- 17.1.2 The dividends — 324
- 17.2 Highlights of the previous year — 324
- 17.2.1 Structure of the market — 324
- 17.2.2 Record prices — 325
- 17.2.3 Buyers with cash to spend — 326
- 17.2.4 Leveraged purchases and guarantees — 327
- 17.2.5 Consumer protection — 328
- 17.3 Current developments — 329

Contents xix

17.3.1	Cosmopolitan buyers	329
17.3.2	Museum sales and purchases	330
17.3.3	Auctioneer's strategies	330
17.4	Purchasing art and antiques	331
17.4.1	Quality and provenance	331
17.4.2	Fakes and forgeries	331
17.4.3	Choosing an adviser	332
17.4.4	Exporting art	332
17.4.5	National heritage bodies	333
17.5	Characteristics	334
17.5.1	Prospects of capital appreciation	334
17.5.2	Art as investment	335
17.5.3	Costs of ownership	335
17.5.4	Malbin collection	336
17.5.5	Independent sources of information	337
17.6	Taxation	337
17.6.1	Tax planning	337
17.6.2	Capital gains	338
17.6.3	Capital transfer	339
17.6.4	Inheritance tax	341
17.6.5	VAT	342
17.6.6	Stamp duty	342
17.7	Mechanics	343
17.7.1	Suitability	343
17.7.2	Sources of information	344
17.7.3	Advisers	344
17.7.4	Commercial galleries	346
17.8	Maintenance	347
17.8.1	Safeguarding the investment	347
17.8.2	Insurance	348
17.8.3	Security	349
17.9	Preview of the year ahead	349
17.9.1	The May 1990 sales	349
17.9.2	Japanese interest	350
17.9.3	Chinese interest	351
17.9.4	The desire to invest	352
17.10	Conclusion	352
	Sources of further information	352

18 Collectibles 353
18.1	Introduction	353
18.1.1	Collectibles as alternative investments	353
18.1.2	Collectible cars as a case in point	354
18.1.3	Numismatic coins as a further case	355
18.2	Highlights of the previous year	355

	18.2.1	Auctions of collectibles	355
	18.2.2	Auctions of automobiles and automobilia	356
	18.2.3	Scope for creative imagination and knowledge	357
	18.3	Current developments	358
	18.3.1	Classic stamps	358
	18.3.2	Rare books	358
	18.3.3	Syndicated buying of numismatic coins	359
	18.4	Purchasing collectibles	360
	18.4.1	Strategies	360
	18.4.2	Collectibles in general	360
	18.5	Taxation	363
	18.5.1	Tax planning	363
	18.5.2	Sets of collectibles	363
	18.6	Suitability and mechanics	364
	18.6.1	Risks	364
	18.6.2	Precautions	364
	18.7	Preview of the year ahead	364
	18.8	Conclusion	365
		Sources of further information	365

Index 369

Other titles 378

1 Introduction

Robert Brown, Director, CS Investment Management Ltd, Vice President, Union Bank of Switzerland

1.1 Annual publication

This guide, which was first published in 1980, is aimed primarily at the investment adviser and aims to provide an annual update. Accordingly, most chapters include a section designed to cover:

(1) Highlights of the previous year including the principal developments since the previous edition;
(2) A preview of the coming year where appropriate; and
(3) A view of the next five to ten years, based on current thinking.

The principles of investment discussed later in this chapter continue unchanged indefinitely, and it is only the influences on investment policy that are likely to change over the years. These influences are primarily, but not necessarily, of a political and economic nature, that is to say the world economic climate and, for the UK investor, the economic and taxation policies being pursued by the government of the day.

A significant influence affecting investment policy in recent years was the abolition of UK exchange control in 1979. For many years significant numbers of UK investors have sought to invest a part of their portfolio overseas. However, since the Second World War investment outside the Sterling Area involved compliance with exchange control and dealing through the investment currency market—two major deterrents. In 1979 the UK resident found himself free to send money abroad, to open bank accounts abroad, to create offshore settlements, to buy villas and apartments abroad and to make investments abroad. This led to greater interest in overseas investment which has gathered pace in recent years. 'Investment' in foreign currency itself has become fashionable notwithstanding that the volatility of exchange rates makes this a hazardous operation best left to the expert.

The Conservative Government abolished exchange control but it could always be reintroduced by a future administration. However, the risk seems small at present and one can only speculate as to what form controls might take if they were to be reimposed at some future date. Hedges have been created such as offshore funds and non-resident trusts to protect, as far as possible, the investor's foreign portfolio from future restrictions. However, investors intending to go down such roads will need professional advice, for there are many traps for the unwary.

Although references are made both here and in some of the following chapters to overseas investments, this guide, of necessity, deals primarily with UK investments.

1.2 The investment adviser

This guide has been written with the needs of persons who give investment advice specifically in mind. However, it can also be read with profit by the intending investor himself. The investment adviser nowadays has an unenviable burden, being as much a victim of the 'information explosion' (and its concomitant, an embarrassing richness of choice) as any other member of a modern industrial society. Today more investment media exist than ever before: they are described in an ever-growing mass of literature, whether of the sales, the Press comment or the specialist legal textbook variety; they are marketed and advised on by an army of experts with widely differing qualifications, specialist knowledge, 'back-up' resources, general shrewdness and integrity; and they live in, and are sometimes choked by, a proliferating jungle of regulation.

Not the least reason for pitying the investment adviser is that he is the adviser, not the client. Assuming that the adviser has no particular axe to grind (ie, that his livelihood does not depend on the buying and selling of a particular type of investment), his duty is to try to see the problems of his clients in the round and to fit investment advice into that wider framework. Traditionally, this was the family solicitors' role, but the solicitors' monopoly in giving strategic investment advice has been eroded.

Today, the investment adviser—solicitor, accountant, stockbroker, insurance broker, bank manager or anyone else—should recognise his own limitations. He needs to know which investment media are available—and the first purpose of this guide is to identify the media available in the UK—and to establish which are suitable for the particular needs of his client or customer. This is particularly so following the passing of the Financial Services Act 1986 which broadly speaking prohibits a person from carrying on an investment business (which is widely defined) in the UK unless he is duly authorised under that Act. The adviser also needs to know which basic questions to ask about each investment medium and where to find the answers if, as will increasingly be the case, he does not know them himself.

Finally, the adviser must be able to make, either himself or through someone instructed by him, arrangements for a particular investment or disinvestment to be made on behalf of the client or customer; and indeed the adviser will usually find that it is financially advantageous to himself if he can do this. This guide identifies the media; identifies the investor for whom they are suitable or unsuitable, posing the main questions which should be asked about each medium; and provides signposts to the specialist consultants or dealers and to the legal, fiscal and other technicalities.

1.3 Types of investor

While Chapters 4–18 concentrate on the investments, this chapter focuses on the investor and comments on the types of investor that the investment adviser is likely to meet; and identifies so far as it can the most suitable types of investment for particular types of investor, acting as a pointer to the later chapters.

Although institutional investors are nowadays of immense importance and by their very nature cannot act without advice, this guide is not written for such investors or their advisers. It is concerned with and is written for individual investors (including trustees and family investment companies) and their advisers.

Because this guide is concerned with individual investors, it is perhaps reasonable to remind the investment adviser that all investment decisions ultimately reflect one facet or another of the human condition, whether the particular investor's ultimate motivation is fear and insecurity; greed; love of family; a wish to live comfortably, spaciously or ostentatiously; a wish for status and power; or a delight in risk-taking. Whether the investment under consideration is Broadacres or bearer bonds, diamonds or a piggy bank, the investment adviser always does well to consider the real as well as the professed motivation of the investor. Even though today we live in such an 'instant society', and notwithstanding that taxation considerations so often distort or even thwart investment intentions, the mainsprings of investment decision lie, as they have always done, far deeper than formal calculation of yield or gain; and the investment adviser ignores those mainsprings at his peril.

It is of the essence of investment advice that the adviser should succeed in identifying the particular category of investor to which the individual (or trustees) whom he is trying to advise belongs. As will be seen in section **1.7**, it would be impossible to devise a precise categorisation which is comprehensive and exhaustive and any categorisation which one might attempt to make would in part be financial-cum-legal and in part one of temperament and motivation.

It follows that the careful investment adviser must take into account a number of personal factors, special to the particular investor, in appraising both that investor and also the investment and divestment situations with which he is concerned. These factors include, but are not necessarily limited to, the investor's age; his health; his intentions with regard to his place of residence and/or domicile; his willingness to accept risk or his preference for spreading the risk; his willingness to participate in selecting, administering and reviewing investments; and his capacity to delegate.

1.4 Ways of arranging and holding investments

The foregoing paragraphs assume considerable sophistication on the part of the investment adviser and also a willingness to give his time, for which he will obviously expect to be remunerated properly. It is because investors of moderate means cannot afford to have access on the individual level to such sophistication or to pay an economic fee or charge for the adviser's time that collective investment media have developed hand-in-hand with the relative decline in importance of the personal or trustee investment portfolio, which in the past could be tailored by the adviser, or (as often as not) advisers, to the particular needs of the individual or of the beneficiaries concerned.

A corollary of the development of collective investment media is that an ever-growing body of legislation and regulation has had to be developed to protect the small saver against fraud or unscrupulous salesmanship. It is outside the scope of this guide to examine these protections. However, it is worth reminding those who criticise the complexity of, for instance, the Financial Services Act 1986, the Insurance Companies Act 1982 and the Banking Act 1987 (to take but three examples) that those enactments are designed for the protection of savers and investors.

In respect of many of the specific investments, comment is made on methods of arranging and holding those investments. However, a number of such methods are common to many investment media. It is outside the scope of this guide to give detailed explanations or advice on either the mechanics of establishing and conducting the particular 'vehicle' or its taxation incidents. The professional investment adviser will be aware that the principal ways in which investments can be arranged and held are:

(1) by personal direct investment by the individual;
(2) through a trust or settlement (including a will trust);
(3) in partnership with others; or
(4) through a family investment company.

1.5 The nature of an investment

The approach adopted in this guide is to attempt to state principles rather than express personal and therefore subjective opinions. Nowadays an investor has to be an economist, politician, historian and crystal ball gazer as well as a student of the markets with which he is concerned, and his perception of the basic nature of an investment may in consequence become blurred. Some thoughts on the nature of an investment are offered here.

The two basic elements of an investment are capital and income. At one end of the scale the capital invested remains constant while the income produced by the investment may vary (eg, money invested in a building society or placed on deposit at a bank). At the other end of the scale there are non-income-producing investments (using that word in the wider sense), such as commodities and works of art, where no income is produced but the capital value fluctuates. Between the two extremes there are many variations, of which only a few examples can be given. A short-dated gilt-edged security is probably the most predictable form of investment. One with a high coupon, ie, a high rate of interest, can be purchased at about par and redeemed at par to show little or no capital appreciation but a high income; one with a low coupon, ie, a low rate of interest, can be purchased below par and on redemption will show some capital appreciation but, until then, little income. Longer-dated gilts can be predictable if held to maturity, but in the meantime their value will alter in line with fluctuations in interest rates generally. Investments in real property or equities, whether by design or not, will produce variations in both capital value and income yield. Life assurances, such as single-premium bonds, in theory produce no income while they are held as an investment, but in practice this disadvantage can now be overcome by the various withdrawal plans which are available (see Chapter 13).

An essential third element in evaluating investments is inflation and the connected topic of the changing values of money, although inflation rates during the past few years have been considerably lower than they were in the mid 1970s. The need for a hedge against inflation has always influenced investment policy. As inflation rates fluctuate opinions will also vary widely on what represents an effective hedge; inflation means different things to, and has different consequences for, different people. Money—paper money—is basically a token which expresses the market values for the time being of an infinite number of commodities, goods and services. The intrinsic value of a loaf of bread (a concept which some might say could relate only to its nutritional value) ought to be the same however it is expressed, and the same applies to a bushel of wheat which is its main constituent. However, many other factors come into play; the most obvious used to be that a glut leading to greater supply tended to reduce the price and, conversely, a shortage leading to increased demand tended to increase the price (even these free market principles are increasingly eroded in the modern world by factors such as government intervention). Thus, although the intrinsic value of that loaf arguably remains unaltered, its value relative to those of other commodities, goods and services fluctuates.

On the bushel of wheat analogy, commodities, works of art or tangible assets are perhaps a good hedge against inflation, but the same hope of finding a good hedge often underlies investment in bricks and mortar, land, trees, overseas investment, manufacturing industries and service industries. The list is endless; and the investor must take his pick according to his own philosophy or instincts.

A fourth investment dimension is the time factor. In most, if not all, of the following chapters references are made to fluctuations, trends and fashions affecting the various markets. Within a long-term trend there are likely to be many short-term fluctuations, as often as not caused by political influences. When to buy and when to sell are therefore difficult decisions for the investor. He can be guided by professional advisers who have knowledge of the technical factors affecting a particular market but who can only express an opinion on political factors and the general state of a country's economy and who can therefore make only intelligent general forecasts not amounting to precise predictions.

Since the abolition of UK exchange control the opportunities for investing overseas are much greater. For those who do invest overseas, exchange rates form a further element in the evaluation of investments.

1.6 Investment policy—general principles and special factors

1.6.1 Diversification

The first maxim for practically every investor should be diversification. Indeed, for trustees the Trustee Investments Act 1961 prescribes diversification, although its provisions can be expressly excluded when a trust is created.

Diversification can be achieved by investing in investments of the kinds described in all or some of Chapters 4–18 but can also be achieved within a particular class of investment described in any one chapter; and this applies particularly to investment through The Stock Exchange (see Chapter 5).

As with all generalisations, there must be exceptions to the general rule. There will be the investor who has to commit, or to leave committed, a substantial part of his capital in one particular way (eg, the landed estate owner or the man who has built up a substantial business). It might be thought that the small investor who has little money to invest, and therefore little scope for diversification, would be an exception, but he can, for example, invest in unit trusts (see Chapter 8) or bonds (see Chapter 13), which themselves indirectly provide diversification.

1.6.2 Balance

The investor should as far as possible have a balanced portfolio. A part of his capital should be earmarked for security and invested in, for example, gilt-edged securities and real property, and a part invested in equities. It is axiomatic that the investor should look for capital appreciation for this should produce profits and in the process more capital, which in turn should increase both income and the overall value of the investment fund as a hedge against inflation. The precise balance will depend on the individual circumstances and personality of the particular investor.

Generally speaking, capital profits and high income yield do not go together and one instance of this is low-coupon long-dated gilts. However, it can happen that some high-yielding equities produce better growth than some low-yielding ones.

Most balanced investment portfolios will now contain an element of overseas securities usually in the form of indirect investment. As to direct investment overseas, see **1.8.1**.

1.6.3 Advice of specialists

The investor should be guided by the advice of a specialist in the appropriate field. There are brokers, agents, dealers or experts for all the markets discussed in this guide and they all provide a service which, if well performed, is a valuable service and for which they quite properly charge fees, either directly or indirectly. The old cry of saving agents' fees (which in practice too often amounts to not taking expert advice) frequently proves to be a false economy.

The only warning note to be sounded, and one which has already been given, is that the specialist in a particular field naturally wishes to sell his wares and, accordingly, another reason for a policy of diversification is the desirability of avoiding total dependence on the judgment and integrity of a particular specialist.

The investor who seeks to invest his money overseas should pay particularly close regard to the advice of specialists, particularly those familiar with the markets in the countries concerned. The advice that he will require will not be limited to the nature of the investment in question, but will also cover other factors, such as marketability, banking arrangements and (particularly in the case of purchase of land, houses, villas or flats) legal advice to ensure that he obtains a good title.

1.6.4 Taxation

The general rule for special factors such as taxation should be that full cognisance should be taken of their implications but that the investor's investment policy should not be dictated by them. Some basic taxation factors are mentioned below.

At 5 April 1979 the highest rate of income tax on unearned income was 98 per cent. Patently, this had a marked influence on the investment policy of the high rate taxpayer. To illustrate the point consider the purchase of five-year dated gilts. If the 98 per cent taxpayer had invested in such a gilt with a 12 per cent coupon, his net income return would have been a mere £2.40 per annum (£12 in five years) for each £1,000 invested with no capital appreciation. However, had he purchased a similar dated gilt with a 3 per cent coupon at say £82 his £1,220 stock would have produced an annual income of merely 73p but, at the expiration of the five years when the gilt matured, he would have received a capital gain of £220 free of capital gains tax. Clearly on this analysis, the higher rate taxpayer would have been advised to invest in the low coupon gilt.

With the reduction of the highest rate of income tax to 40 per cent, the higher rate taxpayer may still be better off by investing for capital appreciation though with the differential significantly reduced. Using the above figures at today's income tax rates he would receive £72 per annum on the high coupon gilt (£360 in all) as compared with £21.96 per annum (£109.80 in all), ie, a total of £329.80 including capital appreciation of £220 on the low coupon gilt.

For the high-rate taxpayer there is now more incentive than there was to invest for income. However, for this investor, investing for capital appreciation is likely to remain more attractive than investing for income.

Investments with favourable tax treatment include national savings certificates, which are entirely free of income tax and capital gains tax (see Chapter 4); and life assurances, both regular premium policies and single-premium bonds, which continue to have capital gains tax benefits (see Chapter 13) and, in the case of certain trust policies, inheritance tax benefits. These tax benefits are a good reason for investing in this way. However, there is no guarantee that over a given period one form of investment which has a favourable tax treatment will necessarily produce a better overall performance than another which has no tax benefits at all but has other compensating benefits, eg, better capital appreciation. Furthermore, future taxation legislation could alter or even nullify tax benefits that are now available (as has happened with the income tax treatments of woodlands); providing yet another reason for a policy of diversification.

Investment policy has sometimes tended to be unduly influenced by capital gains tax considerations. When considering a sale of an investment, the investor has to balance the right time (according to the market conditions prevailing and such ability as he may have to avoid or reduce his tax liability) to sell an investment which has shown a profit against the loss of the money (and of its use) which has to be applied in paying the tax. To put it another way, 60 per cent (or 75 per cent, depending upon the individual's income and the size of the gain) of a gain (ie, after deduction of tax) is worth having, and as a matter of general investment policy, all other things being equal, the profit should be taken at the right time in the market.

The investor investing overseas must consider not only UK tax implications but also the taxes of the country concerned and the interaction of those taxes with UK taxes.

1.6.5 Commissions and expenses of buying and selling

At one end of the scale there is no commission at all on investing money in, say, a building society or placing it on deposit at a bank. The commission on the purchase of gilt-edged securities is also small, and for equities it is reasonable but ad valorem stamp duty on purchases will be payable (see Chapter 5). These commissions vary from broker to broker following the abolition of fixed commissions on 27 October 1986. Relatively speaking, the commissions in the property market are reasonable but purchases involve ad valorem stamp duty. At the top end of the scale comes the art market. Here, the total commission on a sale and purchase can be as high as 20 per cent, plus VAT (see Chapter 17). The investor who purchases a work of art with a view to making an eventual gain must realise that immediately after he has purchased it the item may be worth only 80 per cent of the amount that he paid for it (or even less, when VAT is taken into account). Generally, wherever a commission is payable, VAT on that commission will also be payable.

1.6.6 Buying and selling prices

On The Stock Exchange separate buying and selling prices are quoted, the difference between these prices being the market-maker's turn or commission. The same principle can apply to other markets and with certain assets (jewellery is an example) another factor, namely that the asset acquires a second-hand value the moment it has been purchased, must be taken into account.

1.6.7 Investing for the future

When making a purchase the investor must look to the future performance of the investment and when making a sale he should compare the prospects of the investment to be sold with those of the investment which he intends to make with the sale proceeds. Past performance, trends, fashions and other historical matters are relevant, but only as a guide to future performance. If an investment has done well in the past it may do well in the future, but so-called recovery stocks also exist which have failed in the recent past but look as though they may improve in the future. The investor who has made a loss and does not want to sell until the value of the investment recovers to its cost might nevertheless be well advised to look to the future, by cutting his losses and reinvesting in something with better prospects.

1.6.8 Other benefits

Investments cannot be considered only by reference to pure investment criteria. Property may be purchased as a home or, for example if a farm, to provide a livelihood. Life assurance is a form of investment which brings with it also the element of family protection. Works of art (unless stored in a safe deposit) bring pleasure to the owner and collector.

1.6.9 Methods of investment

The normal method of investment is for the investor, either himself or preferably through a broker or other agent, to buy and sell individual investments. He can, however, give to his agent a discretionary power to buy and sell on his behalf. (This can generally be withdrawn by the investor on short notice.)

Moreover, as indicated in various chapters, the investor can either buy outright the investment itself or acquire options or, in the case of commodities, futures (see Chapter 15).

The same type of investment can sometimes be acquired through different types of investment media. For example, a man who prefers to invest his money in property or bricks and mortar can do this by direct purchase of property (see Chapters 9, 10 and 11), shares in a property company (see Chapter 5), units in a property unit trust (see Chapter 8) or property bonds (see Chapter 13). The person wishing to invest overseas can do so directly through the medium of investment trusts or unit trusts (whether based in the UK or offshore) holding overseas investments, or in UK companies with substantial overseas activities.

1.6.10 Gearing

Borrowing is a sensible strategy for the investor if tax relief is available on the loan interest, ie, if the loan interest can be set off as a charge against the investor's income for tax purposes, but while high interest rates subsist borrowings are not really practicable where relief is unavailable, except in special situations such as bridging loans.

Under the present law, tax relief for loan interest is available for loans for the purchase of a house as a principal residence, the 'ceiling' being £30,000; relief is available without limit on a borrowing for the purposes of a business in which one is actively engaged. For the investor with small capital resources, eg, the young man buying a home or setting up a business, borrowing is a necessity. If he pays tax at the higher rate on the top slice of his income, the borrowing will be relatively cheap, but if he is a low taxpayer, the borrowing will inevitably be expensive. For the man with a little more capital such borrowing will be desirable to enable him to have a fund of liquid capital available in case of need.

For the wealthy, borrowing often becomes a question of gearing. By way of illustration, consider an investor with say, £500,000 who buys a house for £150,000. If he buys the property without a mortgage he will have a £150,000 stake in the property market and £350,000 invested elsewhere. If he borrows £75,000 his stake in the property market will be only £75,000 and he will have £425,000 to invest elsewhere. The object of the exercise is to make better use of the £75,000 which (for him) can be borrowed very cheaply, and such borrowing will appeal to the adventurous investor who thinks he can invest his free assets so as to produce greater capital appreciation. It would be pointless, however, for the cautious investor to borrow £75,000 from a building society and then reinvest it in a building society or another equally safe but mundane investment because, although he would have protected his savings, the interest he paid would exceed the interest he received and the only beneficiary would be the building society itself.

1.7 UK investors

1.7.1 Introduction

Investors can be categorised by wealth (eg, wealthy, medium and not-so-wealthy) or by age (young, middle-aged and old), as well as by other factors mentioned in the Introduction. To attempt to categorise each separate type of investor, eg, widow, married man with family, football pools winner and so on could not be done with any acceptable degree of precision and to seek a comprehensive categorisation by listing suitable investments in respect of each category would involve numerous sub-divisions to take account of wealth and age factors alone—and would still not be comprehensive.

Consequently, as will be seen, investors are here categorised by wealth. The investor, and his adviser, therefore, will have to read the whole of the comparatively short section appropriate for his wealth in which, so far as is possible, other relevant factors have been incorporated. There is then a section (**1.7.6**) devoted to trustees.

1.7.2 The wealthy

Uncommitted wealth

For the investor who has very substantial free liquid capital the world is his oyster and he is referred to all the following chapters, since he could be interested in virtually any of the investments discussed in this guide.

His income is likely to attract the higher rate of tax and consequently he should be looking for capital appreciation (in property which does not attract capital gains tax) and a hedge against inflation.

He is advised to invest the major part of his capital in investments in which he has an interest or expertise, whether it be land, works of art or anything else.

He may like to become a 'name', ie, a member of a Lloyd's underwriting syndicate (see Chapter 12, **12.7**).

He may well like to set up a charitable trust, in the running of which he himself takes an active part. If so, he is directed first to **1.7.6**.

If he is a family man and/or wishes to pass on his fortune to others, he will be considering ways of mitigating inheritance tax. The principal investment areas which he should consider are agricultural land, works of art and setting up a business, all of which attract inheritance tax concessions. Chapter 11 discusses briefly the concessions for agricultural land and woodlands and Chapter 17 those for works of art. Setting up a business is not really within the scope of this guide, although brief reference is made to the enterprise agencies and Business Expansion Scheme relief in Chapter 12.

Committed wealth

High capital/low income

In this category is probably the agricultural estate owner and farmer, most of whose capital is tied up in the land and in the farming business conducted on that land.

An investor in this category may tend to invest for income and may restrict himself largely to The Stock Exchange. He should not invest entirely in high-yielding shares attracting income tax, but should also to some extent acquire growth shares as a hedge against inflation.

Depending on his capital resources, he is referred to Chapters 4–18.

Low capital/high income

The investor who has built up a substantial business may come into this category, but it is likely that with the development of the business his capital has grown as well. Clearly, he should invest for capital growth.

For the investor with substantial uncommitted capital, inheritance tax on his death (or on chargeable gifts during his lifetime) is no problem, in the sense that the money required is readily available. The investor who has substantial capital committed and only little readily realisable capital available can take out life assurances written in trust as a means of creating funds for his beneficiaries to satisfy the inheritance tax liability which they will have to bear.

This investor should where possible take advantage of pension policies which at present offer 100 per cent tax relief on premiums within specified limits.

1.7.3 The medium-wealthy

The upper and lower limits of investors in this category are difficult to define in monetary terms, bearing in mind inflation and the changing value of money. At the top end of the scale the considerations discussed in relation to the wealthy will tend to apply, with the exceptions that the money available for each type of investment will be that much less and/or that the overall spread will be that much narrower. At the lower end the considerations discussed in relation to the not-so-wealthy could apply.

In the middle of this category is typically the middle-aged, reasonably successful professional or businessman with a family. He will have a substantial earned income, will own his house with or without a mortgage and in all probability will have a second property, eg, a pied-à-terre for himself, a country cottage, a flat for his children or a villa overseas. He will also probably have his children educated privately.

If he owns more than one property, this will represent an investment in the property market. If he is interested in making any other form of investment in land or bricks and mortar he will probably not have sufficient money for direct investment and will instead invest through the medium of property companies or property bonds.

He will be looking for capital appreciation (as a hedge against inflation, if for no other reason) but should maintain a reasonably balanced portfolio. In that part of the portfolio which is devoted to fixed interest investments designed for security of capital, he should consider holding low-coupon dated stocks, bearing in mind that in an inflationary age the protection conferred by a 'long' stock is illusory.

A fairly standard portfolio for long-term investment would be at least fifty per cent in equities for capital growth, a proportion in gilts and proportions in other forms of investment, such as unit trusts, single-premium bonds, commodities or works of art, according to the inclination of the investor. The more adventurous will invest more for capital appreciation, regarding a proportion of his portfolio as 'risk' capital, whereas the more cautious will have a greater proportion of fixed interest stocks in his portfolio.

In this group there will also be the man who has fairly substantial capital, possibly from inheritances, but does not have a substantial earned income. He will therefore require investment income, but again he should have a balanced portfolio providing for capital appreciation, which both generates increased income and also enables him to live on capital profits. His income-producing investments will tend to be those with a high coupon and with an above-average yield. This investor may well be interested in investing in businesses without taking part in the management (see Chapter 12).

All investors in this category will be involved with life assurance in one way or another, not the least of which will be pension policies (see Chapter 14).

1.7.4 The not-so-wealthy or small investor

This category includes those with comparatively small means: young people starting out in life; and old people, particularly widows, who have to a large extent to live without the benefit of earned income.

Such investors are recommended to invest, first of all, in the purchase of a home for themselves (see Chapter 9); secondly, in safe investments, such as building society shares and deposits and gilts, for easily realisable money, and National Savings Certificates (see Chapters 4 and 5); thirdly, for their 'risk' or growth capital, through the collective investment media (see Chapters 7 and 8); and fourthly, possibly more as family protection than as investment, in life assurance (see Chapter 13).

The young may tend to invest for capital appreciation, eg, low coupon gilts and unit trusts with the emphasis on capital, whereas the elderly widow may invest more for income, eg, high coupon gilts and unit trust with the emphasis on income.

As the investor's capital resources increase, either by his own efforts or by inheritance, he can acquire a more diversified portfolio of his own. For example, if he is so inclined he can enter the art market, build up a stamp collection or make other investments of the kinds mentioned in Chapters 16–18.

1.7.5 Widows

As mentioned above, widows can fall into any number of investment categories and accordingly Table 1.1 is not fully comprehensive.

Table 1.1

Category	Suitable investments
1 *Wealthy* All ages with or without children	All types of investment
2 *Medium wealthy* (a) *Elderly* (assuming that children, if any, are adequately provided for)	All types of investment
(b) *Middle-aged* Children, if any, provided for	All types of investment
Children to maintain	House as residence. Primarily, Stock Exchange investments, including proportion of gilt-edged securities, unit trusts and insurances. Balanced investment policy aiming for both income yield and capital appreciation.
3 *Not-so-wealthy* (a) *Elderly*	House as residence, if possible; gilt-edged securities and unit trusts; national savings index-linked retirement certificates or bonds;

building society deposits or shares, but these may not be suitable for a low taxpayer. Investment policy aiming for high income rather than for capital appreciation.

(b) *Middle-aged*

    Without children — House as residence; gilt-edged securities and unit trusts; national savings certificates; building society deposits or shares, but these may not be suitable for a low taxpayer. Investment policy should be aimed more for capital appreciation than income, though this will be dependent on the widow's ability to earn income.

    Children to maintain — House as residence; gilt-edged securities and unit-trusts; national savings certificates; building society deposits or shares, but these may not be suitable for a low taxpayer. Investment policy: the widow's ability to earn income will probably be limited and cashflow will be important, so the investment policy should aim more for income than capital appreciation.

(c) *Young*

    Without children — House as residence; gilt-edged securities and unit trusts; national savings certificates; building society deposits or shares, but these may not be suitable for a low taxpayer. Investment policy: presumably the widow will be able to earn income and will have reasonable prospects of remarriage, so the investment policy should aim for capital appreciation.

    Children to maintain — House as residence; gilt-edged securities and unit trusts; national savings certificates; building society deposits or shares, but these may not be suitable for a low taxpayer. Investment policy: the widow's ability

> to earn income may be limited and cashflow may be important, so the investment policy should aim at as high an income as possible, but with some capital appreciation.

1.7.6 Trustees

Trustees are usually appointed by a settlement or a will. They can, however, be bare trustees, nominees or attorneys for others (under a power of attorney) who might well be infants or persons under some disability. They also include anyone who owes a fiduciary duty of care to others.

For investment purposes their 'bible' is the Trustee Investments Act 1961, although some of its provisions are often expressly excluded by the trust instrument itself. The principles that the Act lays down are discussed below.

Suitability of investments for the trust
Normally the question of what investments are suitable for a particular trust involves considering the interests of the beneficiaries under that trust. If there is a life tenant and remaindermen, then the trustees must ensure that the income produced for the life tenant is reasonable, but at the same time they must consider security of capital and possible capital appreciation for the remaindermen. Where there are infant beneficiaries, a special duty of care is required.

The principle of balancing the interests of all the beneficiaries is seldom specifically excluded, but can be excluded where the settlor has reason for requiring particular consideration to be given to the needs of some of the beneficiaries.

Diversification
In a normal trust the trustees could be in breach of trust if they do not diversify the trust investments. In a small trust diversification can be achieved through the medium of, for example, unit trusts or investment trusts. However, diversification can be a problem in the fairly common case where a settlor has built up a business through a company and settled shares in that company upon trust for his children. In this case the trust instrument should include the appropriate authority for the trustees to continue to hold that investment notwithstanding that diversification would thereby be effectively precluded.

Expert advice

Trustees must obtain and consider proper advice from a specialist in the relevant field of investment. This principle is seldom expressly excluded. Unless there is a specific provision in the trust instrument to the contrary, trustees must make investment decisions personally (and cannot delegate this to the expert adviser).

Authorised investments

The Act specifies the kinds of investment in which trustees are authorised to invest and states that at least half the trust fund should be invested in the 'narrower range' and that the balance can be invested in the 'wider range'. Investments in the 'narrower range' include deposits with approved banks and building societies, gilt-edged securities, mortgages on property and debentures of companies that, first, have an issued and paid up share capital of at least £1 million and, secondly, have paid dividends (however small) on the whole of their ordinary share capital in each of the previous five years. The 'wider range' includes unit trusts and ordinary shares in companies satisfying the conditions stated above for debentures in the narrower range.

It is fairly general practice nowadays for trust instruments to confer express powers of investment, overriding the provisions of the Trustee Investments Act 1961 in this respect, and it is quite usual for the trustees to be given very wide powers in the interests of flexibility. The investment clause will always require close examination because, either by design or as a consequence of bad drafting, the powers actually given may not be so wide as appears at first sight. An investment in its narrow legal sense is an income-producing investment. Consequently, if trustees are to be given powers to buy houses as residences for beneficiaries or to use capital for improving or repairing them, specific powers must be included. Again, if trustees are to be permitted to invest in assets such as capital shares with no participation in the profits of the company or chattels or commodities or currency, specific powers must be given. Specific powers must also be given in respect of insurances and assurances.

Suitability

In their own interests trustees should tend to be cautious and adopt a conservative policy. They must act within the principles laid down in the Trustee Investments Act 1961. Their first duty is to familiarise themselves with the powers of investment that they have been given and whether these are restricted as specified in the Act or whether, as is often the case, they are given the powers of an absolute owner, but even then they must ensure that they are given *all* the powers of an absolute owner.

If a known liability arises (and this commonly occurs on the death of a testator, where a liability to inheritance tax may arise), the trustees or the personal representatives should set about covering that liability, if necessary by realising investments and placing the money on deposit with a bank or with building societies or even by investing in short-dated gilts. A prudent trustee who does this cannot be criticised if the market in those investments then goes up, but, conversely, a trustee who does not do this is open to criticism if the market goes down.

1.8 Overseas investors

1.8.1 Exchange control

A resident in the UK can now invest in any country in the world without UK exchange control restriction, although he will be subject to whatever restrictions the country in which he plans to invest may impose. Conversely, an overseas investor can freely invest in the UK, but he may be subject to exchange control provisions imposed by his country of residence.

1.8.2 Taxation

Since detailed advice on taxation is outside the scope of this guide, the investor should take professional advice where necessary, and the comments made below are necessarily only in very general terms. Overseas investors (and also immigrants and emigrants) have to be particularly aware of taxation considerations, which for them depend on domicile and residence. It is impossible to give an all-embracing definition of an overseas investor. He may be both domiciled and resident outside the UK, domiciled outside but resident in the UK, or domiciled in and resident outside the UK, and his taxation position will vary accordingly.

For tax purposes, a person is regarded as 'resident' in the UK if he is physically present in this country for six months or more in any tax year, or, if over a period of four such years, he is present in this country for an average of three months or more in each tax year, or, if he has 'accommodation available' for his use (regardless of whether he owns it or it is the whole or part of a house or flat) and he visits the UK for any time at all in a tax year. He will be regarded as 'ordinarily resident' if he is habitually resident in the UK year after year and will continue to be so regarded if he usually lives in this country but is in fact physically absent (eg, on a long holiday abroad) for even the whole of any tax year. At least for the short term, proposals to change these definitions, set out in an Inland Revenue Consultative Paper, are not going to be pursued.

Introduction 21

Inheritance tax
Liability to UK inheritance tax depends basically on domicile. The investor domiciled in the UK will be subject to inheritance tax on his global assets, whereas an investor not so domiciled will be subject to inheritance tax only on his UK property or investments. He can avoid this tax either by forming a non-UK holding company which generally should be owned by an offshore (ie, non-UK) trust under which he is a beneficiary, or by investing in offshore funds, or, if he is both domiciled and resident abroad, by investing in those UK government securities which are free of tax to residents abroad.

The concept of domicile depends on a great number of factors which it is outside the scope of this guide to describe. Briefly, under UK law, domicile means permanent residence (evidenced by an intention to reside for life). An individual starts life with the domicile of his father, known as his domicile of origin, and this remains his domicile unless and until he establishes a domicile of choice (and he will revert to his domicile of orgin if he loses his domicile of choice without establishing another domicile of choice). To acquire a domicile of choice he must establish, first, an actual residence in his country of choice and, secondly, an intention to live there for the rest of his life. Proving a domicile of choice to the satisfaction of the Revenue may be difficult and, conversely, if desired, proving that a domicile of origin has *not* been lost may be equally difficult. In this connection a non-UK domiciliary who has been resident in the UK for seventeen out of the previous twenty years is deemed to be domiciled in the UK for inheritance tax purposes and, therefore, will be within the UK inheritance tax net unless or until he has established three complete tax years of residence outside the UK. (However, on the death of such an investor there may be some relief from inheritance tax under the provisions of an appropriate double taxation agreement.) As with the definitions of residence and ordinary residence, there are no short term plans to change the rules regarding domicile.

Capital gains tax
Liability to capital gains tax depends on UK residence or 'ordinary residence' for tax purposes. The former can be established by mere physical presence in the UK for more than six months in any tax year. The general rule is that the investor ordinarily resident in the UK is subject to capital gains tax and the investor not so resident is exempt from it. An investor resident abroad who intends to establish a residence in the UK should therefore consider whether he should first sell investments which have shown a gain before he sets up residence in the UK, repurchasing them later if he so wishes. Special rules apply for UK domiciliaries.

Income tax

Liability to income tax depends on residence, but there are certain concessions for a non-UK domiciliary. Many factors, including provisions of double taxation agreements, are relevant, and the investor must take professional advice.

1.8.3 Other restrictions

Normally an overseas investor can invest in any form of UK investment described in this guide without any other form of UK restriction. Difficulties could arise, however, where the investment involves a liability in the UK (eg, investment in leasehold property involving the usual covenants on the part of the lessee, because the UK-resident landlord might not accept covenants from a lessee residing outside the jurisdiction unless he can provide a UK resident guarantor satisfactory to the landlord) or where the investor might ultimately want to export the investment, in particular where it is a work of art.

1.9 Conclusion

If there is any conclusion to be drawn for the investor and the investment adviser from the foregoing analysis, it is that nothing is constant and that continual review and permanent vigilance are essential. The investment strategies appropriate in one generation, or for one particular generation of investor, are likely to be wholly inappropriate in the next generation, when the investment climate and the law may have changed, the investor will have aged and his needs and his family circumstances will have changed.

2 The Finance Act 1990

Allied Dunbar Assurance plc

Although the Chancellor's budget on 20 March contained no real surprises, it enabled one of the most historically significant Finance Acts to come into force by recognising the individual fiscal position of married women. Independent taxation provides new opportunities for married couples to save and invest in a more tax efficient manner. The relevant highlights of the 1990 Finance Act are shown below:

2.1 Income tax

Basic rate of income tax—remains unchanged at 25 per cent.

Higher rate of income tax—remains unchanged at 40 per cent. Threshold is also unchanged at £20,700.

Personal allowances—main personal allowance increased to £3,005 which is in line with inflation. The new Married Couples Allowance is set at £1,720. The Blind Person's Allowance is to be doubled to £1,080.

Mortgage interest relief—loan limit remains unchanged at £30,000.

Independent taxation—the Chancellor confirmed the introduction of proposals announced in the 1988 Budget, to take effect from 6 April 1990.

2.2 Capital taxes

Capital gains tax—annual exemption to be £5,000 per individual. No changes to rates (25 per cent to 40 per cent depending on individual's tax position). Retirement relief on sale of business assets allows the first £125,000 of chargeable gain to be tax free and the next £375,000 to be taxed at half the CGT rate.

Inheritance tax—Nil-rate band increased from £118,000 to £128,000 to apply to transfers made on or after 6 April 1990. Above £128,000, the flat rate of 40 per cent continues to apply.

2.3 Indirect taxes

VAT—Standard rate of 15 per cent remains unchanged. Registration threshold is raised from £23,600 to £24,400 and will usually be based on turnover in the last 12 months rather than anticipated turnover. Bad debt relief is extended to debts which have been written off in the trader's accounts and have been outstanding for two years. VAT incurred on domestic accommodation for directors is no longer to be eligible for deduction. Change to take effect from royal assent.

Stamp duty—all stamp duties on transactions in shares and unit trusts to be abolished from late 1991 or early 1992. Stamp duty on transfers of land and property remain unchanged.

2.4 Savings and investments

Tax exempt special savings account (TESSA)—Proposed new savings account to be introduced from 1 January 1991 where interest earned can be free of tax in certain circumstances. Its main features are:

(1) a TESSA will remain tax exempt for five years provided the capital remains untouched for this period;
(2) savings may be monthly (maximum £150) or annual (maximum usually £1,800);
(3) a lump sum of £3,000 may be invested in the first year provided the overall maximum investment over the five years does not exceed £9,000;
(4) cash sums equivalent to the interest earned net of basic rate tax may be withdrawn at any time. Provided no more than equivalent to the net interest is withdrawn, there will be no tax to pay on interest left to accumulate;
(5) accumulated interest will be totally exempt from income tax at the end of the five year period.

Composite rate tax (CRT)—to be abolished from 6 April 1991. Instead, income tax will be deducted at the basic rate from the interest credited to the individual's account. Excess tax deducted may be reclaimed at the end of the tax year. Higher rate tax will continue to be collected separately. Special arrangements will enable non-taxpayers' accounts to be credited in full. During the 1990/91 tax year the rate of CRT will be 22 per cent.

Personal equity plans—from 6 April 1990 overall investment limit increased from £4,800 to £6,000 per annum. Limit for unit and investment trusts increased from £2,400 to £3,000 per annum. The proportion required to be invested in UK equities for unit and investment trusts is reduced from 75 per cent to 50 per cent. Where these requirements are not met the annual maximum investment is increased from £750 to £900.

Futures and options—With effect from royal assent, trading income from futures and options is to be exempt from tax in the hands of pensions schemes and authorised unit trusts.

Employee share ownership plans (ESOPs)—From budget day new CGT rollover relief was available on sale of shares to qualifying ESOPs in certain circumstances.

Convertible and indexed securities—The Act introduces new rules, affecting both investor and issuer, for the taxation of 'qualifying convertible securities', amends existing rules taxing indexed securities and excludes certain bonds issued on or after 9 June 1989 from the rules for 'deep gain' securities.

Unit trusts, investment trusts and offshore funds—the Act:

(1) extends to all authorised unit trusts, the tax regime now applying to trusts freely marketable in the European Community. This means that they will pay a lower corporation tax rate of 25 per cent and will get relief for management expenses and interest. This will apply from 1 January 1991;
(2) removes indexation from units and offshore funds mainly invested in assets not themselves qualifying for indexation—this applied from budget day;
(3) frees unit trust managers from rule preventing the conversion of income from units into capital gains. This will apply for accounting periods ending after 5 April 1970;
(4) relaxes the rule on distributions by investment trusts to remove existing conflicts between company and tax law. This will apply to accounting periods ending on or after royal assent.

Capital limits for income-related benefits—the amount of capital above for which individuals are ineligible for income-related benefits is increased. For housing benefit and community charge benefit, the limit is doubled from £8,000 to £16,000 with effect from 1 April 1990. For income support and family credit the limit increased from £6,000 to £8,000 with effect from 9 April 1990.

Save as you earn (SAYE)—banks to offer SAYE contracts in addition to building societies and the Department for National Savings. This will apply from royal assent.

Pensions-earnings cap—in some cases a cap applies to limit the amount of earnings to be taken into account when calculating the contributions or benefits under approved occupational and personal pension schemes. This cap is increased from £60,000 to £64,800 with effect from 6 April 1990.

Friendly societies—limit on premiums for tax exempt life and endowment policies offered by friendly societies increased from £100 to £150 per annum with effect from 1 September 1990.

2.5 Businesses

Corporation tax rate—remains unchanged at 35 per cent.

'Small companies' rate—remains unchanged at 25 per cent. The limits for marginal relief increase to £200,000 and £1m. The effective marginal rate remains at 37.5 per cent for 1990/91.

2.6 Charities

Payroll giving—increase in annual limit on charitable gifts through employer from £480 to £600 per annum with effect from 6 April 1990.

Gift aid—introduction of income tax relief for single charitable gifts by individuals. The minimum single gift is £600, maximum gift is £5m in any tax year. The donor pays net of basic rate tax and gets higher rate tax relief if applicable. Charities can claim back basic rate tax. This relief applies from 1 October 1990.

Company gifts—introduction of corporation tax relief for single charitable gifts by companies, on a similar basis to gift aid.

Covenants—the Inland Revenue has issued guidance to help charities and individuals ensure that covenants to charities obtain tax relief, suggests model forms of words and deals with other practical points, including the restriction of backdating deeds and escape clauses.

2.7 Implications for the investment and savings industry

Overall, the Budget was largely neutral with regard to the investment and savings industry as a whole. The absence of any major changes provides a welcome respite from the repeated upheavals of the past few years, some of which are still to take full effect.

The increase to investment limits on the already popular personal equity plans is to be welcomed as there can be little doubt that many investors would have preferred to have greater amounts. The popularity of PEPs can be clearly demonstrated by the fact that around £750m was invested into 300,000 plans in 1989. The 25 per cent increase in the annual limit will ensure continued buoyancy in sales of these highly tax-efficient savings vehicles.

The introduction in 1991 of the new tax exempt special savings accounts (TESSAs), offering the potential for tax free growth, may well provide further competition within the financial services industry, particularly in the area of short to medium term investments. Unlike PEPs, distributed income will still be subject to basic rate tax at source and the reclaiming of the tax deducted is subject to the capital remaining invested for the full five-year period. PEPs will, therefore, still have a clear advantage.

The removal of composite rate tax on deposit accounts for non-taxpayers will typically be of benefit to the smaller account holder, notably accounts held for children or by pensioners and married women who are not working (following the introduction of independent taxation on 6 April 1990). However, for taxpayers, the rate of tax deducted will be increased from the current 22 per cent to 25 per cent.

The attractiveness of pensions, with tax relief on contributions and tax free growth within the funds, remains unchanged with the exception of the expected increase in the 'earnings cap' introduced in the 1989 Budget. Surprisingly, there was no announcement in relation to the widely expected changes to the taxation of life policy gains.

The Budget was clearly aimed at encouraging savings and this should be favourably reflected in the investment industry by the increased public awareness of the need for savings through a growing range of investment media.

3 Investor protection

Peter Howe, LLB, Barrister, Divisional Director, Allied Dunbar Assurance plc

3.1 Introduction and background

The Financial Services Act 1986 was enacted following widespread concern at the collapse of a number of investment firms in the early 1980s. The legislation is based on the recommendations of Professor Gower who, on behalf of the Government, carried out an investigation which revealed a lack of consistency (and in some cases the absence of any controls at all) in the regulatory systems controlling different types of firms.

Professor Gower's approach was to recommend regulation only in so far as necessary for the protection of investors and that the regulatory structure should remain flexible so as not to impair market efficiency. The aim was to introduce a consistent regulatory structure which would produce a 'level playing field' (ie, rules which do not put some firms at a competitive disadvantage compared with others). His view was that regulation should not try to do the impossible by protecting investors from their own folly but rather to prevent reasonable people from being made fools of.

Finally, Professor Gower recommended self-regulation by the industry as preferable to the regulatory system in the United States where the Securities Exchange Commission is a Government Agency. Although the UK system is backed up by statute, the day-to-day regulation of investment businesses is undertaken by self-regulatory organisations made up of practitioners drawn from the various types of investment business which operate in the market.

The Financial Services Bill was enacted in 1986 and brought into force by a number of Commencement Orders. The key provisions were implemented in 1988. During this time a Securities and Investments Board (SIB) had been created, responsible for several self regulatory organisations (SROs) which are referred to in the paragraphs below. They each produced their own rules and determined their compliance and monitoring approach.

3.2 Basic framework

The key provision in the Financial Services Act 1986 (FSA) makes it a criminal offence to carry on investment business in the UK unless the person concerned is authorised or exempt. Investment business is defined as carrying on certain activities eg, buying and selling, advising, arranging or managing 'things' which are investments under the FSA. The definition of investments includes most 'paper' securities such as stocks and shares, collective investment schemes, most life and pension policies, gilt-edged securities and futures and options. The definition excludes real property, bank and building society accounts or alternative investments such as antiques and works of art.

3.2.1 Authorisation

Firms carrying on investment business may obtain their authorisation from the SIB or more likely from one of the five SROs which the SIB has recognised:

(1) The Securities Association (TSA) which regulates the activities of those who deal in, advise or manage securities;
(2) The Investment Management Regulatory Organisation (IMRO) which regulates the managers of investments including the managers and trustees of collective investment schemes eg, unit trusts;
(3) The Life Assurance and Unit Trust Regulatory Organisation (LAUTRO) which regulates the marketing activities of Life Companies, Friendly Societies and collective investment scheme managers;
(4) The Financial Intermediaries Managers and Brokers Regulatory Association (FIMBRA) which regulates the many intermediaries who advise and arrange deals in life and pension products, collective investment schemes and other investments;
(5) The Association of Futures Brokers and Dealers (AFBD) which regulates those who advise on and deal in futures and options including those handled by the commodity exchanges and the London International Financial Futures Exchange.

Another way in which authorisation to carry on investment business can be obtained is through membership of a recognised professional body (RPB). Many solicitors and accountants obtain their authorisation from their respective professional bodies (eg, The Law Society or one of the accountancy bodies) where their investment business is only a small proportion of their overall professional activities.

Finally, there are firms such as insurance companies and friendly societies which obtain their authorisation under separate legislation from the Department of Trade and Industry and the Registrar of Friendly Societies respectively. These firms do not need to seek additional authorisation under the FSA although their marketing activities are subject to regulation by LAUTRO or in a very few cases the SIB.

3.2.2 Exemptions

Some firms are exempted from the requirement to obtain authorisation under the FSA. These include the Bank of England, recognised exchanges and clearing houses and members of Lloyds.

An important category of exempt person is the appointed representative. This is an individual or firm which acts as the agent of an authorised person and for whose activities (within the limits of the authorised person's business activities) the authorised person takes legal responsibility. Although it is open to any firm which is authorised to appoint such representatives, the practice is most common in the case of insurance companies and companies that market collective investment schemes.

3.2.3 Authorisation criteria

In deciding whether to authorise a firm the SIB, SROs or RPBs consider such matters as whether those involved in the business are fit and proper persons having the competence and financial resources to operate the business in a way which is unlikely to result in unreasonable risk to investors. In addition, the SIB have published 10 Principles (pages 32–33) which it expects all firms to observe. The breach of any principle might call into question whether the firm was fit and proper to carry on investment business.

3.3 Rules and regulations

The FSA contains only the bare framework of the total investor protection legislation. The detailed rules and regulations with which authorised firms are expected to comply are contained in rule books maintained and enforced by the SIB and the relevant SRO or RPB. The original rule books of individual SROs and RPBs were required to give investor protection which was equivalent to that given by the rules of the SIB itself. In an effort to avoid unnecessary duplication whilst preserving the ability of SROs and RPBs to make practitioner-based rules relevant to the particular business in which their members

The Principles

(1) **Integrity**
A firm should observe high standards of integrity and fair dealing.

(2) **Skill, care and diligence**
A firm should act with due skill, care and diligence.

(3) **Market practice**
A firm should observe high standards of market conduct. It should also, to the extent endorsed for the purpose of this principle, comply with any code or standard as in force from time to time and as it applies to the firm either according to its terms or by rulings made under it.

(4) **Information about customers**
A firm should seek from customers it advises or for whom it exercises discretion any information about their circumstances and investment objectives which might reasonably be expected to be relevant in enabling it to fulfil its responsibilities to them.

(5) **Information for customers**
A firm should take reasonable steps to give a customer it advises, in a comprehensible and timely way, any information needed to enable him to make a balanced and informed decision. A firm should similarly be ready to provide a customer with a full and fair account of the fulfilment of its responsibilities to him.

(6) **Conflicts of interest**
A firm should either avoid any conflict of interest arising or, where conflicts arise, should ensure fair treatment to all its customers by disclosure, internal rules of confiden-

tiality, declining to act, or otherwise. A firm should not unfairly lace its interests above those of its customers and, where a properly informed customer would reasonably expect that the firm would place his interests above its own, the firm should live up to that expectation.

(7) **Customer assets**
Where a firm has control of or is otherwise responsible for assets belonging to a customer which it is required to safeguard, it should arrange proper protection for them, by way of segregation and identification of those assets or otherwise, in accordance with the responsibility it has accepted.

(8) **Financial resources**
A firm should ensure that it maintains adequate financial resources to meet its investment business commitments and to withstand the risks to which its business is subject.

(9) **Internal organisation**
A firm should organise and control its internal affairs in a responsible manner, keeping proper records, and where the firm employs staff or is responsible for the conduct of investment business by others, should have adequate arrangements to ensure that they are suitable, adequately trained and properly supervised and that it has well-defined compliance procedures.

(10) **Relations with regulators**
A firm should deal with its regulator in an open and cooperative manner and keep the regulator promptly informed of anything concerning the firm which might reasonably be expected to be disclosed to it.

Source: *The Securities and Investments Board*

operate, some amendments have been made to the FSA. These amendments allow the SIB to make certain core rules which are directly applicable to all investment firms (except members of RPBs) whichever SRO they belong to. It is hoped that the proposed designated core rules (of which there are likely to be some 40) will provide a degree of uniformity and common standards which the individual SROs can supplement by additional rules geared to the activities of the firms which they regulate. Instead of having to convince the SIB that their rule books are equivalent the new proposals will require the SIB to agree that the rule books, together with the SRO's monitoring and compliance arrangements, provide adequate protection to investors.

3.3.1 Business conduct

The detailed rules and regulations cover a number of areas relating to the conduct of investment business by authorised persons. These include:

(1) the way in which authorised firms and their appointed representatives seek new business;
(2) the ongoing relationship between authorised firms and their customers where such relationships exist;
(3) the way in which authorised firms must deal with complaints by investors.

3.3.2 Seeking business

There are detailed advertising rules which prohibit misleading statements, and statements and claims which cannot be substantiated. There are rules which require authorised firms to know their customer before making a recommendation or arranging an investment transaction and to make sure that any investment that is recommended or transacted is suitable having regard to the investor's personal and financial requirements.

In the case of packaged product investments such as life assurance, pension plans and collective investment schemes the polarisation rule requires intermediaries to disclose in a Buyer's Guide and on business stationery whether they are independent, in which case the obligation is to recommend a suitable product from those available on the market or company representatives, who must recommend a suitable product from the product range of the particular company they represent.

Independent intermediaries and company representatives are permitted to make unsolicited calls (personal visits or oral communications other than at the investor's invitation) which cannot be made in relation to non-polarised investments. Investments which can be the subject of unsolicited calls normally give the investor cancellation rights enabling the investor to cancel an investment transaction within a reasonable period (normally 14 days) from entering into the contract. Detailed product disclosure rules are designed to provide sufficient information about the product to enable the investor to decide whether to continue with the contract.

3.3.3 Customer agreements

The rules prescribe the terms of customer agreements between authorised firms and their customers including how such agreements are made, how instructions are to be communicated and how such agreements are terminated.

There are also rules requiring authorised firms to place client money in designated trust accounts to ensure that investors' money is kept separate from other money belonging to the firm.

3.3.4 Complaints and compensation

There are rules requiring authorised firms to operate detailed monitoring and compliance procedures to ensure that the rules are obeyed and to have suitable procedures for dealing with complaints from investors.

Authorised firms are required to contribute a levy to a compensation scheme established by the SIB under which, in the event of an authorised firm going into liquidation, investors may recover up to a maximum of £48,000 if the firm is unable to meet its liabilities.

3.4 Complaints and remedies

3.4.1 Basic procedure

If an investor has a complaint about an authorised firm the investor should raise the matter initially with the firm's compliance officer who is an employee of the firm with responsibility for ensuring that the firm complies with the rules. If the firm does not handle the complaint to the investor's satisfaction the investor may refer the matter to the relevant complaints body. The appropriate complaints body will depend upon the arrangements which that firm's SRO or RPB has made. For example, many life assurance and unit trust companies are members of the Insurance Ombudsman Scheme and it is this body that would deal with the investor's complaint. It is the authorised firm's responsibility to inform the investor as to the appropriate complaints body. The complaints body has a range of sanctions which can be imposed including awarding appropriate compensation for any losses suffered by the investor.

Referring a complaint to one of the relevant complaints bodies does not normally prevent the investor from pursuing any other legal remedies. In addition to bringing civil actions for breach of contract or negligence, the private investor is given a right, under the FSA, to sue an authorised firm for any breach of the investor protection rules which causes the investor loss.

Individual SROs as well as the SIB have a range of intervention powers which can be used in the interests of investor protection. These include the SIB's power to prohibit the employment of persons considered to be unfit, to apply for an injunction or restitution order where a breach is threatened or where investors have suffered loss, to restrict the business of investment firms, to restrict any dealings with a firm's assets or even to vest those assets in a trustee.

3.5 Overseas aspects

Overseas firms are subject to the FSA if they carry on investment business in the UK. Unless an overseas company is authorised to carry on investment business in the UK, it is difficult for it to market its products and services to UK investors. It is possible for the overseas firm to promote its products and services in the UK by advertising provided that it can come to some arrangement whereby an authorised person in the UK ensures that the advertisement satisfies the UK rules and takes responsibility for it or alternatively by promoting it through an authorised person.

If the investment is a recognised collective investment scheme or an insurance policy issued by a recognised insurer which it may be if the scheme or insurer is authorised in another EC member state or in a territory designated by the Secretary of State for Trade and Industry (eg, the Isle of Man, the Channel Islands) the authorised firm may market it freely within the UK. Although such a scheme may not be subject to the UK compensation scheme it is possible that it will be subject to a compensation scheme set up in the home country or territory concerned.

If the collective investment scheme or insurance policy is not a recognised scheme then there are severe restrictions on the extent to which it can be promoted in the UK. For example, an authorised person is able to promote such a scheme to established customers under the terms of a subsisting customer agreement but cannot market to investors generally.

3.6 Conclusion and future developments

The FSA provides the framework for the most comprehensive investor protection system ever seen in the United Kingdom or elsewhere in Europe. In the past two years considerable progress has been made by the SIB and the SROs in putting the flesh on the bare bones provided by the FSA.

Changing circumstances brought about by an innovative and competitive financial services industry will require further adaptations of a system which needs to be responsive to such changes. Significant amendments have already been made to the FSA to reduce the duplication and ensure common standards whilst retaining a system of self regulation. Further developments are expected aimed at harmonizing the rules relating to the marketing of various types of packaged product and introducing common standards of competence amongst intermediaries. There is also the challenge of Europe and the need to agree a workable investor protection system across member states of the EC.

The FSA introduced a dynamic system capable of responding to change. There is little doubt that the system will be severely tested during the next few years.

Sources of further information

Useful addresses

LAUTRO (Life Assurance and Unit Trust Regulatory Organisation)
Centre Point
103 New Oxford Street
London
WC1A 1QH

Tel: (071) 379 0444

IMRO (Investment Management Regulatory Organisation Ltd.)
Broadwalk House
5 Appold Street
London
EC2A 2LL

Tel: (071) 628 6022

SIB (Securities and Investments Board)
3 Royal Exchange Buildings
London
EC3V 3NL

Tel: (071) 283 2474

AFBD (Association of Futures Brokers and Dealers)
Fifth floor, sixth section
Plantation House
5–8 Mincing Lane
London
EC3M 3DX

Tel: (071) 626 9763

FIMBRA (Financial Intermediaries, Managers and Brokers Regulatory Association)
Hertsmere House
Marshwall
London
E14 9RW

Tel: (071) 538 8860

TSA (The Securities Association)
The Stock Exchange
Old Broad Street
London
EC2N 1HP

Tel: (071) 256 9000

The Law Society (of England and Wales)
The Law Society's Hall
113 Chancery Lane
London
WC2A 1PL

Tel: (071) 242 1222

The Institute of Chartered Accountants (in England and Wales)
PO Box 433
Chartered Accountant's Hall
Moorgate Place
London
EC2P 2PJ

Tel: (071) 628 7060

The Insurance Ombudsman Bureau
31 Southampton Row
London
WC1B 5HJ

Tel: (071) 242 8613

4 Unlisted investments

John Smithard, of Greenwell Montagu Stockbrokers

4.1 Introduction

4.1.1 Types of unlisted security

This chapter deals with the most commonly available forms of investment which do not have an official quotation or market price. It includes investments issued by the government through national savings, by local authorities and by other financial institutions wishing to raise money, and in general can only be redeemed by the borrower.

With some exceptions, these securities provide the investor with interest until they mature, whereupon he receives the return of his original capital. Although the rates of return on some of these investments might not always compare favourably with returns on other forms of investment, some have taxation advantages up to a specific amount, particularly for the higher-rate taxpayer. Other investments covered in this chapter may produce no income in the course of their lives, but give a guaranteed improvement in capital value on maturity. Premium bonds give no guarantee of income or capital appreciation but offer the holder a chance in draws for tax-free prizes. A comparison of rates of return, the limitations on amounts invested, and conditions of withdrawal are set out in Table 4.1 on pages 40–41.

4.2 Highlights of the previous year

With the Government keeping interest rates on national savings instruments at distinctly uncompetitive rates as set against other similar forms of savings, it is not surprising that the total size of National Savings has continued to decline since the start of 1989. While privatisation and taxation receipts were so strong during the later part of the 1980s, the government used the opportunity to pay back some of the national debt and so did not want to attract new borrowing through the national savings movement; indeed it was

Table 4.1 Current rates of return and conditions (July 1990)

Investment	Return (% pa) Gross*	Return (% pa) Net*	Amount invested Min	Amount invested Max	Withdrawal notice (days)	Notes
1 National Savings Bank: Ordinary accounts	2.5–5[0]	1.9–3.8[0]	£5	£10,000	£100 on demand	[0] Depending on balance, first £70 free of tax
Investment accounts	12.8	9.6	£5	£25,000	30	
2 National savings certificates (35th issue)	9.5[1] (tax free)		£25	£1,000	8	[1] Equivalent to 12.7% to basic-rate taxpayers; further £10,000 if from re-investment of expired NSC
3 National savings index-linked certificates (5th issue)	Increase in RPI[2] (tax free)		£25	£5,000	8	[2] Paid on withdrawal if after one year, with tax-free interest
4 National savings income bonds	13.5	10.1	£2,000	£25,000	3 months	
5 National savings capital bonds	13	9.8	£100	£100,000	3 months	
6 National savings yearly plan	9.5[4] (tax free)		£20pm	£200pm	14	[4] If held for full five-year period
7 Premium savings bond	Chance of prize[5] (tax free)		£100	£10,000	8	[5] Monthly prize fund; one month's interest at 6.5% on each bond eligible for draw
8 Local authority mortgage bonds: 1 year	15.2	11.4				Other terms available

Unlisted investments 41

						Notes
9 Commercial banks: Deposit accounts (7 day)	4	3	25p	None	7[6]	[6] But may be withdrawn on demand subject to deduction of 7 days' interest from balance
High Interest cheque	6.7–13.6	5–10.2	£1,000	None	None	
Certificates of deposit	14.5[7]	10.9	£50,000	None	Marketable security	[7] 3-month term and 6-month term
10 National Girobank deposit accounts	6.7	5	£1	None	4–5	Depending on amount
High interest deposit	12.5–16	9.4–12	£500	None	3 months	
11 Building societies: Share accounts	9.5	7.1	£1		On demand[9]	[9] Up to £300 in cash or £5,000 by cheque; above £5,000 branch refers to head office
Premium accounts	12–15.3[10]	9–11.5[10]	£500	None	0–3 months	[10] Rates vary according to size
12 Certificates of tax deposit	11.5–13[11] 5.0[12]	8.6–9.8[11] 3.8[12]	£2,000	None	0–12 months	[11] If withdrawn for payment of tax [12] If withdrawn in cash
13 Treasury bills	14.3	10.7	£5,000	None	Marketable security	

*Based on tax at the basic rate of 25%

actively encouraging holders of many certificates, for instance, to have their holdings repaid by offering them a paltry return if they were retained. The government may turn to a net borrowing position once again and for national savings this may imply a better balance of return against other instruments, especially with the tax benefits taken into account.

In 1989, the amount of cash held through national savings declined, and stood at the end of February 1990 at £18.4 billion.

As for other forms of deposit, the banks and building societies were forced to follow the trend of higher interest rates, while improving the number of products available to depositors. The change over the last two years or so to an emphasis on interest-bearing current accounts has been most noticeable, and beneficial to most depositors, but needs to be encouraged further.

4.3 Types of unlisted investments

4.3.1 National Savings Bank accounts

The National Savings Bank is guaranteed by the government and is operated by the Post Office as agent. Two types of account—ordinary accounts and investment accounts—are available.

Anyone aged seven years or over can open an account in his own name, and an account can be opened on behalf of a younger child by his parent or legal guardian although withdrawals and encashments are not allowed until the child is seven. Friendly societies and other classes of investor can also open accounts.

Interest on both types of account is credited annually on 31 December. In the case of ordinary accounts, this is for each complete calendar month. For investment accounts, interest is calculated from the day funds are deposited until the day prior to withdrawal. There is a maximum amount which can be withdrawn daily from an ordinary account, and all withdrawals from an investment account require one month's notice.

Interest is paid gross (ie, without deduction of tax at source). In the case of ordinary accounts an individual is given exemption from basic- and higher-rate income tax for the first £70 interest. If a husband and wife each have an account, they can each claim exemption up to this level, although if they hold a joint account the exemption is £140. However, there is no such exemption for the higher gross interest earned on investment accounts.

Although the limit on income tax exemption for ordinary accounts is relatively low, a holding up to this level may be attractive for higher-rate taxpayers.

Accounts can be opened by completing a simple form available from almost any branch of the Post Office. The account holder receives a pass book in which all deposits and withdrawals are entered. The minimum for each deposit is £5.

The pass book no longer needs to be sent in once a year for the adding of interest, as this will be done on the next occasion that it is received by the National Savings Bank.

4.3.2 National savings certificates

National savings certificates are guaranteed by the government. They cannot be sold to third parties. A number of different issues of certificates have been made over the years.

A maximum individual holding is specified for each issue of national savings certificates. Trustees and registered friendly societies and charities approved by the director of savings can also buy certificates.

No interest is paid, but after a stated period of time the certificates can be redeemed at a higher value than the original purchase price. The total rate at which the value appreciates during this period is indicated on the certificate and in the prospectus. However, the value builds up by the addition of increments at the end of the first year and each subsequent period of three months. The full table, showing how the value rises more steeply towards the end of the period and levels off after the end of the period, is available from the details issued by the National Savings Bank. Certificates from the seventh issue earn interest at the general extension rate after maturity. The general extension rate is a variable rate of interest for matured certificates when they have completed their fixed period terms.

The capital appreciation is free from both income tax and capital gains tax. The minimum holding is £25 and the maximum £1,000 in the current issue, but holders may have a further £10,000 certificates if these arise from reinvestment of a holding in an earlier issue.

The certificates can be a suitable form of savings for children. For the pure investor they are not suitable for non-taxpayers or for short-term savings; but for the investor paying tax at the higher-rate, the certificates may be attractive. Application forms are available from most branches of the Post Office and banks.

Holdings should be reviewed from time to time, particularly since new issues may carry more attractive rates of capital appreciation than those already held. A review of holdings should certainly be made at the end of the specified period.

Any number of certificates can be cashed at one time, on at least eight working days' notice, and repayment forms are available at most branches of the Post Office and banks.

4.3.3 National savings index-linked certificates

As with national savings certificates, these certificates are guaranteed by the government. They cannot be sold to third parties.

There is no lower age limit for holding these certificates, although encashment is not allowed until a child reaches the age of seven, except in special circumstances. No more than 200 certificates of £25 ie, £5,000 at initial purchase price can be held in the current issue unless they came from a reinvestment of mature certificates in which case the limit is £10,000. The minimum holding is one certificate.

If a certificate is encashed within the first year, the purchase price only is repaid. If the certificates are held for more than a year, the redemption value is equal to the original purchase price, increased in proportion to the rise in the retail prices index between the month of purchase and the month of redemption. In the event of a fall in the RPI, the certificates can be encashed for the original purchase price. After the death of a holder, indexation can continue for a maximum of 12 months.

The latest issue guarantees a return above the rate of inflation for a five year term by offering extra tax-free interest as well as indexation. The amount of extra interest credited to the holding rises in each year of the life of the certificate after its second anniversary and is itself inflation-proofed. Details of these calculations are shown in the prospectus available at post offices.

After the fifth anniversary certificates continue to earn interest and index-linking, but on such terms as the Treasury may decide. As with national savings certificates, capital appreciation is exempt from income tax and capital gains tax.

Certificates are suitable for individuals who do not need immediate income but are seeking protection in real terms for the amount invested. Higher-rate taxpayers in this category will find the certificates particularly attractive. Application forms are obtainable from most branches of the Post Office.

4.3.4 National savings income bonds

As with national savings certificates, these bonds are guaranteed by the government. Anyone aged seven years or over can buy income bonds and they may be bought for children under seven, but there are two special conditions:

(1) interest is normally credited to a national savings bank account in the child's name;
(2) the bond is not normally repayable until the child reaches seven.

Friendly societies and other classes of investor can also buy these bonds.

Gross interest is paid on a monthly basis but the interest is subject to tax. Investors may cash in part of their holding in multiples of £1,000, but they must keep a minimum balance of £2,000. Investors should be aware of the following terms of repayment:

(1) for repayments in the first year, interest is credited at half the rate from the date of purchase to the date of repayment on the amount repaid;
(2) for repayments after the first year, interest is paid in full.

Three months' notice of repayment is required. The maximum holding is £25,000 for new holders after 1 January 1990.

If the investor dies, the money can be withdrawn without any formal period of notice and with interest paid in full up to the date of repayment.

The bonds are particularly suitable for investors who require high regular income, who can afford to tie up at least £2,000 for a minimum period of 12 months and are not subject to tax. Income is paid monthly, on the fifth of each month. The first payment is made on the next interest date after the bonds have been held for six weeks. Application forms are obtainable from branches of the Post Office.

4.3.5 National savings capital bonds

The bonds are guaranteed by the government. They may be held by individuals, by children and by trustees of a sole individual.

Bonds are bought in multiples of £100 with a £100 minimum and no maximum. Although called capital bonds, they accrue interest which is capitalised on each anniversary of the purchase date, and this accrued interest must be notified to the Inland Revenue on the individual's tax return (and income tax paid, if necessary, before actual receipt of the capitalised interest at the date of maturity). An annual statement of value, showing the capitalised interest, is sent to the bondholder.

The capitalised interest accrues at an increasing rate during the life of the bond and the full advertised compound rate will only be received if held to maturity. This occurs on the fifth anniversary of the purchase date, before which the bondholder will have been reminded by the bond office of the imminence of maturity.

Repayment can be requested at any time for a minimum amount of £100, provided this leaves at least the minimum holding. Three months' notice is required. No capitalised interest accrues before the first anniversary.

Depending on the level of interest rates available elsewhere, capital bonds may prove an excellent investment for an individual who pays little or no income tax and who can tie up his funds for five years, assuming that interest rates will move downwards in the intervening period.

4.3.6 National savings yearly plan

Following the termination of the index-linked save-as-you-earn contracts, the yearly plan has been introduced to give a competitive tax-free return. Security of investment is guaranteed by the government.

Yearly plan contracts are available solely to individuals over seven years of age and to trustees of a sole beneficiary.

The individual contracts to subscribe by standing order a fixed monthly amount of between £20 and £200, in multiples of £5, for a period of 12 months at which time he receives a yearly plan certificate. Each monthly payment is credited with interest for each whole month that it has been invested, and the certificate when issued has a value equal to the capital and accumulated interest for that year. To ensure the highest return, the certificate should be held for a further four years as the interest rate is higher during that period. After these four years, interest is added at the published general extension rate.

If monthly payments are continued after the first year, a further yearly plan will have been entered into, with an overall return dependent on the level of interest rates ruling at the time of the new first payment. Holders will be notified.

The return is free of income tax and capital gains tax and is fixed through the five year period. Yearly plan is a sound method of saving a set sum each month in a tax-efficient manner and with a highly competitive return.

Repayment forms are available at branches of the Post Office and redemption takes around 14 days. A holder may encash his certificate early but the rate of return will then be lower. No interest is given if the yearly plan is ended within the first year.

4.3.7 Premium savings bonds

Premium bonds are guaranteed by the government. They cannot be sold to third parties.

Any person aged 16 or over can buy the bonds, and a parent or legal guardian may buy bonds on behalf of a child under 16. A bond cannot be held in the name of more than one person or in the name of a corporate body, society, club or other association of persons. Prizes won by bonds registered in the name of a child under the age of 16 are paid on behalf of the child to the parent or legal guardian.

The minimum purchase for a child under 16 is £10. Bonds are otherwise sold in units of £1 and purchases must then be in multiples of £10 subject to a minimum purchase at any time of £100 up to a maximum of £10,000 per person.

No interest is paid, but a bond which has been held for three clear calendar months following the month in which it was purchased is eligible for inclusion in the regular draw for prizes of various amounts. The size of the monthly prize fund is determined by applying one month's interest at a predetermined rate to the total value of the eligible bonds at that time. This rate is reviewed from time to time. Bonds can be encashed at any time. All prizes are free of income tax and capital gains tax.

Premium bonds are suitable for higher-rate taxpayers who do not wish to receive income and can set aside some savings with no guaranteed return but with the chance of receiving a tax-free prize.

Application forms are available at branches of the Post Office and from banks. Winning bond-holders are notified in writing at their last recorded address and lists of winning numbers are advertised in newspapers. Repayment forms are available at branches of the Post Office and from banks.

4.3.8 Local authority mortgage bonds

These borrowings are secured on the revenues of local authorities, which have the power to levy rate and community charges. It is generally assumed that the government would stand behind such borrowings, although it has no legal commitment to do so.

A minimum investment is usually specified: this varies between authorities but is smaller than for local authority negotiable bonds (ie less than £1,000).

Local authority mortgage bonds are issued for a fixed term, usually between two and seven years and, unlike local authority negotiable bonds, in which there is a free market on The Stock Exchange, they cannot normally be sold to third parties.

Interest is subject to income tax and is paid after deduction of basic-rate tax. Non-taxpayers will therefore have to claim a rebate of tax, while higher-rate taxpayers will be assessed for the balance of tax due.

Deposits are suitable for the investor who is seeking a competitive rate of interest and is prepared to tie up his capital for a fixed term. An investor who may require to realise his investment more quickly should explore the possibility of negotiable bonds (as to which, see **5.5.2**).

Authorities seeking deposits advertise in the national press, stating the period, rate of interest paid and details of where applications should be made. Deposits are acknowledged by the issue to the holder of mortgage bonds.

4.3.9 Commercial banks—current accounts, deposit accounts, savings accounts and certificates of deposit

Deposits with banks carry no government guarantee and their security therefore lies in the reputation and viability of the bank concerned. Certificates of deposit (CDs) are bearer documents and can be sold to third parties, whereas deposit and savings accounts represent a non-assignable debt from the bank to the holder.

There are normally no pre-conditions to opening a deposit or savings account with a commercial bank. However the minimum sum for an investment in CDs is usually fairly high.

Interest, which is paid at regular intervals on accounts, can be varied by the bank as the general level of interest rates and the bank's own base rate change. Seven days' notice of withdrawal is required for deposit accounts. The interest on CDs is fixed for the duration of the certificates—normally between three months and five years. CDs are negotiable, mainly through the London discount market, at prices which reflect the rate of interest and the unexpired life of the CD. Dealings can be carried out through a stockbroker, money broker, bank or discount house.

Interest on deposit and savings accounts is paid until the 1991/92 tax year net of composite rate tax which cannot be reclaimed. From then a non-taxpayer will be able to reclaim basic tax rate deducted at source.

Deposit and savings accounts are useful means of investing funds which may be needed at short notice. CDs are suitable for large deposits and consequently earn a higher return than deposit or savings accounts. From 1 January 1991, banks will also be able to offer tax exempt special savings accounts (TESSAs), see **4.3.12** and also Chapter 6.

Deposit and savings accounts may be opened, and CDs purchased, by instruction and transfer of cash to the bank concerned.

Bank account statements should be kept for reference. Since CDs are bearer documents, they should be held in safe custody.

4.3.10 National Girobank deposit accounts

National Girobank is a specialist banking subsidiary of the Post Office. It operates both current and deposit accounts and high interest accounts.

To open a deposit account the investor must first have opened an ordinary (ie, current) account, for which the minimum age is 15.

Interest is credited to the deposit account or may be transferred to the current account at the depositor's option. Interest is paid net of composite rate tax and cannot be reclaimed.

Like the deposit and savings accounts of commercial banks, National Girobank deposit accounts are suitable for investors who may require to withdraw money at short notice. The return on the account should be compared with that available on commercial bank deposit accounts.

Current accounts and deposit accounts may be opened by completing application forms available at most branches of the Post Office. Withdrawals can be made by cashing cheques at up to two nominated Post Office branches.

4.3.11 Building society accounts

Building societies offer share accounts, various higher interest accounts, term bonds and save-as-you-earn contracts. None of these investments can be sold to third parties. Security lies in the reputation and viability of the building society concerned. From 1 January 1991 building societies will be able to offer tax exempt special savings accounts (TESSAs), see **4.3.12** and Chapter 6.

The minimum age for entering into an SAYE contract is 16, but any of the other forms of savings may be undertaken by children aged seven or over. For younger children an account may be opened in the name of trustees (normally the child's parents). SAYE contracts are only open to individuals and cannot be undertaken on joint accounts.

Building societies compete for deposits not only with banks but also with each other (their offices are often open to the public for longer hours than the banks during the week and are also open on Saturday mornings). On lump sum investments, interest is usually paid every six months, although in some cases monthly. On SAYE contracts the bonus is fixed at the outset and paid at the end of the fifth and the seventh years, but other savings plans bear interest rates which, although specified at the time of investment, vary from time to time with the general level of interest rates. A period of notice is specified for withdrawals from share accounts but is in practice seldom required except for large sums. There may be penalties for early withdrawal from term bonds.

In most cases interest is paid net of composite rate tax, which is paid by the building society although, with effect from 6 February 1989, building societies have been able to pay interest gross to depositors in certain instances. Non-taxpaying investors have no claim for repayment of tax; but, on the other hand, investors who pay income tax at higher rates are liable for the balance of tax at those rates on the grossed-up amount. Following the abolition of composite rate tax from 6 April 1991 non-taxpayers will be able to reclaim the basic rate tax deducted at source.

The simplicity of building society deposit and share accounts and the ease with which small withdrawals can be made on demand, coupled with the sound record of building societies, make them attractive for basic or higher-rate taxpayers. Application forms are available from local branches of the building societies. Passbooks are issued for most types of investment, although certificates are in some cases issued in respect of fixed term contracts.

4.3.12 Tax exempt special savings accounts (TESSAs)

TESSAs were announced in the 1990 budget and are introduced on 1 January 1991. They provide a means of longer term saving, tax-free, and will be operated on a commercial basis by the banks and building societies.

Each individual over 18 will be allowed one TESSA lasting for five years, following which a new TESSA can be opened under the regulations then in force. A total of £9,000 can be placed in a TESSA, either by monthly deposits of £150, or by lump sum payments of up to £3,000 at the start of the first year, followed by annual payments of up to £1,800 in the three succeeding years and up to £600 in the final year.

Interest accrues during the five year period and is credited net of basic rate tax. At the end of the five years a bonus of the basic rate tax is credited to the account so that in effect the deposit interest is tax-free. During the life of the TESSA up to the full amount of the net income can be withdrawn but any repayment of capital will bring the account to an end, without the bonus. Interest on a TESSA will not need to be declared on tax returns.

Any investor with cash savings, and especially the higher rate taxpayer, should consider a TESSA in combination with his other deposits. Although there is a five year life to the account, he can withdraw his capital and net accrued income at any time (but losing the right to the tax bonus), so the position is not dissimilar to an ordinary deposit account. However, except in cases where the accrued income has been continually withdrawn, an investor thinking of closing his account early should give consideration to the fact that all accrued income will be deemed to have been paid at the time of closure and may increase that year's income tax liability.

4.3.13 Certificates of tax deposit

Certificates of tax deposit are not strictly speaking a form of investment but a scheme operated by the Inland Revenue whereby future tax liabilities can be provided for in advance. The deposits are therefore guaranteed by the government.

Certificates are available to any taxpayer—individual, trustee or corporate—and can be surrendered to meet tax liabilities of any kind, except PAYE income tax or income tax deducted from payments to subcontractors. Different rates apply to deposits below £100,000; there is no maximum deposit.

Interest is paid for a fixed maximum period at a rate specified by HM Treasury when purchased, but the rate varies in line with money market rates. If the deposit is not used to meet tax liabilities but is instead withdrawn for cash, interest is paid at a much lower rate. Interest is paid gross and is subject to income tax.

These certificates are only suitable for taxpayers facing known future tax liabilities, although such taxpayers should consider whether a better return could be obtained by investing elsewhere until such times as the liability has to be met.

Deposits are made by applying to any Collector of Taxes, who issues a certificate specifying the date of receipt and the amount of the deposit. Any request for a deposit to be withdrawn for cash should be made to the collector of taxes, accompanied by the relevant certificates.

4.3.14 Treasury bills

Treasury bills are bearer documents issued by the Bank of England and guaranteed by the government. There is a £5,000 minimum holding.

A Treasury bill is initially a 91-day loan to the Bank of England. No interest is paid but bills are issued at a discount. The difference between the discounted price and £100, the redemption price, is the capital gain accruing to the investor, and the annual rate of discount which it represents is called the Treasury bill rate. Although the holder may not encash the bills at the Bank of England before the due date, they can be sold through the discount market at any time at the prevailing market price.

The difference between the discounted price and the price at which the bills are redeemed at the Bank of England or sold in the market is subject to tax. In the unlikely event of a private investor holding a Treasury bill, the gain would be liable to income tax. Treasury bills are suitable for companies rather than individuals and confer total security on short-term deposits.

Tenders for Treasury bills must be made on printed forms (available from the Chief Cashier's Office, Bank of England) and must be submitted through a London clearing bank, discount house or stockbroker. The value of bills tendered for and the price at which the investor is prepared to buy them must be specified. On the day tenders are received the Bank notifies persons whose tenders have been accepted in whole or in part. Since Treasury bills are bearer documents, they should be held in safe custody.

4.4 Comparing different types of security

The investor, in making a choice between different types of security, should take into account not only the relative importance to him of income and of capital gain but also:

(1) the degree of security against default;
(2) the expected rate of return;
(3) the tax advantages or disadvantages attaching to the security;
(4) the convenience and cost of dealing in the particular security; and
(5) the ability to realise the investment.

4.4.1 Security against default

The British government has the power to levy taxes and to print money and it is in the highest degree unlikely that it would ever default on any of its borrowings, which include national savings certificates, national savings bank deposits, premium bonds and government-guaranteed fixed interest stocks. It is generally assumed that the government would stand behind borrowings of local authorities, which in any event have the power to levy local charges. All these securities, therefore, have an intrinsic safety which the private sector cannot emulate.

4.4.2 Rate of return

The rate of return on securities may be specified and fixed, as it is for conventional national savings certificates, local authority deposits, Treasury bills and fixed interest stocks issued by public and private sector organisations. In most other cases the rate of return is specified initially but may be subject to variation to reflect the general movement of interest rates. Returns on some investments may be linked to the prevailing rate of inflation.

4.4.3 Tax advantages

Certain securities carry tax advantages, which may be of particular benefit to higher-rate taxpayers. Examples are national savings bank ordinary accounts (up to a specified limit), national savings certificates, index-linked national savings certificates and prizes on premium bonds. British government guaranteed stocks are free of capital gains tax (see also Chapter 6).

4.4.4 Convenience and cost of dealing

The securities described in this chapter can (with the exception of certificates of tax deposit and Treasury bills) be negotiated conveniently through high street outlets such as the Post Office, banks and building societies. In many cases no commission or other dealing costs are incurred.

4.4.5 Ability to realise the investment

With the exception of Treasury bills, the securities covered in this chapter cannot be sold to third parties. Thus the investment can only be realised by withdrawing the money from the borrowing organisation. This can be done on demand or at fairly short notice in the case of National Savings Bank accounts and certificates, national savings index-linked certificates (after one year if indexation is required), premium bonds, and bank, Girobank and building society accounts. In other cases the capital initially invested is tied up for a particular period: this applies to local authority deposits and building society term investments as well as national savings income bonds. If certificates of tax deposit are encashed instead of being used to meet tax liabilities, a lower rate of interest is paid. Early withdrawal in these cases will either be impossible or entail a financial penalty. This disadvantage also applies to commitments to save regular amounts through yearly plan schemes.

4.4.6 Maintenance

The investor should retain safely all documents (particularly bearer documents) relating to the investments covered in this chapter. Each time he changes his address the investor should notify the appropriate body.

4.5 Preview of 1991 and conclusion

Until the changes to some rates of return in Summer 1990, there was little to entice the saver into the Post Office. However, full use should be made of the facility of income paid without deduction of tax in order to take a non-working partner's gross income up to the level of his/her personal allowances. Although the return on the investment account and income bonds at the time of writing is not fully competitive with that given by banks and building societies, it has to be remembered that the latter is subject to irreclaimable composite rate tax.

Looking to the future, the government will still need to improve the return on national savings products if it hopes at all to compete with the banks and building societies after the abolition of composite rate tax in the 1991/92 tax year, and the introduction of tax exempt special savings accounts (TESSAs) from 1 January 1991. Over the last few years, as the government attempted to pay back some of the national debt through a contraction of the gilt-edged market, it hardly wished to attract new money through the national savings movement and so kept returns (especially on conventional certificates) at a distinctly uncompetitive rate, forcing redemption of matured certificates; the Chancellor announced in Spring 1990 that his was a 'budget for savers' but only a little help seems to have been offered them through the national savings movement.

The commercial banks and building societies will be competitively enticing depositors to make use of their TESSA schemes and this should attract a good deal of longer term money formerly earmarked for national savings certificates.

Some useful addresses will be found at the end of Chapter 5.

5 Listed investments

John Smithard, of Greenwell Montagu Stockbrokers

5.1 Introduction

This chapter is concerned with securities created when bodies such as the government and individual companies wish to raise money. These securities can be traded on The Stock Exchange, where they are listed. However, this chapter does not deal with shares in private companies. Unlisted securities are covered in Chapter 4.

This chapter contains an introduction to The Stock Exchange and also deals with the distinction between market-makers and agency dealers, the mechanics of dealing in listed UK and overseas securities, as well as those traded on the unlisted securities market, and sources of information.

Sections **5.5** and **5.6** cover fixed interest borrowings ('stocks'), section **5.5** deals with those issued by the public sector and which are traded on The Stock Exchange, and section **5.6** with analogous private sector stocks. The purchaser of either kind of stock knows precisely what interest payments he will receive during the life of the stock, since, with very few exceptions, these are fixed. He also knows what he will receive if he retains the stock until redemption, and since this amount is normally more than the purchase price, he will realise a known capital gain. He also has the option of selling in the market before redemption, although the price obtainable in the market fluctuates from day to day.

Section **5.7** covers companies' ordinary shares traded on The Stock Exchange. Shareholders normally receive dividends the total of which may vary from year to year, reflecting the changing profitability of the company. In addition, the market price of shares may also fluctuate from day to day. There is thus no certainty as to the level either of income return or of capital gain, although the hope is that over a period of years the general level of share prices will rise to reflect inflation and growth in the economy.

5.2 Highlights of the previous year

With 1989 proving much more exciting for UK and other world equity markets than the previous year, the rise in interest rates around the world together with domestic economic and political problems eventually forced UK shares down in the first few months of 1990.

In tandem with many of the world's major markets, London reached a peak as the decade turned, showing a rise of 35 per cent over 1989 as measured by the FTSE-100 Index. The re-rating of equities in the spring of 1989, which followed the 1988 lull, continued to April but excitement was further generated by corporate activity, most notably the takeovers of Consolidated Gold Fields and Plessey by Hanson and the GEC/Siemens consortium respectively, and then the attempted takeover of BAT Industries by the Hoylake consortium. This bid, which was finally abandoned in April 1990, forced BAT's management to seek ways of improving the company's value to its shareholders by splitting off non-essential parts and asset sales. However, the late 1980's phenomenon of bids backed by high borrowings rather than cash or equity seems to have been dealt the death blow by difficulties in the US where acquisitive companies have not been able to generate the necessary cash-flow or asset sales to pay the interest on the junk bonds issued in bids.

The takeover market lost a good deal of its lustre in the UK also when a number of management and leveraged buy-outs turned sour, most notably in the retail sector, which was already feeling the pinch of falling consumer expenditure from higher interest rates. However, corporate activity saw one or two highlights in the second half of the year, first through the July flotation of Abbey National, which produced a huge number of first-time shareholders, and then in December from the successful offer of the water companies, raising over £5bn and producing a good profit for all subscribers.

The total money raised in the primary market during 1989 was £17bn, a 25 per cent rise over 1988's figure. At the end of 1989 the total value of listed investments on the London Stock Exchange was just under £2,300bn, of which UK shares accounted for £500bn, UK public sector stocks £127bn, Eurobonds £120bn, and the balance of around £1,500bn by overseas stocks listed here.

Other activity included RTZ's June acquisition of BP's mineral interests closely followed by the sale of its own chemicals division, the Ford takeover of Jaguar, the takeovers of Pearl and the Halfords chain Ward White, and the acquisitions of Morgan Grenfell and

Dickinson Robinson Group. There were gloomy moments however: many smaller property companies felt the brunt of declining values of portfolios and land-banks, and both Ferranti and British & Commonwealth shareholders must have wished that expensive acquisitions in the past had not been made.

The mini-crash in October, on the second anniversary of the stockmarket crash of 1987, saw share prices retreating rapidly and a bearish view prevailed until sentiment returned as the eastern European countries moved towards democratic control. A strong rise in share prices both here and elsewhere saw markets reach peaks in the new year and then decline as interest rates and inflationary expectations started to rise and Tokyo cracked.

Reduced levels of consumer activity and the contracting UK economy tended to ensure that smaller companies underperformed larger capitalisation stocks, which in general were better exposed to growing overseas economies through exports and overseas manufacturing capacity, and less hurt by the high interest rate regime. Among sectors, those most exposed to domestic consumers suffered most; builders, stores and property underperformed, while health and oils (both high overseas earners) and insurances (on takeover speculation) fared best.

Having been net sellers of gilts, and placing the lowest amount in UK equities for some time, UK institutions put £11bn in overseas equities in 1989, easily a record. For the UK, cash was generally thought to be a safe haven.

In overseas markets, Tokyo's 1990 crash knocked it from the status of the world's largest capitalised market, allowing Wall Street to regain its long-held position by the end of the first quarter. By then Tokyo accounted for 33 per cent of world capitalisation, compared to the US's 35 per cent, and the UK's 10 per cent. These were followed by West Germany at 5 per cent and France at 3 per cent. Japan's problems of higher interest rates, a weak currency and political instability after a number of scandals gave rise to a plummeting market, which had little spill-over effect in the other markets by the time of writing, being perceived as a purely Japanese phenomenon. The US economy was moving towards a measured slow-down and the dollar once again became the beneficiary of world economic tension, helping share prices along even though corporate earnings were starting to drop away. However, it was West German share prices which put on the best performance of major markets, buoyed by the expectation of strong corporate growth arising both from reunification and the single European market in 1992.

Figure 5.1 FTSE 100 Price index

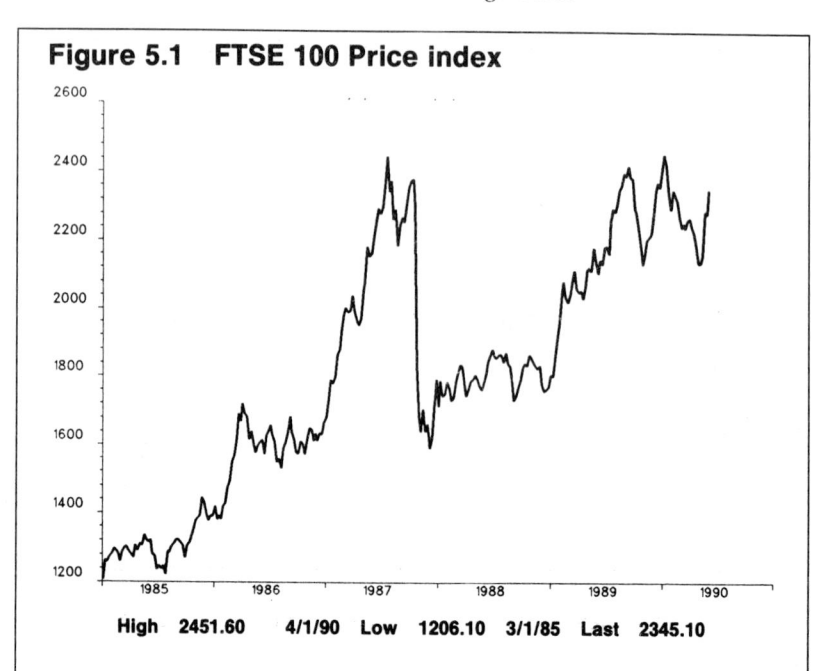

High 2451.60 4/1/90 Low 1206.10 3/1/85 Last 2345.10

Figure 5.2 London FTA All share price index

High 1238.50 16/7/87 Low 581.88 3/1/85 Last 1154.24

Listed investments 61

Figure 5.3 London — FTA Government all stocks price index

High 143.21 17/4/86 Low 114.92 26/4/90 Last 120.73

Figure 5.4 London clearing banks base rate – middle rate

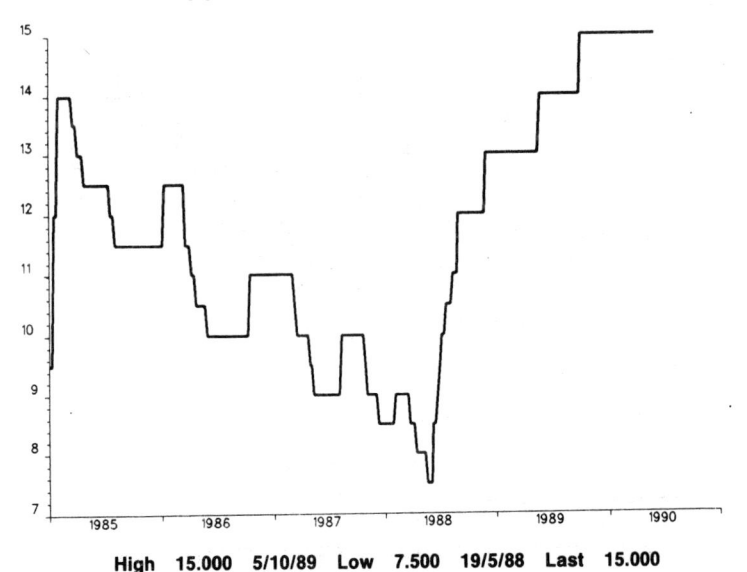

High 15.000 5/10/89 Low 7.500 19/5/88 Last 15.000

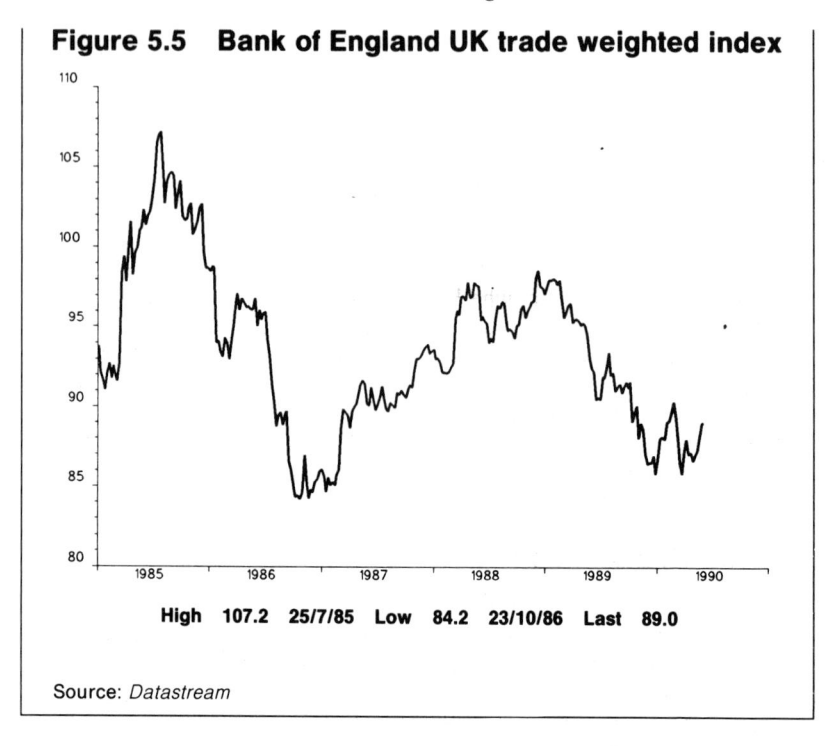

Figure 5.5 Bank of England UK trade weighted index

High 107.2 25/7/85 Low 84.2 23/10/86 Last 89.0

Source: *Datastream*

The graphs on pages 60–62 illustrate:

(1) the performance of ordinary shares (measured both by the familiar FT-SE 100 Share Index and the more representative FT Actuaries All Share Index);
(2) the performance of government securities (gilt-edged stocks, measured by the FT Actuaries All Stocks Index);
(3) the movement in UK interest rates;
(4) the movement of sterling on a trade-weighted basis.

5.3 Comparing different types of security

The investor, in making a choice between different types of security, should take into account not only the relative importance to him of income and of capital gain but also:

(1) the degree of security against default;
(2) the expected rate of return;

(3) the tax advantages or disadvantages attaching to the security;
(4) the convenience and cost of dealing in the particular security; and
(5) the ability to realise the investment.

5.3.1 Security against default

The British government has the power to levy taxes and to print money and it is in the highest degree unlikely that it would ever default on its borrowings whether as national savings (see Chapter 4), gilt-edged securities or Treasury bonds. It is generally assumed that the government would stand behind borrowings of local authorities, which in any event have the power to levy rates and the community charge. All these securities, therefore, have an intrinsic safety which the private sector cannot emulate. The safety of private sector borrowing lies in the reputation, integrity, viability and good management of the body concerned.

5.3.2 Rate of return

The rate of return on securities may be specified and fixed, as it is for fixed interest stocks issued by the government and by public and private sector bodies. In many other cases the return is specified initially but may be subject to variation to reflect the general movement of interest rates. Returns on some investments may be linked to the prevailing rate of inflation. Finally, the return may be dependent, as in the case of ordinary shares, on confidence in and the performance of the company. The more uncertain the return, the more attractive it has to be to compensate for the risk of underperformance. On the other hand, the investor should beware of overvaluing the certainty of return in money terms, since the real value of such returns can be eroded by inflation.

5.3.3 Tax advantages

The basic-rate income tax payer is likely to find little tax advantage in individual forms of listed security and he must choose whether the emphasis in his portfolio is to be on high income, the prospect of capital gain, or a balance between the two. Naturally, both among fixed interest stocks and ordinary shares, the investor will find a range of income yield from which to choose, and a stock which offers a good net return to a basic-rate investor may not appeal so much to an investor who pays the higher-rate. In terms of capital gains tax, British government stocks are exempt, no matter how long they have been held, and individuals will find that they have an exemption also for the first £5,000 of capital gains on disposals in the 1990/91 tax year, after the indexation of book cost. Most trusts have an exemption of the first £2,500 of indexed capital gains on disposals in this tax year. In equities, including unit and investment trusts (to a limit), each individual can also take advantage of a personal equity plan, in which dividend income is free of all income tax and capital gains are exempt from CGT.

5.3.4 Convenience and cost of dealing

In general, investments listed on The Stock Exchange are liquid within reason and no investor should feel tied into any holding unless it is of unmarketable size. Dealing on The Stock Exchange, whether direct through a stockbroker, or indirect through an agent, will generally involve the payment of commission and other expenses.

5.4 The Stock Exchange

5.4.1 Constitution and regulatory role

Historically the burden of supervision of the securities industry has lain with The Stock Exchange. However, under the Financial Services Act 1986, Stock Exchange member firms must now be monitored by a self-regulatory organisation (SRO) which, in turn, is approved by the Securities and Investments Board (SIB). In the SIB's hands rests the responsibility, delegated by the Department of Trade and Industry, for the entire securities industry—this includes Stock Exchange business, life assurance, unit trusts and commodities—both to regulate and to defend standards. Rules of any SRO must be equivalent in effect to those of the SIB and the remainder of the industry.

In 1986, fearful of the consequences of the drift in trading in major equities away from The Stock Exchange, a merger was agreed between it and the International Securities Regulatory Organisation (who were predominantly dealing in Eurobonds but increasingly in equities) to form The Securities Association; this would act as the SRO to cover the joint membership and would combine the individual functions of each organisation. Dealings formerly done on The Stock Exchange would then take place on one Recognised Investment Exchange (RIE) with Eurobond trading on another. The Stock Exchange is known more formally as the International Stock Exchange of the United Kingdom and the Republic of Ireland Limited.

From its earliest origins in the coffee houses, through the establishment of an elected membership at the beginning of the nineteenth century, practice and regulation have developed together. The rules had evolved to meet changing circumstances and to deal with abuses. Under the Financial Services Act 1986 the position has now changed in that The Securities Association (as SRO) has taken over a number of the regulatory roles, such as the authorisation of members, their conduct of business with clients and compliance matters. The Stock Exchange (as RIE) remains responsible for the dealing rules, the listing of new securities and the provision of market related information services amongst many other matters. There is a close working relationship between the two bodies.

5.4.2 The primary and secondary markets

The Stock Exchange provides the main securities market in the UK, representing both a new issue and a trading market. The new issue, or primary, market provides the mechanism for the raising of capital by means of the issue of securities. Users of capital, be they government, local authorities or public companies, all seek funds of a long-term nature, and a large part of these funds is obtained by the issue of securities through the primary market.

Suppliers of capital, whether they are institutional or individual savers, need to invest their money in such a way that it is readily realisable. Hence the existence of the secondary, or trading, market in which it is possible to deal in several thousand securities listed on The Stock Exchange. It is also possible to deal in traded options (see **5.7.2**). The overall market capitalisation of securities listed on The Stock Exchange at 31 December 1989 was £2,281bn of which gilts accounted for £127bn and UK equities for £507bn. The balance was made up by overseas stock with a London listing and eurobonds.

5.4.3 The Unlisted Securities Market, the Third Market and other markets

In November 1980 the Council of The Stock Exchange established the Unlisted Securities Market, to provide a market for smaller or less mature companies for whom a full listing is inappropriate. Securities of companies admitted to this market are not officially listed for statutory purposes, so that there are restrictions on the extent to which they can be purchased by certain investors, such as investment and unit trusts. This market is regulated by The Stock Exchange but in general the requirements for companies admitted to the USM are less onerous than those for listed companies.

Following directives under European Community legislation, it seems likely that the Third Market will have been phased out by

1 January 1991. One of these directives demands an upgrading of the legal requirements for prospectuses for entrants to both the Unlisted Securities Market and to the Third Market, reducing also the trading history needed for an entrant to full listing. Demand for entry to the Third Market will decline sufficiently for it to be abandoned. It had been launched in January 1987 in order to bring a number of over-the-counter market-makers under the umbrella of The Stock Exchange and give a degree more respectability to an area which had seen some problems in the past. The initial response was not high. Companies whose shares are traded on this market are generally at the start-up and early-development stages and investors are advised to be more cautious before committing their funds due to a limited trading history. There will always be companies which will develop strongly, but potential investors must research their target and be prepared sometimes for a long wait until fruition. Turnover in the market is low and so marketability of shares, especially when selling, can prove difficult. The relationship with The Stock Exchange is through the sponsoring broker.

Permission may also be obtained from the Council of The Stock Exchange under Rule 535.2 for specific bargains in the securities of some companies which are neither officially listed on The Stock Exchange, nor admitted to the USM or the Third Market. This makes it possible for a shareholder in such a company to sell his shares through The Stock Exchange (subject to prior permission) and, for an investor wishing to do so, to take an interest in an unlisted company which may be known to him from a local or other source. Companies whose securities are dealt in under Rule 535.2 have not been subjected to the same critical examination which has been undergone by listed companies and by those admitted to the USM or the Third Market; and there is no formal relationship between The Stock Exchange and such companies. Accordingly, The Stock Exchange will not allow a 'market' to develop in such securities and restricts the number of bargains allowed. Deals are done on a 'matched bargain' basis.

5.4.4 Overseas securities

This chapter is primarily concerned with UK securities, but British investors should remember that they can also deal in foreign securities, not only those listed on The Stock Exchange in London, but also those listed on foreign exchanges. In 1979 the exchange control regulations which had been in force for about forty years were abrogated so that currently UK investors can invest throughout the world without any restriction imposed by UK regulations, although such investors may be affected by local regulations.

Residents of the UK are no longer required to deposit all foreign currency securities with an authorised bank or other authorised depositary in the UK, although on grounds of security and to protect the investor's interests on dividends and stock issues, it is still advisable for some foreign stocks, in particular those which are in bearer form, to be held by a bank or agent, either in the UK or overseas. Neither should investors overlook the withholding tax of the country in which they invest, since this is not always allowable against UK tax. Should bearer bonds be lost, the expenses incurred and work involved in obtaining duplicates can be considerable.

5.4.5 Dealing on The Stock Exchange

Following Big Bang in October 1986, the distinction between firms acting as stockbrokers and stockjobbers became blurred. Formerly, a member firm of The Stock Exchange would deal only as one or the other: as a broker it would advise and transact business for its clients, either individuals (private clients) or institutional, with a jobbing firm whose role was to buy, and to sell securities owned by it, for its own profit. Investors could not deal direct with a jobber, but were obliged to deal through a stockbroker who would charge a commission for this (the amount being laid down by The Stock Exchange). This commission also covered ancillary services such as advice, valuations and tax calculations.

The current position is that broking and jobbing (now called market-making) subsidiaries can belong to the same parent. Although institutional investors can now deal direct with market-makers, not being charged commission but trading at net prices, they will not receive advice or recommendations. Many institutions, and all private clients, will continue to use the broking arm of a firm exercising both roles, or a firm which concentrates solely on broking. Broking continues in the same manner as before: advice, recommendations, dealing at best price, settlement and protection of benefits accruing to the investment until registration.

The minimum rates of commission (formerly set by The Stock Exchange) have been abandoned and firms have been left to charge their own rates. For the private client, it may be that the commission charge has changed very little, and firms are now moving towards charging for ancillary services in order to keep dealing commissions competitive.

Generally, the method of dealing in stocks and shares is as follows (see Figure 5.6 (flowchart) on page 68). The client will speak or write to the stockbroker looking after his affairs and is likely to discuss

68 *Allied Dunbar Investment and Savings Guide*

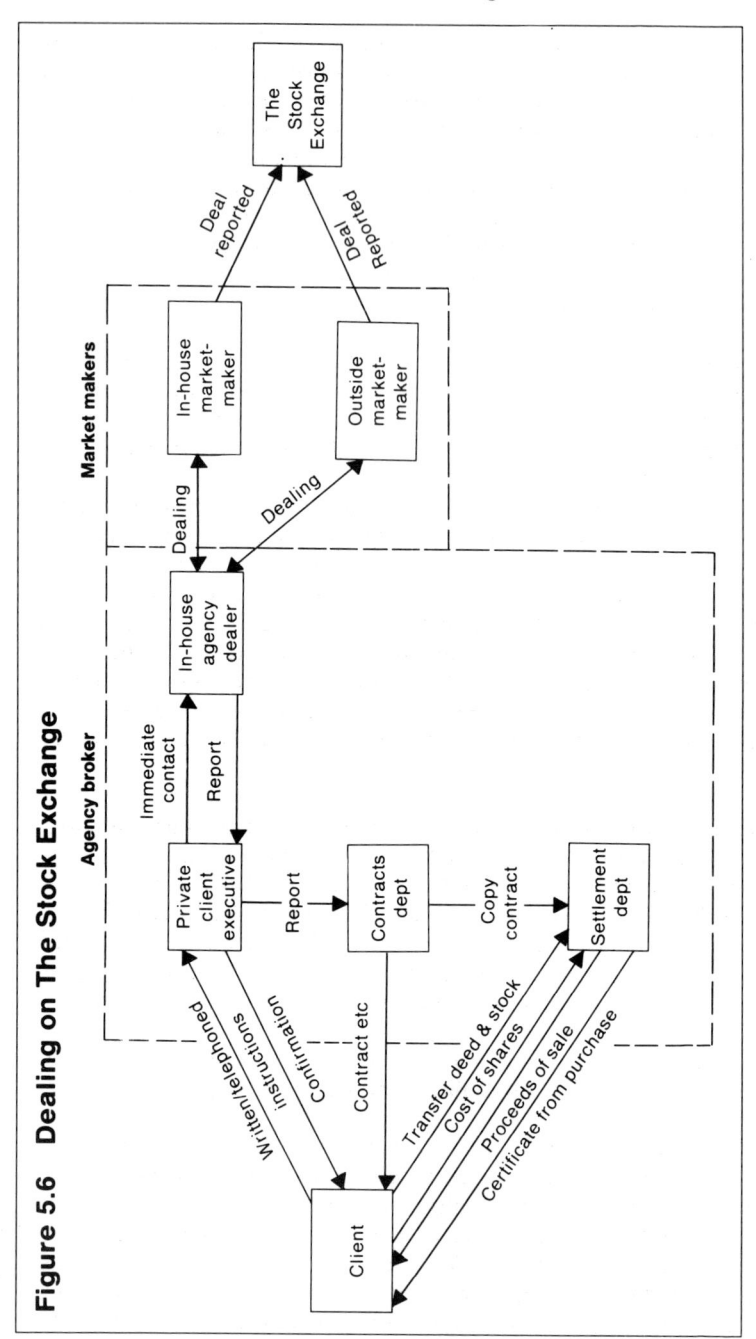

Figure 5.6 Dealing on The Stock Exchange

what he wishes to do. The initial contact might alternatively have been made by the stockbroker. At this stage, if a sale is intended, it may be necessary for the broker to estimate potential tax liabilities as this may have some bearing on the discussions—many brokers will keep a running record of earlier transactions for the client to help them. By referring to sources of information to hand, primarily the screen-based TOPIC service, the broker will be able to give some indication of the current trading price. If an order is given by the client, it will be attempted immediately unless an unobtainable price limit has been given.

The broker then contacts his dealing staff whose function is to deal with the market-maker in that share who is offering or bidding the best price in the size (number of shares) required by the client. The change from face-to-face encounters on The Stock Exchange floor to a screen-based system means that the agency dealer needs only to look at his monitor to find the best price available in the most frequently traded 500–600 stocks (known as alphas and betas) where market-makers' two-way quotes are firm; but those shown for the smaller-capitalised and low turnover gammas and deltas are indicative only and are not necessarily true dealing prices. The dealer will complete the order, occasionally with reference to the private client executive if there is some difficulty in dealing, with one or more market-makers including, in many cases, the in-house market-making side. The dealer should always try to improve on the prices quoted by the market.

With investor protection being of paramount importance, any deal for a client transacted through the in-house market-maker has to be done at the best price available in the market at that time, whether made by the in-house team or others. It will often be the case that the in-house team will match the best available price elsewhere, when they are not making it themselves, as the private client order is on average relatively small set against the size of institutional orders.

The Stock Exchange floor was closed in 1987, except for the Traded Options Market, and all dealing is now inter-office.

The dealer, having completed the bargain, will report to the private client broker who in turn, if requested, will contact the client with oral confirmation. The time of dealing will appear on the contract note so that no confusion will arise as to price, especially important in shares whose prices are volatile. The contract note, which will indicate whether the bargain has been made with a connected party, will then be produced together with any other documentation required to cover a sale. An example of a bought contract note appears on page 71 (Figure 5.7)—a sold contract note would not include stamp duty. The costs would be deducted from the sale consideration, rather than being added.

The settlement date appears on the contract note. Generally, settlement for a gilt is made on the next working day although delayed settlement can be agreed in advance. For equities, settlement is on account day. The Stock Exchange dealing year is divided into account periods of two weeks (there are the occasional three week accounts when bank holidays occur) commencing on the Monday of the first week and running to 4.30 pm on the Friday of the following week. For the private client, deals during the account are netted off and a balance one way or other is paid on account day, usually the second Monday after the end of the account. Settlement for all purchases is the due date, but payment of proceeds of sales can be delayed if the correct documentation is not with the stockbrokers by settlement day.

When selling, a client can expect to receive immediately in the post the contract note, which should be kept for tax purposes, and a transfer form. The transfer must be signed by the registered holder of the investment and returned to the brokers (together with the certificate representing the holding). The transfer form for sales of gilts eventually shows both seller and purchaser, although only the seller's name appears initially. Sales of unit trusts are covered by the same type of form, or through endorsing the reverse of the certificate. As to UK registered shares and corporate loans, a different transfer form is completed allowing settlement through the TALISMAN system.

TALISMAN was introduced in 1979 to speed up and simplify the transfer of shares from sellers to buyers. It uses a centralised settlement system in which shares from all sellers are transferred into The Stock Exchange's own nominee company, SEPON Limited, which holds them until the correct form is lodged to transfer the shares to the buyer's name. The earlier system linked buyers and sellers on the same transfer form, causing lengthy delays in cases where sellers could not produce certificates or did not sign the transfer in time. It is true that if there is no balance of shares in a particular company in SEPON, the buyer cannot yet be registered on that company's books but, where there have been a number of buyers and there is a balance, shares are now apportioned out of SEPON in date order, and the average waiting time for registration of the buyer is much shorter. TALISMAN has been extended to cover actively-traded South African, Australian and Irish shares.

Figure 5.7 Contract note

Name and address
of stockbrokers

Bargain ref: Bargain date:
                                                                    Time of deal:

As agents we have bought for Mr J Smith

       10,000 United Sprockets ord 25p at 56p   £5,600.00

                Commission at 1.5%   £84.00
                Stamp duty   28.00
                PTM levy   0.10
                                                112.10
                                          £5,712.10

Bargain effected with connected company   Settlement date:

Subject to the rules, customs, usages and   (Signature of stockbrokers)
interpretations of The Stock Exchange   Members of the Stock Exchange

Transfer of bearer shares—mostly overseas companies—passes on good delivery. North American shares are in bearer form once the registered holder has signed the pre-printed form on the reverse of the certificate.

The buying client will not see a transfer form but will immediately receive a contract note. This should be kept for taxation purposes. If so arranged, he may also be sent a dividend mandate form, to be signed and passed to his bank, which will authorise the company (or the Bank of England for a gilt) to pay all dividends direct to his bank account instead of his registered address. There is little more for him to do, except to arrange payment to his broker on settlement day. Depending on the speed of registration (usually out of the broker's hands) he would expect to see a certificate for his new holding within eight weeks of purchase. The company's registrars must be informed of any change of the investor's address.

When a company intends paying a dividend, it must temporarily halt the registration of new shareholders in order to produce dividend warrants and tax vouchers in time for the dividend date. The registration process for that dividend stops on the 'record' or 'books-closing' date, shortly after account day for the last Stock Exchange account in which the company's shares were being dealt in cum-dividend form. Dealings in this form include the right to the forthcoming dividend. On the first day of the following account the shares are marked ex-dividend; sellers then retain the right to the dividend and purchasers do not buy the coming dividend with the shares. Even under the TALISMAN system, shares bought cum-dividend are occasionally not able to be re-registered in time for the record date and the company is obliged to pay the seller, as his name still appears on its books. It is then for the seller's broker to claim the dividend from his client and for the buyer's broker to pay the dividend to his client. The dividend will be passed from selling broker to buying broker.

If a company makes a capitalisation issue (often called a scrip, bonus or free issue) or a rights issue, a record date is used once again, although The Stock Exchange will not usually mark the shares ex-entitlement until the working day immediately after new certificates or documents of title are posted. It is the buying broker's duty to claim from the selling broker any entitlement received by the seller which belongs to the buying broker's client. Where a seller is unable to produce documents of title for a rights issue by the time that new shares have to be accepted, then his broker must protect the buyer's entitlement so that those new shares do not lapse.

Listed investments 73

Stamp duty is payable on purchases of shares, warrants and convertible loan stocks: it is collected by the buying broker and accounted for on the bought contract note. The current rate is 0.5 per cent on the consideration after rounding up to the next £100. There is no stamp duty payable on purchases of gilts or corporate loan stocks. For unit trust purchases, the stamp duty is covered by the initial charge. Stamp duty at differing rates may be charged on purchases of overseas shares. In certain transactions, eg, purchase and sale by an investor of the same shares within a Stock Exchange account or purchase of renounceable letters of acceptance or allotment, stamp duty reserve tax is payable at the rate of 0.5 per cent on the amount or value of the consideration. In his 1990 budget the Chancellor announced that stamp duty on Stock Exchange transactions would be abolished from 1992 to coincide with the introduction of the paperless settlements system TAURUS.

The scale of minimum commissions set by The Stock Exchange has now been abolished and brokers are able to charge competitive rates. A new client should ensure that he knows what rate of commission will be charged on his dealings: firms have started to charge non-advisory clients, requiring only a dealing service, different rates from those charged to clients needing advice and periodic valuations.

Deals showing consideration of £5,000 or more also attract a flat 10p levy to help fund the costs of the Panel on Takeovers and Mergers.

5.4.6 Stockbroker services and licensed dealers in securities

Stockbrokers, market-makers, licensed dealers in securities and all others in the industry are subject to regulation by self-regulatory organisations, answerable to the Securities and Investments Board with wide-ranging powers.

Stockbrokers provide a variety of services in addition to buying and selling on behalf of clients. Brokers act on the specific instructions of their clients and give advice when called on to do so. They can also provide routine valuations of a portfolio at regular intervals and make recommendations. Alternatively a client may choose to give his broker discretion to manage his investments on his behalf, buying and selling when the broker considers it to be advantageous and reporting his actions to his client. Charges, if any, for these services (over and above the commission that they charge for dealing) vary from firm to firm.

The stockbroker, with access to economic and analytical material, often produced by his own firm's research department, is able to advise on investment policy and help in the choice of securities which best match his client's objectives. The investor can approach a firm of stockbrokers direct, or can instruct his bank, accountant, solicitor or other financial adviser to approach a stockbroker on his behalf.

5.4.7 Sources of information

Every weekday the previous day's dealing and closing prices of listed securities are published in The Stock Exchange Daily Official List. The last recorded marks are also shown for securities traded in the Unlisted Securities Market and the Third Market. The *Financial Times* and other newspapers also give a list of closing prices—generally the middle market price of each (ie the average of the buying and selling prices), although many are now showing the two-way price.

A number of indices are published, of which the FT-SE 100 Share Index is the best known: it is widely quoted in the press and used as a barometer of price movement of shares. More sophisticated indices are published in respect of government securities, fixed interest and gold mining shares. The most representative indices for ordinary shares are the *Financial Times* Actuaries Share Indices, covering at present 682 shares and 35 different sections of the market. These are compiled daily. The FT-SE 100 Share Index is an arithmetically weighted index of 100 leading UK shares, revalued each minute, giving an immediate picture of market movements. The companies appearing in the index are, in general, the largest in market capitalisation terms and account for almost 70 per cent of the total capitalisation of the UK equity market.

Daily indices of government securities, corporate fixed interest securities and gold mining shares are published in the financial press, together with indices of overseas markets.

Apart from primary sources of information such as political and economic news and statements, and annual accounts and other reports and circulars issued by companies, a wide range of information and comment is available from financial columns in newspapers, financial journals and newsletters. In addition, the results of stockbrokers' research covering both individual companies (many of which have been visited by the stockbroker), and sectors of the market are published together with economic forecasts, and various publicly available statistical services provide immediate access to relevant information. All this information provides the raw material for what is termed 'fundamental analysis'.

Technical analysis—the use of charts—provides data expressed in three forms: line, bar and point-and-figure charts. It is not the purpose of this chapter to explain these three forms of chart in detail, still less to comment on methods of interpreting them. However, charts are often a useful source of further information, for instance, apart from displaying the levels of the main markets, they can also be used to show a price level of a particular share or stock in relation to an appropriate index and how the performance of the particular investment has changed over a period of time in relation to the market generally.

Information issued by The Stock Exchange, such as the total number of daily bargains and the volume of equity turnover, has for some time been used as a measure of the current level of activity in the market. Other more sophisticated charts, such as confidence and over-bought/over-sold indicators, are now increasingly used and from these and many others the technical analyst tries to assess what is likely to happen in the future. In essence, chartists use technical analysis as a tool for demonstrating the existence of complex interrelationships between events and expectations, with a view to determining from established trends and patterns the direction in which the market generally, or a particular share, will move.

5.5 Listed public sector securities

5.5.1 British government stocks

Legal nature
British government stocks (also called 'British funds' or 'gilt-edged securities') represent borrowings by the British government or borrowings of certain nationalised industries which are guaranteed by the government. The investor can be entirely confident that interest will be paid and the principal repaid in accordance with the terms of the loan. A number of names are used for specific stocks—Treasury, Exchequer, Funding, Gas, etc—but these have no practical significance for the investor.

Pre-conditions
Gilt-edged securities listed on The Stock Exchange may be held by all categories of UK investor—governmental, personal, corporate or trustee. However, friendly societies or trustees acting without specific

investment powers in their trust deeds must observe the Trustee Investments Act 1961.

Characteristics

British government stocks, with certain limited exceptions, carry a fixed rate of interest (the 'coupon') which is expressed as an annual rate on £100 nominal of the stock. Thus the holder of £100 nominal of Treasury $8\frac{3}{4}$ per cent 1997 will receive £8.75 per year until that date (subject to deduction of income tax at the basic rate), irrespective of the price which he may have paid or of the market price from time to time. In March 1981 the first issue of a gilt-edged stock on which both capital and interest were linked to the retail prices index was launched and currently stocks are available with redemption dates ranging to 2024. With the exception of Consols $2\frac{1}{2}$ per cent, on which interest is paid quarterly, interest on all British government stocks is paid at six-monthly intervals.

In addition to paying interest during the lifetime of the stock, the government has an obligation to redeem its stock, ie, to repay each loan at the nominal, or par, value of £100. The precise nature of this obligation is different for different stocks: it may be to redeem either:

(1) on a fixed date (eg, Treasury $8\frac{3}{4}$ per cent 1997 must be redeemed on 1 September 1997); or
(2) within a specified range of dates (eg, Exchequer Gas 3 per cent 1990/95 must be redeemed at some time between 1 May 1990 and 1 May 1995); or
(3) on a small number of low coupon stocks (eg, Consols $2\frac{1}{2}$ per cent, Treasury 3 per cent and War Loan $3\frac{1}{2}$ per cent) at any time chosen by the government.

The government is unlikely ever to redeem the stocks in the last category unless the general level of interest rates falls below the coupon. They are purchased mainly for the interest payments, which give a high level of fixed income; but capital growth on them depends on interest rates falling rather than on the passage of time to a certain redemption date. The government is also unlikely to redeem a stock in category (2) above before the last date for redemption if the general level of interest rates remains higher than the coupon.

The period still unexpired before redemption is used to classify government stocks, as follows:

(1) Short-dated stocks ('shorts') are defined as stocks with less than five years until redemption.

(2) Medium-dated stocks ('mediums') are stocks with between five and 15 years still to run to redemption.
(3) Long-dated stocks ('longs') are stocks with over 15 years until redemption.
(4) Undated or irredeemable stocks are those with no final date specified for redemption.

Although all the irredeemable stocks have low coupons, there is a wide choice of different coupons in the other categories, ranging from $2\frac{1}{2}$ per cent to $15\frac{1}{2}$ per cent. The investor should therefore be able to find a stock which combines the redemption date which he is seeking with his preferred rate of coupon.

The two benefits of buying gilt-edged stocks are (1) the interest received; and (2) the capital profit which can be made when a stock bought below par is repaid at par or when a stock is sold through The Stock Exchange at more than the purchase price. Two kinds of yield can be calculated to help in assessing the benefits: running yield and redemption yield.

The running, flat, or interest yield ignores the possibility of capital profit and takes into account only the interest. It is calculated by dividing the coupon by the price paid by the investor, ignoring any accrued interest, and multiplying by 100 to produce a percentage.

The redemption yield takes account of both the interest and the capital gain (or, in some cases, loss) which would occur if the stock was held until redemption. The most common form of redemption yield is the gross redemption yield, which ignores the effect of income tax. A net redemption yield can be calculated after deducting tax (at the rates incurred by the investor). A grossed-up net redemption yield can also be calculated, to indicate the rate of interest which cash put on deposit would need to earn to give the same return as the stock, allowing for tax at the particular investor's highest marginal rate. Where the stock is redeemable within a specified range of redemption dates, the redemption yield is calculated assuming the last possible redemption date if the stock is standing below par, but assuming the first possible date if it is standing above par. Redemption yields cannot of course be calculated for undated stocks, since there is no prospect of redemption.

The price of gilts is determined by such factors as the amount of new stock which the government might have to issue to fund its borrowing requirement, the amount of new money flowing into the institutional investors (such as pension funds), and the attractiveness of gilts compared with other investment opportunities. Thus, if the general interest rates and yields on other investments rise, the yields on gilts will also rise, ie, the price of gilts will fall. With the probable exception of index-linked stocks, gilt prices will also fall if inflationary expectations rise. Any kind of political, economic, financial or industrial news may affect gilt prices, in so far as it affects the market's expectations about inflation, interest rates or the government borrowing requirement.

Although gilt prices do not tend to fluctuate as much as those of ordinary shares, the timing of both purchases and sales still requires careful consideration.

Following the introduction of new rules in February 1985 designed to prevent 'bond-washing' or the substitution by investors of tax-free capital gain for taxable income, the market price of all gilts excludes the interest which has accrued since the last interest date and a separate payment is made in respect of this. In a 'cum dividend' transaction (one where the purchaser will receive the next dividend payment) the purchaser pays to the seller the amount of interest which has accrued to the date of sale since the last interest payment, as the purchaser will later be receiving interest for the full six-month period. In an 'ex dividend' transaction (where the seller will receive the next dividend payment) the seller pays to the purchaser the amount of interest which will accrue between the date of sale and the next interest date.

In March 1981, the government made its first issue of an index-linked gilt, whose redemption value and annual income return were linked to the change in the retail prices index in order to compensate the holder to maturity for the effects of inflation. Since this date, and with inflation at lower levels, these stocks have been a cheaper method of finance for the government than conventional higher-coupon fixed interest gilts and a number of further issues have been made.

Income from index-linked stocks is relatively low as the main advantage to a holder is through the inflation proofing afforded to the invested capital. The income payments increase every six months to reflect changes in the RPI.

The timing of market purchases and sales requires consideration since dealing prices do not necessarily reflect the underlying value of the stock. A comparison might here be made with index-linked national savings certificates which increase in value each month in line with the change in the RPI (see Chapter 4, **4.3.3**).

As with conventional gilt-edged stocks, the market price of index-linked stocks will not include interest which has accrued since the last payment date.

Taxation

Interest is paid net of basic rate income tax, except in the case of War Loan 3½ per cent and any stock bought through branches of the Post Office. Interest received by individuals is treated as investment income and is subject to higher-rate income tax, where appropriate.

With some exceptions, overseas holders of gilts who are both resident and ordinarily resident outside the UK are exempt from all UK taxes on a large number of British government securities. Exempt individuals should be able to arrange with the Inspector of Foreign Dividends to have interest on the appropriate stocks paid gross. In choosing stocks in which to invest, overseas holders should take care to ensure that they choose *approved* stocks, as certain issues do not have the facility for paying interest free of tax to non-residents. Also a non-resident holding an approved stock should be careful when selling, because to be certain of receiving the gross dividend it is not sufficient to sell the stock ex-dividend. To be absolutely safe the sale should not be made until the dividend payment date.

For transfers of certain interest-bearing securities made on or after 28 February 1986, the provisions of the accrued income scheme, introduced by the Finance Act 1985, apply. The securities affected include any loan stock or similar security (but not shares in a company) whether of the UK government, any other government, any public or local authority in the UK or elsewhere or of any company.

Where such securities are transferred the scheme provides for apportionment of interest on a daily basis with the result that, for tax purposes, the seller is treated as having received interest accruing up to and including the settlement day and the purchaser is treated as having received the interest accruing thereafter. Interest is therefore deemed to have been received by the seller on a sale 'cum div' and by the purchaser on a sale 'ex div' and, in each case, there is a corresponding rebate for the other party to the transaction. The charge to tax is calculated by reference to interest periods which will usually end on each normal interest payment date. If deemed interest exceeds rebates for a given interest period, the difference is chargeable to income tax under Schedule D, Case VI (or, where the securities are non-UK securities, Schedule D, Case V).

No charge will arise if the taxpayer concerned is an individual and at no time in the year of assessment in which an interest period ends, or the previous year of assessment, does the nominal value of securities held by him exceed £5,000. Husband and wife are treated separately for this purpose.

Stamp duty is not payable on purchases of British government stock.

Suitability

Investment in British government stocks is a convenient way of providing for future commitments, the timing and size in money terms of which are known or can be confidently predicted. On the other hand, if the size of the commitment is uncertain because of the impact of inflation in the intervening period, the investor should consider a portfolio comprising both fixed interest stocks, index-linked stocks and ordinary shares.

Because default is virtually inconceivable and interest and redemption value are both fixed, with the exception of the irredeemable issues and the index-linked stocks, gilts are also ideal for the investor for whom security is paramount. Most investors through The Stock Exchange will place some value on security and are therefore well advised to include a proportion of such stocks in their portfolios. Trustees, if they have not been given express powers by their particular trust deed, are obliged by the Trustee Investments Act 1961 to invest a proportion of the trust funds either in this sector of the market or in other fixed interest stocks carrying 'trustee' status.

Further, the advantages of ready marketability and reasonably high yields should not be overlooked.

Mechanics

There are four ways of dealing in gilt-edged stocks:

(1) by a direct approach to a stockbroker;
(2) by an indirect approach to a stockbroker;
(3) through the Post Office; or
(4) by application for newly issued stock direct to the Bank of England.

Direct approach to a stockbroker

An investor may place his order to buy or sell with a stockbroker who will execute the transaction on The Stock Exchange for a commission. For information on dealing see **5.4.5**.

Indirect approach to a stockbroker

The investor can instruct his solicitor, accountant, bank or other financial adviser to place the order to buy or sell on his behalf with a stockbroker. The stockbroker may share the commission earned from an agent's client with that agent.

Dealing through the Post Office

Members of the public can buy certain stocks (on the National Savings Stock Register) through branches of the Post Office, from which application forms can be obtained. Interest on stocks purchased in this way is paid gross. The maximum amount that may be invested in any one stock on any one day is £10,000, and there is no limit to the total amount of stock which may be held. Execution of orders takes longer than if they are placed direct with the stockbroker, leaving the price paid or received more open to chance. Moreover, the Post Office, unlike stockbrokers, will only accept orders to buy or sell at the best price obtainable, and it cannot give advice, manage portfolios or take orders to buy and sell when prices reach particular levels. On the other hand, fees charged by the Post Office on both purchases and sales may be lower than Stock Exchange commissions.

The Post Office maintains a separate register from the Bank of England Register. Any stock on the National Savings Stock Register may be transferred to the Bank of England Register, but only £5,000 nominal of a particular stock may be transferred by any one investor from the Bank of England Register in a calendar year.

Purchase of newly issued stocks

The above methods of dealing in stocks concern those already issued and trading on The Stock Exchange. When a new stock is first issued by the Bank of England, application forms (obtainable from the Bank of England, banks or stockbrokers or cut out from newspaper advertisements) must be sent to the New Issue Department of the Bank of England. Prior to 1979 all new stocks were issued by the fixed-price method, whereby the government announced the price of the stock (not necessarily at its par value, and sometimes in partly paid form) and the investor applied for the amount required. Occasionally the stock would be over-subscribed at that price, but more frequently the government would have to adjust the price gradually over the following weeks in order to sell it all. However, an experimental 'tender' method was introduced in March 1979. Under this method the terms of issue specify a minimum price, subject to which applicants state the price at which they are prepared to buy and the amount required. The stock is then sold to the highest bidders at the price of the lowest successful bid. Remaining stock, if any, is issued by the tap method, whereby the government, through the Bank of England, supplies further amounts from time to time provided there is sufficient demand from the market.

The names of holders (other than those who bought through branches of the Post Office) are registered with the Bank of England, and holders receive certificates which are evidence of registration. By sending the appropriate form to the Bank of England it is possible to convert registered holdings of a number of specified stocks to bearer bonds. Holders of bearer bonds should arrange for them to be held in safe custody.

The direct cost of dealing is limited to the commission charged by the stockbroker, the Post Office or other agents. For dealing on The Stock Exchange see **5.4.5**.

As a rule, prices per £100 nominal of stock are quoted in multiples of £$\frac{1}{32}$. Three months before redemption, prices are quoted in pounds and pence.

Safe custody
The contract note, which constitutes evidence of a sale or purchase, is relevant, *inter alia*, for taxation purposes and should be kept in a safe place. For stocks where a register is maintained, certificates are evidence of title and should also be kept in a safe place. If certificates are lost, duplicates can only be obtained against an appropriate form of indemnity.

In the case of bearer bonds, no register is maintained and possession is evidence of title. Bearer bonds should therefore be held in safe custody.

5.5.2 Local authority negotiable bonds

Legal nature
These borrowings are secured on the revenues of local authorities, which have the power to levy rates and the community charge. It is generally assumed that the government would stand behind such borrowings, although there is no legal commitment on it to do so.

Pre-conditions
Negotiable bonds are issued with lives of up to five years but most are for one year ('yearling bonds') where the terms are fixed. The minimum holding for bonds is £1,000.

Characteristics
Interest is payable half-yearly and accrues daily.

Taxation
Interest paid on local authority negotiable bonds is subject to income tax, with basic-rate tax being deducted at source.

Suitability
Negotiable bonds are best suited for short-period deposits where the investor seeks a competitive rate of interest on funds which may be required at fairly short notice.

Mechanics
Negotiable bonds are listed on The Stock Exchange and are transferable by a stock transfer form in multiples of £1,000 stock. Issues of bonds usually take place each Tuesday, but applications should be received by stockbrokers a day earlier. Commission on a successful application is likely to be charged by the stockbroker.

Safe custody
The contract note, which constitutes evidence of the sale or purchase is relevant, *inter alia*, for taxation purposes and should be kept in a safe place. Bond certificates are evidence of title and should also be kept in a safe place, although if certificates are lost, duplicates can usually be obtained against an appropriate indemnity.

5.5.3 Other public sector stocks

Certain public boards are entitled by act of parliament to borrow on the security of their revenues without government guarantees, stated or implied. Examples are the Agricultural Mortgage Corporation, the Metropolitan Water Authority and the Port of London Authority.

Commonwealth stocks carry no British government guarantee and are the obligation of the issuing authority.

Commission on both public board stocks and Commonwealth and overseas government stocks is likely to be charged by the stockbroker. In most respects they are similar to debenture stocks (see **5.6.1**). For dealing on The Stock Exchange see **5.4.5**.

In July 1980 the market for overseas borrowers in sterling re-opened and since then a number of issues of the so-called 'bull-dog bonds' have been made. The issues are usually much smaller than gilt-edged issues, averaging around £50 million nominal. The yields available on these issues are higher than on gilt-edged and, depending on the method of sale, they are quoted either in the debenture market or in the gilt-edged market. Several of the issues have features which are not available on gilt-edged stocks, such as lenders' options for repayment at par after a certain number of years. Interest is paid gross on a number of issues.

5.5.4 Eurobonds

A Eurobond is a stock raised with funds circulating outside the country of origin of the currency in which the bond is denominated. Bonds are normally in bearer form with interest coupons attached. There is no withholding tax on the interest payments.

The major investment consideration is the performance of the currency in which the bond is denominated.

The investor can deal through a stockbroker but small deals (ie less than £25,000) may be difficult to arrange. Normally settlement is seven days—five business days. If a foreign exchange deal is required then the broker concerned will arrange this also. Commission on a Eurobond is likely to be charged.

5.6 Listed company fixed interest securities

5.6.1 Legal nature

Fixed interest stocks issued by companies are a form of borrowing. There are three basic types of security:

(1) debenture stocks;
(2) loan stocks; and
(3) preference shares (which are not borrowings).

Debenture stocks
These are either mortgage debentures, secured by a fixed charge on the company's properties, or debentures secured by a floating charge on some or all of the company's assets. Default under mortgage debentures usually gives the holder rights of foreclosure, ie, the right to take over the mortgaged property, or of sale, in order to recover his money. Under a floating charge, the event of default crystallises the security, converting the floating charge into a fixed charge over the assets covered by the charge at the date of default.

Under the Companies Act and the Insolvency Act, in the winding up of a company certain debts are preferential and have priority over debts secured by debenture with a floating charge. These preferential debts include rates; certain taxes, subject to certain limits; and wages and salaries of employees, again subject to certain limits.

For all debenture stock (and, nowadays also, all listed unsecured loan stocks), a trustee is appointed to supervise the performance of the company's obligations and to act for the holders in the event of default. The trust deed sets out the rights of the lenders, including limitations on the company's freedom to act in ways which might undermine their security (eg, borrowing limits are imposed and changes in the nature of the business and substantial disposals of assets are restricted).

Loan stocks

Loan stocks are unsecured obligations. If the borrowing company fails to meet its obligations, loan stockholders are in the same position as other unsecured creditors: they can sue for their money, but if the company's assets remaining after creditors ranking ahead of the unsecured creditors have been paid off are insufficient to meet the claims of all unsecured creditors, stockholders receive only that proportion of the remaining assets which the outstanding principal amount of the loan stock bears to the company's total unsecured debts.

An important variant is convertible loan stock, which carries the right of conversion into the company's ordinary shares (see further **5.6.3**). Other variants include: subordinated stock, where the holder's rights are subordinated to those of other, or other specified, creditors; and guaranteed stock, carrying the guarantee of another company or companies, normally the borrower's parent company. A trustee is appointed to protect the stockholders' interests.

Preference shares

Preference shares are not debts but are part of the share capital of the company, issued on terms which are usually set out in the company's articles of association. Before any dividend is paid to ordinary shareholders, preference shareholders are normally entitled to receive a fixed dividend, provided that sufficient profits are available to cover it. If the company is wound up, preference shareholders rank ahead of ordinary shareholders up to the nominal value of their capital, but have no further rights unless expressly provided for in the articles.

An important variant is convertible preference shares, which carry the right of conversion into the company's ordinary shares (see **5.6.3**).

Other variants include cumulative, non-cumulative, redeemable and participating preference shares.

5.6.2 Pre-conditions

Fixed interest stocks listed on The Stock Exchange may be held by most categories of UK investor, although friendly societies and trustees acting without specific investment powers in their trust deeds must observe the Trustee Investments Act 1961.

5.6.3 Characteristics

Like dated government stocks, dated debentures, dated loan stocks and redeemable preference shares carry a fixed rate of interest for a specified number of years, at the end of which the principal amount becomes due for repayment. However, unlike the government, the company may have the right to repay before the stated redemption date and may do so if general interest rates fall substantially below the coupon. Debentures and loan stocks may also have sinking funds designed to repay all or part of the loan either by purchases of stock in the market or by drawings of stock. Thus the actual life of the investment may prove to be shorter than the originally stated term.

Private sector securities are less easily marketable than gilt-edged stocks and, with the exception of most convertible stocks, can normally be purchased on higher yields than government securities paying the same rate of interest over the same number of years. This yield differential also reflects the value given by the market to the weaker level of security offered by the loan stock.

Convertible stocks, sometimes referred to as 'deferred equities', have certain additional characteristics. Essentially they are securities issued with a fixed interest payment and fixed redemption date, but conferring the right to convert on a certain date or dates into a stated number of ordinary shares of the company.

Convertible stock usually provides a much higher running yield than the ordinary shares of the company concerned, in addition to being slightly more secure, although an investor who exercises his conversion right will not share in any capital gain achieved up to that point by an investor who had originally invested in the ordinary shares. Until the first conversion date, the market price of convertible stock tends to maintain a fairly steady relationship to the market price of a corresponding block of ordinary shares. However, the price of the convertible stock will not fluctuate to the same extent as the share price, since it will also be influenced by the general level of yields on non-convertible fixed interest securities.

Holders of convertible stocks will receive notification of the conversion option and advice should be sought at that time. It is most important to take action by the final conversion date, either exercising the conversion option or selling the convertible stock. Once the right to convert is lost, the stock will then be valued as a straightforward fixed interest security, which often results in a sharp drop in value.

The decision to exercise the right to convert on one of the conversion dates will largely depend on whether the income on the stock is likely to be less than the prospective return, in the form of dividends, on the holding of ordinary shares into which the stock can be converted.

The majority of the convertible securities in issue are convertible loan stocks, but some convertible debenture stocks and some convertible preference shares exist (see **5.6.1**).

More complicated variants include partly convertible stocks; dual currency loans with conversion rights into non-sterling shares; and stocks with detachable warrants conferring the right to subscribe at a future date and at a fixed price for the ordinary shares of the company while retaining the stock if desired.

5.6.4 Taxation

Stamp duty is not payable on transfer of debentures and non-convertible debenture or loan stocks, but it is payable (by the purchaser) on transfer of convertible stocks and on preference shares, whether convertible or not.

Fixed interest stocks bought after 13 March 1984 and fulfilling the requirements for 'qualifying corporate bonds' in s 64 of the Finance Act 1984 are treated in a similar way to government securities (see **5.5.1**) and disposal or redemption gains are exempt from capital gains tax. Losses are not offsettable.

Interest on loan stocks is paid after deducting income tax at the basic rate. Holders not liable to tax may reclaim it, while those liable at the higher rate will be assessed on the gross amount of the interest, credit being given for the tax already deducted at source. The provisions of the accrued income scheme described in **5.5.1** may apply to the transfer of loan stocks.

In the case of preference shares, the 'imputation system' results in a slightly different treatment. The dividend paid is not subject to deduction of tax; instead it carries a 'tax credit'. The recipient's tax liability is calculated on the total of the dividend and the tax credit, with the result that for a basic-rate taxpayer there will be no further liability to tax after allowing for the credit. Those not liable to tax may claim back the tax credit, while higher-rate tax-payers will be liable to tax on the total of the dividend and the tax credit, the credit satisfying the basic-rate part of their liability. Unlike interest on loan stocks, preference dividends received by a UK-resident company constitute franked investment income.

5.6.5 Suitability

Fixed interest stocks are suitable for investors who have known future commitments to meet or who want to maximise the return on their invested capital through a mixed portfolio of stocks and ordinary shares. Private sector debentures or loan stocks may represent a cheaper route to these goals than gilts if the investor is prepared to forgo the additional security offered by gilts. However, preference shares may not be best suited to the private investor (since he derives no benefit from their dividends being franked investment income for corporation tax purposes).

Convertible stocks are a means of keeping the investor's options open as between investing in ordinary shares or in fixed interest stocks.

5.6.6 Mechanics

The method of dealing is shown at **5.4.5**.

5.6.7 Safe custody

The contract note, which constitutes evidence of the sale or purchase, is relevant, *inter alia*, for taxation purposes and should be kept in a safe place. Certificates are evidence of title and should also be kept in a safe place, although if certificates are lost, duplicates can usually be obtained against an appropriate form of indemnity.

5.7 Ordinary shares

5.7.1 General

Legal nature
A company is a legal person, capable of perpetual succession and distinct from its proprietors, namely the persons who contributed the

Listed investments 89

original capital or their successors. Ownership of a company takes the form of 'shares' in the capital of the company. All companies listed on The Stock Exchange, or the subject of trading in the Unlisted Securities Market and the Third Market, are limited liability companies, and the shareholders usually have no liability to creditors if the company defaults on its obligations. If a share is partly paid (nowadays relatively rare for listed shares), a shareholder can only be called on to subscribe for the unpaid balance of the nominal or par value of the shares, unless he has agreed to pay a premium for the shares, in which case he will be liable to pay that premium.

Shareholders are the proprietors (or members) of the company. Subject to a company's memorandum and articles of association, and to whatever dividends the company in fact pays, ordinary shareholders have the right to all profits after payment of prior charges on the company's revenue, such as interest, wages, other running expenses, taxes and dividends on preference shares. In the same way, if the company is wound up they are entitled to all assets remaining when prior claims have been met. Thus they own the residual assets or 'equity' of the company—hence the term 'equities' to describe ordinary shares.

A company's memorandum of association states, *inter alia*, the objects of the company and whether shareholders' liability is limited or unlimited. Its articles of association define, among other things, the shareholders' rights in relation to the issue and transfer of shares, the company's borrowing powers, and the procedures for appointing directors and paying dividends. The articles also define shareholders' voting rights: normally each ordinary share carries one vote but some companies have non-voting shares. Plural voting rights may be given to 'founders' shares'. The exercise of voting rights may be restricted to certain circumstances.

Ownership of most shares listed on The Stock Exchange is established by registration; the name of the owner is entered on a share register by the company's registrars (sometimes an agent office of the company and sometimes a bank or other specialist organisation), which then issue share certificates. In the case of 'bearer' shares, the certificate itself is evidence of ownership and such shares are therefore simpler to transfer between seller and buyer.

Extensive and up-to-date information is required from companies when they seek an initial listing on The Stock Exchange (or permission for trading on the Unlisted Securities Market or Third Market), issue new shares or other securities for cash, make a take-over offer, to seek to effect a merger or reconstruction. Such information requirements may be prescribed by legislation, by The Stock Exchange or by the Panel on Take-overs and Mergers.

Pre-conditions

Shares listed on The Stock Exchange can be held by most categories of UK investor, although friendly societies and trustees acting without specific investment powers in their trust deeds must observe the Trustee Investments Act 1961.

Characteristics

Ordinary shares are a company's risk capital; the investor expects a reasonable and rising level of dividend income and perhaps a rise in the share price, but there can be no certainty about this. If his expectations are fulfilled or exceeded, he is rewarded for taking the risks that dividends might have been low or non-existent and that the share price might have fallen.

Dividends are paid out of profits, normally following the recommendation of the directors. From time to time the amount of a company's dividends may be limited statutorily as part of a government incomes policy although no such limitations exists at the present time.

The market price of a company's shares will fluctuate from day to day and will in part reflect objective data such as its past records on profits and dividends and its assets; but prices will also be affected by subjective judgments about the company's probable future performance. News about the company (including its regular profit announcements) will influence the price, but so too will news concerning the sector or sectors in which the company operates and, indeed, news affecting the political situation and/or economy as a whole. Prices are also influenced by the amount of new money which the institutional investors, in particular, have to invest, some of which is likely to find its way into company shares, the proportion depending on how attractive shares are considered by comparison with other investments.

Taxation

Ordinary shareholders in receipt of dividends also receive a tax credit (corresponding to the advance corporation tax paid by the company in respect of the dividend). Non-taxpayers may claim repayment of the tax credit, while the liability of basic-rate taxpayers is satisfied by the credit. For those liable to tax at the higher-rate, tax is calculated on the total of the dividend and the tax credit, and the tax payable is reduced by the amount of the credit. Dividends received by a UK-resident company constitute franked investment income (see Chapter 7, **7.6.3**).

In order to conserve cash flow and to give shareholders a method of accumulating more shares, many companies now allow their shareholders to elect to take the forthcoming dividend in the form of shares in lieu of cash. This is commonly known as a scrip dividend. As the company is issuing new capital direct to its shareholders there are no brokers' costs nor stamp duty, but there are no tax savings for the recipient. Only the net dividend on his holding is used to acquire new shares at a pre-ordained pricing formula but the credit on the dividend cannot be reclaimed where a shareholder does not have to pay income tax at the basic rate. A higher rate taxpayer must also eventually find the difference between the tax credit deemed to be his and the tax liability on the dividend's gross equivalent out of cash from other sources as he will have received no cash from the company, save perhaps for a small balancing item. The active share investor ought also to bear in mind before accepting scrip dividends that records will need to be kept completely up-to-date for the purposes of capital gains tax as each new allotment of shares has a separate indexation factor.

Capital gains realised from the sale of shares may be liable to capital gains tax, and capital losses can be used to offset other gains. As a general rule capital losses can only be carried forward, but they may be used to offset earlier capital gains where they all occur in the same fiscal year.

Capital gains tax considerations are important and investors should try to make full use of the annual exemption for capital gains tax available in each tax year to individuals. This implies that an investor should endeavour either to switch from investments where the income or growth potential has run its course to others where the return is likely to be greater, or to increase the base costs of his shares (within the CGT exemption) by the action widely known as 'bed and breakfasting'. This entails a sale of shares one afternoon and their repurchase the next morning in the expectation that the share price has not moved. As these transactions are completed within a single Stock Exchange account period and as the investor's name need not have to be deleted from the company's share register, it is not necessary for him to provide a share certificate to the broker or to sign a transfer deed. The costs of 'bed and breakfasting' are relatively low, limited only to the stockbroker's commission and the market-maker's 'turn' (the difference between the selling and the repurchase price) together with stamp duty. Not only can an investor 'bed and breakfast' a gain which would be covered by the annual exemption but he could also 'bed and breakfast' a loss to offset chargeable gains made elsewhere during the tax year.

The Finance Act 1982 provides for indexation relief on capital gains from the 'appointed date'. The 'appointed date' is 6 April 1982 in all cases with the exception of companies, for which it is 1 April 1982. The calculation of the indexation relief, where there has been a single purchase of shares, is straightforward. For shares bought after March 1982, their historic cost is increased by a factor equal to the change in the retail prices index from the month of acquisition to the month of disposal. For those bought before April 1982, the Finance Act 1988 brings forward the deemed acquisition date to 31 March 1982 and the deemed book value of the holding to the value on that date, as adjusted by capital issues made by the company in the intervening period. Some sales will produce indexed gains under the new system where these would have been losses under the old, and vice versa, and these will be treated as 'no gain, no loss' situation. Naturally, at the time of disposal, it is impossible to calculate the indexation relief exactly as the RPI figure for that month is not issued until the following month, but an estimated figure can be given by financial advisers or a certain amount of leeway can be left to cover this unknown element. Indexation relief can be used to increase a loss, or to create a loss from a profit in pure money terms.

Where a shareholding has been built up in a company over a period the calculation of the capital gains tax position on disposal including any indexation relief can be extremely complicated, and accurate records of dates of purchase should be kept by all investors. This is especially the case where scrip dividends have been taken in lieu of cash.

Suitability

Ordinary shares are suitable for the investor who is able to accept an element of risk and is looking for rising income and a hedge against inflation, particularly if he follows attentively the fortunes of companies in which he invests.

For the investor who needs to estimate with a degree of confidence the timing and size in money terms of his future commitments, shares are not as suitable as fixed interest stocks.

Unlike some of the fixed term savings schemes described in section **4.3**, most ordinary shares in public listed companies are readily marketable at a moment's notice. However, since share prices are subject to a considerable degree of fluctuation (greater than that in fixed interest stocks), an investor who is likely to be faced suddenly with unexpected commitments should endeavour not to rely on ordinary shares to meet such commitments.

Mechanics
For the mechanics of dealing see **5.4.5**.

Safe custody and maintenance
The contract note, which constitutes evidence of the sale or purchase, is relevant, *inter alia*, for capital gains tax purposes and should be kept in a safe place. Share certificates are evidence of title and should also be kept in a safe place, although if certificates are lost, duplicates can usually be obtained against an appropriate indemnity.

In the case of bearer shares no register is maintained and possession is evidence of title. Bearer shares should therefore be held in safe custody.

The investor is well advised to keep his portfolio under review, either continuously or periodically. Some stockbrokers and other agents will automatically review and revalue the portfolios of their private clients at intervals of three, six or 12 months and will be prepared to offer advice. Between these reviews they may also contact their clients to make recommendations affecting individual holdings or the balance of the portfolio between the main investment areas.

In addition to regular reviews, which are essential, the investor who follows the economic, industrial and financial news and who is prepared to buy when a good investment opportunity arises at a reasonable price or to sell a share when its prospects have dimmed or its price is high, will do better than a more passive investor, provided of course that his judgment and the advice that he receives are good.

All shareholders will receive the annual report and accounts of the company in which they hold shares. Companies listed on The Stock Exchange or the subject of trading on the Unlisted Securities Market also have to make an interim report, normally containing profit figures for the first six months of the company's financial year and reporting any interim dividends declared. The interim statement need not be sent to shareholders but, if not sent, must be advertised in the press. The interim dividend, which is paid at the board's discretion, and the final dividend which is recommended by the directors at the company's year end (subject to the approval of its shareholders at the annual general meeting), normally make up the total dividend for the year. Some major international companies issue interim statements every quarter.

Although annual and interim reports provide natural occasions on which to consider increasing or reducing shareholdings, such action should not necessarily be taken straight away, since the impact of the report will immediately be reflected in the share price. Few tactics can be worse than trying to sell when others are selling and the price is low, or trying to buy when the price is high. Having formed a judgment on whether to buy, sell or merely retain an existing holding, the prudent investor will await a suitable opportunity before acting.

Personal equity plans

PEPs were introduced in the 1986 Budget and allow investors to commit now up to £6,000 each year, in a tax-efficient form of saving.

A new plan is entered into each year and for plans commenced after 5 April 1989 the year of each plan is deemed to coincide with the fiscal year. Formerly the year of the plan was the calendar year. After 31 December 1989 all calendar 1987, 1988 and 1989 plans can be merged into one. Investment changes within the plan are allowed. The tax advantages continue until the investor ends the plan.

Only UK registered shares listed on The Stock Exchange or dealt on the USM may be included in the plan although up to £3,000 may be initially invested in investment trusts or authorised unit trusts which themselves are at least 50 per cent invested in UK equities. Cash may be held in a PEP but all interest on cash will be subject in 1990/91 to composite rate tax.

Shares arising from new issues, including privatisations, can be transferred into a PEP within 30 days of the announcement of allocation, at the issue price. This issue value will count towards the annual investment limit. There is no liability to income tax at basic rate or higher rate on dividends on shares held in the PEP, nor is there any liability to capital gains tax on any disposal in the duration, or at the end of the plan. PEPs are therefore an advantageous method of saving through risk investment for all equity investors, but especially so for those on the higher rate of income tax or who generally have an annual capital gains tax liability.

PEPs can be held by anyone aged 18 or over who is resident and ordinarily resident in the United Kingdom or, though non-resident, is a Crown employee serving overseas.

Listed investments 95

Each plan must be managed by an investment adviser, authorised under the Financial Services Act 1986, and registered with the Inland Revenue. The manager will arrange for investors to receive annual reports of each investment, although often charging a fee for this service and ensure that all rights of that shareholder are made available to him. All records, dealing and other paperwork will be the responsibility of the manager, who should liaise on the investor's behalf with the tax authorities (see also Chapter 6).

5.7.2 Warrants and options

Legal nature
An alternative to buying a security outright is to purchase the right to buy a security. There are three ways of doing this:

(1) Warrants give holders the right to buy a particular company's ordinary shares at a fixed price. The right can normally only be exercised between two specific dates in the future.
(2) Conventional share options confer the right to deal in a specified number of company's shares at a fixed price (the 'striking price') at any time during the option period (normally three months). To obtain an option the investor pays a price ('option money' or 'premium'), often expressed in pence per share. A 'call' option confers the right to buy at the striking price. A 'put' option confers the right to sell at the striking price. A 'double' option entitles the investor either to buy or to sell at the striking price.
(3) Traded options—'calls' or 'puts'—are available in a limited but increasing number of leading companies, the FT-SE index and both a short and long gilt, and, in the case of company shares, take a standardised form, each unit normally representing 1,000 shares in the underlying equity. At any time before the expiry date (either three, six or nine months after the commencement of the option), the holder can exercise the option. Alternatively, he can sell the option on The Stock Exchange, where another investor can buy it.

Pre-conditions
Before dealing in traded options it is essential for the investor to have read the brochures prepared by The Stock Exchange which cover in detail this specialist area of the market. There are no other special preconditions to investment in warrants or conventional options over and above those applying to ordinary shares. However, such investment would not ordinarily qualify under the Trustee Investments Act 1961.

Characteristics

There are clearly two sides to any option transaction. On the one hand, the purchaser of the option is paying a premium in the hope that the underlying share price will rise or fall depending on the type of option. Since the premium will be low relative to the share price, the investor is able to obtain gearing (buy the option to acquire or sell more shares than if he dealt in the underlying shares). At the same time, should the share price decline substantially, his risk is limited to the option money (which can be lost entirely).

On the other hand, there must be a writer of such an option, who will take the option money and any dividends on the underlying shares (if he is a covered writer and already holds the stock) in exchange for an agreement to supply to, or take up the shares from the option buyer if the price rises or falls sufficiently. This role will appeal to the shareholder who wishes to hedge.

Taxation

The short-term nature of transactions in traded options may involve their being treated for taxation purposes as trading rather than capital transactions or even possibly as transactions falling within Case VI of Schedule D. Traded options disposed of after 5 April 1980 are no longer treated as wasting assets. The full cost of acquisition is taken into account in the capital gains tax computation. The abandonment of a traded option is treated as a disposal.

Suitability

Options are suited to the active investor, prepared to risk a small premium on his judgment about likely movements in share prices over the short-term. If he has little capital to invest, he might well consider traded options. The longer-term investor wishing to back a judgment that a particular company's shares will improve might consider purchasing warrants, although the number of companies with warrants is limited.

Mechanics

The mechanics of investing in options are similar to those applicable to private sector stocks (see **5.4.5**), except that, for traded options, the London Options Clearing House supervises the registration and settlement of transactions.

Safe custody

Warrant or option contract notes should be kept for tax purposes and certificates for warrants should be kept in a safe place.

5.7.3 Offers from companies

Whereas earlier sections were concerned with dealings by an investor in the market on his own initiative, this section is for the most part concerned with opportunities which may arise suddenly and may require an investor to respond rapidly to them. However, as will be seen, an application for shares under an offer for sale has often, though not always, to be actively sought out by an investor, and a takeover offer comes not from the company in which the investor has invested but from some other company.

It is a common feature of all the transactions referred to below that strict time limits are laid down for the taking of decisions by the investor, who should therefore allow adequate time for taking advice.

Offers for sale
Although there are several ways in which a company may obtain an initial listing of its shares, only one of them, the 'offer for sale', normally involves the private investor, although very occasionally the well-connected private investor is given an opportunity to participate in a private placing of shares on an initial listing or on entry to the Unlisted Securities Market or the Third Market.

In the most normal type of offer for sale, an unlisted company seeks an initial listing (or permission for trading to take place in the Unlisted Securities Market or the Third Market) for all its shares and makes a substantial proportion of its issued share capital (normally not less than 25 per cent) available to the general public. The shares may be made available either by means of a sale by existing shareholders of part of their holding or by the offer of subscription for new shares, the subscription moneys being paid into the company. Sometimes an offer for sale combines a sale and a subscription.

The offer is made by means of a prospectus, usually prepared by the company in conjunction with an issuing house or a firm of stockbrokers and with the help of professional advisers. The prospectus and accompanying application form are available from the issuing house, the stockbrokers acting for the company and selected branches of banks, and are also advertised in newspapers. If members of the public wish to participate in the offer, they must take steps to obtain a copy of the prospectus and complete and lodge the application form, with the application moneys, within the (very short) period prescribed by the prospectus.

In the past, shares were generally offered for sale at a discount of perhaps 10 per cent of the price at which it was estimated that dealings would commence in the market. The purchase of or subscription for shares at the offer price was thus an attractive investment proposition, both for speculators who applied for shares, hoping to sell them again almost immediately in the market at a profit (the so-called 'stags'), and also for long-term investors who saw not only an immediate, although unrealised, capital appreciation, but also the prospect of longer-term growth. However, these features of a new issue could result in extensive over-subscription and the scaling down of applications, and sometimes the offer is made by means of a tender with a pre-announced minimum tender price. The investor is left to judge the price which he is willing to pay for the shares on offer and, once the company's financial advisers have been able to see the various levels of subscription, an announcement is made concerning the striking price at which all the shares on offer will be sold to investors. Applications for shares at prices below the striking price will be unsuccessful and subscription moneys returned; where investors have tendered for shares at, or above, the striking price, they will usually be allotted shares, although in some circumstances there may be a ballot amongst applicants for an allotment.

Occasionally investors receive an opportunity to participate in an offer for sale by reason of a holding of shares in another company which is 'floating of' a subsidiary.

Rights issues

A company wishing, subsequent to obtaining its initial listing or permission to enter the Unlisted Securities Market or the Third Market, to raise capital by the issue of new shares or of securities convertible into shares will normally have to do so by means of an issue by way of rights to its existing shareholders. If it wishes to issue shares to third parties for subscription in cash, it will normally, in accordance with the requirements of The Stock Exchange, have to seek the prior approval of shareholders.

An issue by way of rights will almost invariably be made on terms considered to be favourable to the shareholders, with a view to persuading them to take up the offer. Generally, a shareholder who does not wish to take up the whole of the offer (whether because he does not have available funds or for some other reason) may sell, prior to the payment of subscription monies (ie, nil paid), the rights subscribed, either through the market or privately, or simply fail to accept the offer and pay the subscription monies, leaving it to the company to sell the rights on his behalf and account to him for any premium. He may, if he wishes, accept the offer in part.

However, there has been a discernible move towards a form of disguised rights issue, known as a placing with clawback, where a company making an acquisition will raise sufficient funds, subject to agreement by its shareholders in general meeting, by placing new shares with institutions while allowing current shareholders to apply for these shares in proportion to their present holdings. Entitlements not taken up by shareholders may be transferred but cannot be sold through the Stock Market in nil paid form. The higher the level of acceptance shown by shareholders, the greater the clawback from the institutional placees. The benefit to the company is in its being allowed to allot new shares at close to market price, rather than at the discount that a rights issue would entail. There is also no need for underwriting although placees do receive a commitment fee.

A rights issue is made by means of a prospectus, which typically consists of a provisional allotment letter and an accompanying, or previous, circular. The provisional allotment letter is a temporary bearer document of title, which is negotiable for the period during which the offer is open for acceptance (a minimum of three weeks) and for a further period of weeks when the shares are dealt in on these documents. Thereafter, the shares become registered.

Capitalisation issues

From time to time companies also make capitalisation issues—from the company's viewpoint, merely a book-keeping exercise, reflecting the incidence of accumulated and undistributed profits and/or the effects of inflation. Although shareholders receive 'free' shares, which can be dealt in on a temporary bearer document of title (either a fully paid renounceable allotment letter or a renounceable certificate) for a period of weeks, the issue of these shares represents no more than a rearrangement of existing shareholdings and any disposal of the new shares may give rise to a liability to capital gains tax. Special rules apply for arriving at the acquisition cost for capital gains tax purposes.

Take-over offers

From time to time shareholders in a particular company may receive offers from another company wishing to acquire their shares in exchange for cash and/or shares and/or other securities of the other company. Most take-over bids are conditional upon a reference not being made to the Monopolies and Mergers Commission. Under the Fair Trading Act 1973 the Director General of Fair Trading has the power to recommend to the Secretary of State for Trade and Industry that a proposed merger be referred to the Monopolies and Mergers Commission if (*inter alia*) (1) the value of the assets being taken over exceeds £30m, or (2) he believes that the merger involves the national or public interest. Whether the takeover proposal has or has not been agreed with the directors of the target company, the directors of that company will have to give to shareholders a recommendation as to whether to accept the offer. Shareholders can expect to receive not only that recommendation, but also offer documents and (particularly in the case of a contested take-over offer) a flood of circulars. The prudent course for the shareholder is to take careful note of the timetable for accepting the offer prescribed in the offer document and to delay taking any decision or action until a day or two before the closing date under the offer, in the hope that a higher offer may be forthcoming either from the original offeror or from a counter-bidder. If a higher offer is made by the original offeror, an earlier acceptance of the offer at the lower level will not preclude the shareholder from accepting the higher offer, and if a competing offer is made by a third party, an earlier acceptance of an offer can be withdrawn in certain circumstances.

Maintenance
The investor should retain safely all documents (particularly bearer documents) relating to the investments covered in this chapter. Each time he changes his address the investor should notify the appropriate body.

5.8 Preview of the year ahead

World economic growth has declined from the rapid rates of the late 1980s but should stabilise at comfortably above 3 per cent in 1990. With a successful soft-landing of the US economy pointing to economic growth of about 2 per cent from America, it will be up to the continental and far eastern economies to take up the slack. So much depends on interest rates, which remain rather too high after the rises in the first quarter of 1990.

As far as the UK investor is concerned, domestic markets will be driven by fears of inflation and worries on the government's standing. Corporate earnings and dividend growth, though still healthy, are unlikely to match 1989's figures except for those companies with a high exposure to the stronger overseas economies. Once again, we shall probably see out-performance of larger over smaller companies due to a higher proportion of export sales and manufacturing capacity. The high interest rate regime will remain until most of the problems of inflation, excessive consumer expenditure and high pay settlements are past, but with an election to be held by May 1992, interest rates will need to start falling by early 1991 to stimulate economic growth and give a boost to the flagging property market. If this proves difficult, 1992 might see a change of government and gilts will remain unsettled. However, the UK will not be able to go it alone on reducing interest rates without help from the major economies or sterling will suffer and inflation prove even more tenacious. Entry into the ERM will come in due course.

Although continuing to slow down from the unsustainable levels of 1988, economic growth may well be around 2 per cent in 1990, rising to 3 per cent in 1991. Inflation will end the year closer to 10 per cent than 5 per cent, probably not falling to the latter figure until well into 1991.

On any more than a short-term view, equities still seem to offer good value on the assumption of continued economic growth through the early part of the 1990s. A portfolio of good quality, larger UK equities exposed to strong export markets, index-linked stock and some direct or indirect overseas holdings should prove as good as any on a medium to longer term view. Investors should continue to make full use of the tax concessions, either through personal equity plans (where the limit for the 1990/91 tax year is £6,000 for each individual) or through the structural changes brought about by the separate taxation of husband and wife. This will allow couples to improve their net return by sensible use of the capital gains tax allowance and the band rates for income tax.

In the meantime The Stock Exchange will be making further moves towards the acceptance of investments as a savings medium, and continuing its efforts to introduce the TAURUS paperless settlements system.

5.9 Conclusion

Historically, listed investments have presented a good means of saving with the flexibility of choice between income or growth, or a balance of the two. However, potential investors must give full regard to the detrimental effect that inflation can have on the return on fixed interest securities, and the damage to capital values that a decline in the general level of a stockmarket can create even to a quality list of blue chip equities. Most investment is on a long-term basis, regard being given to the real economic growth potential of the chosen investment area, and provided that the individual can accept the risks involved in this form of investment, balanced against the twin benefits of the potential for reward and the ease of encashment, if necessary, listed investments would seem an excellent place for savings over and above more immediate cash requirements. The spate of privatisations during the 1980s has done a lot to draw back the veil of mystery over equities in particular; they can now be accepted as part of the savings of all individuals as, especially in the case of personal equity plans, the level of entry is now within the reach of so many more people. No longer can equity investment be thought to be limited to the very rich.

Sources of further information

Legislation

Building Societies Act 1962
Companies Act 1985
Stock Transfer Acts 1963–1982
Trustee Investments Act 1961
Fair Trading Act 1973 (as amended)
Capital Gains Tax Act 1979
Finance Acts
Financial Services Act 1986
Income and Corporation Taxes Act 1988
Insolvency Act 1986

Bibliography

Admission of Securities to Listing (looseleaf), The Stock Exchange

The Stock Exchange Unlisted Securities Market (2nd edition), The Stock Exchange, 1982.

The City Code on Take-overs and Mergers, and the Rules Governing Substantial Acquisitions of Shares (looseleaf), The Panel on Take-overs and Mergers, 1985.

Self-defence for Investors, Securities and Investments Board, 1986

Financial Services—A Guide to the New Regulatory System, Securities and Investments Board, 1986.

An Introduction to The Stock Market, The Stock Exchange, 1986

An Introduction to Buying and Selling Shares, The Stock Exchange.

Introduction to Traded Options, The Stock Exchange.

The Unlisted Securities Market, The Stock Exchange.

The Third Market, The Stock Exchange, 1988

The International Stock Exchange Official Yearbook, The Stock Exchange, 1989

Useful addresses

The Public Relations
 Department
The Stock Exchange
Old Broad Street
London
EC2N 1HP

Tel: (071) 588 2355

Director of Savings
National Savings Bank
Boydstone Road
Glasgow
G58 1SB

Tel: (041) 649 4555

The Director
Department of National
 Savings
Bonds and Stock Office
Preston New Road
Blackpool
FY3 9XR

Tel: (0253) 66151

The Director of Savings
Savings Certificate and SAYE
 Office
Milburngate House
Durham
DH99 1NS

Tel: (091) 3864900

National Girobank
Bridle Road
Bootle
Merseyside
G1R 0AA

Tel: (051) 928 8181

The Building Societies
 Association
3 Savile Row
London
W1X 1AF

Tel: (071) 437 0655

Finance Houses Association
18 Upper Grosvenor Street
London
W1X 9PB

Tel: (071) 491 2783

Bank of England
Threadneedle Street
London
EC2R 8AH

Tel: (071) 601 4444

The Association of Investment
 Trust Companies
Park House
6th Floor
16 Finsbury Circus
London
EC2M 7JJ

Tel: (071) 588 5347

Financial Intermediaries
 Managers and Brokers
 Regulatory Association
Hertsmere Road
Marsh Wall
London
E14 4AB

Tel: (071) 538 8860

The Securities and Investments
  Board
3 Royal Exchange Buildings
Cornhill
London
EC3V 3NL

Tel: (071) 283 2474

Inland Revenue
Public Enquiry Room
West Wing
Room 62
Somerset House
London
WC2R 1LB

Tel: (071) 438 6622

The Securities Association
The Stock Exchange Building
Old Broad Street
London
EC2N 1HP

Tel: (071) 588 2355

The Panel on Takeovers and
  Mergers
PO Box 226
The Stock Exchange Building
Old Broad Street
London
EC2P 2JX

Tel: (071) 382 9026

Unit Trust Association
65 Kingsway
London
WC2B 6TD

Tel: (071) 831 0898

6 Tax beneficial investments and savings

Tony Foreman and Andrew Grant of Pannell Kerr Forster, Chartered Accountants

6.1 Introduction

As already pointed out, the most important aspect of savings planning is to identify appropriate investments which offer good value—tax benefits and privileges are only one aspect of this.

An investment which is appropriate for one person will not necessarily meet the needs of another person in different circumstances. Some of the questions to be asked are:

(1) How long can the savings be tied up?
(2) Are the savings for a particular purpose (school fees, daughter's wedding, retirement, etc)?
(3) When will the money be needed?
(4) Is income required?
(5) Will fluctuations in stock market and/or property prices be such a worry that the investments become unattractive?

Another aspect is that you may want to strike a balance. The criteria for investing the short term part of the portfolio should be different from the method of investing in more volatile investments on a longer term basis. Striking the right balance is one of the hardest aspects. If savings are fairly modest they may have to be invested on a conservative basis—and the return will reflect this. At the other extreme, a high net worth individual who has covered all his short term requirements may deploy a proportion of his capital in more risky investments which offer the prospect of a very high return.

Once these decisions have been made, the next step is to identify investments which meet the specifications and offer good value. An investment may offer good value if the managers' charges are reasonable and the tax treatment is favourable.

This chapter starts by looking at tax privileged investments from the standpoint of the most cautious investor who may want access to capital at short notice and who is, therefore, not well disposed towards investments which may fall in value from time to time. Then a look is taken at tax privileged investments which involve a degree of risk arising from fluctuations in the Stock Exchange, etc. Finally consideration is given to bank deposits and 'near cash' investments most of which involve little or no risk but do not have a privileged treatment. Many of these investments are provided by the government through the department of national savings or local authorities.

6.2 Tax privileged investments

6.2.1 TESSAs

One of the government's recent innovations are TESSAs (tax exempt special savings accounts). These will be available from 1 January 1991 to any individual who is resident in the United Kingdom and aged 18 or over.

This investment will normally run for five years. It offers a secure return since the money has to be deposited with an authorised bank or building society and the risk of capital loss is therefore remote. The investor can withdraw his capital but the tax benefits will be forfeited if such withdrawals exceed certain limits. Subject to this, the benefit of having a TESSA is that the investor receives tax-free interest.

The maximum amount which may be withdrawn during the first five years without jeopardising the tax benefits is the interest credited to the account less the basic rate tax which would have been deducted if the account had not enjoyed its special tax exempt status.

Example

Sid deposits £2,000 in a TESSA. In year one the bank credits interest of £250. The interest has not borne any tax. Sid can withdraw £250 less 25 per cent notional tax ie, £187.50 without affecting the exempt status of the account. The remaining £2,062.50 will continue to attract tax-free interest. However, if Sid withdraws £187.51 the bank will have to account to the Inland Revenue for the tax of £62.50 and the account will thereafter be treated as an ordinary deposit account. Once five years have elapsed, Sid can withdraw the entire amount with no tax consequences.

There are limits on the maximum amount which may be invested in a TESSA. An individual may invest up to £3,000 in the first year and up to £1,800 each year thereafter, subject to the total not exceeding £9,000. Alternatively, an individual can invest up to £150 per month.

An individual can not have two TESSAs at any one time. However, the above limits apply separately in relation to husband and wife. The terms under which banks and building societies accept deposits for TESSAs will vary. The government regards it as a matter of choice as to whether the deposit carries a rate of interest which is fixed for five years or a variable rate. TESSAs are 'portable' so an investor will be able to transfer his savings from one financial institution to another without losing his tax benefits.

Uses of TESSAs
Older investor who needs income
The prime user of a TESSA is an older person who needs to take a regular income and who would rather avoid fluctuations in the value of his or her savings.

School fees provision
TESSAs are also suitable investments for individuals who wish to accumulate capital to cover school fees and similar costs—especially school fees payable in the medium term.

Quite sizeable sums can be accumulated. Thus if an individual makes the maximum deposits allowed, and interest is earned at an average rate of $12\frac{1}{2}$ per cent, he will accumulate a total of £13,750 at the end of five years (this assumes interest is credited on a six monthly basis). Thus a married couple could accumulate £27,500 over five years. If we assume that they have put this aside to cover school fees payable when their son reaches 13, and the fees are currently £2,500 per term and likely to rise with inflation at 8 per cent per annum, they will still have covered the first three years fees and this will allow other savings plans (such as PEPs—see below) to fund later years.

Why waste the tax exemption?
TESSAs may also be attractive to wealthy individuals who happen to have £10,000 on deposit and who may or may not keep it there for five years but would like to obtain the tax exemption if it is held for the full period.

6.2.2 National savings certificates

These are another investment which provides a totally tax free return. However, the yield reflects this and so TESSAs offer better value for most people.

National savings certificates are a five year investment, although they can be encashed early and a tax-free addition which corresponds to interest is currently credited at the following rates:

Encashment within first 12 months	Nil	
next 12 months	6.5%	from date of purchase
next 12 months	7.0%	
next 12 months	7.75%	
next 12 months	8.5%	
at fifth anniversary	9.5%	

Once certificates have matured, they attract tax free interest at the national extension rate (currently 5.01 per cent) until they are redeemed.

Practical aspects

The certificates are a suitable form of savings for children. They are not, however, suitable for non-taxpayers or for short-term savings; but for the investor paying tax at the higher rate, the certificates may be attractive.

Application forms are available from most branches of the Post Office and banks. Between £25 and £1,000 can be invested in the 35th issue, plus up to £10,000 re-investment of earlier issues which have matured.

Holdings should be reviewed from time to time, particularly since new issues may carry more attractive rates of capital appreciation than those already held. A review of holdings should certainly be made at the end of the specified period.

Any number of certificates can be cashed at one time, on at least eight workings days' notice, and repayment forms are available at most branches of the Post Office and banks.

6.2.3 National savings yearly plan

Following the termination of the index-linked save-as-you-earn contracts, the yearly plan has been introduced to give a competitive tax-free return. Security of investment is guaranteed by the government.

Yearly plan contracts are available solely to individuals over seven years of age and to trustees of a sole beneficiary.

Tax beneficial investments and savings 109

Figure 6.1 Yearly plan

Year 1: 6%
Year 2: 10%
Year 3: 10%
Year 4: 10%
Year 5: 10%

Return for the five years comes to 9.5% pa

Source: *Department for National Savings*

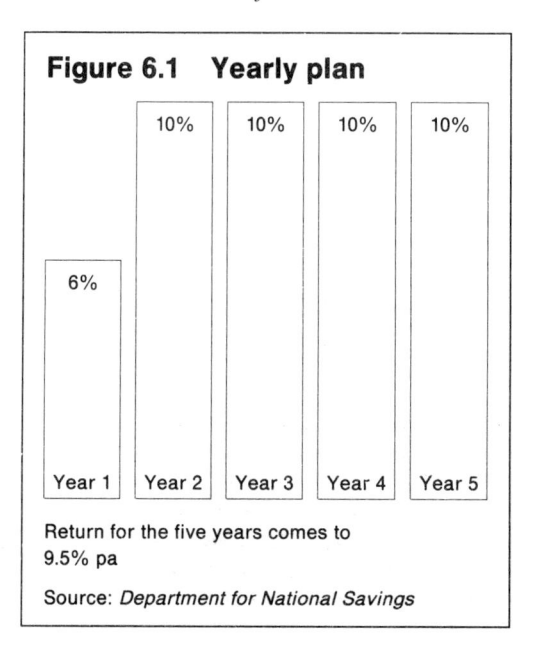

The individual contracts to subscribe a fixed monthly amount of between £20 and £200, in multiples of £5, for a period of 12 months at which time he receives a yearly plan certificate. Each monthly payment is credited with interest for each whole month that it has been invested, and the certificate when issued has a value equal to the capital and accumulated interest for that year. To ensure the highest return, the certificate should be held for a further four years as the interest rate is higher during that period. After these four years, interest is added at the published general extension rate.

If monthly payments are continued after the first year, a further yearly plan will have been entered into, with an overall return dependent on the level of interest rates ruling at the time of the new first payment. Holders will be notified.

The return is free of income tax and capital gains tax and is fixed through the five year period. Yearly plan is a sound method of saving a set sum each month in a tax-efficient manner and with a highly competitive return.

Repayment forms are available at branches of the Post Office and redemption takes around 14 days. A holder may encash his investment at any time but no interest is given if the yearly plan is ended within the first year.

6.2.4 National savings index-linked certificates

As with national savings certificates, these certificates are guaranteed by the government. They cannot be sold to third parties.

There is no lower age limit for holding these certificates, although encashment is not allowed until a child reaches the age of seven, except in special circumstances.

If a certificate is encashed within the first year, the purchase price only is repaid. If the certificates are held for more than a year, the redemption value is equal to the original purchase price, increased in proportion to the rise in the retail prices index between the month of purchase and the month of redemption. In the event of a fall in the RPI, the certificates can be encashed for the original purchase price. After the death of a holder, indexation can continue for a maximum of 12 months.

The latest issue guarantees a return above the rate of inflation for a five year term by offering extra tax-free interest as well as indexation. The amount of extra interest credited to the holding rises in each year of the life of the certificate and is itself inflation-proofed.

As with national savings certificates, capital appreciation is exempt from income tax and capital gains tax.

Certificates are suitable for individuals who do not need immediate income but are seeking protection in real terms for the amount invested. Higher-rate taxpayers in this category will find the certificates particularly attractive. The investment limit here is £5,000 in addition to holdings of all other issues of savings certificates.

Application forms are obtainable from most branches of the Post Office.

Comparison with TESSAs
There are circumstances where index-linked certificates could provide a better return than TESSAs. Interest rates are affected by a number of factors other than the rate of inflation and if you are very pessimistic about the likely rate of inflation over the next five years index-linked certificates constitute a low risk alternative.

6.2.5 Premium bonds

Premium bonds are guaranteed by the government. They cannot be sold to third parties.

Any person aged 16 or over can buy the bonds, and a parent or legal guardian may buy bonds on behalf of a child under 16. A bond cannot be held in the name of more than one person or in the name of a corporate body, society, club or other association of persons. Prizes won by bonds registered in the name of a child under the age of 16 are paid on behalf of the child to the parent or legal guardian.

The minimum purchase is £10. Bonds are sold in units of £1 and purchases must then be in multiples of £5 up to a maximum of £10,000 per person.

No interest is paid, but a bond which has been held for three clear calendar months following the month in which it was purchased is eligible for inclusion in the regular draw for prizes of various amounts. The size of the monthly prize fund is determined by applying one month's interest at a predetermined rate to the total value of the eligible bonds at that time. This rate is reviewed from time to time. Bonds can be encashed at any time.

6.2.6 Personal equity plans

PEPs were introduced by the Chancellor of the Exchequer in the 1986 Finance Act to encourage wider share ownership by individuals in UK companies by offering investment tax incentives. Successive Finance Acts have introduced changes which make PEPs even more attractive.

Anyone who is over 18 years old and resident in the UK for tax purposes can take out a PEP. Crown employees working overseas are deemed to be resident for this purpose. Should a plan holder subsequently become non-resident, the plan can be maintained and its tax benefits preserved.

The tax benefits take the form of total exemption from capital gains tax and income tax on the appreciation and investment income earned from equities, unit trusts and investment trusts held within the plan. A plan can be terminated at any time and the funds withdrawn without loss of the tax benefits.

There are two distinct types of plan, discretionary or managed, and non-discretionary (usually referred to as 'self-select'). As the terms imply, the first type of plan is operated along the lines of a unit trust and is managed on the investors behalf. The second type of plan is only administered by the plan manager with the investor himself selecting the underlying investments and taking all portfolio management decisions. The charges on self-select plans are normally significantly lower.

There is no restriction on the investment switches that can be made within the fund and no liability to income tax or capital gains tax arises. A PEP can be transferred from one manager to another.

The maximum investment into a plan is currently £6,000 per tax year. Both husband and wife can invest this sum. The investment must generally be in the form of cash although shares acquired through a public offer may be transferred into a plan within 30 days. In addition, many managers offer share exchange schemes or will reduce their normal charges for selling shares so that cash can be raised for investment in a PEP.

The cash held within the PEP can be held on deposit. The interest earned is currently subject to composite rate tax but will be subject to basic rate tax from 6 April 1991. Provided the interest is subsequently invested in qualifying investments, there will be no charge to higher rate tax.

Up to £3,000 may be invested in authorised unit trusts or investment trusts who in turn invest at least 50 per cent of their funds in UK equities. As an alternative, up to £900 may be invested in any authorised unit trust or investment trust. The balance of any investment over these two limits must then be invested in either UK equities, which includes shares quoted on the Unlisted Securities Market, or left in cash.

Although no relief is available on the investment into the fund, the plan is virtually a gross fund in the same way as a pension fund. There is an important advantage over most pension funds in that all proceeds are tax free when drawn whereas at least part of what emerges from a pension scheme will be taxable. It is therefore a useful addition for individuals to enhance retirement benefits. The fund can be used in the same way as a pension ie, tax free cash can be taken or the fund could be used to purchase an annuity.

Personal Equity Plans are not 'no risk' investments but in the past a combination/selection of unit/investment trusts and direct investment in blue-chip or 'alpha' stocks have generally produced a reasonable return where the investment was kept for between three and five years.

6.2.7 Insurance policies

Insurance policies are another type of tax privileged investment. Investors in qualifying policies are not subject to any tax on the maturity of the policy. We look at such investments in greater detail in Chapter 13.

6.2.8 Friendly society investments

Friendly societies issue qualifying insurance policies and there is no tax charge for investors when such policies mature. In this respect the position is no different from policies issued by insurance companies. The difference lies in the way that friendly societies are treated for tax purposes. Friendly societies are treated favourably as they are not normally subject to tax on life assurance business and this has generally enabled them to produce attractive returns.

Friendly society policies are however essentially a long term investment since they are prevented from paying a surrender value within the first ten years which exceeds the amount of premiums paid. In any event the surrender value can be very low where plans are cancelled or surrendered before the ten year term has expired as penalties tend to be heavy and frequently the charges on friendly society plans are high.

The maximum premiums are very low, for contracts arranged after 1 September 1990 the maximum annual limit is £150. Some societies do permit a lump sum investment to be made to cover the full ten-year plan. Policy holders must be between the age of 18 and 70.

At least 50 per cent of the underlining fund of a friendly society must be invested in narrower range securities as defined in the Trustee Investment Act 1971. This could put restraints on the investment performance although on the other hand it offers a reduced level of risk. All investment income and capital gains within the fund are free of all UK tax which enhances the rate of return.

Finally, the Policyholder's Protection Act 1975 does not extend to friendly society plans and there is no compensation scheme in the event of a friendly society having financial difficulties.

6.2.9 Pension policies

Personal pension policies and additional voluntary contributions to approved pension schemes are amongst the most favourably treated of all investments. Full tax relief is available for the individual's contributions and the fund enjoys total exemption from tax. This is discussed in Chapter 14.

6.2.10 Enterprise zone property trusts

These trusts are effectively collective schemes whereby an individual acquires an interest in a portfolio of properties located in one of the designated enterprise zones. The minimum investment is usually £5,000 but unlike the business expansion scheme investments there is no maximum, and it is therefore possible for investors to shelter very large or exceptional income during a tax year. Investors are issued 'units' or 'shares' but in law they hold an interest in the properties as members of a syndicate.

The investment is allowable as a deduction from the investors' taxable income to the extent that the managers invest the cash raised by them to construct buildings or purchase newly constructed and unused buildings within an enterprise zone. There is usually a small part of the investment which attracts no tax relief representing the cost of purchasing the land on which the building has been constructed. Generally this is between 4 per cent and 8 per cent of the total investment.

Example

Mark invests £50,000 in an enterprise property trust on 3 March 1991. He has income which is subject to the 40 per cent top rate of £75,000.

The managers of the trust invest all the money raised in qualifying property before 6 April 1991. The land element is 4 per cent. Mark, therefore, gets a tax deduction of £50,000 × 96 per cent ie, £48,000. This deduction saves Mark tax of £19,200 so the net cost of the investment is £30,800.

Current yields on such investments are between 6 per cent and $7\frac{1}{2}$ per cent of the gross investment. The income is paid gross and is treated as rental income for the investor. The final investment return on such an investment is difficult to predict. Investors should expect to retain their units for a term of 25 years. A disposal within this term could give rise to a clawback of some or all of the income tax relief given in year one (although no such clawback need arise in the case of a gift).

The yield becomes more attractive when one compares it with the net cost of the investment, after tax relief. Thus if the trust yielded 6 per cent on the gross cost, the yield on Mark's net cost becomes 9.7 per cent.

These investments are tax privileged because of the relief due to the investor when he makes the investment. However, they are not risk free as the investment produces income only if the properties are fully let. In practice this risk can be minimised.

The trust managers can generally secure rental guarantees of at least two years where they buy properties from developers. Sometimes the developer offers a further guarantee which in the short term provides effectively a guaranteed income. In most cases the managers buy enterprise properties which have been 'pre-let' and this means the investor is securing a guaranteed income, usually with upward only rent reviews for a 25-year period. If good rent reviews are achieved the capital value of the investment can be expected to appreciate.

Investors may also take a qualifying loan to acquire the units. The interest being set first against the rental income from the properties and any surplus is then available to be set off against any other Schedule A rental income for the same year. The balance of any unused interest relief is available to carry forward against rental income of future years.

In addition to the long term nature of these investments, it is often difficult to dispose of the units as there is no established market through which units can be bought and sold. The managers do, however, offer to assist investors on a matched bargain basis.

Planning in later years

One planning possibility involving the use of these investments relies upon the fact that the clawback (or 'balancing charge') need not arise on a gift. Thus, Mark might transfer the shares in the enterprise property trust to his wife if she is not subject to the 40 per cent rate. If she had no other income at all she would have no tax liability on the rents she received of £3,000 per annum.

6.3 Conclusion

Some of the tax benefit investments offer the prospect of outperforming inflation. The return on a TESSA might very well be 12 per cent or more per annum. PEP's invested in a range of equities should produce a comparable return over the medium to longer term. Index-linked national savings certificates are guaranteed to do so.

The return on some of the other privileged investments looks positively miserly. Where savings certificates have matured the rate of interest added (5 per cent) is significantly lower than the rate of inflation.

The various types of deposit schemes offer a poor long term return to anyone who cannot enjoy the income gross. They are, therefore, sensible investments for a married woman with little or no other income, but less attractive for a person who is subject to tax at 25 per cent or 40 per cent. That is not to say that these investments are not appropriate from time to time, as a way of investing money short term or in order to secure a known commitment or liability.

7 Investment trusts

Jeremy Burnett Rae, MA (Oxon), Barrister, Investment Secretary, Allied Dunbar Asset Management plc

7.1 Introduction

Collective investment media enable a number of investors to pool their resources so as to create a common fund for investment by professional managers. The two great benefits of this collective approach to investment are to provide investors with (1) more efficient and economical investment management; and (2) greater security through the spreading of risk over a wide range of investments.

To meet these needs, various different media, such as investment trusts, unit trusts and offshore funds (see Chapter 8) and insurance bonds (see Chapter 13) have evolved from separate legal and financial origins, subject to varying regulation and tax treatment. The choice between the different media in practice may depend on the investor's convenience as much as the features of the collective media, which are nowadays increasingly given a 'level playing field' by legislation. Nevertheless there are still some marked differences in the ways these investments are marketed, priced and taxed, quite apart from the management of the underlying assets.

The most straightforward of these media is the investment trust, which is actually not really a trust, but simply a limited company in which investors buy shares so as to benefit indirectly from its assets and income. An investment trust is constrained by its authorised capital, which cannot generally be changed or repaid to shareholders, and the shares are bought and sold by investors on The Stock Exchange at market prices determined only by supply and demand.

7.2 Historical background

The first investment trust to be established in England was the Foreign and Colonial Government Trust, which was created as a trust in 1868 and in 1879, owing to doubts concerning the legality of its original structure, was reorganised as a public limited liability company under the Companies Act 1862. The original objective of this trust was, in the words of its initial prospectus, to provide '... the investor of moderate means the same advantage as the large capitalists in diminishing risk in foreign and colonial stocks by spreading the investment over a number of stocks.' By the early twentieth century a number of other investment trust companies had been incorporated in England and Scotland and the investment trust had become firmly established in the UK as an investment medium. Some of these early trusts (including the Foreign and Colonial Government Trust which is now known as 'The Foreign and Colonial Investment Trust plc') still exist today despite two World Wars and many serious economic crises. During the last 100 years, investment trust companies have provided much new capital for listed companies in the UK by underwriting or subscribing for public issues of securities and accepting private placings, thus giving an important support to capital investment in the UK.

Investment trusts are probably the most flexible of the collective media, free to invest in any kind of assets, and the individual companies vary widely. In comparison with the other media, two distinctive characteristics are their ability to 'gear-up' their sensitivity to the markets by borrowing, and the fact that the shares are generally priced by supply and demand in the market at significantly less than the value of the underlying assets of the investment trust. Both these factors tend to make investment trusts more sensitive to movements in the markets as a whole, while still spreading the specific risks of investments in individual stocks.

As explained in **7.7**, certain capital gains tax concessions are given to those investment trusts which have been approved by the Inland Revenue for the purposes of the Income and Corporation Taxes Act 1988, s 842. In order to obtain approval the investment trust must, among other requirements, be resident for tax purposes in the UK and have its ordinary share capital listed on a recognised stock exchange. This chapter deals primarily with investment trusts which have been so approved for tax purposes and which have been incorporated in the UK. Unapproved investment trusts can generally be treated like any other company.

7.3 Highlights of the previous year

Investment trusts have for a long time been at a marketing disadvantage against the modern 'open-ended' media, since their shares are subject to the same advertising and dealing restrictions as those of any ordinary company. Accordingly neither the trusts themselves nor ordinary high street insurance brokers can market the shares, and there can be problems in arranging small purchases, regular investment schemes or reinvestment of income. The retail review committee of the Securities and Investments Board made proposals in March 1990 for parity of treatment with unit trusts and bonds in some cases. Thus the requirements for brokers to give 'best advice' and to disclose commissions on other investments may perhaps improve the competitive position of investment trusts, and so increase their market prices towards their net asset values (see **7.6.4**).

More dramatically, the £1bn Globe Investment Trust (the UK's largest) was taken over and liquidated by the British Coal Pension Funds after a bitter battle with the managers. Whether or not this is a welcome development (and it was evidently accepted by a majority of the shareholders), the graphic demonstration of the disciplines of a free market will keep the investment trusts on their toes and up-to-date with the demands of their investors.

7.4 Legal nature

An investment trust is constituted as a limited liability company with a share capital, and is a legal entity separate from its shareholders or managers. In practice the trusts are often promoted and managed by fund management groups who run a number of investment trusts and other funds, which, in some cases, own the management group or control its Board. However, the shareholders are always entitled to vote to replace the management, and recently there has been much take-over activity, and more trusts wound up than new ones launched.

Investments are made by buying stocks, shares and warrants of the trusts. Apart from ordinary share capital, a trust may issue debenture stock (secured by a charge on its assets), unsecured loan stock or preference shares and may take out bank loans and overdrafts. The holders of such securities are entitled to receive interest or preference dividends at the applicable rate before any dividends are paid to the equity shareholders. Such securities may, in the long run, prove less profitable, but on a winding-up of the company, the equity shareholders are only entitled to any surplus assets remaining after payment of all other liabilities, including the repayment of principal and income due to holders of loan capital or preference shares. If an investment trust has a high proportion of its capital in the form of loan capital and preference shares, major fluctuations in the value of the underlying assets attributable to the holders of its equity share capital can result. This topic is discussed in more detail in **7.6.5**. (Debenture stocks, loan stocks and preference shares are discussed in Chapter 5.)

Like any limited liability company, an investment trust company is constituted by the contract with its shareholders contained in its memorandum and articles of association. Objects clauses in the memoranda of investment trusts usually contain wide powers to invest the funds of the company in securities and property and to borrow, but, for tax reasons, commonly prohibit trading (as opposed to investing) in securities or property; and their articles of association normally contain a provision prohibiting the distribution of capital profits by way of dividend. However, the desirability of approved status for tax purposes (see **7.7**) will impose certain practical limitations on the exercise of these wide investment powers.

An investment trust is not permitted to advertise its shares for sale except by reference to Listing Particulars, registered with the Registrar of Companies and complying with the requirements of the Financial Services Act. However, investment trusts publish informative annual reports and an increasing number of schemes are advertised by the managers to facilitate investment. Further advice and information are available from stockbrokers, through whom the shares are often bought.

7.5 Conditions for purchase

There are in general no limitations on the purchase of UK investment trust shares. Investors must of course satisfy any restrictions imposed by their own powers (eg as trustees), or any foreign laws to which they are subject. Investment trusts are normally a wider-range investment under the Trustee Investments Act and collective investment media generally help to satisfy trustees' duty of diversification.

7.6 Characteristics

7.6.1 Spread of risk and flexibility

An important feature of investment trust shares, like other collective investments, is the spread of risk which can be achieved by the investor. Investment trust shares represent an indirect interest in all the underlying assets of the trust, which can give the small investor a well balanced portfolio with a good spread of risk which would be too expensive and impracticable to obtain and manage by direct investment. But larger investors (personal or corporate), also invest through investment trusts in order to obtain professional or specialised investment management, currency management or gearing, and their attention to the trust's management of their interests may benefit all shareholders.

The wide investment powers of most investment trusts enable them, subject to the limitations acceptable for tax purposes, to follow a reasonably flexible investment policy. In response to changes in investment or fiscal conditions, they are able to adjust the emphasis in their portfolios on income or capital appreciation or on a particular sector of the market or geographical location. In addition, they are able, within limits, to invest in real property (although usually through the securities of listed property companies) in shares of unlisted companies and in other assets and, although they do not deal or trade in securities themselves for tax reasons, they may establish dealing subsidiaries to take short-term positions in securities. Due to regulations under the Financial Services Act, the investment policy of an authorised unit trust must necessarily be less flexible than that of an investment trust.

The basic investment characteristics of a particular investment trust are stated in its prospectus and may be indicated in its name. However, since investment trusts are flexible vehicles and investment conditions are constantly changing, a better indication of an investment trust's current policy can be obtained from its latest report and accounts.

As well as considering the stated investment objectives and financial record of a particular investment trust, the potential investor should check its size. A small investment trust may be able to out-perform a larger one by adopting a more flexible investment policy, but its shares could be less marketable than those of a bigger trust, with a greater spread between buying and selling prices.

7.6.2 Income and capital gains

Income and capital gains from investments are taxed differently and may be separately owned, so the balance between the two is very significant to many investors. Some markets, particularly in the far east, offer negligible dividend yields and correspondingly greater expectations of gains, but investment trusts may be chosen with a wide range of divided policies.

Certain investment trusts, known as 'split-level' trusts, have their equity share capital divided into income shares and capital shares, and are incorporated for a fixed period. During that period the holders of the income shares are entitled to all or most of the income arising from the investment portfolio, and on the liquidation of the trust at the end of the period the holders of the capital shares are entitled to all or most of any capital appreciation on the trust's portfolio. The capital shares are particularly suitable for higher-rate taxpayers who currently wish to defer the returns from their investment (for example, pending retirement), and the income shares for those (such as some trustees) who require an above-average income. The approach of a fixed liquidation date helps to reduce the discounts to net asset value discussed at **7.6.4**. For similar reasons, more sophisticated structures, including zero-coupon and stepped preference shares and index loan stocks are continually being developed.

7.6.3 Investment overseas and currency management

Although most investment trusts adopt a flexible investment policy and are not rigidly committed to maintaining a particular proportion of their investments in any one geographical area, some of them specialise in one or more overseas areas in which they have acquired special knowledge and investment expertise. These trusts provide a useful medium for overseas investment.

Many trusts use foreign currency loans for overseas investment, so that the exposure of the trusts to the foreign exchange markets can be managed independently of the investments made in any country. At the same time the trust may be geared-up (see **7.6.5**) but whenever the managers choose to reduce the exposure of the trust to the market a sterling deposit can be made from the trust's original capital. For example, a foreign investment which gains by 20 per cent in local currency terms would still show a 20 per cent sterling loss if the exchange rate fell by a third. However, the portfolio can be insulated from exchange rate volatility by borrowing the amount of the investment locally, since if the exchange rate falls the liability to repay is reduced as well as the assets. At the same time the trust's original capital could also be invested in any market.

Another, sometimes cheaper, way of hedging against exchange rate exposure is the 'currency swap' under which a UK investment trust swaps an amount in sterling with, say, a US company for an equivalent amount of US dollars. The US dollars received by the investment trust are used for portfolio investment. At the end of the agreed period the investment trust simply hands back the same amount of dollars to the US company in return for the sterling amount which it originally agreed for the swap. Accordingly, the risk of a default by the other party is limited to the possible exchange loss and attributable expenses.

The investment trust has always been a useful medium for overseas investment by UK residents because such investment is a difficult matter for most private investors, having regard to the distances involved and the taxation and other problems which may arise in the overseas territories concerned. The average UK investor does not possess sufficient expertise to undertake the effective management of his own UK investments and is even less qualified to manage a portfolio of overseas investments.

7.6.4 Stock market price and underlying net asset value

An investment trust incorporated in the UK in general cannot purchase or redeem its own shares. Consequently investment trust shareholders are normally only able to realise their investment by selling their shares through the stock market to other investors, or if the trust is wound-up or taken over. The market prices of investment trust shares are dictated by supply and demand and for many years have generally stood at a discount to the value of their underlying net assets. These discounts and valuations are regularly published for most trusts. Formerly, part of this discount may have been due to contingent capital gains tax liabilities in the portfolio, but approved investment trusts are exempt from CGT but still regularly stand at a price in the stock market which is 15 or 20 per cent lower than the amount per share which would be paid to shareholders on a liquidation of the company. The obvious explanation for these substantial discounts is a lack of demand for investment trust shares in the market. It is due, in part, to lack of publicity, competition from pension and insurance funds and unit trusts (whose managers are free to advertise their units for sale and to offer commissions to selling agents), and the fact that investment trust shares are often held by long-term investors. All these factors have contributed towards a comparatively low level of regular dealing activity in investment trust shares and so reduced their marketability.

In order to realise the profit inherent in the discount on net asset value a number of investment trust companies have been reconstructed by their managers, taken over by other companies, placed in voluntary liquidation or 'unitised'. Unitisation is a scheme under which the shareholders pass a special resolution to wind up the investment trust and transfer its investments to an authorised unit trust in exchange for units of the unit trust to be issued direct to the former shareholders in the investment trust. Subject to Inland Revenue clearance, unitisation does not of itself involve the investment trust shareholders in any liability to capital gains tax and on a subsequent disposal of units in the authorised unit trust, the original acquisition cost of those units for capital gains tax purposes is the acquisition cost of the shares in the investment trust from which the units arose. Following the unitisation, the former shareholders in the investment trust are able to sell their new units in the authorised unit trust at a price based on the underlying assets of the unit trust (see Chapter 8) and so the discount will have been effectively eliminated.

The discount on net asset value has also been eliminated for some investment trust shareholders by take-over offers being made for their shares at prices near their underlying net asset value. Some of these take-over offers have been made by predator companies, while others have been made by institutions, such as pension funds, which see the acquisition of an investment trust company as an inexpensive means of acquiring a 'ready-made' investment portfolio and perhaps eliminating a competitor. However, a take-over, unlike a unitisation, may unexpectedly crystallise a liability to capital gains tax.

Having regard to the possibility of the discount being eliminated in one of the ways mentioned above or narrowing simply as a result of increased demand in the stock market, it can be said that the discount may in the end prove highly beneficial to purchasers of investment trust shares, who acquire an interest in underlying assets at a discount and are then sometimes able to dispose of that interest at a price equal to or near the true underlying value of those assets. When the investor comes to sell his shares, so long as the discount is not larger than when he bought them, he should not suffer loss solely by reason of its existence and in the meantime will have benefited from the income on the assets.

Another factor which will affect the stock market price of investment trust shares is the market-maker's turn, ie, the difference between the higher offer price (at which the market-maker is prepared to sell to the investor) and the lower bid price (at which the market-maker is prepared to buy from the investor). The spread between the market-maker's bid and offer price will usually be wider in the case of shares of the smaller, less marketable trusts.

This assumes that there is a sufficient market for the shares to enable them to be sold at all. In practice, a small investor in most of the larger investment trusts should not experience any difficulty in disposing of his shares subject to the applicable discount on net asset value.

7.6.5 Gearing

In addition to its equity share capital, an investment trust may raise further capital by issuing debenture or loan stocks or preference shares and borrow money in sterling and foreign currencies. On a liquidation of the investment trust, holders of such stocks or preference shares and lenders of funds to the investment trust are entitled to repayment of fixed amounts of capital or principal from the assets of the trust in priority to equity shareholders. Only the surplus assets remaining, after discharge by the investment trust of all its other liabilities, are distributable to the equity shareholders. In effect, any increase or decrease in the value of the assets of the investment trust is primarily attributable to its equity share capital. An overall increase or decrease has a greater effect on the underlying value of its equity share capital in the case of a trust which has raised most of its capital in the form of loans or preference shares than in the case of a trust which has raised most of its capital by issues of equity shares. In UK securities terminology, if the proportion of a company's capital which has been raised in the form of loans and preference shares is large in relation to its equity capital, the company is described as 'highly geared' and, if small, the company's 'gearing' is said to be low; the US term is 'leverage'.

The following examples will illustrate the consequences of gearing; taxation and other factors have been ignored in the interests of simplicity.

Example 1

A new ungeared investment trust raises £1 million by an issue of equity shares and invests the proceeds of the share issue in a portfolio of securities. If the value of the portfolio doubles to £2 million the assets of the trust attributable to the equity shareholders will increase 100 per cent. If the portfolio halves, the net value for ordinary shareholders will, likewise, decrease by 50 per cent.

Example 2

Suppose a new geared investment trust raises £1 million by (a) issuing 250,000 preference shares at £1 each, (b) borrowing £250,000 and (c) issuing equity shares at an aggregate price of £500,000, and then invests the total proceeds of £1 million in a portfolio of securities. If the portfolio doubles in value to £2 million, on a liquidation, the investment trust will have to pay (a) £250,000 to the preference shareholders and (b) £250,000 to the provider of the £250,000 loan; but, after these payments have been made, the amount attributable to the trust's equity shares will have increased by 200 per cent from £500,000 to £1.5 million. On the other hand, if the value of the portfolio halves, the preference shareholders and lenders will each be repaid £250,000 leaving nothing for the ordinary shareholders a 100 per cent loss.

The ability of investment trusts to gear their portfolios in this manner is one of the principal differences between investment trusts and unit trusts. The latter can only have very limited powers to borrow money without gearing up, principally for foreign currency loans in respect of portfolio investment overseas.

The examples given above illustrate the effect of gearing on the *capital* assets of an investment trust, but, if the lenders of money to an investment trust or its preference shareholders are entitled to payment of interest or dividends at a fixed rate, gearing will also have an effect on the *income* of the trust from its investments which is distributable to its equity shareholders. An increase (or decrease) in the income arising from a geared trust's investments will have a greater impact on the amount of income available for distribution to equity shareholders of the trust by way of dividend than will a similar fluctuation in the income of an ungeared trust.

Equity shareholders of investment trusts will benefit from investing in highly geared investment trusts when the assets in which those trusts have invested are rising in value but that they are at greater risk when such assets are falling in value. One of the more difficult tasks of a professional investment manager is to utilise gearing successfully. The investment manager must decide when to gear up the trust and when to undertake a rapid 'de-gearing' exercise by repaying borrowings or turning substantial portions of the investment portfolio into cash or assets which are not likely to fluctuate significantly in value.

7.7 Taxation

7.7.1 Approval of investment trusts

This chapter deals with 'approved' investment trusts as opposed to 'unapproved' investment companies. Only approved investment trusts (and authorised unit trusts) attract the capital gains tax exemption outlined below. An approved investment trust is one which is not a 'close company' and which, in respect of an accounting period, has been approved by the Board of Inland Revenue for the purposes of the Income and Corporation Taxes Act 1988, s 842. The Inland Revenue appears to have discretion under s 842 to withhold approval, even in the case of an investment trust which would otherwise qualify for approval under that section. It will approve a company that can show that:

(1) it is resident for taxation purposes in the UK;
(2) its income is derived wholly or mainly (which in practice means approximately 70 per cent or more) from shares or securities;
(3) no holding in a company (other than another approved investment trust or a company which would qualify as such but for the fact that its shares are not listed as required by (4) below) represents more than 15 per cent by value of its investments;
(4) all its ordinary share capital is listed on a recognised stock exchange in the UK; and
(5) the distribution as dividend of capital profits on the sale of its investments is prohibited by its memorandum or articles of association.

It is expressly provided in s 842 that an increase in the value of a holding after it has been acquired will not result in an infringement of the 15 per cent limit referred to in (3) above. However, the holdings of an investment trust in its subsidiary companies are treated as a single holding for the purposes of this limit, as are its holdings in other companies which are members of the same group of companies. In addition, any loans made by the trust to its subsidiaries are treated as part of its investment in the subsidiaries for the purposes of ascertaining whether the limit has been infringed.

7.7.2 Approved investment trusts—capital gains

Investment trusts are corporations and their income is subject to corporation tax in the same manner and at the same rates as other corporations, but capital gains accruing to approved investment trusts are wholly exempt from capital gains tax in the hands of the trust. Thus active management of the trust's investments need not be constrained by tax on realising gains and the investor may only be subject to tax on disposing of his investment trust shares.

7.7.3 Approved investment trusts—income

The taxation of the trust's own income, and of the income and gains of investors in the trust, is exactly the same as for other limited companies (see Chapter 5). The corporation tax system is complicated and a detailed explanation of it is outside the scope of this guide but a brief summary may help.

Income
Franked income
This is income received by a trust in the form of dividends paid by a UK company in respect of which that company has paid advance corporation tax (ACT). ACT is effectively a payment by a UK company on account of its own corporation tax liability and is made in respect of dividends paid by it. The rate of ACT is expressed as a fraction of the dividend paid. The current fraction is 25/75, or one third, which means that if a company pays a dividend of £75 to a shareholder it must pay £25 ACT in respect of that dividend and the shareholder will receive a tax credit of £25. The amount of the dividend plus the ACT is known as a 'franked payment'. A trust is itself liable to pay ACT on paying dividends to its own shareholders, but if its dividend is paid out of franked income, it can deduct the amount of the tax credit received from the paying company from its own ACT liability. This means that franked income received by a trust can be passed on by way of dividend to its own shareholders without any payment of ACT by the trust. Further, the franked income is not liable to corporation tax in the hands of the trust.

Unfranked income
This is all other income (such as interest on gilt-edged securities, bank deposit interest and dividends paid by foreign companies) which does not carry a tax credit indicating that ACT has been paid in respect of it. Unfranked income is less favourably treated, being subject to corporation tax. However, interest paid by the trust and the fees paid to its investment managers are set primarily against unfranked income, reducing the amount liable to tax.

7.8 Unapproved investment companies

Unless an investment company has the status of an approved investment trust (see **7.7.1**), it is subject to ordinary forms of corporate taxation and will not qualify for the capital gains tax exemption mentioned in **7.7.2**. Thus both the investment income and capital gains made by such a company will also be taxed, under the terms of the Finance Act 1987, at the full corporation tax rate. Under the Finance Act 1989, a closely-held investment company that does not distribute the bulk of its income will suffer corporation tax at a rate equivalent to the higher rate of income tax, currently 40 per cent. In addition, if an investment company disposes of its assets and is then liquidated there is effectively a double capital gains tax charge, because (1) the company will be liable to corporation tax on capital gains realised by it on the disposal, and (2) its shareholders will be liable to capital gains tax in respect of any capital gains realised by them on the disposal of their shares in the investment company, which will occur by reason of the distribution of cash proceeds to them in the liquidation. (Considerations affecting investment in a *private* investment company are discussed in Chapter 12, **12.4**.)

Having regard to these disadvantages and to the fact that, so long as the investment company continues in existence, profits on the sale of investments may only be distributed to its shareholders by way of comparatively highly taxed dividends, the investment company has become unpopular as an investment medium. In fact, in order to mitigate this unsatisfactory taxation position, many unapproved investment companies have been 'unitised' (see **7.6.4**). However, a side effect of the Finance Act 1980, which exempted authorised unit trusts from capital gains tax, is that the transfer of the assets out of an unapproved investment company into an authorised unit trust has become a disposal for capital gains tax purposes. Accordingly, the only advantage which such a unitisation offers to a disposing shareholder is that it defers the capital gains liability on the company shares until the ultimate disposal of the units issued as the result of an investment company unitisation. Taken together with the use of the capital gains tax exemption for one year or more, such a deferral will still, in many cases, make a reconstruction scheme an attractive proposition.

7.9 Suitability

Investment trusts are a suitable investment medium for small and large investors who are resident in the UK for tax purposes, who wish to spread their investment risk and who do not have the expertise or the resources to make direct investments such as in foreign securities. However, the investor in investment trusts should be aware of the possible advantages and disadvantages which may result from the existence of the discount on net asset value (see **7.6.4**) and from the ability of investment trusts to gear their portfolios (see **7.6.5**). If the investor is unwilling to accept the risks involved for the sake of the possible greater rewards, the unit trust is probably a more suitable investment medium. On the other hand, investment trusts have frequently shown better long term returns.

7.10 Mechanics

Investment trust shares may be acquired on The Stock Exchange through stockbrokers, banks and other investment advisers. They may be included in personal equity plans up to a limit of £3,000 on condition that the trust must be at least 50 per cent invested in UK equities. A number of stockbroking firms specialise in the investment trust sector and will be able to provide detailed information relating to individual trusts, including analyses of past performance, level of discount on underlying net asset value and investment policy. Information relating to investment trusts can also be obtained from the Association of Investment Trust Companies and from the cards produced by the Extel Statistical Services. Alternatively information on individual trusts can be obtained from the managers, who may also offer shares for sale through 'Savings Schemes'.

Investment trust savings schemes are operated by managers to avoid some of the restrictions on marketing shares. Typically they offer lump sum, regular savings and dividend reinvestment options. The contributions are pooled by the managers and used to buy shares on The Stock Exchange, and the saving in transaction costs may reduce the investor's brokerage as low as 0.2 per cent, although some schemes provide for the payment of substantial commissions to intermediaries, the cost of which is naturally passed on to the investor.

Costs of both acquisition and disposal on The Stock Exchange will normally include stockbrokers' commission, which is subject to negotiation, but for a private investor is likely to be something between 1 per cent and 1.65 per cent (plus VAT), depending on the extent of the service the client requires from the broker; there will usually be a minimum, perhaps £25 (plus VAT) and a lower rate for large deals. On purchases, there will also be stamp duty at 0.5 per cent (until its abolition, expected in 1991), and the spread between bid and offered prices may be around 1.5 per cent, though it will usually be less on the freely traded shares of large companies. There is no initial charge payable to the managers, but further brokerage will be payable on final realisation of the shares by sale.

7.11 Maintenance

Running costs vary from one investment trust to another, but management fees, often in the region of 0.5 per cent per annum on the value of the portfolio, are usually payable by the trust at half-yearly intervals in addition to its day-to-day operating expenses. New and converted specialist trusts, such as those involved in providing venture capital, often pay higher fees, sometimes approaching 1.5 per cent. Economies can often be achieved in cases where the managers act as managers for several investment trusts and are therefore able to spread the burden of management and administrative expenses among a number of different trusts. These management fees and expenses are normally deductible from the income of the trust for corporation tax purposes, whereas the management fee of a private portfolio manager generally has to be found out of his client's after-tax income. In the case of investment trusts, the level of management fees and the extent to which operating expenses may be charged to the trust are not controlled by any governmental body.

Like any other investment, holdings in investment trusts should be periodically reviewed by the investor or his adviser. Performance of the investment trust may be monitored by observing the movements in its quoted stock exchange price (published in the daily newspapers) and the changes in its underlying net asset value and by reading the half-yearly financial statements and annual directors' reports and audited accounts which will be sent by the trust to its registered shareholders and are generally available free on request. The annual report and accounts will contain detailed financial and other information relating to the trust and will usually include details of its investment portfolio as at the date of its balance sheet. The trust will also convene an annual general meeting of shareholders to adopt the annual report and accounts and to conduct other business. Any registered shareholder may attend and vote on the resolutions proposed at these meetings or, if he does not wish to attend, he may appoint a proxy to vote on his behalf.

7.12 Preview of the year ahead

The SIB's Retail Review Committee proposed, in March 1990, to liberalise the marketing of certain investment trust savings schemes. If adopted, this long-awaited development could fundamentally enhance the investment trust sector by raising its public profile, so improving prices and thus the values to existing holders, whether or not they use savings schemes.

132 Allied Dunbar Investment and Savings Guide

The proposals would apply to schemes for trusts which are:

(1) approved by the Inland Revenue;
(2) listed on The Stock Exchange, and complying with the current requirements for new listings;
(3) liquid or readily realisable;
(4) of conventional capital structure; and
(5) managed by authorised persons subject to conduct of business rules.

If adopted the proposals will allow door-to-door sales and sales via press coupons, and will require brokers to consider investment trust schemes along with other 'packaged' investment products such as unit trusts, in order to give best advice. Correspondingly, standardised projections, risk warnings, product particulars and cooling-off periods would be introduced, as with the other packaged products.

7.13 Conclusion

While the market prices of investment trust shares generally remain below their underlying asset values, there will continue to be opportunities to profit from this discount, either on a reconstruction, take-over or winding-up of the trust or if rule changes increase demand for (and so prices of) investment trusts. Predators continue to give every incentive for good performance to trust managers, who have started to respond with 'poison pill' measures such as investment in unquoted shares or the issue of warrants. The freedom of investment trusts to use new and sophisticated financial structures, techniques and instruments which are largely denied to other collective media may become of increasing importance, as other differences are reduced. For example, because investment trusts do not have to contend with fluctuating capital flows, they are particularly suitable for index-matching investment policies. The first conversion of a trust into a fully indexed fund was approved by the New Tokyo Investment Trust's shareholders in January 1989 against the managers' wishes, in order to track the Tokyo First Section market index. Other trusts may well follow, but the flexibility of investment trusts in the hands of their professional managers will ensure they remain efficient and attractive investment vehicles for small and large investors alike.

8 Unit trusts and offshore funds

David Ballance, MA (Oxon), Investment Manager, Allied Dunbar Assurance plc

8.1 Introduction

Another form of collective investment medium (see Chapter 7) is that of unit trusts. A unit trust is a trust fund, in which the investors hold direct beneficial interests. It is normally open-ended, meaning that units are created or redeemed at the current fair prices, and so the managers buy and sell units as required by investors (see **8.7**).

Obviously the honesty and competence of the managers of such trusts is of fundamental importance, and the constitution, management and marketing of trusts are all regulated in the UK, primarily under the Financial Services Act 1986. These powers are exercised by the Securities and Investments Board (SIB) and a number of self regulatory organisations with delegated powers over member firms. Only authorised persons may conduct investment business. The European Community Directive on Undertakings for Collective Investment in Transferable Securities (the UCITS Directive) requires all member states to assimilate their regulations for certain collective schemes, which may then be sold throughout the Common Market.

8.2 Historical background

Units in the first unit trust in the UK were offered to the public in April 1931 by the M & G Group, which still exists today as one of the leaders of the industry. Allied Investors Ltd, now Allied Dunbar Unit Trusts PLC, followed in 1934 and is now the second largest unit trust group. The first trusts were 'fixed' trusts and offered virtually no flexibility in investment policy once the trust deed had been executed. Each new subscription was invested in the fixed portfolio and each unit was thus unchanged in its composition. Each unit was normally divided into sub-units for sale to the public.

The first 'flexible' trust (the type of trust which is marketed today) was not offered to the public until 1936. When the Prevention of Fraud

(Investments) Act 1939 came into force, supervision of the new industry was made the responsibility of the (then) Board of Trade. Under that Act, revised and re-enacted as the Prevention of Fraud (Investments) Act 1958, the Department of Trade and Industry (DTI) laid down regulations for the conduct of unit trusts, supervised charges and 'authorised' unit trusts complying with its requirements until 1988. The power of authorisation for new unit trust schemes then passed from the DTI to the Securities and Investments Board (SIB).

8.3 Authorisation

The main requirement for authorisation of a unit trust by the SIB is that a trust deed conforming with the Board's regulations is executed, between a company performing all management functions for the trust (the managers) and an independent trust corporation (the trustee) to hold the trust's investments and supervise the managers. Both the managers and the trustee must be incorporated under the law of, or of some part of, the UK or any other member state of the EC, must maintain a place of business in Great Britain and must be authorised persons to conduct investment business and so subject to the regulators' rules for conduct of business. The persons who are to be directors of a unit trust management company must be approved by the SIB. The trust deed and regulations must provide for, *inter alia*:

(1) managers' investment and borrowing powers and limits on investment of the trust's assets;
(2) determining the manner in which prices and yields are calculated and the obligation of managers to repurchase units at the 'bid' price;
(3) setting up a register of unitholders, with procedures for issuing certificates and dealing with transfers;
(4) remuneration of the managers and trustees;
(5) periodic audits of the trust and the issue of financial statements to unitholders, with reports by the managers, trustees and auditors;
(6) meetings of unitholders under certain circumstances.

Authorisation makes it possible for unit trust managers to advertise units for sale to the public and carries with it tax privileges for the trust. These taxation aspects are discussed in detail in Section **8.9**. This Part deals only with unit trusts which have been authorised by the SIB, and the expression 'unit trust', when used in this Part, means an authorised unit trust unless otherwise indicated. (As to unauthorised unit trusts, see Section **8.12**.)

8.4 Highlights of the previous year

Sales of unit trusts in 1989, compared with the previous two years were as follows:

	1987 £m	1988 £m	1989 £m
Industry sales	14,545.1	7,675.7	10,609.0
Industry repurchases	8,214.3	5,880.4	6,743.0
Net new investment	6,330.8	1,795.3	3,866.0

At 31 December 1989, the total funds invested in authorised unit trusts were £52.8bn.

One hundred and twenty four new trusts were launched in the year making a total of 1,379, operated by 162 management companies, compared with 153 at the end of 1987.

Share prices continued their recovery from 1988 levels. In particular the UK and US markets rose sharply through the year, and European markets benefitted from the perceived liberalisation of Eastern Europe. However, the new sales figures failed to recover to 1987 levels, and net outflows continued from several management groups. Some smaller groups suffered from high compliance or administration costs; the debacle of the Duménil group, a small specialist group managing mainly single country trusts would be an example of this. More recently, concern over the UK political scene, and the weakness in the previously resolute Japanese market have conspired to cloud the scene.

8.5 Pricing of units

Since 1 July 1988, unit trust managers have been free to choose whether to deal on 'forward prices', ie, at the next price to be calculated, or at prices already calculated and published, as had been usual. Many management companies have availed themselves of this opportunity. With forward pricing, a buyer does not know exactly how many units he will receive, but he does know that he will deal at a fair, up-to-date price. If, on the other hand, a management company is dealing on historic prices and the value of a trust is believed to have changed by more than 2 per cent since the valuation on which the company is offering to deal, a new price must be calculated (using an index if the trustee agrees). Alternatively, the company can change to forward pricing.

More information now has to be given with the unit prices published in newspapers. In addition to bid and offer prices, the initial charge and the cancellation price must now be shown. The cancellation price is that at which the company can cancel units that it has created or bought back from the public. If the trust is on a bid basis, the bid and cancellation prices will be the same.

The Financial Services Act 1986 became effective in 1988, superseding the Prevention of Fraud (Investments) Act 1958. As a result, much of the regulation of unit trusts, including authorisation, will be transferred from the DTI to other bodies. The regulation of borrowing powers and permitted investment remains with the DTI, and the constitution of unit trusts is regulated by the DTI and the SIB, but the management of trusts is regulated by the Investment Management Regulatory Organisation (IMRO) and the marketing by the Life Assurance and Unit Trust Regulatory Organisation (LAUTRO) and the Financial Intermediaries and Brokers Organisation (FIMBRA).

The 1990 Budget raised further limits on annual investment in personal equity plans, this time to £6,000, from £4,800. The maximum investment in unit and investment trusts was raised from £2,400 to £3,000 and there continued to be no restriction on the proportion of trusts to the whole. Qualifying trusts now need to have at least 50 per cent invested in the UK, down from 75 per cent previously required.

8.6 Legal nature

As mentioned in **8.3**, a unit trust scheme is constituted by a trust deed which is made between the managers, who are the promoters of the scheme and who will subsequently be responsible for the conduct of the investment and for administration, and the trustee (usually one of the clearing banks or major insurance companies), which is responsible for ensuring that the managers act in accordance with the provisions laid down in the trust deed and which holds the assets of the trust on trust for the unitholders. Regulations determine the content of the trust deed and other binding requirements, and both the trustee and the management company are subject to the Conduct of Business Rules.

The underlying securities are registered in the name of the trustee or, if in bearer form, held in the custody of the trustee, which also holds any cash forming part of the fund. The trustee, as the legal owner of the underlying assets for the unitholders, receives on their behalf all income and other distributions made in respect of such assets.

The trust deed and regulations also lay down a formula for valuing the trust to determine the prices at which units may be sold to the public by the managers and at which units must be bought back by the managers from the public (see below). Additional units may be created to meet demand from the public or existing units may be cancelled as a result of the subsequent repurchase of units from the public. A unit trust is thus 'open-ended' and can expand or contract depending on whether there is a preponderance of buyers or sellers of its units.

Three prices are quoted for unit trusts. These are the 'offered' price, at which units are offered for sale to or subscription by the public, and the 'bid' price, at which the managers buy units back and the cancellation price, at which the managers may arrange for units to be redeemed out of the assets of the trust. These prices are, broadly speaking, ascertained in the following manner:

(1) the offered price is calculated by reference to the notional amount which would have to be paid to acquire the underlying assets held by the trust, to which are added the notional acquisition costs (such as brokers' commission and stamp duty) and the preliminary management charges (see **8.11.1**);
(2) the bid price is calculated by reference to the notional amount which would be received on a disposal of the assets held by the trust, from which are deducted the notional costs of the disposal, ie, brokers' commission and contract stamp.

An investor must never be required to pay more for his units than the offered price as calculated under the trust deed, nor may the unitholder on a sale of his units be paid less than the bid price as so calculated. When an investor buys units, the managers may either create them or sell units that they have previously repurchased. The spread between the offered and bid prices under the DTI rules is normally between 8 and 11 per cent, but in practice most unit trust managers quote spreads for their own dealings in units between 5.5 and 7.5 per cent, which may be positioned anywhere between the maximum offered and minimum bid prices applicable on subscription for new units and cancellation of existing units.

Managers normally base their buying price for units in a particular trust on the strict bid valuation if they are buying back more units than they are selling, since this is the price at which units must be cancelled. Conversely, if the managers are selling more units than they are buying, their selling price is normally based on the full offered price, at which units must be created.

A unit trust cannot 'gear' its portfolio by borrowings, either unsecured or secured on the assets of the trust. The only circumstances in which borrowing is permitted are to anticipate known cash flows (such as dividends due) or to hedge against currency losses on holdings of foreign securities. The gearing effect of hedge borrowing is almost eliminated by the requirement that a matching sterling deposit must be made (see **8.8.2**).

The trust deed, which takes effect subject to any regulations under the Financial Services Act, may make provision for the trust to be terminated and also specifies circumstances in which the approval of unitholders at a general meeting needs to be sought. Such approval is required, among other things, for proposals to vary the provisions of the trust deed, to change the investment objectives of the trust or to amalgamate it with another trust. Unitholders' interests are thus protected despite the fact that no annual general meeting is held, since certain material changes affecting their interests may only be effected with their approval in general meeting.

8.7 Conditions for purchase

Any individual, corporate body or trustee may acquire and hold unit trusts without any condition or restriction, subject to any limitation which may be imposed on its own investment powers.

Unit trusts are specifically mentioned as approved 'wider range' investments under the Trustee Investments Act 1961. Unit trusts whose portfolios consist exclusively of investments suitable for 'narrow range' investments under the same Act may themselves be included in the narrow range investments. Trustees should, however, satisfy themselves of their powers to invest in unit trusts by reference to their trust instrument.

Nearly all unit trust managers specify a minimum investment, usually in the range of £250–£1,000. Certain specialist funds have higher minima. These minima do not apply to monthly saving schemes, where amounts from £10 per month may be invested on a regular basis.

Since a unit trust is open-ended, there is no maximum holding, though a corporate or trustee unitholder may be restricted by his own investment limitations.

In the case of some 'exempt' unit trusts, purchasers will still have to satisfy the managers that they enjoy tax-exempt status (eg, they are pension funds or charities) (see **8.13**), despite the fact that 'exempt' unit trusts' fiscal privileges have been outmoded by the exemption of all authorised unit trusts from tax on their capital gains.

Persons resident outside the UK may acquire and hold unit trust units, subject to the local exchange control rules in their country of residence or domicile. But for reasons of taxation, it is usually preferable for such people to invest in 'offshore' funds, see **8.15**.

8.8 Characteristics

Unit trusts must invest the greater part of their portfolios in securities listed on recognised stock exchanges. Trust deeds usually contain power for unquoted investments having an aggregate value not exceeding 5 per cent of the value of all the investments of the trust to be held. Depending upon their trust deeds, trusts may also be allowed to hold a proportion of their investments in shares on the London Unlisted Securities Market.

The investments of the majority of unit trusts are usually in equity shares. Preference shares are, however, occasionally held for reasons of yield, since the income from these, unlike interest on bank deposits or gilt-edged securites, is 'franked' investment income (see **8.9.2**). Following the Finance Act 1980, fixed interest funds (ie, those investing in gilt-edged and other bonds) became increasingly common (see **8.9.2**), but some have lost a part of their attraction now that the taxation of income on an accrual basis has removed much of their tax efficiency compared with direct investment.

Traditional authorised unit trusts may, in general, invest only in securities, although new classes of unit trusts will be authorised this year to invest in other financial instruments, or property, and mixed funds will invest in several different classes, including commodities. These new schemes will have separate regulations of investment and borrowing powers, and from 1990, may have a separate tax regime. All trusts, including traditional schemes may use certain traded option techniques for hedging purposes. Call options written and put options bought must be covered by the relevant securities held in the trusts.

It is not, at present, possible for a unit trust to adopt the 'split form' whereby all the income accrues to one class of holder and all the capital appreciation to the other.

The specific investment characteristics of unit trusts will vary depending on the stated objective of any particular trust. However, all unit trusts share certain general characteristics.

8.8.1 General characteristics

Spread of risk
By acquiring an interest in a portion of all the investments in the underlying portfolio of a unit trust, an investor can achieve a much wider spread of risk than he could himself achieve economically with limited resources. By spreading his investment across a large number of companies in a wide variety of industries in a number of different countries, the investor can much reduce the risks inherent in a holding of shares in only one company or a small number of companies. The result is likely to be a much more even progression of capital and income growth. Regulations covering the maximum investment of a trust's assets in a single company or issue, ensure that a wide spread of risk is achieved. In practice, unit trusts usually hold something between 30 and 100 investments, considerably more than the required minimum.

Professional management
By committing his investment funds to the purchase of a holding in a unit trust the investor is in effect delegating the day to day management of his portfolio to the managers of the trust. Virtually all unit trust management companies employ a team of investment specialists whose aim is to maximise capital and/or income performance, and who are given a wide discretion within the limitations imposed by the trust deed to increase or decrease the liquidity of the trust or to switch investments as they consider appropriate. The advantage to the investor is that his investments are under the continuous supervision of people whose business it is to keep abreast of economic, political and corporate developments at home and abroad.

Simplicity and convenience
The sometimes tedious paperwork associated with owning a portfolio of securities is largely eliminated. Day-to-day decisions on such matters as rights and scrip issues, mergers and take-overs are all taken by the managers. Dividends are received by the trustee and distributions of the trust's income are made, usually twice a year, to unitholders together with a report on the progress of their trust during the preceding accounting period.

Marketability

In view of their open-ended nature, as a result of which units can be created or cancelled to meet the requirements of investors, unit trust units can be regarded as a totally liquid investment, with none of the constraints on marketability sometimes encountered in connection with investment in some of the smaller listed companies. As a result of the pricing structure, referred to in **8.6**, purchases and sales of units take place at prices which reflect the underlying value of the trust's assets.

8.8.2 Types of unit trust

While all unit trusts share the investment characteristics listed above, there are a very wide range of trusts which offer different investment objectives designed to suit different categories of investors. The main types are described below.

Balanced trusts

These invest in a portfolio which is usually composed of leading 'blue chip' shares with the aim of achieving a steady growth of both capital and income. These trusts are designed for the investor who wishes to invest in a wide spread of ordinary shares. They are suitable for the first-time investor in equities, who wishes to hold the units for longer term investment or saving.

Income trusts

These aim to achieve an above-average yield to the investor whose primary need is for a high and growing income. Normally, such trusts give a yield between 1.2 and 1.5 times that available on shares generally. These trusts are most suitable for retired people, widows, or others who depend on investment income. Such trusts may purchase convertible shares as a way of achieving their yield objectives.

Capital trusts

These are designed to seek maximum capital growth. The income from such trusts is usually low. These characteristics make them particularly suitable for those who want to build up a nest-egg.

Fixed Interest trusts

These generally invest in a portfolio of government bonds, corporate bonds and convertible shares and may be either income or capital trusts. Such trusts may be suitable for those requiring a high income, although prospects for income growth are unlikely to be as good in equity income trusts.

Overseas trusts

These aim to provide the investor with an opportunity to invest through stock markets in other countries of the world. Investment overseas is a particularly complex and difficult task for the private person, but can be rewarding in times when sterling is weak against other currencies or when economic conditions in some region overseas are particularly buoyant. For these trusts, the 'back to back' loan can be a useful investment tool to neutralise currency fluctuations while preserving the exposure to the stock market in the chosen country. The term 'back to back' is used to describe the need for unit trusts to make a sterling deposit equivalent to the amount of foreign currency borrowed. The need to make this deposit arises from the restrictions on gearing by unit trusts (see **8.6**).

Specialist trusts

Certain trusts, sometimes referred to as 'specialist trusts', are promoted to invest in particular sectors of the securities market (eg, commodities or smaller companies). These trusts are suitable for the larger or more sophisticated investor who wishes to concentrate on a particular sector while still achieving a spread of risk. The specialist nature of such trusts means that the investor may be somewhat more at the whim of fashion; UK smaller companies unit trusts, for example, after many years of above-average returns, did not enjoy a buoyant 1989 unlike their balanced counterparts.

Accumulation trusts

Certain trusts within all the categories referred to above are structured and promoted on the basis that they will accumulate the net income within the trust rather than distribute it to unitholders. This income is nonetheless subject to taxation as if it had been received by unitholders.

'Tracker' trusts

Certain trusts are structured to imitate a stock market index and so achieve a performance matching that market. Because of their essentially passive nature, with investment managers taking fewer active decisions, such trusts normally have lower management charges. These trusts are also referred to as indexed trusts.

8.9 Taxation

8.9.1 Introduction

Sections **8.3** of this chapter dealt with 'authorised' unit trusts, as opposed to 'unapproved' investment companies and 'unauthorised' unit trusts. Only approved investment trusts and authorised unit trusts attract the capital gains tax concessions outlined below. This section on taxation also refers briefly, by way of comparison, to the tax treatment of unauthorised unit trusts.

Authorised unit trusts

An authorised unit trust for taxation purposes is a unit trust which, for any accounting period, is a unit trust scheme that has been authorised by the Securities and Investments Board, in accordance with the Financial Services Act 1986. The conditions which must be fulfilled before the SIB will confer authorisation have been discussed in **8.3**. By virtue of the Income and Corporation Taxes Act 1988, s 468, for taxation purposes an authorised unit trust is effectively treated as a company, its unit-holders are treated as shareholders in a company, and any distributions of income made to its unitholders are treated as dividends paid by a company to its shareholders. The exception is fixed interest trusts (**8.8.2**), which are taxed as trusts. Following the 1990 Budget, the corporation tax payable by all unit trusts that come within EC rules will, from 1 January 1991, be at a rate equal to the standard rate of income tax. This will remove a discrimination against unfranked income in the hands of trusts other than fixed interest trusts (see below). An authorised unit trust and its unitholders are given the same capital gains tax concessions as equity shareholders in other vehicles.

8.9.2 Taxation of approved and authorised unit trusts

Taxation of the trust

As mentioned above, authorised unit trusts (other than fixed interest funds) are effectively treated as corporations for taxation purposes and are granted the same capital gains tax concessions as approved investment trusts. The corporation tax system is complicated and a detailed explanation of it is outside the scope of this guide, but a brief statement of the position as it relates to the income and capital gains of approved investment trusts and authorised unit trusts is set out below.

Income
Franked income
This is income received by a unit trust in the form of dividends paid by a UK company in respect of which that company has paid advance corporation tax (ACT). ACT is effectively a payment by a UK company on account of its own corporation tax liability and is made in respect of dividends paid by it. The rate of ACT is expressed as a

fraction of the dividend paid. The current fraction is 25/75, or one third, which means that if a company pays a dividend to a shareholder of £75 it must pay £25 ACT in respect of that dividend and the shareholder will receive a tax credit of £25. The amount of the dividend plus the ACT is known as a 'franked payment'. A trust is itself liable to pay ACT on paying dividends to its own shareholders, but if its dividend is paid out of franked income, it can deduct the amount of the tax credit received from the paying company from its own ACT liability. This means that franked income received by a trust can be passed on by way of dividend to its own shareholders without any payment of ACT by the trust. Further, the franked income is not liable to corporation tax in the hands of the trust.

Unfranked income
This is all other income (such as interest on gilt-edged securities, bank deposit interest and dividends paid by foreign companies) which does not carry with it a tax credit indicating that ACT has been paid in respect of it. Certain unfranked income received by certain unit trusts (not investment trusts) is treated differently, as described in **8.9.1**. Unfranked income is less favourably treated for tax purposes, being subject to corporation tax (currently at 35 per cent or 25 per cent if the smaller company rate is applicable) in the hands of a trust (other than an authorised unit trust established especially to invest in UK government securities). However, interest paid by the trust and the management fees paid to its investment managers are set primarily against unfranked income, thereby reducing the amount of income which will be subject to corporation tax. However, following the 1990 Budget this discrimination against unfranked income will be removed from 1 January 1991. From that time the rate of corporation tax for all unit trusts that come within the EC rules for undertakings for collective investment in transferable securities (UCITS) will be equal to the standard rate of income tax.

Income received by authorised unit trusts complying with the provisions of the Income and Corporation Taxes Act 1988, s 468(5)—Section 468(1) Income and Corporation Taxes Act 1988 provides that authorised unit trusts are to be treated as if the trustees were a company resident in the United Kingdom and the rights of the unit holders were shares in the company. However, if the terms of the trust deed require that the trust fund must be invested only in assets which produce income which would be taxable under Schedule C (interest on gilt-edged securities) or Case III of Schedule D (interest on deposits, debentures and loan stocks), subs (5) of s 468 provides that the general treatment under subs (1) will not apply. The effect of this is that such trusts are liable only to income tax at the basic rate. This provision, introduced in the Finance Act 1980, effectively removed the disadvantages previously suffered by unit trusts set up to invest in fixed interest securities and allowed the creation of a new range of unit trusts. On the other hand, the management expenses of such trusts cannot be set against their income for calculation of their tax liability. However, as mentioned above, as from 1 January 1991 all unit trusts that are UCITS within the EC rules will be able to do so, as well as paying corporation tax at a rate equal to the standard rate of income tax.

It will be seen from the above that income accruing to a trust in the form of dividends on ordinary and preference shares in UK companies (ie franked income) is, until 1 January 1991, treated more favourably for corporation tax purposes than other forms of income. Subject to any relevant double taxation treaties, the amount of any foreign withholding tax borne by the trust in respect of income received from its overseas investments may be deducted from the corporation tax payable by the trust in respect of its income. This may prevent full set-off of ACT paid by the trust on the distribution of that income.

Capital gains
Capital gains accruing to authorised unit trusts are exempt from capital gains tax.

Taxation of the trust's shareholders
Income
The shareholder in a trust (other than an authorised unit trust established to invest wholly in UK government securities) who receives a dividend in respect of his shares will receive a tax credit for the ACT attributable to that dividend. In the example given in **8.9.2**, if he receives a dividend of £75 from the trust he will receive an associated tax credit for £25, which can be set against his liability to income tax. If he is not subject to income tax at the basic rate (currently 25 per cent) he will be entitled to reclaim all or part of the tax credit from the Inland Revenue. However, if he is liable to income tax at the higher rate of 40 per cent, he will have a further liability to tax in respect of an amount consisting of the dividend received plus the tax credit.

Capital gains
Capital gains made on units in authorised unit trusts or shares in approved investment trusts are treated exactly the same as gains made on any other type of security; ie, the gain, after allowing for indexation, is added to the taxpayer's income for tax purposes.

For 1990/91, capital gains up to £6,000 are exempt from tax. In addition, acquisition costs for capital gains are adjusted for changes in the Retail Prices Index from March 1982 or the date of purchase, if later, under FA 1982, ss 86 and 87 and FA 1985, s 68. Gains and losses accruing on the disposal of assets held on 31 March 1982 may be computed on the basis that those assets were acquired at their market value on that date. This rebasing cannot, however, increase either the amount of a gain or the amount of a loss as compared with what the gain or loss would have been under the previous capital gains tax regime.

The concessions given to trustees of settlements by the Finance Act 1978 (now contained in the Capital Gains Tax Act 1979, Schedule 1) in relation to capital gains tax are more restrictive. Where the settlement was made before 7 June 1978 the Trustees will not be liable to capital gains tax, if the net gains made by them in 1989/90 do not exceed £2,500. For settlements made after 6 June 1978 this limit may in certain circumstances be reduced. For certain disabled persons' trusts there is an exemption which is the same as for individuals, ie, £6,000 of gains in 1990/91.

8.10 Suitability

Unit trusts are suitable for investors, large or small, whether trustees, corporations or private individuals who wish to invest in a portfolio of either general or specialist securities in the UK or overseas, but who do not wish, or are not investing sufficient sums, to run their own investments.

Because the income from and the value of all securities can fluctuate, investors should understand that unit trusts are risk investments. 'The value of the units as well as the income from them may go down as well as up' is the caveat which must appear in all unit trust advertisements and literature soliciting purchases of units issued by managers who are members of the Unit Trust Association. However, the fact that unit trusts cannot, by law, gear up and that present regulation ensures a reasonable level of diversification within the trust, considerably reduces the inherent risk of the investment.

8.11 Mechanics and maintenance

8.11.1 Mechanics

Unit trust units may be acquired through any professional adviser (stockbroker, bank, accountant, solicitor or insurance broker). Many have departments specialising in advice on the selection of unit trusts. There are also several firms which offer unit trust portfolio management and advisory services. If there is any doubt as to the suitability of unit trusts to the investor's needs, professional advice may be desirable in any case.

Alternatively, unit trusts units may be acquired directly from the managers on either telephoned or written instructions. The disposal of units can be achieved in exactly the same way.

The names, addresses and telephone numbers of unit trust managers are given in many leading newspapers, together with a list of the current prices of the trusts they manage. All managers will supply more comprehensive information and copies of recent reports on particular trusts on request.

The Unit Trust Association can supply a comprehensive list of members and other general information about unit trusts on request.

When units are purchased, an initial charge payable to the managers is usually included in the unit price. There is no restriction on the initial charge, but the trust deed must contain a figure for the maximum permissible charge and all advertisements or literature must give details of the actual current charge. Initial charges are normally in the region of 5 per cent to 6 per cent.

Most managers pay commission to accredited agents. This is borne by the managers from the permitted initial charge.

The unitholder receives a contract note giving details of this purchase and subsequently receives a certificate showing the number of units of which he is the registered holder. Payment of the proceeds of sale is normally made by the managers within a few days of their receiving the certificate signed on the reverse by the unitholder.

8.11.2 Maintenance

Annual management fees based on the value of the trust are deducted by the managers from the income of the trust. As in the case of investment trusts, these fees are deductible from the income of the trust for tax purposes. The exception is the type of gilt or fixed interest trust made possible by the Finance Act 1980 (see **8.9.2**), in which fees can only be deducted from net income after tax. From the annual charge the managers must meet the costs of trustees' fees, audit fees, administration, and investment management. The maximum permitted level of annual management fees must be laid down in the trust deed and the actual level charged set out in all advertisements and literature. If managers wish to increase the fees to a level not exceeding the maximum figure, unitholders must be given three months' notice in writing. Increases in the maximum figure must be approved by unitholders at an extraordinary meeting. Fees charged usually vary between 0.75 and 1.5 per cent per annum, although management charges for certain indexed trusts may be as low as 0.5 per cent.

Certain other costs, including agents' fees for holding investments in safe custody overseas and the cost of collecting foreign dividends, may be charged to the income of the trust. These costs are usually small in relation to the total income.

The stamp duty and brokerage on the purchase and sale of underlying investments are borne by the trust but are reflected in the pricing structure (see **8.6**).

Like any other investment, unit trust holdings should be periodically reviewed by the investor or his adviser. The investor should be able to monitor the performance of the managers by reading the half-yearly (or sometimes annual) reports which they are required to send him. These reports should contain:

(1) a statement of the capital and income performance of the trust during the period, compared with appropriate indices;
(2) an assessment of portfolio changes during the period or any change in investment philosophy;
(3) the managers' view of the forthcoming period;
(4) a list of the current investment holdings;
(5) the figures for the income distribution; and
(6) a ten-year capital and income record.

8.12 Unauthorised unit trusts

Unauthorised unit trusts are unit trusts which have not been authorised by the Securities and Investments Board (see **8.3**). In some circumstances, authorised status for a unit trust may, for somewhat technical reasons, carry with it certain taxation disadvantages. In particular, if an authorised unit trust (other than one established specially to invest in UK government securities) is to receive a substantial proportion of its income other than by way of distributions from companies which are tax-resident in the UK (ie, in unfranked form), it will have income which is liable to corporation tax because of the rule deeming an authorised unit trust to be a company for taxation purposes. In these circumstances an authorised unit trust would have to pay corporation tax on a substantial proportion of its income, thus reducing the amount of income available for distribution to unitholders. This may be contrasted with the position where an authorised unit trust is in receipt solely of dividends from UK companies, in which case all the income which it receives will be 'franked investment income' and thus not liable to corporation tax. Accordingly, in cases where a material proportion of foreign income or other income liable to corporation tax is to be received, a unit trust may be established in unauthorised form in order to ensure that its income is liable only to ordinary income tax at the basic rate (presently 25 per cent), the payment of which is reflected in distributions to the unitholders. The treatment for income tax purposes of an unauthorised trust which receives a high proportion of its income in unfranked form will be more favourable than that of an authorised unit trust which receives a like proportion of unfranked income. But usually the advantage will be small compared with the disadvantage relating to capital gains (see **8.9.2**), and it will be negated, from 1 January 1991, by changes announced in the 1990 Budget (see **8.9.1**).

An unauthorised unit trust does not benefit from the capital gains tax exemption of authorised unit trusts. Capital gains tax will therefore be payable in full, putting such a trust at a disadvantage in comparison with an authorised trust so far as capital gains tax is concerned, unless the unauthorised trust is an exempt trust.

8.13 Exempt unit trusts

Exempt unit trusts are unit trusts designed for particular types of unitholders. While many such funds exist, their rationale was destroyed by the exemption of unit trusts from tax on chargeable gains in the Finance Act 1980. Exempt unit trusts may be in authorised or unauthorised form.

8.14 Preview of the year ahead

The present outlook for world stockmarkets is uncertain, with world interest rates set to remain high and with the Japanese market having fallen sharply, so the more subdued industry conditions compared with 1987 can be expected to continue. The costs of compliance are also affecting some of the smaller groups. The growth of indexed trusts (see **8.8.2**) where trusts seek to imitate a stock market index, and where managers are therefore, more passive may continue and possibly make some inroads into the traditional market. However, the increased personal equity plan limit (see **8.5**) should boost investment over time and when world interest rates fall one can reasonably expect investors to return to greater levels of activity.

8.15 Offshore funds

The expression 'offshore fund' is applied loosely to any investment medium, whether it be a unit trust or an investment company, which is based outside the UK in one of the many tax havens around the world and which is designed to produce a common fund for investment by professional investment managers on behalf of a number of investors. Offshore funds are usually based in jurisdictions where their activities attract little or no local tax, such as the Channel Islands, the Isle of Man, the Bahamas, Bermuda, the Cayman Islands, the British Virgin Islands and Luxembourg. The exact taxation effects will depend on several factors, including where the trust is resident, where it invests, and the existence, or otherwise, of relevant double tax treaties. As a general rule, such funds do not benefit from double tax treaties on dividends received but, at the same time, no corporation tax is payable within the fund and no withholding tax imposed on distribution of income to investors. The activities of offshore funds tend, in general, not to be as strictly regulated as those of UK investment trusts and unit trusts and are regulated by local authorities. Potential investors should therefore check carefully the structure, charges and credentials of the managers of such funds before making investments. Recently there have been cases, for example, where the very high yields being advertised on certain offshore gilt funds, were only being achieved by funds paying out of capital, with corresponding adverse implications for investors. Offshore funds may or may not be recognised by the Securities and Investments Board and contact with the management company in question or with a reliable newspaper should be able to furnish such information.

There are many different types of offshore funds, investing in different forms of assets and operating under different jurisdictions. As with unit trusts (**8.8.2**) they may be general or specialist, be invested in UK or overseas equities or fixed interest securities. They may, subject to tax or exchange controls in investors' countries of residence, be a suitable medium either for persons temporarily or permanently resident outside the UK for tax purposes, or for investors of non-UK domicile, who are resident in the UK who wish to take advantage of remittance basis taxation. Such investors will wish to ensure that their investment income and realised gains arise outside the UK's tax jurisdiction. Offshore funds may also be attractive to UK residents, especially those defining an investment medium where distributions are paid gross, perhaps because they are non-taxpayers, but any UK residents considering investing in offshore funds should seek expert advice on taxation implications before making such an investment.

8.16 Unauthorised property unit trusts

Direct investment in property and investment in property shares has been covered elsewhere in this publication. However, there also exist a number of property unit trusts all of which are unauthorised (see **8.2** and **8.3**) and which were initiated to allow tax-exempt pension funds to have a stake in property with the benefits of diversification provided by a large property portfolio. The operation of an unauthorised property unit trust is free from statutory control to a similar extent to a private investor, being governed primarily by the terms of the trust deed (see **8.3**). As these unit trusts are tax-exempt funds both in terms of CGT and income tax, allocation of units is limited strictly to investors in a similar exempt situation. Section 81, Finance Act 1980 provided that gains accruing to all authorised unit trusts, irrespective of their investors' tax status, should be exempt from CGT, and thus the distinctive position of property unit trusts limited to exempt investors is no longer as important as it was before 1980.

Property unit trusts raise funds through subscription by certificate holders. The value of the units is assessed by independent valuation of the property assets within the fund, usually on a monthly basis. The annual reports and accounts normally provide extensive information on the content of the property portfolio.

8.17 Suitability

Property unit trusts are suitable for small pension funds and other tax-exempt funds seeking a stake in property but without sufficient capital to create a properly diversified direct portfolio. The main drawback in practice is the lack of flexibility in making withdrawals, particularly on a substantial scale, as these are dependent on similar subscriptions from other investors or a sale of underlying assets.

However, the main advantages of these unit trusts are the wide spread of investments for an investment of relatively small sums of money and the fact that the investor can 'buy' property expertise in the form of property unit trust managers in several different trusts.

8.18 Authorised property unit trusts

As yet, all property unit trusts are unauthorised (see **8.12** and **8.16**). However, there have been recent moves, following both the Financial Services Act 1986 and activity by the DTI and SIB, to allow the creation of authorised property unit trusts. Such unit trusts, if sanctioned, would operate under an identical framework to other authorised unit trusts (see **8.3**) and would be open to investment from private investors and not just tax-exempt bodies such as pension funds and charities. Such a development could reasonably be expected to take place within the next 12–18 months, in the absence of unforeseen circumstances.

Sources of further information

Legislation

Capital Gains Tax Act 1979
Companies Act 1985
Finance Act 1980
Finance Act 1982
Finance Act 1984
Finance Act 1985
Finance Act 1986
Finance Act 1987
Finance Act 1988
Finance Act 1989
Financial Services Act 1986
Income and Corporation Taxes Act 1988
Prevention of Fraud (Investments) Act 1958

Bibliography

Investment Trusts Explained (2nd edition), Arnaud, Woodhead-Faulkner, 1983

Unit Trusts: What Every Investor Should Know (3rd edition), Gilchrist, Woodhead-Faulkner, 1982

Unit Trusts (FT Guide series), Stopp, Financial Times Business Information

Unit Trusts and the Financial Services Act, Unit Trust Association/ Touche Ross, 1988

Various explanatory leaflets available on request from the Unit Trust Association and the Association of Investment Trust Companies

Unit Trusts: A Guide for Investors, Williams, Woodhead-Faulkner Money Guides

Useful addresses

Unit Trust Association
65 Kingsway
London
WC2B 6TD

Tel: (071) 831 0898

Association of Investment
  Trust Companies
6th Floor
Park House
16 Finsbury Circus
London
EC2M 7JJ

Tel: (071) 588 5347

Department of Trade and
  Industry
Companies Division
10–18 Victoria Street
London
SW1H 0NN

Tel: (071) 215 7877

The Association of Corporate
  Trustees
2 Withdean Rise
Brighton
East Sussex
BN1 6YN

Tel: (0273) 504276

The Stock Exchange
Old Broad Street
London
EC2N 1HP

Tel: (071) 588 2355

Securities and Investments
  Board
3 Royal Exchange Buildings
London
EC3V 3NL

Tel: (071) 283 2474

9 Residential property

Catherine Paice, MA (Cantab), freelance journalist

9.1 Introduction to real property

This chapter is the first of three which covers property investment. Chapter 10 deals with commercial property, Chapter 11 agricultural, woodland and miscellaneous. Sections **9.1** and **9.2** act as a general introduction to all three chapters.

Real property is by definition essentially tangible. It is land and buildings of four principal types: *residential, commercial, agricultural* and *woodlands.*

Ownership of land can vary in type. Within England and Wales the superior ownership is the freehold interest, but more than one interest, indeed several, can be held in the same piece of land in the form of leases or licences. In addition to these interests, rights may be enjoyed by other people over land, such as easements, rights of way or restrictive covenants to prevent certain happenings on that land (eg, restrictions against a certain type of development).

In Scotland there is a different system of ownership of land. Feudal tenure still exists, with the major interest that of the superior and, below this, the interest of the vassal or feuar. The feuar's interest is one of property and is commonly called a heritable interest, which is an approximate equivalent to the freehold interest in the remainder of the UK. As with the rest of the UK, the same piece of land can be subject to several different types of interest in the form of leases, rights of way, etc.

These interests in land and rights or restrictive covenants over them are normally created by private agreement, but in addition extensive and increasing legislation affects all land within the UK.

An interest in property may satisfy three separate needs: enjoyment, investment and security. Enjoyment in its broadest sense might be considered as the actual use of that land, whether agricultural, a place to live, a place to manufacture, a place from which to extract minerals or a place of employment or entertainment.

The most common form of investment in land involves the ownership of an interest which does not entitle the investor to have any direct enjoyment of the land but simply to participate in an agreed share of the income or produce obtained from it. For example, one of the basic clauses in leases is included to ensure that the occupational tenant (as opposed to the landlord investor) has quiet enjoyment and exclusive use of the land, and to allow the investor to enter upon the land or interrupt such use only when there has been a breach of covenant on the part of the tenant or for purposes of inspection.

It is the investment aspects of real property that are principally considered in this chapter, although it will be appreciated that enjoyment and investment are commonly combined – for example, owner-occupiers of residential property rarely consider their home as an investment, although for the great majority of individuals it is the largest single investment that they will ever make.

Property is generally considered as one of the most secure forms of investment in that it is almost totally indestructible and immovable (it cannot be lost or stolen) and is usually capable of producing an income. However, an investment in property is by its very nature fraught with complications and pitfalls, and a thorough understanding of all its implications is necessary to ensure that optimum results are obtained from the specific investment selected.

Today, ownership of land and property is in many hands, the principal types of investor being:

(1) the private individual;
(2) the trust fund (the settled estate, the accumulation and maintenance trust, the discretionary trust and the charitable trust);
(3) public and private investment and trading companies; and
(4) the institutions.

All these investors invest in property because over the years property has normally maintained a stable value and indeed increased in value relative to other forms of investment. In particular, commercial and agricultural property has historically provided a real rate of return in inflationary times, due to the opportunities provided for increasing the rental income to be obtained from the property at each rent review. Furthermore, in the case of commercial property in the UK the costs of repairing, insuring and operating the building and, more particularly, increases in these expenses, are traditionally borne by the tenant.

Investment in property falls into two main categories:

(1) direct investment, which is dealt with in detail in this chapter; and
(2) indirect investment (eg, property bonds and other unit-linked schemes), which is touched on at the end of this chapter and is also considered in Chapter 13.

The principal types of direct investment in property may be identified as follows:

(1) residential;
(2) commercial;
(3) agricultural;
(4) woodland.

In addition, investment may be made in mineral-bearing land, leisure property, caravan sites, and certain other types of property with a specialised use.

9.2 Legal, taxation and cost factors of real property

9.2.1 Legal

Property legislation is extensive and increasing. Real property has always had political implications and these are becoming more important as the community becomes increasingly aware of the need to preserve the environment. The main purpose of property legislation has therefore been to establish ground rules governing the way in which owners, landlords and tenants should behave to each other.

In England and Wales the law has evolved over the centuries through the common law, the rules of equity, the law of contract and tort and increasingly, through Acts of Parliament. In Scotland separate rules of equity have never applied and the law of contract and *delict* (tort) are themselves affected either by common law or Acts of Parliament.

Legislation affecting landlord and tenant

Probably the most fundamental legislation affecting the investor is that which provides the basis of the landlord and tenant system and which is briefly summarised below.

England and Wales

All property: the common law, equity and the 1925 property legislation.

Commercial property: Landlord and Tenant Acts 1927 and 1954.

Agricultural property: Agricultural Holdings Act 1986 (consolidating all legislation since 1948), Agriculture Act 1986, and numerous Statutory Instruments.

Residential property: Rent Act 1977, Housing Act 1985, Landlord and Tenant Act 1985, and Housing and Planning Act 1986, Landlord and Tenant Act 1987 and Housing Act 1988.

Scotland

All property: common law and conveyancing statutes.

Commercial property: common law and Tenancy of Shops (Scotland) Act 1949 (as amended).

Agricultural property: Agricultural Holdings (Scotland) Act 1949, Agriculture Act 1958, Succession (Scotland) Act 1964, Land Compensation (Scotland) Act 1973 and Agriculture (Miscellaneous Provisions) Act 1968 and 1976 and the new Agricultural Holdings (Scotland) (Amendments) Act, 1983.

Residential property: Rent (Scotland) Act 1984.

The general effect of legislation has been to favour the occupier against the owner, especially in the residential and agricultural sectors. However, apart altogether from legal considerations, any prospective investor in property would be well advised to remember that with the ownership of property goes a social as well as a legal responsibility to the people who live or work in that property and to neighbouring owners.

Legislation to protect the community

The principal legislation designed to protect the community includes the Town and Country Planning Acts, Building Regulations,

National Parks and Access to the Countryside Act and the Land Compensation Acts.

Central and local government now have very considerable powers over the use and development of land, and the ownership of an unencumbered freehold interest no longer automatically confers complete control over the particular land. Not only do the authorities have extensive control over new development but, generally, permission has also to be sought to change the use of an existing building from one purpose to another (eg, a change from a shop to an office use). Values of residential and commercial property are affected more by this area of legislation than by any other single factor. In addition, under the Land Compensation Acts, central and local authorities have powers to acquire land compulsorily for statutory purposes, such as the construction of a new road.

9.2.2 Taxation

General rates
Property has always represented one of the major sources of taxation revenue and today, for example, local rates are, after grants from central government, the largest source of local government finance. Rates are a tax on occupation rather than on investment income, although an investor may find that he is liable for rates on empty property. Successive governments have promised to review the whole of the rating system and a flat-rate poll-tax (or 'community charge') is being introduced from 1990 (in Scotland from 1989) to replace domestic rates. A non-domestic rating system will be based on rental values at 1 April 1988.

Taxation
Specialist advice in the tax field is an essential prerequisite to an investment in real property. It is important to tailor the investment to the investor and from time to time to rearrange the investment in line with political, fiscal and legislative changes. Taxation varies with each investor and this bears upon the criteria of liquidity, yield and reversion. The principal taxes to be taken into account when dealing with real property are detailed below.

Capital taxes
Individuals may be chargeable to the following capital taxes.

Capital gains tax: prior to the 1988 Budget, this was a tax on the gain realised on disposal, being the difference between base value (or acquisition cost) and disposal value, subject to indexation relief and also subject to re-basing. For CGT purposes 5 April is the year-end. There is an annual exemption for gains up to a specific amount in any tax year. For the year 1990/91 the exempt amount is £5,000 (£2,500 for trusts). (See example.)

Example

Gross sale proceeds (January 1990 contract)				say £250,000
Less: sale costs				
agents—say 2%		£5,000		
advertising expenses etc, say		750		
		£5,750		
VAT 15%		863		
			£6,613	
Legal—say 0.75%		£1,875		
VAT 15%		281		
			2,156	
				8,769
Net sale proceeds				£241,231
Less: Revaluation at 31.3.1982	say £140,000			
Indexation Allowance 0.397 (January 1990)			£55,580	
				195,580
Chargeable gain				£45,651
Individual's Annual Exemption (1990/91)				5,000
Taxable gain				£40,651
Rate of tax—say				× 40%
Capital gains tax payable on 1.12.1989				£16,260

Notes:
(1) Rates of tax for individuals. For 1988/89 onwards, chargeable gains are taxable at the rate or rates which would apply if the gains formed the top slice of individual's income. Therefore, they are chargeable at 25 per cent where the aggregate of taxable income and chargeable gains does not exceed £20,700 in 1990/91, and at 40 per cent on any amount in excess of £20,700.
(2) If the sale was by a person or body registered for VAT, the VAT on sale costs could be recovered and the above figures would consequently change.

Residential property 161

The Finance Act 1982 introduced an indexation allowance from March 1982 based on original acquisition cost. The Finance Act 1985 removed the restriction that the asset had to be owned for 12 months before the allowance was available; permitted indexation to produce losses; removed gilt-edged securities from indexation entirely; and made the radical change that in calculating the indexation allowance for assets held at 31 March 1982, this can (at the option of the owner) be done by reference to the market value of those assets at that date rather than by reference to expenditure incurred on the asset prior to that date; and exempted from capital gains tax disposals of gilt-edged securities made after 1 July 1986. The detailed provisions are very complicated and professional advice should always be sought.

The Finance Act 1988 changed the CGT regime. From 6 April 1988:

(1) The base value is market value at the later of 31 March 1982 or the date of acquisition.
(2) Indexation is still applied to the 31 March 1982 base value or later cost.
(3) The resultant gain/loss has to be compared with the position under the old regime. If, as shown in the example, the new regime has changed a gain into a loss or vice versa then, subject to certain exceptions, the transaction will be treated as giving rise to no gain/no loss.
(4) Any taxable gain resulting will be added to the taxpayer's income for the purposes of assessing the rate of CGT applicable.
(5) The annual exemption for 1988/89 and 1989/90 is reduced to £5,000 (£2,500 for most trusts).

Development land tax: The Finance Act 1985 abolished this tax for all future disposals. Pre-19 March 1985 disposals will still pay DLT at 60 per cent of realised development value in excess of £75,000.

Capital transfer tax/inheritance tax (IHT): The Finance Act 1986 introduced IHT which is an amended version of CTT and also seems to reintroduce some elements from the old pre-1974 Estate Duty. Prior to the Finance Act 1988, IHT was a sliding rate tax based on the diminution in value of a person's estate with liability arising when the person makes gifts in his lifetime or upon his death. It is not necessarily merely the value of the property given that is taxed. IHT now needs to be dealt with in three parts:

(1) *Lifetime gifts*—'potentially exempt transfers': Gifts made between individuals or to Accumulation and Maintenance settlements or to trusts for the disabled, or (since the Finance Act 1987) transfers involving Life Interest Settlements in certain

circumstances, do not now bear tax unless the donor dies within seven years of making the gift. If this happens there is a tapering scale (20 per cent after three years rising to 80 per cent after six years) of relief based on the death rates of tax. There are complicated rules relating to potentially exempt transfers such as the fact that there must be no reservation of benefit by the donor, and professional advice is essential.

(2) *Lifetime gifts*—chargeable transfers: All gifts or transfers not coming within the definition of potentially exempt transfers, eg, gifts to discretionary settlements, bear tax at 50 per cent of the death rates.

(3) *Death*—prior to 15 March 1988 tax was charged on estates in excess of £90,000 at 30 per cent rising to a maximum of 60 per cent at £330,000 and over. This also applies to transfers made within three years prior to the donor's death.

Since 6 April 1990, tax is charged on estates in excess of £128,000 at a flat rate of 40 per cent.

There is still an annual exemption of £3,000 on lifetime transfers (with the right to bring any unused exemption forward for one year), exemption for transfers between husband and wife, and a threshold of £128,000 below which no tax is paid on lifetime or death transfers. Various reliefs available on certain types of property have the effect, where they apply, of reducing the values for tax purposes. The cumulative period is now seven years, ie, gifts that were made more than seven years previously are left out of account when assessing the tax on a subsequent transfer/death. The legislation on IHT is contained in the Finance Act 1986 and the Capital Transfer Tax Act 1984 (also known as the Inheritance Tax Act 1984), as amended by the Finance Acts 1987, 1988, 1989 and 1990.

Table 9.1   Rates of inheritance tax 1990/91

Value transferred £	Rate of tax
0–128,000	Exempt
128,000 and above	40% flat rate

Notes:
(1) (On chargeable lifetime transfers the flat rate is 50 per cent of the death rate.)
(2) Effective from 6 April 1990.

Companies may be chargeable to the following capital taxes:

(1) Corporation tax in respect of chargeable gains (there is no annual exemption for a company). The effective rate for 1990/91 is 25 per cent for small companies on profits up to £200,000 and 37.5 per cent on profits from £200,000 to £1m. The rate for companies paying the full rate of corporation tax is 35 per cent. All companies must now account for corporation tax nine months after the end of the trading period/year. Interest is payable on unpaid/under-paid tax.
(2) Development land tax. No longer applicable to disposal post-19 March 1985, but pre-March 1985 disposals are still liable.
(3) Inheritance tax: in certain circumstances.

Revenue taxes

Individuals are chargeable to income tax under the relevant provisions of the Income and Corporation Taxes Act 1988, as subsequently amended.

Schedule A tax is charged on rents or receipts to which a person becomes entitled under leases of land, rent charges and other annual payments arising out of land and any other receipts arising by virtue of his ownership of an estate or interest in land in the UK. In arriving at the amount on which tax is payable, deductions may be made for expenditure in respect of maintenance, repairs, insurance, management, etc, properly payable by the taxpayer.

Prior to March 1988, income from commercial woodlands was normally charged to tax under Schedule B. The charge to tax under this Schedule and the corresponding right to elect for taxation under Schedule D were abolished by the Finance Act 1988 with transitional provisions to relief arrangements in existence on 15 March 1988.

Schedule D tax is charged in respect of any profits or gains arising from any trade carried on in the UK or elsewhere; any profession or vocation; any interest on money (yearly or otherwise), annuity or other annual payment (but not including any payment chargeable under Schedule A), discounts and income from securities bearing interest payable out of the public revenue; income arising from securities out of the UK; income arising from possessions out of the UK (not being income from any office or employment); and any annual profits or gains not mentioned above and not charged under any other Schedule.

Corporation tax (1990/91)

Small companies	25% up to	£200,000
Marginal rate	37.5%	£200,001–£1m
Full rate	35% over	£1m

Thus: profit of £800,000 is assessed as follows:

First £200,000 @ 25%	£50,000
Next £600,000 @ 37.5%	£225,000
Total tax	£275,000 (34.375%)

The investment income surcharge at 15 per cent on investment income was abolished for individuals (but not for all trusts) for 1984/5 onwards, but this may be reintroduced by a new government. For those trusts still liable to the surcharge (known as the additional rate), the Finance Act 1988 reduced the rate to 10 per cent.

Rents in the hands of individuals used to be treated as unearned income (thus attracting the investment income surcharge) whilst profits from the occupation of property were treated as earned income. This distinction no longer applies following the abolition of the investment income surcharge.

Value Added Tax

Value Added Tax is charged on services or goods, where annual turnover is in excess of £25,400 from 21 March 1990 based on past turnover. Goods and services are subdivided into three categories as follows:

(1) exempt items (including rent);
(2) zero-rated items (including food and livestock); and
(3) other items (including goods, services and bloodstock), taxed at 15 per cent.

VAT is not usually charged on rents for real property but may be relevant where a business is carried on.

From 1 June 1984, zero-rating has been broadly restricted either to the construction of new buildings and new civil engineering works, or to the demolition of a complete building and it is possible that zero-rating will cease to apply to construction of commercial buildings in the United Kingdom in line with the rest of the EC. With the exception of approved alterations to protected buildings, alterations no longer qualify for zero-rating, and so all work that is done to existing buildings is standard-rated.

The principal changes in the Finance Act 1985 were:

(1) Advertisements in newspapers and periodicals are taxable at standard rate (15 per cent) from 1 May 1985 thus increasing the cost of property sales.
(2) Some relaxation of the rules on recovery of VAT on bad debts.
(3) Wider ranging and severe enforcement powers.

The Finance Act 1986 introduced a number of minor changes, principally redefining certain 'supplies' to clarify what is and what is not subject to VAT.

The Finance Act 1987 introduced (from 1 October 1987 subject to EC permission) effective relief for bad debts for companies with a turnover of less than £250,000 by allowing such companies to account for VAT on a cash basis (paid and received).

Following an adverse ruling by the European Commission, sales of non-residential property (development land and new buildings) will become liable for VAT at standard rate, with effect from 1 April 1989. Landowners who are not registered for VAT, but who sell non-residential development land, will be deemed to be registered for the purposes of the sale.

9.2.3 Costs

Acquisition costs
In connection with the purchase and subsequent management of any property investment, a number of costs need to be borne in mind in ascertaining the net yield. These costs can vary substantially, depending on the nature of the transaction and the degree of management involved. Specific references are made to costs under the various categories of investment, but the following are general comments.

In England and Wales the scales of charges for legal fees have been abolished, with limited exceptions, with the result that there is no set scale of charges for legal advice and services on the sale or purchase of a property. Generally, however, in relation to sales and purchases these charges tend to be between 0.5 and 0.75 per cent of the purchase price, although the percentage may be considerably higher if the transaction is complicated or the purchase price is very low. In all cases, VAT is charged in addition.

Before property is acquired solicitors carry out searches, principally in the local land charges registers, in order to establish that the property is free of unexpected burdens. The cost of these searches may prove to be wasted but is small relative to the problems that may be disclosed. It is also necessary to provide (at all events in those areas in which registration of title is compulsory) for registration costs, which on larger transactions range up to £900.

In Scotland, in years past, there was a scale of legal fees for property transactions laid down by the Law Society of Scotland. That scale was abolished in 1985, and fees can now be expected to vary from firm to firm. Deeds relating to heritable (real) property are recorded in the Register of Sasines, which has been in existence since 1617. The registration fees are now £11 per £5,000 for conveyances and £11 per £10,000 for security deeds with an additional charge of £10 if the property falls to be registered under the Land Registration (Scotland) Act 1984, with a maximum fee of £550 for conveyances exceeding £250,000 and £275 for security deeds of the same value. The system of purchasing property is entirely different in Scotland from the remainder of the UK. A formal offer in probative form is made at an early stage and acceptance of this offer, also in probative form, creates a binding contract which is normally subject to a number of conditions being fulfilled before the purchaser takes entry to the property. (A probative document is one which provides proof of its facts in court, without the need for further substantiating evidence.)

A fundamental change in Scottish conveyancing law was introduced by the Land Registration (Scotland) Act 1979. This Act set up a Land Register for Scotland and, over a period of years, all documents which were previously recorded in the Register of Sasines will have to be recorded in the new Land Register. This new register is taking effect gradually and, after a two-year preparatory period to set up all the machinery for the transfer of writs from the Register of Sasines to the Land Register, is being phased in over a period of years, registration being applied to different areas of Scotland year by year. The Land Register currently only applies to the counties of Renfrew, Dumbarton, Lanark and the county of the Barony and the Regality of Glasgow.

Stamp duty

Stamp duty is charged in England, Wales and Scotland at the rate of 1 per cent on the whole value of the purchase consideration where this is in excess of £30,000. For small transactions, no duty is payable on a purchase at less than £30,000. Special scales are applicable to the grant of leases, but provisions have also been introduced to counter the avoidance of stamp duty on the transfer of interest in land and

Surveyors' fees
Where a surveyor is instructed to act by a purchaser on his behalf for surveying, valuing and negotiating the purchase of a property, the fee varies between 1 and 2.5 per cent of the purchase price, although this percentage may increase for smaller transactions. Where a surveyor is instructed merely to survey and value, the usual fee would be about 0.25 per cent of the valuation. In all cases VAT is charged in addition.

Other professional fees
In certain circumstances, where other expertise is necessary, additional fees will need to be incurred, such as those of accountants, structural engineers, quantity surveyors and architects.

Overall acquisition costs
Assuming a normal and straightforward investment, total acquisition costs would be in the order of 3.5 to 4.5 per cent of the purchase price (see example below).

Example

Agreed purchase price			say £200,000
Costs of acquisition:			
Stamp duty 1%		£2,000	
Legal, say 0.75%	£1,500		
VAT 15 %	225		
		1,725	
Surveyor, say 1.25%	£2,500		
Expenses, say	150		
VAT 15 %	398		
		3,048	
Acquisition costs (= 3.4% incl VAT)			6,773
Total cost of acquisition			£206,773

Note:
If the purchase was by a person or body registered for VAT, the VAT on the acquisition costs could be recovered and the above figures would consequently change.

Management costs

Whereas stocks and shares are essentially a passive investment, property is an active investment. Management costs will depend on the type of property and the location. The property will at some stage need to be repaired, insured, altered, re-let, improved or redeveloped. In general, management costs are deductible for tax purposes. Good management will help to provide capital appreciation and revenue growth. Lack of liquidity and the desire to maximise the returns of property holdings place a premium on positive asset management. This is achieved by systematic monitoring of market conditions and opportunities, together with a sustained programme of inspection and assessment of individual assets which implies regular and preventive maintenance and well-planned schemes for refurbishment or redevelopment.

The level of management costs will depend much on the type of investment. On fully let offices where the tenant is responsible for all repairs and other outgoings, it might be as little as 2 to 3 per cent of the gross rents, to cover supervision of repairs, insurance and management (communal 'service charges' and sometimes management costs are charged and recovered separately from the tenants), whilst at the other extreme, for a small shop in a small market town on a standard repairing lease, 5 to 10 per cent is more likely to be applicable. Management costs for farms might vary from 5 per cent on full repairing and insuring leases (ie, where the tenant is responsible for all repairs, insurance and landlord's outgoings) to between 7.5 and 10 per cent on standard repairing leases. VAT and expenses are charged in addition to management fees.

Agents' managing fees are usually agreed at the outset and are paid out of rental income as and when received. Other costs might include general rates, water and sewage rates, drainage rates (for farms), corn rents and parochial charges, although in the majority of cases these charges are paid by the tenant, under the terms of the tenancy agreement/lease.

Where a surveyor is instructed to negotiate or advise on a rent review, lease renewal or re-letting, fees may be incurred in the range of 7.5 to 10 per cent of either the first year's rental obtained or the amount of the increase over the previous rent, depending on the circumstances of each case, with VAT and expenses in addition.

Disposal costs

Sales—On disposal of larger properties the costs are between 2 and 3 per cent—less than on an acquisition (due to the absence of stamp duty). There is no scale legal charge for solicitors when selling a property; however, generally, the costs will be less than those set out previously. Surveyors' fees vary, depending on the type of property, ranging from 1.5 per cent on large sales to 2.5 per cent on the sale of houses. However, the vendor may, in addition, incur the costs of sale procedure (advertisements, brochures, plans, etc), which can often be as high as 1 per cent of the value of the sale of assets in the region of £100,000, although the costs decrease for larger transactions.

Tenancy agreements—Stamp duty is charged on tenancy agreements but is usually payable by the tenant. The costs vary according to the circumstances of the agreement but in general they are minimal for the landlord.

Professional advisers generally

Real property should never be acquired, sold or developed without the investor first obtaining competent professional advice. The leading professional bodies in the property world, to which the partners of most of the reputable firms of surveyors and valuers belong, are the Royal Institution of Chartered Surveyors, the Incorporated Society of Valuers and Auctioneers and the National Association of Estate Agents. Prospective investors should select advisers from one of these professional bodies. A valuer or surveyor may be the first adviser whom the investor calls in, but with certain types of investment it may be necessary for the investor and the valuer to secure the services of an expert planner, architect, developer, structural engineer, banker or accountant, and a solicitor will in all cases need to be instructed.

Through their regular involvement in the property market the principal firms of surveyors have a close knowledge of the services required and through their connections can secure any additional expertise needed; but it will invariably be to the investor's advantage to ensure that his team of legal, valuation and financial advisers is properly co-ordinated so as to ensure that investment decisions are made in the light of the best possible overall advice. For example, certain investment situations, particularly where development is involved, will require 'project management' with the surveyor co-ordinating the expertise of a specialist team of advisers. It is noticeable that at least one of the larger firms of surveyors has now extended its services and established a corporate financing department in addition to expanded investment management skills. This type of new alignment will permit a broader and more comprehensive role to be played by surveyors in meeting institutional requirements.

Residential property

9.3 Highlights of the previous year

The bubble burst in the residential sector. Those who were fortunate enough to sell at or near the top of the 1988 market had seen the value of their houses soar to as much as twice or three times their value five years earlier. In 1989 very little changed hands. Although prices in Scotland continued to rise, houses elsewhere found a very sticky market. Turnover is estimated to have dropped by 40 per cent compared with 1988, and prices by 15–25 per cent. Houses at the bottom end of the market suffered most, particularly where there was oversupply due to enthusiastic new building over the last two years. Bargains and special incentives were openly offered on many new developments. Mid-market property sales depended on 'chains' being completed, but where cash purchases prevailed prices were more resilient. At the top end of the market, factors such as location, access, design or style and realistic pricing became crucial but some houses rose further in value if all these ingredients were right. The second home market virtually dried up, but some spare cash continued to find its way into cheaper properties on the Continent, particularly France.

9.4 Direct investment in residential property

9.4.1 Personal homes

The purchase of a home is perhaps the one investment which the great majority of us make without ever considering it as such. It is the only form of property investment where capital gains are normally tax-free. The owner, if he has more than one home, may elect which is his 'principal residence' in order to obtain exemption under s 101 of the Capital Gains Tax Act 1979. He may vary this election from time to time subject to notifying the Inland Revenue. A person required to reside in employer-provided accommodation may acquire a house and enjoy CGT exemption in respect thereof provided he intends in due course to live in it. The exemption usually applies to a house and up to one acre of grounds, but there are exceptions above and below this amount and professional valuation advice should be sought.

The purchase of a home has long been and will continue to be the safest and soundest form of property investment. The purchaser enjoys absolute control over his investment and may obtain tax relief at the higher rate in respect of interest on loans up to £30,000 for house purchase. Although the investment produces no income, historically it has more than maintained its value in real terms against inflation. Funds for purchase are traditionally obtained on mortgage from building societies, insurance companies or local authorities, although the major clearing banks entered this field in 1981 and now provide a large part of the mortgage funds to the residential market.

The method of purchase is usually by private treaty, but in England and Wales sometimes by auction for the higher priced property. Factors to consider on house purchase include its structural condition; the availability of main services (gas, water, electricity, telephone, drainage); the local standard community charge (poll tax); location and potential planning factors. Houses built after 1965 may well have a certificate from the National House-Building Council—a body sponsored by the building industry which lays down minimum standards for the construction of private houses and guarantees that maintenance work will be carried out for a specified period. Unmodernised houses may be eligible for local council improvement grants.

Insurance of property should usually be on the estimated cost of replacement, notwithstanding that the cost may exceed the purchase price of the property, and should be index-linked to increase the sum insured in line with inflation of building costs.

The length and cost of the journey to work will normally be an important factor with the rising cost of all forms of transport.

Conclusion
A home is the best and safest form of investment in real property for the small investor.

9.4.2 Holiday homes and time sharing

With increasing leisure caused by a reduction in working hours, the demand for holiday homes (which vary from a site on which to park a caravan to a substantial secondary house) has increased very considerably in recent years. The value of these properties is very much related to the personal choice of the purchaser, who is greatly affected by the ease of access to and from the major conurbations. Lettings of these properties for holiday purposes are exempt from Rent Act protection. They are likely to show a good capital appreciation, with the added advantage that they provide cheap holiday accommodation for the family. Up to twice the standard community charge is payable on second homes.

Holiday homes may be purchased abroad. Specialist advice needs to be taken with regard to such matters as local exchange control, the mechanics of purchase and availability of services. Good agents and lawyers are even more essential abroad than in the UK. It is particularly important to enquire as to the property's eventual saleability and any problems which might arise with regard to the repatriation of funds. The abolition of exchange control increased the opportunity for this type of investment. Partly as a result of this a new concept of property ownership known as 'time sharing;' has become popular. In essence, this provides for the investor to acquire an interest for a stated period (a week or a month) in each year in perpetuity. It effectively widens the spectrum of investment to encompass the smaller investor who can secure holiday accommodation abroad with the added benefit of capital growth on an investment in property. It is too early to judge the success of this type of investment, but it is an interesting concept for those who have limited funds of between £5,000 and £15,000 which would otherwise be insufficient to purchase a holiday home. If the owner does not wish to use the accommodation each year, the property can be exchanged if the location is in a major resort. The method of sale varies according to the country, some properties being sold freehold and others on long leaseholds. An annual services payment is payable to the vendor, together with the cost of electricity, water and other services used during a vacation. There are a number of companies specialising in this market who advertise nationally.

Holiday homes are a sound investment but location is critical and, if abroad, there are many possible pitfalls, not the least of which is guaranteeing sound title. Prospective purchasers should, however, consider the consequences of reintroduction of exchange control in the event of a change of government.

9.4.3 Let houses and flats

Let houses and flats produce rental income. The principal problems are rent control and security of tenure. The Rent Acts allow tenants or the landlord to apply to the Rent Officer (an official of the local authority) to fix a fair rent for the property. It is then illegal to charge more than that rent for the property. The Rent Officer's idea of a fair rent is usually well below what the landlord regards as an economic rent. The Rent Acts give protection to tenants of unfurnished and furnished lettings, although s 52 of the Housing Act 1980 provides that in the case of lettings of not less than one year and not more than five years (protected shorthold tenancies) the landlord can recover possession at the end of the tenancy, provided certain conditions are fulfilled. There is now no longer any requirement to register a fair rent under a protected shorthold tenancy prior to the commencement of the tenancy (wherever the property is situated) but this will not prevent the tenant from being able to apply to the Rent Office to fix the rent. Nevertheless, this legislation has increased the number of residential tenancies being offered in the market. There are proposals being considered for further adjustment to these and other types of private rented property agreements.

The Housing Act 1988 provides for recovery of market rents from tenants under the new *assured tenancies* for lettings after 15 January 1989 not entered into as a result of contracts made prior to 15 January 1989. The rent officer system does not apply to such tenancies. Assured tenancies require a tenant to occupy the property as his only or principal home. It is possible to draft rent review clauses in certain circumstances under the contract of tenancy to maintain market rents. After the contractual term finishes a landlord can apply to increase the rent annually but the tenant can challenge the increase. For the most part (the most notable exception being assured shorthold tenancies) the tenant is given security of tenure at the end of the contractual term, but with wider powers for landlords to recover possession than existed under old Rent Act tenancies.

Assured shorthold tenancies must provide that the landlord may not terminate the tenancy during the first six months of the term. The landlord may determine the tenancy by obtaining a court order for possession at the end of the contractual term of at least six months. There is no maximum term for an assured shorthold tenancy and successors in title to the landlord acquire the original landlord's right to obtain possession by court order at the end of the term. The tenant has the right to apply to the Rent Assessment Committee during an assured shorthold tenancy for a determination that the rent payable under the tenancy is set at a level equivalent to the market rate of similar tenancies let on the same terms and in the same area. The underlying principle is to establish a market rent for these forms of tenancy in the same area, rather than using the criteria that the rent officers use under the Rent Acts for determining a fair rent.

Corporate tenants are excluded from the security of tenure provisions under the Rent Acts although for tenancies granted prior to 15 January 1988 they may apply to the Rent Officer to set a fair rent. Corporate tenants are also excluded from the security of tenure provisions under the Housing Act 1988 and there is no 'fair rent' control. It is important, however, that any sub-letting by such corporate tenants is made to licensees only and that the corporate tenants are granting bona fide licences to their employees to avoid any such letting arrangements being regarded as a sham and creating a tenancy direct to the 'licensee' to which the security of tenure provisions will apply.

Management involves written tenancy agreements, regular maintenance and rent reviews. Disagreement on rent is referred to the Rent Officer and rent increases must be phased. Tax relief, except in certain circumstances, is not available for interest on loans for the purchase of let properties by individual investors. Professional advice should be sought as mortgage tax relief may be forfeited on houses that are let and insurance costs will be increased. If property is selected to ensure minimum vacant periods and optimum quality of tenants, the yields can be between 7 and 12 per cent gross or between 6 and 10 per cent net of management costs and outgoings.

Let houses and flats are a safe and secure form of investment if the location is selected carefully and management standards are high. Security of tenure, possible rent freezes, repair costs and the possibility of enfranchisement rights are the principal disadvantages. Let houses and flats are probably suitable for the small investor whose income does not attract the higher rate of tax (40 per cent). However, they are also worthy of consideration as a speculative investment with a view to negotiating tenants' vacating the property and so securing for the investor a vacant possession premium.

9.4.4 Blocks of flats

The investment considerations in respect of blocks of flats are similar to those for let houses and flats. However, the market in blocks of flats has in recent years been determined by their 'break-up' value rather than by the income which is produced. This break-up value arises through an investor being able to acquire a complete block of flats at a figure which will enable him subsequently to dispose of the flats either to the occupying tenants or with vacant possession, if obtained, and so realise an overall capital gain.

The competition for flats having a break-up value is such that a block is unlikely to show a sufficiently high yield to warrant holding it as a long-term investment. It is a high risk form of investment, as there is little guarantee of obtaining vacant possession, having regard to the high degree of security of tenure enjoyed by the tenants. Recently tenants have formed their own associations to try to control their landlords' operations, and the political and social problems for an investor operating in this market are considerable.

The Landlord and Tenant Act 1987, which came into operation on 1 February 1988, requires a landlord to offer to sell his interest to the tenants should the landlord wish to sell. A prospective purchaser can also serve notices on tenants in a block to establish whether a prospective disposal might be frustrated by the tenants. There is then a statutory framework for registration which can take seven months, so an investment in a block of flats is therefore difficult to dispose of quickly, and this increases the risk of the investment.

For the investor who is seeking longer-term income from blocks of flats, considerable regard must be paid to the ratio between gross income and net income. The provision of services and maintenance can be very high, often as much as 30 or 40 per cent of the gross income, and in addition, the costs of replacing lifts, boilers and other plant and machinery may be incurred.

9.5 Preview of the year ahead

Providing serious upheaval in the economy is avoided, it is generally believed that the market will stabilise. House prices are continuing to fall in some areas, however, and there is little prospect of turnover increasing. Bargains will be had by those with money to spend. But the cost of borrowing now looms large. Existing mortgages are a heavy drain on resources, and despite numerous incentives offered by building societies and banks for new mortgages, first-time buyers are not keen to enter the market. Severe financial pressure will continue to be felt not only by home owners who are overborrowed but by the lenders themselves. Building societies and insurance companies who bought up chains of estate agents two years ago will be forced to prune their offices. Some builders and developers who have overstretched themselves financially, or who are left with expensive land banks, will go into liquidation.

9.6 Conclusion

The residential market is in a period of reassessment. Recovery is inevitable, and private residences will remain one of the most secure investments in the medium to long term. Early in 1990 the Woolwich Building Society predicted that a £58,000 dwelling today would cost £200,000 by the year 2000. Rarely, however, do short-term yields match those of the mid- to late-1980s.

10 Commercial property

Andrew Bull, ARICS, Partner, Jones Lang Wootton

10.1 Introduction

The end of the 1980s heralded a dramatic change, finishing with the highest levels of institutional investment in property for some time and the end of a long bull market. Prospects for the 1990s with European capital deregulation, an election and rising inflation will ensure that the early part of the new decade will be exciting.

Property has often been regarded as a hedge against inflation in that, understandably, values have tended to rise as prices have risen. However, a hedge also implies a year by year correlation between capital growth and inflation and analysis has to date revealed no such correlation between annual inflation and capital growth.

The purchase of a commercial property involves the giving up of a capital sum now in exchange for future returns which can be either the benefits of owner occupation, income flow and/or capital gain. Underlying any property investment decision will be the option of alternative investments, namely stocks, shares, cash, unit trusts and even works of art. In selecting an investment the investor will seek the highest real rate of return on capital invested but, depending upon the object of the investment, may 'trade-off' a reduced rate of return in consideration for increased liquidity or security of income. The tax status of an investor will also be an important factor.

10.1.1 Types of investors

Property investments can be broken down into sub-sectors in which different types of investors will be interested. Properties can be subdivided according to location, type and size. Small industrial units and multi-million pound office investments are unlikely to be of interest to the same investor. Risk-averse investors such as insurance companies and pension funds will prefer to invest in 'prime' properties in established locations let to blue chip tenants on standard full repairing and insuring leases. A factor of considerable importance to these investors is the security of rental income and capital gain. Other investors will, however, be prepared to accept a higher level of risk by purchasing 'secondary' properties if the return on capital is considered to be sufficiently attractive.

10.1.2 Property valuation

This is, in its simplest form, the basis of the property valuation process. The rental income of a property is capitalised over a term of years or in perpetuity (depending on whether the property is leasehold or freehold) at an investment rate which will reflect all the elements of risk associated with that property (security of income, obsolescence of the building, economic factors and the cost/inconvenience of management). The capitalisation rate chosen to value the property will also reflect the expectation of future rental growth and consequently tends to be significantly lower than the yields available from fixed-interest securities. This phenomenon (also illustrated by the dividend yield of equities) is known as the 'reverse yield gap' and since the 1970s has varied between about 3 per cent and 8 per cent.

10.2 Types of commercial property

Direct investment in commercial property falls mainly into the following categories:

(1) retail including supermarkets and retail warehouses;
(2) offices including town centre, out of town and campus;
(3) industrial including factories, warehouses and hi-tech; and, to a much lesser degree—
(4) farm land and forestry;
(5) leisure.

Most investors with a significant long-term investment portfolio will aim to hold the majority of the investments balanced between the shop, office and industrial categories, where there is a well-defined investment market.

10.2.1 Purchase of commercial property

Due to the large amounts of capital required for the purchase of even the smallest commercial property, the commercial property investment market is, like the equity market, generally confined to UK and foreign insurance companies, pension funds and property companies, together with a number of wealthy private individuals or family trusts. UK insurance companies and pension funds began investing in commercial property in the mid-1950s, broadening their asset bases beyond the equities and government securities which had hitherto formed their principal media for investment. UK pension fund investment reached a peak as a percentage of their assets in 1979 and significant net new investment was not then seen until the late 1980s.

10.2.2 Lease of commercial property

Commercial buildings are generally leased for a term of 25 years with five-yearly rent reviews to the current open market rental value of the property. Recently, there has been a trend towards shorter leases with options for tenants to terminate leases on predetermined dates. Under the terms of what is known as a 'full repairing and insuring' lease, the occupational tenant will be responsible for (or for at least the cost of) carrying out all repairs to and insurance of the property. Whilst the day-to-day management of a commercial property investment is of vital importance in terms of maintaining the performance of the investment, and in particular in achieving the best possible rent on review, in the case of a letting of an entire building (as opposed to one which is in multiple occupation) the process is essentially one of collecting the rent and checking that the repairs and insurance are in place. In occupied buildings the repairs and insurance are carried out by the landlord, or his managing agents, with the costs being recovered from the tenants. An investment in commercial property has historically been regarded as a passive investment, with the day-to-day and portfolio management responsibilities being undertaken by a firm of managing agents.

10.2.3 Rent reviews

Investments in commercial property provide regular opportunities for increasing the income obtained from the property through the medium of rent reviews. Since the Second World War market practice with regard to the time period between rent reviews has altered. Formerly leases were granted with a period of 21 years between rent reviews, but latterly this decreased to 14 years, then to seven years and is currently five years. Generally, rent reviews result in the rent increasing to the then open market rental value of the property. It is now a standard provision to review the rent upwards only.

10.2.4 Rental growth

As can be seen from the two graphs on pages 180 and 181 showing rental growth in the three major investment sectors throughout the decade of the 1980s, and also the mean asking yield for the three sectors through the same time period, the rate of rental growth has

Figure 10.1 Rental growth by sector

% p.a.

Office
Shop
Industrial

Year to March

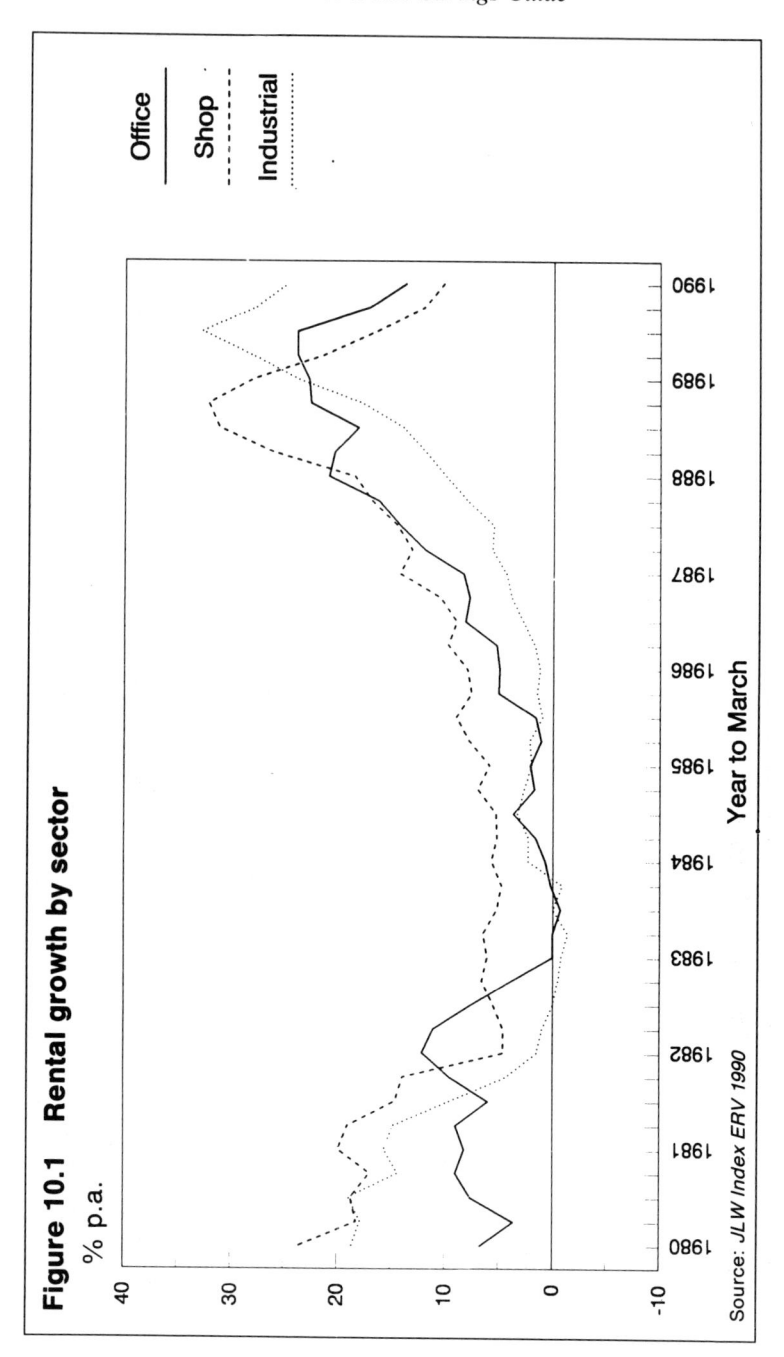

Source: JLW Index ERV 1990

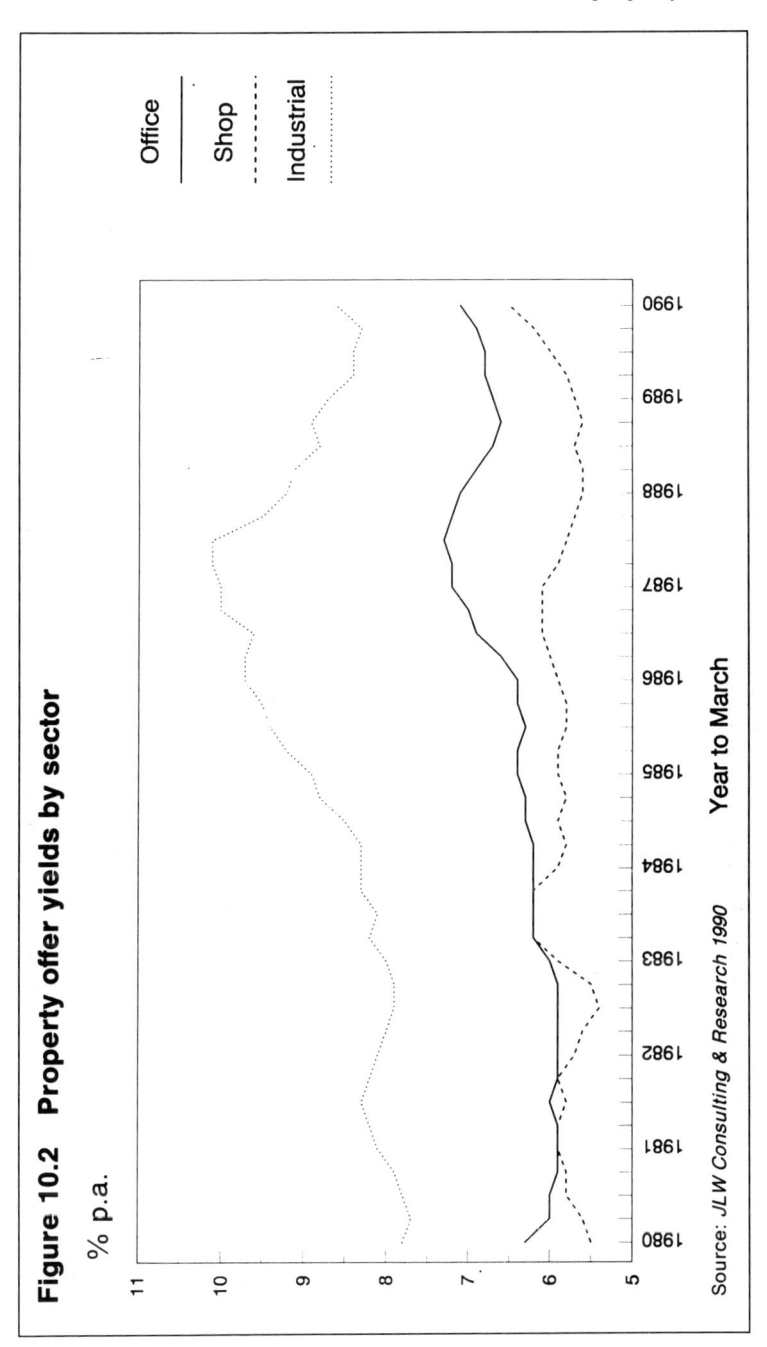

Commercial property 181

Figure 10.2 Property offer yields by sector

Office ———
Shop – – –
Industrial ....

% p.a.

Year to March

Source: *JLW Consulting & Research 1990*

varied enormously from a peak of about 30 per cent per annum to an actual decline in real terms. At the same time yields have altered by as much as 25 per cent. It is these two factors and the perceived future which affect the value individuals ascribe to buildings and their willingness to invest or divest.

10.3 Shops

10.3.1 General

Historically, three factors have affected the rental and capital value of shops: location, location and location. Due to the fact that the quality of the location can readily be ascertained, shops have been regarded as one of the most secure forms of commercial property investment. In the past, principal high street locations were rarely subject to major change, except when a town centre redevelopment scheme or a new shopping centre was planned, when it was usually possible to predict the effect that these new centres would have on the existing shopping patterns within the high street. However, the future impact of out of town retail schemes and retail warehouse parks on high street shopping patterns is uncertain. With the announcement of the intentions of major retailers such as Marks & Spencer to set up a number of large-scale operations in out of town locations, the indications are that only those town centres with an adequate supporting infrastructure combined with sufficient and accessible car parking and an attractive environment will continue to prosper on the same levels as before; otherwise, traditional town centres will be left to become fashion-dominated, durable-good centres, with food shopping moving out of town. The retailing sector is undergoing significant change, with many retailers repositioning in the market, restyling their outlet and merchandise, and taking over competitors. In addition there has been dramatic growth in 'speciality' retailing in the past two years where a number of retailers have been successful in targeting specific markets and responding quickly to changes in consumer demand. Hence the more established chains have experienced greater competition for prime pitches in the high street.

In the property investment market, shops are categorised as prime, secondary and tertiary.

A large number of the best shop units in the UK are now owned by the institutions, although a proportion are still owned and occupied by the major retailing organisations. In recent years rental growth has been considerable throughout the retail sector. There has been keen competition to make further investment in this category, whilst the availability of suitable investments is extremely limited in relation to the amount of investment money available. Over the past two years substantial institutional investment has spread out into the best located shops in the smaller towns.

10.3.2 Prime

Prime shops are those situated in the best trading locations along the principal high streets in the larger towns where major multiple retailers, such as Boots, WH Smith and Marks & Spencer, are to be found. The rental income obtainable from shop units within these locations varies enormously depending on the importance of the particular town.

10.3.3 Secondary

Secondary shops are shops either on the fringes of the best trading positions within the larger towns or in the best shopping positions in the smaller towns. Due to the shortage of prime shop units now available for commercial investment, the institutional demand for this type of property has grown in recent years. Since the prospects for rental growth in these locations have proved more erratic than those in prime locations, investors expect a higher yield.

10.3.4 Tertiary

Tertiary shops are shops on the fringes of the secondary trading positions and shops in neighbourhood shopping parades, including 'the corner shop'. There is a negligible demand from multiple tenants for representation in these locations. Therefore, covenant strength is lower and the management load, heavier. Consequently, demand for these properties derives principally from private investors. This market is usually very active with sales of all sizes taking place by private treaty or auction.

10.3.5 Out of town shopping

Out of town shopping has evolved through the recognition of the car-borne shopper and may generally be divided into food and non-food retailing. The main DIY specialists (Sainsbury's Homebase, WH Smith Do-It-All, Texas Homecare and B & Q) are often found grouping together and require units of 35,000–50,000 sq ft. Out of town food retailers now include most of the major food chains. Good surface car parking and main road prominence are essential criteria.

10.4 Offices

10.4.1 General

In the early 1970s many provincial towns, as well as central London, became seriously over-supplied with office accommodation and rents either remained level or fell. This has, it appears, started to happen again to a lesser extent in the late 1980s. A factor in the demand/supply imbalance is the lengthy period from planning to completion of a development.

The quality of an office building is of greater importance than the quality of a shop unit. Occupational tenants are setting ever higher standards, requiring good quality finishes, modern lifts, central heating, adequate car parking facilities, the ability to accommodate a growing range of sophisticated office equipment (notably computers, word processors and communications equipment) and, particularly in central London, double-glazing and air conditioning. The costs of maintaining offices, especially the mechanical services, the unified business rates, and the cost of refurbishing the accommodation mean that the tenant and investor are subjected to high outgoings. These have increased as a direct result of technological changes having shortened the lifetime of buildings and services.

The most expensive office locations in the UK are the West End and City of London. Since the tenant will be responsible for all outgoings under the terms of his lease, the actual cost of occupation will probably be double the cost of the rent alone. Due to the exceptional security and perceived prospects for long-term rental growth offered by buildings within the West End and City of London, there has been a strong institutional demand for investments. Increasingly foreign investors as well as UK investors have been active during the late 1980s.

The other principal office areas in London follow a similar but less expensive pattern to that of the City and West End, although in the late 1980s an upswing in demand coupled with relatively restricted supply resulted in these locations experiencing dramatic growth in rents. Outside London, rents vary from centre to centre, with the towns immediately to the west of London along the M4 corridor being the highest outside London.

10.4.2 Conclusion

Offices form the backbone of most commercial property investment portfolios, due to the amount of money involved and the past performance of rental growth on rent review. They are likely to remain a dominant feature of institutional portfolios and the preferred areas are those in central London and certain selected provincial centres. However, it is becoming necessary to spend large capital sums more frequently to maintain the quality of the investment. Over many years the cost of central London office occupancy and the inconvenience of commuting have encouraged companies to move their operations to suburban and provincial locations.

10.5 Industrial

10.5.1 General investment: factories and warehouses

The declining importance in Great Britain of the industrial and manufacturing sectors, the volatility of the economy and the relatively short economic life of industrial buildings have resulted in investors requiring higher yields for factories and warehouse premises than for shops and offices. In this context, institutional investors tend to prefer warehouse buildings, as opposed to factories, due to the fact that these tend to be less specialised and therefore require fewer remedial works when a tenant vacates the premises. Industrial processes also tend to have a more destructive effect on the actual fabric of the property.

10.5.2 Location criteria

Although the uses of factories and warehouses are different, both in practical and in legislative terms, it is convenient to categorise them together, since the locational and investment criteria are similar. The most desirable investments in this category are situated on well-located industrial estates, close to the major conurbations or motorway access points or the national airports. It is interesting to note that proximity to rail service is not an important criterion in the UK, being less important than a good supply of labour and good estate services for the factory owner.

10.5.3 Institutional criteria

The insurance companies and pension funds have developed certain criteria which they look for in modern industrial and warehouse buildings. These criteria relate to clear working height, floor loading capacity, the presence of sprinklers, the proportion of office space to warehouse space within the unit, the number of loading doors, the presence of a concreted hard standing in front of the unit and adequate car parking. Whilst these institutional criteria are often in excess of the criteria required by occupiers, the investor would be wise to purchase units meeting institutional criteria, since they will find a wider market in which to sell the property in the future.

10.5.4 Yields

Yields available on prime industrial and warehouse investments are higher than those on prime shops and offices. Rental growth experienced over the late 1970s was, generally, very satisfactory but was static in the early and mid-80s during the economic recession. Investment in modern industrial and warehouse buildings is a more recent trend than investment in offices and shops but now forms around 25 per cent of a typical portfolio. Opportunities do exist for non-institutional investment where very high yields can be obtained from obsolescent or poorly located properties, but these carry commensurate risk.

10.6 Hi-tech

Whilst many areas of traditional manufacturing industry were affected by the economic recession, the hi-technology field experienced considerable growth. This has resulted in a new direction in the design and use of industrial buildings with tenants becoming increasingly discerning as to their preferences in building design and working environment. The most radical change has been the introduction of the building which comprises a two- or three-storey structure designed to permit the interchangeability of functions such as offices, research and development, laboratories or industrial. An edge of out of town location, extensive car parking and landscaping with imaginative and functional finishes both internally and externally create a high quality corporate image. For occupiers, the first and still largest business park in the UK was Stockley Park off the M4 very close to Heathrow airport. Both back office and headquarters type functions are now moving to such business parks.

10.7 Agriculture

Having experienced growth in popularity with institutional investors, at one point forming in excess of 5 per cent of some investment portfolios, farm land and forestry have been increasingly less popular as a result of falling values and the perception of a continued fall in values. In addition, investors have begun to appreciate that in many instances the economic support or tax benefits of these investments have been and are likely to be subject to political tinkering thus in many instances dramatically altering the value of such investments at a stroke.

Smaller, more picturesque farms, especially those with attractive houses have, however, become increasingly attractive and prices have continued to rise for the successful businessman desirous of changing his place of domicile and lifestyle. (See also Chapter 11.)

10.8 Leisure

Investments in the 'leisure industry' include hotels, marinas, golf courses, sports centres and entertainment facilities. The growing demand for leisure facilities, both home-based and from tourists, is resulting in increasing investment in this field. It is, however, regarded as an investment in management expertise rather than in the property which the particular leisure activity occupies, and great caution is therefore necessary. Quite often an investor's return will be geared to the operator's turnover or profitability rather than to the rental value of the premises, which can sometimes be very difficult to determine.

Whilst the returns from leisure industry investments, in terms of capital gains, can be substantial for the astute investor, the risks are considerable and they are not recommended to small investors.

11 Agricultural land, woodlands and miscellaneous

Catherine Paice, MA (Cantab), freelance journalist

11.1 Introduction

There has been a dramatic change in the perception of agricultural investment over the last ten years. In the long term, investment in vacant possession or tenanted land has traditionally been more than satisfactory. The short-term outlook for investors is unstable as the government comes under increasing pressure and attitudes towards financial support, and the countryside itself, change.

This chapter outlines the various investment opportunities and likely returns. But two factors should be borne in mind. Efficient management plays a crucial role, particularly during a time of change. It is unlikely that investment in agricultural property will ever again be in monoculture or single commodities. Food surpluses have led to radical changes in attitudes towards farming and to severe pressure on farm incomes. However, the second factor is that traditional investment in agricultural land has also been for pleasure and personal reward. More and more people are seeking the sort of life they believe the countryside can provide. With increased leisure time and spending power now more widespread in the community, combined with a greater appreciation of sport, recreation and all things 'green', the opportunities for investors are more diverse than ever.

11.2 Highlights of the previous year

Despite the vagaries of the residential market, the vacant possession agricultural property market held up remarkably well. It was clearly impossible for it to repeat the extraordinary 20–50 per cent price increases witnessed in 1988 on the back of the residential boom. But two sources of funds helped make it a resilient year for farm sales.

The huge demand in 1988 for old farmbuildings for residential or industrial conversion and the demand for building land generated hundreds of millions of pounds for landowners. The provisions of roll-over tax relief allowing 100 per cent of the gains to be reinvested in a business mean that a great deal of that money is filtering back into the agricultural market. Existing landowners were once again one of the main forces in the market, reinvesting in the business they know. Others who had sold farms to non-farming individuals in areas of residential popularity were keen to trade up accordingly.

Although many have been prepared to pay dearly to secure a sizeable, good quality farm in what is an increasingly thin market, they were meeting continued competition from outside investors seeking new challenges, opportunities and residences in the countryside.

However, prices in East Anglia, where the largest volume of land was offered, came under some pressure particularly in the commercial arable areas. Pure commercial arable farmland has suffered the most because of surplus cereal production which has resulted in the price of corn today being at the same real level as 10 years ago. Prices at £1,000 per acre or less in the Fens were at their lowest for 15 years.

By far the happiest was the dairy sector, sitting on its highest profits since milk quotas were introduced. Well-equipped units were snapped up, often at a considerable premium.

But as summer began to parch the fields, so interest rates began their relentless hike. Almost half farm income in 1989 was swallowed in servicing debts. Equally, developers curbed their purchase of land, and the value of rural building land fell by 50 per cent. By the end of the year, the number of prospective buyers had considerably reduced, and important sources of funding were drying up.

In the tenanted sector, let land came back into vogue. Interest is rarely from the major financial institutions who flooded the market more than a decade ago and have largely since pulled out, disillusioned with returns.

A far wider range of investors emerged, including the more traditional institutions, entrepreneurial funds and property companies, trust funds and private individuals. Yields that had risen to between 7 and 9 per cent fell back to around 6 per cent as capital values rose on the back of a belief that let agricultural property has become cheap enough to make an attractive bargain.

The prospects for buying at a 50–60 per cent discount from the vacant possession market, for reversion, for deals to be struck with tenants to compensate them for the surrender of a tenancy, for development and alternative use, and enjoyment of rural amenities started to make sense. Many tenants have also been buying their farms, at prices midway between vacant and tenanted value.

11.3 Agricultural land

11.3.1 Vacant possession land

Of the usable acreage of agricultural land in the UK, about 60 per cent is owner-occupied freehold land (vacant possession—VP—land), and held in blocks varying from five acres to 5,000 acres or more. Of this total, between 1 and 2 per cent changes hands annually in varying-sized parcels throughout the country. The market in VP land is made up of owner-occupiers, private investors, the institutions and a small number of foreign buyers. (The average unit size of farms in the UK is currently well above the average of the other members of the EC—farms over 120 acres: UK 31.1 per cent, EC 5.7 per cent.)

The value of land has historically outpaced the equity investment market. Until 1972/73 the rise in values was gradual, with only rare drops in value. In 1972 the VP market rose from about £300 per acre to £1,000 per acre, but in 1975 fell back rapidly to between £300 and £500 per acre.

From 1976 values rose sharply to a peak in 1979/80 when the market fell back by between 15 to 20 per cent until 1983, when the vacant possession value index exceeded the high of 1979/80 for the first time but subsequently fell in 1984 and continued to fall back in 1985 and 1986 and 1987. Statistics on land prices are of necessity historical but the market position at December 1989 was recorded by the indices extracted from Farmland Market No 33 (see table).

The earning capacity of VP land is directly related to farming profitability, which in turn is affected by such factors as land quality (established by reference to the Ministry Land Classification, by which the Ministry of Agriculture grades land qualities in the UK between I and V and prepares maps showing these gradings: only 3.3 per cent of all land in the UK is Grade I), rainfall, drainage, size, shape, fixed equipment (comprising buildings, houses, cottages, roads, services and special installations) and finally, the occupier's farming ability. Returns, therefore, will vary considerably but assuming that the farming capital varies between £300 per acre on an arable farm and £600 per acre on a livestock farm, the net yield to the owner can be between £50 and £110 per acre. For example, if a figure of £1,500 per acre is assumed for vacant possession freehold, the gross return will vary between 3 and 7 per cent. Difficult harvests in recent years with reduced yields, combined with falling commodity prices have produced losses on many businesses which were over-geared.

Table 11.1

Source	Date	Vacant possession £ per acre			Tenanted £ per acre		
		1987	1988	1989	1987	1988	1989
Farmland Market (Auction)	Dec	£2,421	£2,916	£3,263	–	–	–
Inland Revenue (England only)	Sept	£1,375	£1,422	£1,708	£838	£947	£1,239*
ADAS/CLA AMC (England only)	Dec	£1,488	£2,639	£2,128	£714	£706	£909*
AVERAGE		£1,761	£2,326	£2,366	£776	£826	£1,074*

*includes sales & sitting tenants and mixed tenure sales

Revenue taxation will depend on the method of trading (ie, partnership, company or individual). There are certain taxation advantages namely;

(1) Profits may be averaged over two years where profits differ by more than 25 per cent. (This does not apply to companies.)
Since April 1986 the tax allowance (depreciation) for farm equipment has been 25 per cent per annum on a reducing balance basis. There is a 'balancing charge' (or 'balancing allowance') on disposal—if the sale realises more (or less) than the written-down value.
(2) The writing down allowance in respect of agricultural buildings is now only 4 per cent per annum on a reducing balance basis. There is no initial allowance.
(3) A proportion of car and house expenses is tax deductible, the exact proportion being the subject of agreement with the Inland Revenue in each individual case.
    (a) Losses can be carried forward and, in certain circumstances, backwards or offset against other income, but 'hobby farming' (ie, where the occupier cannot show that the enterprise is carried on on a commercial basis with a view to realisation of profit) is penalised if losses continue for more than five consecutive years.

(b) VAT on expenses (if the trader is registered) is recoverable, but is not chargeable on produce, which is zero-rated.

The capital taxation advantages of VP land as an investment are substantial:

(1) Agricultural Property Relief is available. There is an automatic reduction of 50 per cent of the agricultural value for IHT purposes provided the land is vacant or can be vacant within a period of twelve months from the date of transfer. The conditions for this relief are less stringent than for the previous Working Farmer Relief (which in certain circumstances, is still available), ie, either that the land was owner-occupied for the previous two years or it was owned throughout the previous seven years and whilst not occupied by the owner it was occupied for the purposes of agriculture. There are no longer any area or value limits to this relief (except when Working Farmer Relief is being sought). Since the introduction of IHT in 1986, the question of relief has become complicated by the rules relating to the recipients of potentially exempt transfers. Where the donor dies within seven years of making such a transfer, it is the recipient of the transfer who will have to qualify for the relief, eg, if he has sold the land and not replaced it then no relief will be available. Professional advice should be sought.

Example

Mr A owns and farms 600 acres of arable land. He retires and gives his farm to his son Mr B on 24 April 1986 who continues farming on the land in partnership with his brother. The land was valued at £1m. However, to raise additional working capital 50 acres of land are sold in 1987. Mr A dies on 3 March 1989. The value of Mr A's estate at death amounted to £300,000. (Annual exemptions have been ignored.)

(1) No IHT was paid on the gift of the farmland because it was a potentially exempt transfer.
(2) On death IHT is payable on the value of the land at the date of the gift, *viz* £1,000,000 less agricultural relief which is restricted to reflect the sale of land before death.

IHT payable on gift of farmland:
Value of land	£1,000,000	
Less: agricultural relief		
$50\% \times \dfrac{550}{600} \times \dfrac{1,000,000}{(acres)}$	458,334	
Chargeable value	£541,666	
IHT thereon (1988/89 rates)	£216,666	
Less taper relief (death more than 2 years but less than 3 years from gift)	43,333	£173,333

(Payment by interest free instalments over ten years will be permitted.)

Balance of estate on death	£300,000
Add value of gift of land	541,666
Assessable estate on death	£841,666
IHT payable thereon (1988/89 rates)	£336,666
IHT payable on gift of land before taper relief	216,666
IHT on residue	120,000
Total IHT payable	£293,333

Since the Finance Act 1988, if Mr A died in June 1988 and all other matters remain constant:

Chargeable value (as above)	£541,666	
IHT thereon (Post 15.3.88)	£172,666	
Less taper relief		
20% as above	£34,533	£138,133

(Payment by interest free instalments as above)

Balance of estate on death	£300,000
Add value of gift of land	£541,666
Assessable estate on death	£841,666
IHT thereon	£292,666
IHT on gift (before taper relief)	£172,666
IHT on residue	120,000
Total IHT payable	£258,133

(2) Business assets relief is still available in certain circumstances but since agricultural property relief is now automatic (providing the conditions are satisfied) Business Assets Relief will not be so widely used. Relief at either 50 per cent or 30 per cent may be available.

(3) A ten-year period is allowed for payment of IHT in respect of transfers on death and on certain lifetime transfers by annual instalments which are free of interest provided that they are paid on the due dates.

(4) Up to 100 per cent roll-over relief is available in respect of capital gains on sale of qualifying business assets and reinvestment into another business, and relief on a more limited basis on retirement. Hold-over relief is available for gifts to individuals and

also for gifts to trusts and transfers out of trusts. In all cases where hold-over relief applies, the recipient effectively inherits the inherent capital gain of the transferor. The relevant base value is subject to indexation relief. For disposals of assets held on 31 March 1982, the Finance Act 1988 introduced re-basing to the market value of the assets at 31 March 1982.

Owners and occupiers of land can benefit from Ministry of Agriculture grants for *some* capital improvements. The old agriculture and horticulture grant scheme closed on 31 December 1985 and has been replaced by a more limited scheme, The Agriculture Improvement Scheme, AIS. This scheme provides grants towards the cost of approved expenditure on improvements such as greenhouses, replacement drainage, hedge planting and effluent and waste handling. Generally, the new scheme is intended to direct grants to conservation orientated and energy saving improvements with increased assistance for the Less Favoured Areas. Grant rates vary from 15 per cent to a maximum of 50 per cent. From 1 January 1988 the Farm Diversification Grant Scheme has provided grants of up to 25 per cent of eligible expenditure for a wide range of alternative uses (eg, farmshops, recreational and sports facilities, holiday accommodation, etc) up to £35,000 and full details are available from divisional offices of the Ministry of Agriculture, Fisheries and Food.

Grants may also be available for special purposes from Food From Britain (usually for projects of a co-operative nature), the Rural Development Commission, tourist boards and other specialist organisations. These may be for capital items, for marketing and training or for diversification.

Grants and subsidies for agricultural land are moving away from commodity support towards conservation and reduced output. For example, Set-aside payments are payable if a minimum 20 per cent of arable land on a holding is taken out of arable production for five years and put into permanent or rotational fallow, permitted non-agricultural use or woodland. Payments range from £50–£80 per acre, and can be topped up providing certain conservation criteria are met. Compensation for severely restricting arable farming practices in specified Nitrate Sensitive Areas range from £20–£35 per acre, also with conservation premiums available.

Government policy can and does influence the profitability of farming and the price of land. Historically, controls, such as rent control, have from time to time been imposed and special grants and taxation reliefs have been introduced to stimulate output. Politically the price of food is an important factor in the national economy.

From 1 April 1990 any non-domestic property is liable for assessment for the new non-domestic rate, with the exception of agricultural property used for agricultural purposes. Based on the rental value of the property as at 1 April 1988, it is not yet clear how great its impact will be on agricultural properties, which have been encouraged to diversify into non-agricultural ventures over recent years.

Many landowners who had paid rates on employees' tied dwellings are now contributing to those employees' standard community charge.

There is an anomaly on empty farm cottages. In Scotland, the charge is fixed at nil but in England and Wales owners are required to pay an additional charge, in some cases twice the personal charge, unless cottages are deemed uninhabitable. A consultation paper was being circulated in August 1990 proposing this was cut to half the standard community charge.

The uniform business rate is payable on self-catering holiday lets of over 140 days, and the standard community charge on lets of less than 140 days.

The investor may manage his farm personally, or he may farm in partnership with another farmer, or he may have a contractual or profit-sharing arrangement with another farmer. The selection of the method will depend on the investor's income requirement, managerial ability and capital situation, and will affect the amount of farming capital required, the level of return obtained, and the extent of involvement and risk in the day-to-day running of the investment. Special care is needed in structuring management by a partnership or contractual arrangement so as not to convert VP land into tenanted land, thereby losing the premium (which currently can be up to 150 per cent or more of tenanted value).

Intensive livestock farming is a specialist form of farming and is restricted mainly to pigs, poultry (chickens and turkeys), veal, barley beef and trout. These enterprises are usually capital-intensive in buildings and equipment and are restricted to small acreages (two to 20 acres). The investment can be speculative and the return is very dependent on expert management.

11.3.2 Tenanted land

The percentage of tenanted (or let) land comprises about 30 per cent of the total usable acreage in the UK. Historically let land has been a good long-term investment. For many years there has been a VP premium, reflecting the flexibility of the owner-occupier, the income and capital tax advantages of VP land and the fact that all the earnings belong to the owner. In the last decade the VP premium has generally been at a level of about 50 per cent of tenanted value (ie, when VP land was £300 per acre, let land was about £200 per acre). With the disappearance of the 45 per cent estate duty relief and the absence of any CTT relief on let land until the Finance Act 1981, and with the advent of the 1976 tenancy succession legislation (which already existed in Scotland), the VP premium rose in 1979 to 100 per cent of let value. In 1980/81, however, it fell back to the historic level of about 50 per cent of tenanted value but has increased again since 1983 to the present position of at least 100 per cent.

Tenanted land in 1990 might be valued at between £500 and £1,000 per acre producing an income of between £40–£80 per acre (which should equate roughly to approximately 50 to 60 per cent of farm profits) to the landlord giving a net yield varying from 4 per cent to 8 per cent.

Rents are subject to income tax. Management costs, insurance and repairs are allowable against rental income (these may amount to 20 to 25 per cent of gross rents) and improvements are eligible for agricultural building allowances. Some grants are payable to landowners. The Finance Act 1989 made provisions for landowners to elect to tax agricultural rents as from 1 August 1989. Such an option makes all subsequent transactions affecting that land irrevocably taxable. However, it also means VAT charges can be covered when a tenant retires and VAT can be charged on rent and recovered on certain expenditure. There has been some speculation as to whether VAT is properly payable on the surrender value of a tenancy when payment is made in exchange for a surrender.

The capital tax position on let land is:

(1) Agricultural Property Relief is available. This was introduced by the Finance Act 1981 and there is now an automatic reduction of 30 per cent of the agricultural value for IHT purposes provided the land has been owned for seven years and has been occupied for the purposes of agriculture. Where the donor dies within seven years of making a potentially exempt transfer it is the recipient of the transfer who will have to qualify for relief, eg, if he has sold the land and not replaced it, no relief will be available. Professional advice should be sought.

The example on pages 193–4 is also applicable here, but would

need to be re-worked to show the agricultural property relief at 30 per cent for tenanted land, instead of the 50 per cent on vacant possession land shown in that example.
(2) In certain cases, and subject to certain stringent conditions, land let to a family partnership of which the owner is a partner, may qualify as let land but it may also get the benefit of the old 50 per cent Working Farmer Relief.
(3) A ten-year period is allowed for payment of IHT in respect of transfers on death and on certain lifetime transfers by annual instalments free of interest.
(4) The Finance Act 1982 introduced CGT roll-over relief for let land where the disposal is by compulsory purchase; otherwise on normal sales of tenanted land this is not available. Since the Finance Act 1982 the relevant base value has been indexed. For disposals after 5 April 1988 the value of the land if acquired prior to 31 March 1982, will generally be the market value at 31 March 1982.
(5) As with VP land hold-over relief from CGT is available on let land, for gifts of let land.

Investment opportunities vary from single let farms to large residential estates. The size of the investment varies between a probable minimum of 100 acres, with the majority in blocks of between 300 and 1,500 acres. The institutional market has principally invested in units of between 500 and 1,000 acres or more, but due to the shortage of supply of suitable investments, smaller blocks have been considered, particularly of land classified by the Ministry of Agriculture as Grade I or Grade II. A further alternative is lease-back, where the owner-occupier sells the freehold subject to retaining an annual agricultural tenancy at an agreed rent. On a lease-back it is customary for the tenant to undertake all repairs and insurance responsibilities. The approximate value of the investment after the purchase might be £800 per acre and the rent £50 per acre, giving a gross yield of 6.3 per cent.

Agricultural land is usually let on annual tenancies. Leases for terms of years revert on expiry to annual tenancies unless the parties agree to extend the lease itself. Lettings are mainly the subject of written agreements but otherwise are governed by the Agricultural Holdings Act 1986. The tenancy agreement *must* be examined by a professional adviser, since it forms the basis for all matters affecting the investment in the future. Tenancy agreements vary but the most important and *essential* clauses are:

(1) a prohibition against sub-letting and assignment;
(2) the allocation of the repairing and insurance liability;

(3) a requirement for the tenant to occupy the farmhouse; and
(4) the right to recover possession for the use of some or all of the land for non-agricultural purposes at less than one year's notice.

Rent is customarily paid half-yearly in arrears, but new agreements should now require it to be paid quarterly in advance.

The Agricultural Holdings Act 1986 (and the Agricultural Holdings (Scotland) Act 1949 as now amended by the Agricultural Holdings (Scotland) (Amendments) Act 1983) confirms that the landlord has the right to review rent every three years to the full open market rent. Rent levels vary and due to the scarcity of farms to let, rents fixed under the Acts have tended to be 40 to 50 per cent below the rents obtainable from vacant farms offered for letting by tender. An example of sitting tenant rents per acre compared to tendered rents in 1989 might be:

(1) for well-equipped arable farms in the Fens: £70 as opposed to £85;
(2) for well-equipped arable farms (not Fens) and well-equipped stock farms: £50 as opposed to £70; and
(3) for bare land or poorly equipped farms; £35 as opposed to £50.

The Agriculture (Miscellaneous Provisions) Act 1976 introduced into England a statutory right, which already existed in Scotland, for eligible and suitable relatives of tenants to claim a tenancy on the tenant's death. This has abolished the reversionary possibilities which existed before December 1976 whereby, when a tenant died, the landlord secured vacant possession and thereby obtained the VP premium value. Reversion is still possible where the tenant has a substantial acreage in addition to the tenanted farm or where there is no one to succeed him, but the opportunities for reversion are much more limited. 1984 witnessed the passing of the most extensive Agricultural Holdings legislation for over 30 years in the form of the Agricultural Holdings Act 1984. The Act made a number of amendments to anomalies under the existing 1948 Act but the two most important changes were in connection with rents and succession:

(1) Rents: Effectively the section dealing with rents was changed to exclude the words 'open market' in the hope that arbitrators would award a rent to sitting tenants that reflected their ability to pay and the productive capacity of the land, and ignored 'appreciable scarcity' due to absence of farms to let. It is too early to judge how successful the new formula will be but

evidence to date indicates that it is much more difficult and more expensive to resolve rental disagreements when they arise than hitherto.
(2) Succession: As mentioned above the 1976 Act introduced a statutory succession right to certain relatives of a deceased tenant. In theory it tied up a farm for up to three generations. The 1984 Act abolished those rights and replaced them with a lifetime right, but only in respect of tenancies granted after 12 July 1984. The impact of this change is therefore likely to be neutral, at least until some of these new tenancies draw close to termination.

All of these provisions are now incorporated within the Agricultural Holdings Act 1986. In Scotland, land is increasingly let on 'partnership' tenancies which allows the tenancy to continue only as long as the 'partnership' agreement between landlord and tenant exists.

Management is customarily undertaken by professional firms of land agents and surveyors or, on large estates, by resident agents. Annual charges vary from 5 to 10 per cent of the gross rental income, depending on circumstances.

11.3.3 Finance

Short-term requirements are usually provided by bank borrowing. This is mainly appropriate for covering seasonal needs and for providing some working capital. Long-term finance is often funded by mortgages. These can be provided by the Agricultural Mortgage Corporation or the Scottish Agricultural Securities Corporation, which provide fixed long-term loans to farmers, with repayment over ten to 40 years. The banks are also moving into this field. Loan interest is a deductible expense if the loan is used to purchase VP land to be used in a business. Relief for interest paid on a loan used to purchase tenanted land or land for commercial letting is also usually allowed. In certain cases individuals may take out life assurance policies to provide for the repayment of the capital at the end of the period of the loan. The amount of money loaned on mortgage will depend on the borrower's ability to service the loan as well as on the value of the property secured, but up to two-thirds of the value can be funded in this way.

Agricultural land has been one of the most secure of all investments. For four decades the productivity of the industry had increased dramatically and with the exception of a few commodities the UK is self-sufficient in almost all its food requirements, a phenomenon which is common to a large number of the EC member states and which has given rise to the problems of ever-increasing financial liability on the CAP. It is because no political consensus has been agreed as to the means to resolve the problems of overproduction that uncertainty has heightened and land values have fallen in real terms since 1979. That the problems will be resolved, is inevitable. What is uncertain is when, but once positive action is taken confidence will be restored and land values will stabilise and real growth will follow, but this may not be for five years or more.

In a mixed portfolio 'spin offs' are likely to occur from time to time and can bring very substantial investment benefits. Some examples might be sales of surplus houses, cottages or barns, commercial or residential development, mineral extraction or leisure activities.

Underdeveloped properties can be attractive to high-rate taxpayers, as expenditure on major repairs may in certain circumstances be offset for tax purposes against income. Substantial grants are available for improvements and only CGT is likely to be payable on a disposal although, following the Finance Act 1988 capital gains tax is now payable by an individual at the rate of income tax which would apply if any gain on the disposal were treated as the top slice of his income. For companies, tax in respect of chargeable gains is paid on the normal corporation tax rate payable by the company.

The disadvantages of agricultural land are the low income yield, the high capital investment both in land and working capital, the poor cash flow (12 months or more before any return), the absence of control of end-product prices and the risk of political intervention, as is currently being experienced.

In conclusion, good quality agricultural land is a sound long term investment. Whilst yields are low, annual rental growth has, until recently, provided a real return to the investor. The long-term capital growth has produced an outstanding redemption yield and the 50 per cent IHT relief after two years is a valuable tax planning tool. For the private investor under current legislation, the investment should be made in VP land in all but exceptional circumstances. However, the smaller institutional investor who may not be able to utilise the taxation benefits of VP land since income and capital taxes may not be assessable, should concentrate on tenanted land. Thus the market for tenanted land is predominantly controlled by the institutional investors, who prefer to accept a lower, more secure return in the form of rent.

11.4 Woodlands

From 15 March 1988 commercial woodlands are wholly removed from the scope of income tax and corporation tax. Subject to the transitional provisions, Schedule B (whereby tax was on a minimal annual value irrespective of receipts) was abolished as from 6 April 1988 and the right to elect to Schedule D (whereby expenditure was available for relief against other taxed income) ceased on 15 March 1988.

Tax relief under the old rules (Schedule D and Schedule B) will continue to be available until 5 April 1993 at prevailing rates of tax for those who are already either existing occupiers of commercial woodlands or will become occupiers as a result of commitments entered into or grant applications received by the Forestry Commission before 15 March 1988.

To replace tax incentives the Forestry Commission announced (subject to EC ratification) increased planting grants on 23 March 1988. Depending on the area to be planted, grants for planting conifers have been increased by between 60 per cent and 156 per cent to between £615 and £1,005 per hectare. Grants for planting broadleaves have been increased by between 31 per cent and 63 per cent to between £975 and £1,575 per hectare. In addition to the above grants, a payment of £200 per hectare will be made where arable or improved grassland is afforested. Occupiers taking advantage of the transitional tax provisions will be restricted to the old rates of grant. Grants under the Farm Woodland Scheme, effective from October 1988 and not to be confused with the Woodland Grant Scheme, are designed to help finance the gap between the establishment of woodland and its first income from thinnings. They range from £240–£505 per hectare for conifers and from £975–£1,375 per hectare for broadleaves. On a maximum area of 40 hectares per holding, each block of woodland must be at least one hectare.

Annual payments ranging from £30 on unimproved or less favoured areas to £190 per hectare on lowland arable or improved grassland are available over 10 to 40 years depending on the type of woodland.

The annual payments under this scheme will be assessed as taxable income, but these woodlands will normally be classed as commercial so all sale proceeds and the initial planting grant will be outside the scope of tax. The holding must remain primarily agricultural.

Growing timber continues to be free of capital gains tax. Provisions exist which defer the payment of inheritance tax in respect of timber comprised in a deceased person's estate, tax being payable on the value of proceeds of the timber on the occasion of a subsequent disposal. Business relief may also be available in respect of the timber and the land on which it stands.

It is too early to assess how the market will react to the changes in the incidence of taxation on forestry but planting land values may drop significantly from their level before March 1988 of about £740 per hectare to less than £600 per hectare in the uplands. The 1989 planting season was a disaster, with less than one-third of the forestry target achieved. Institutional demand for teenage plantations appears to be remaining firm, currently at around £1,700 to £2,900 per hectare and timber processing companies are showing an increasing interest in acquiring stocked woodland. Demand from private individuals has pushed prices for mature, mixed, amenity woodland to as much as £2,500 per hectare.

The current level of imported timber is about 90 per cent of UK requirements and the balance of payments saving potential seems certain to ensure a continuing and satisfactory demand and, therefore, a high price for the right variety of high quality timber. Generalisation on investment yield is dangerous so soon after the changes effected by the Finance Act 1988, but real yields from stocked woodland in the order of 4–5 per cent per annum compound appear achievable.

11.5 Miscellaneous agricultural-linked investments

11.5.1 Mineral-bearing land

All minerals other than oil, gold, silver and coal usually belong to the freehold owner of land but may have been reserved to a predecessor in title. On acquisition purchasers should always check to see if mineral rights are excluded from the sale. The principal minerals are coal, sand, gravel, silica sand (glass), iron-stone, clay (brickmaking or china), limestone and, in certain areas, other special deposits (tin, copper, etc). With limited exceptions all coal belongs to the National Coal Board.

Strict legislation affects mineral excavation, and specified areas are designated in most county plans. Virtually no excavation is permitted on land classified as Grade I or Grade II. Geological maps will indicate the approximate location of minerals and resistivity surveys and test borings can establish mineral deposit patterns, depths and volumes.

Development is usually carried out through a sale or lease to one of the principal operating companies.

The sale of mineral-bearing land will give rise to CGT in respect of chargeable gains. Profits from the commercial operation of mineral workings are liable to income tax (or corporation tax), with capital allowances (including a depletion allowance of, in general, 50 per cent of the royalty rate of the minerals as determined by the District Valuer) available in respect of certain expenditure. Mineral royalties are taxed, broadly, as to one-half as income and as to the other half as a chargeable gain.

Tipping, fishing, boating and water skiing rights may be reserved and provide high levels of income and reversionary asset value on completion of excavation. The 'hole in the ground' can be worth more than the original land but there may be an expensive statutory or contractual obligation to restore the land to its original use.

Minerals are a speculative investment if the land is purchased by an investor other than a mineral operator with mineral exploitation specifically in view, but some farmland can produce high yields from unexpected mineral excavation. High prices should not be paid merely to hold a 'mineral bank', since compound interest reduces the yield to redemption.

11.5.2 Farm shops and garden centres

Farm shops are usually ancillary to farm businesses: they enable the farmer to obtain better prices than he would on the wholesale market by cutting out the middlemen. Garden centres are normally run by individuals or small companies, but in a few cases they are larger enterprises with multiple sites. Planning consent is required. The location of both farm shops and garden centres is important, the best sites being on main roads and close to large centres of population. The increase in leisure has stimulated the popularity of these enterprises, supplying requisites to the keen gardener and also to the housewife, who is increasingly interested in fresh farm produce, especially for the deep freeze. The 'pick your own' method of sale at certain seasons is increasing in popularity and at farms where it is in operation good car parking facilities are essential.

Enterprises of this kind are a valuable source of additional income and capital if correctly developed out of a farm unit (which is usually owner-occupied) but they are seldom sold as investments.

11.5.3 Accommodation land

The Agricultural Holdings Acts have, as previously stated, given long-term security to tenants. There are, however, three major specific exceptions which are detailed below.

Grazing sales for a period of less than one year

The grazing and mowing rights of VP land laid down to permanent or temporary grass can be sold, often by auction, for a period of less than 12 months. The custom varies considerably in different districts, but the most usual period of occupation for the stock is from April to October.

Returns vary considerably and are regulated by the prosperity of the livestock industry. Prices of up to £100 per acre per season have been obtained in the established grazing areas in Northern England, but £50 to £80 would be more likely to be obtained in the South. It is important to document the arrangements carefully to avoid any possibility of the grazier claiming a tenancy.

Leisure grass

There is a keen demand for grass, particularly in or near towns, for the grazing of horses and ponies. Prices of up to £175 per acre per season can in certain circumstances be obtained, but the more usual basis of charge is a rate per head per week.

In order to retain the VP value, it is important, in the case of both these lettings and grazing sales, that there is a vacant period (preferably not less than one month during the calendar year).

Lettings for more than 12 but less than 24 months

The courts have held (see *Gladstone* v *Bower* [1960] 2 QB 384) that an owner may permit the occupation of agricultural land and buildings for more than 12 but less than 24 months without thereby creating an annual Agricultural Holdings Act tenancy. The content and structure of agreements for this type of letting, however, require specialist advice and may not be acceptable in Scotland.

Accommodation land can provide a useful investment for comparatively small sums (£5,000 to £50,000) where VP is retained and amenity occupation enjoyed and where a more speculative and variable rate of return is acceptable to the investor. It is important for the investor to employ professional advisers to prepare agreements and to administer the occupation to ensure that no long-term security is granted to the occupier, thereby destroying the VP premium.

11.5.4 Sporting rights

Sporting rights may be divided into three main categories:

(1) fishing—game and coarse;
(2) shooting—game and rough;
(3) stalking—red and roe deer.

Sporting rights in England and Wales can be a legal estate and are on occasions reserved out of the sale of agricultural land. In Scotland, only salmon fishing rights can form a separate legal estate. In the majority of cases these rights are not a specific investment but form part of an agricultural property investment. In all cases they may be acquired separately from the land for personal use or letting. From 1 April 1989 VAT is payable on that element of the value of a land sale which relates to the value of the sporting facility. It is now accepted that a transaction will only become taxable where a sporting business is concerned. There is a further concession that farm tenants will only be expected to pay VAT on the sporting element of their tenancy agreements if it is greater than 5 per cent of total rent. Customs and Excise have proposed a minimum limit of 2 per cent on all other transactions involving sport.

There is some speculation as to whether the Government has a right under EC legislation to charge VAT on transactions of this nature.

Fishing
Salmon fishing
Capital values of salmon fishing vary enormously according to location but can range up to £6,000 a fish or more. Pollution and salmon disease can have a devastating effect on both rental and capital values. Salmon fisheries cannot be created artificially, although trout and coarse fishing are increasingly being created from man-made lakes and reservoirs.

Trout fishing
This can be on freshwater chalk streams which command the highest rates and prices or on artificial or natural lakes; demand has been high, but there is evidence of some over-supply of man-made trout lakes.

Coarse fishing
This is usually rented by angling associations or smaller syndicates. Prices and rents vary greatly but old ponds may provide a surprisingly large income if let.

Shooting

Shooting rights are readily lettable to the growing numbers of field sports enthusiasts. The shoots may vary from a 2,000 acre grouse and pheasant shoot in the north or east of England which is readily lettable, to a 100 acre rough shoot. Rents for high quality grouse, pheasant and partridge shoots on large (2,000 acre plus) estates can command high prices, while rough shooting can produce a small amount of extra income to the farming business.

Red and roe deer stalking

This is most usually available in Scotland and the north-west. Red deer stalking is much sought after, while roe deer stalking commands lower prices.

General

Sporting rights are much in demand, but, if let away from the land, can have a detrimental effect on rental income and, if game damage is excessive, on farm profits. Best quality fishing, shooting and stalking are all readily saleable and lettable. Poor quality sport is not readily lettable to reputable tenants and is speculative.

The purchase of a sporting investment can provide the investor with a useful income and a retained rod or gun, but management costs are high and income is very susceptible to economic change. Sporting rights can be dealt with in two ways. The investor may:

(1) purchase the land and let the rights, either on a seasonal or daily basis, the latter commanding higher prices but necessitating increased expenditure and supervision; or
(2) purchase the rights (but in Scotland, only of salmon fishing).

In all cases it is important to ensure adequate pedestrian and vehicular access. It is unusual for sporting rights to be acquired as an investment on a tenanted basis, but not uncommon for the investor in land or forestry to supplement the income from the property by letting part or the whole of the sporting rights.

The impact of sporting activities can affect the capital value of an investment, from the point of view not only of the person enjoying the sporting facilities but also of the owner and occupier of the land over which the facilities are enjoyed. Careful investigation must therefore be made into all aspects of these activities before an investment is made.

11.6 Preview of the year ahead

The agricultural property market faces a period of high interest rates, high inflation and continued political pressure. More farmers will be squeezed out of business, but there will be opportunities for others and existing businesses will expand. Moreover, continuing food scares are eroding confidence in the industry.

There is likely to be a firm market for good commercial land in the right areas, but prices for some farms are expected to fall back. The residential element of a farm, and the value of its redundant barns, will no longer add the sort of premium seen in 1988, although location and amenity will be even more important to non-agricultural buyers.

The price difference between poor land and good land will again widen, and although land will not only be bought for agriculture, there may well be bargains for the prudent buyer.

11.7 Miscellaneous direct property investments

11.7.1 Wild life parks, pleasure gardens, riding schools, golf courses and mansion houses

Planning permission is required for wild life parks, pleasure gardens, golf courses and riding schools. Location is of paramount importance since it is essential to be close to urban populations with good road access. Initial development costs are high. It is probable that future legislation and higher design and maintenance standards will further aggravate the position. It is specially important to check the building status for planning purposes since 'listed buildings' are graded under the Town and Country Planning Act 1971 and the Town and Country Planning (Scotland) Act 1972 which impose varying degrees of responsibility on the owner, including the need to obtain permission for demolition, improvements or alterations.

Many large stately homes have been acquired for institutional purposes, such as research centres, out of town offices, training centres and health farms. Houses having historic and amenity value are frequently opened to the public as a trading venture, enabling the owner of the property to continue to live in a family home, with the trading venture supporting the upkeep of the property and its general environment, in addition to the advantages of a 'one estate election'.

Agricultural land, woodlands and miscellaneous 209

An investment of this kind is highly speculative in all but the prime locations. It is more often seen as a means to an end by existing owners rather than as the reason for a purchase.

11.7.2 Stud farms and training establishments

Stud farms

Agricultural land may be developed for the breeding of thoroughbred bloodstock, riding horses or ponies. The demand is increasing since over two million people are now members of the various horse societies. For stud farms in the most favoured locations, such as Newmarket and Lambourn, the demand remains strong, although it has diminished somewhat in locations further from the recognised breeding centres where the main stallions are stabled. The centre of the national bloodstock industry is Newmarket where the National Stud and Tattersalls Sale Paddocks, which have a worldwide reputation, are both based. Stud farms in the favoured areas have commanded a premium over VP farmland of up to 400 per cent, with prices of £5,000–£10,000 per acre not being uncommon.

Investment in racehorses is discussed in Chapter 12.

The environment of a good stud farm is of great importance if the young stock are to grow and develop properly. The type of soil, particularly its need to facilitate the building of bone, is critical and must be free draining. A stud farm normally varies in size from 50 to 250 acres and may be a private stud (where the owner maintains his own animals only) or a public stud (where one or more stallions are kept and the mares visit during the foaling and covering season).

Stables must be of high standard with special boxes and facilities for foaling purposes. The cost of putting up post and rail fencing is high because of the need for small paddocks and double fences. In some cases it is cheaper to buy farmland for the creation of a stud rather than buy a stud already established.

To establish a stud farm can take up to 20 years in order to allow hedges and shelter belts to mature. Good quality residential accommodation at the farm will be required for the stud groom and other employees: for a medium-sized stud a minimum of five to six houses might be required.

Stud farms usually change hands by private treaty and there is a limited and highly specialised market. Purchasers will usually be closely connected with and interested in the bloodstock industry. It is exceptional for stud farms to be bought as an investment on a tenanted basis.

Training establishments

At various centres in the country, but particularly at Newmarket and Lambourn, there are established training centres. Training establishments usually comprise a house in which the trainer lives, together with a number of cottages and hostels for grooms; a minimum of 15 boxes and accompanying food and hay stores; and in many cases special open and covered exercising areas.

There was some doubt about whether or not Agricultural Property Relief for CTT purposes applied to stud farms. The Finance Act 1984 provided (retrospectively to March 1981) that breeding and rearing horses on a stud farm qualifies as 'agriculture' and that any buildings used for such activities qualify as 'farm buildings'.

11.7.3 Caravan and camping sites and mobile home parks

These properties are usually located at or near seaside areas or in areas of scenic beauty. Mobile home parks may be for permanent (all year round) occupation in certain areas specified by local councils. Planning controls are stringent on all large-scale parks or sites. Special facilities are required under the Caravan Sites and Control of Development Act 1960, including washing and toilet facilities, electricity and roads. The Mobile Homes Act 1975 confers on caravan home owners a limited security of tenure.

An investment of this type can be lucrative but is a high risk, demanding considerable pre-acquisition investigation. The Caravan Club provides excellent information on sites and the pitfalls associated with them. Fashions change and the weather greatly affects the income from holiday parks, particularly in coastal areas, where serious storms can result in large losses. The supply of caravans has increased dramatically over the last ten years and with increasingly high prices for hotel and other holiday accommodation this seems likely to be an expanding market.

Agricultural land, woodlands and miscellaneous 211

Sources of further information

Useful addresses

Country Landowners
 Association
16 Belgrave Square
London
SW1X 8PQ

Tel: (071) 235 0511

Department of the
 Environment
2 Marsham Street
London
SW1P 3EB

Tel: (071) 276 3000

Agricultural Mortgage
 Corporation PLC
AMC House
Chanty Street
Andover
Hampshire
SP10 1DP

Tel: (0264) 334344

Ministry of Agriculture,
 Fisheries and Food
Whitehall Place
London
SW1A 2HH

Tel: (071) 270 3000

Agricultural Development and
 Advisory Service (ADAS)
17 Smith Square
London
SW1P 3HX

Tel: (071) 238 3000

Royal Institution of Chartered
 Surveyors (RICS)
12 Great George Street
London
SW1P 3AD

Tel: (071) 222 7000

Incorporated Society of Valuers
 and Auctioneers
3 Cadogan Gate
London
SW1X 0AS

Tel: (071) 235 2282

National Association of Estate
 Agents
21 Jury Street
Warwick
CV34 4EH

Tel: (0926) 496800

Forestry Commission
231 Corstorphine Road
Edinburgh
EH12 7AT

Tel: (031) 334 0303

Development Land Tax Office
Corporation House
73–75 Albert Road
Middlesbrough
Cleveland
TS1 2RY

Tel: (0642) 241144

Royal Institution of Chartered
 Surveyors (Scottish Branch)
7–9 Manor Place
Edinburgh
EH3 7DN

Tel: (031) 225 7078

Department of Agriculture and
 Fisheries for Scotland
Pentland House
Robb's Loan
Edinburgh

Tel: (031) 556 8400

Caravan Club
East Grinstead House
East Grinstead
West Sussex
RH19 1UA

Tel: (0342) 326944

Food From Britain
301–344 Market Towers
New Covent Garden Market
London
SW8 5NQ

Tel: (071) 720 2144

Rural Development
 Commission
141 Castle Street
Salisbury
Wiltshire
SP1 3TP

Tel: (0722) 336255

12 Business ventures (without participation in management)

John W Shock, MA (Cantab), FCA, Barrister

12.1 Introduction

There are always people with experience and no money looking for people with money and no experience. At the end of the day the former sometimes have the money and the latter have had the experience. That is not to say that, in general terms, such arrangements should always be avoided. There are plenty of good ideas which need financing and the rewards to the investor can be substantial, but such investments call for faith in someone else's judgment, nerves of steel and an instinct for gambling. Many ventures have turned out well after being (sometimes more than once) on the verge of disaster. Those who do not like walking along the edge of a precipice should keep to gentler paths.

The seeker after finance will often paint the picture of his prospects in rosy colours, not through dishonesty but because of enthusiasm, and such enthusiasm should always be discounted. Unfortunately it is often highly contagious, so that impersonal, dispassionate, professional advice is essential. The pitfalls should be considered every bit as carefully as the opportunities. It is easier to lose money than to make it; but money is seldom to be made without accepting an element of chance.

In some cases money, once put into a venture, is effectively locked in, come what may. At best it may be possible to withdraw it only at considerable cost. On the other hand, by good judgment and good luck (and any successful venture requires both), there are fortunes to be made. The essential feature of the investments considered in this chapter is that the investor relies wholly on the expertise of someone else—company director, active partner, racehorse trainer and so on—and will probably be involved in matters of which he is ignorant or, at least, inexperienced.

It must never be forgotten that taxation will make inroads into both income and capital gains, and, in this respect, professional advice should always be taken. There may be alternative ways of making investments so that, with this in mind, every scheme requires careful expert consideration. Equally, if losses are incurred, steps should be taken to see that the maximum tax advantage is obtained. The advice of an accountant or a solicitor or probably both can be invaluable, not only in dealing with legal and financial problems that are puzzling the prospective investor but often also in pointing out problems of which the layman may be totally unaware. The effects of taxation are touched on in the following sections, but complex problems can arise which it is impossible to deal with briefly. In every case the solution will depend upon the individual facts.

1981 saw the introduction of the 'Business Start-up Scheme' intended for the encouragement of investment in companies starting new businesses. Provided that the investment complied with the numerous, rigorous and complex provisions set out in no less than 16 sections of and two Schedules to the Finance Act 1981, the amount invested could be deducted from the income of the investor in computing his income tax liability. The scheme was superseded by the 'Business Expansion Scheme' which, while similar in concept, is more generous in amount, wider in its application and subject to even more complicated legal rules set out in ss 289–312 of the Income and Corporation Taxes Act 1988. The scheme has, in many cases, been viewed as a tax-saving vehicle rather than a way to take a stake in new ventures. Although the avoidance of tax is the inducement to make such investments, the legislation provides that, if such avoidance is the main purpose of the investment, the relief will not be given. This might be thought to be carrying the Treasury's anti-avoidance obsession to absurd lengths and it may be that an entirely new approach to the matter is now desirable.

The view is sometimes held that professional advice is an expensive luxury which can be dispensed with. Nothing could be further from the truth. If it seems expensive it is because the mass of all-pervading legislation of recent years has made it dangerous to take any steps in commerce (or indeed in much else) without considering the application of statute law, Statutory Instruments and regulations. Professional advice taken at the outset will often avoid difficulties and disputes at a later stage which may well prove far more expensive in legal costs.

12.2 Highlights of the previous year

In relation to buying a share in a racehorse, the Jockey Club ceased to register new syndicates and now requires such a transaction to be undertaken by way of a partnership of which each partner is a registered owner. As to the Business Expansion Scheme, the earliest issues have now passed the five year mark and it has been revealed that some 36 per cent of the 1983–84 issues failed, losing about £15.5m. About 20 per cent of the 1984–85 issues are said to have failed, losing a further £11.5m. Later issues seem to be faring rather better. In the theatre there has been a substantial (and expensive) set of flops, some on a grand scale. At Lloyd's, in 1989, over 2,300 names resigned making some 4,000 resignations in the last two years, whilst the number of new names was the lowest on record. The chairman of Lloyd's Underwriting Association, Mr John Gordon, said: 'Lloyd's is not for the fainthearted.'

12.3 Minority holdings in private companies

12.3.1 Introduction

It was for many years a feature of company law that a private company was one which restricted the transfer of its shares and any company which did not do so was a public company. Under the Companies Act 1980 (a statute enacted largely as a move towards European uniformity) this distinction was swept away and although the words 'public' and 'private' are retained, their meanings are now quite different. A public company is defined in the Companies Act 1985 (a consolidating Act bringing together the provisions of the Companies Acts of 1948, 1967, 1976, 1980 and 1981) and any company not within that definition will be a private company. The principal distinction is that a public company (denoted at the end of its name by the letters 'plc' or by the words 'public limited company') must have an authorised and allotted minimum share capital which is at present £50,000 but which may be altered by Statutory Instrument by the Secretary of State. At least one quarter of that allotted share capital of a public company must be paid up before it can commence business. No such minimum capital requirements exist in relation to private companies. A company need no longer restrict the transfer of its shares to be a private company under the new Act. References in this part of the chapter to 'private companies' are intended, generally, to refer to the smaller family company where control rests in the hands of a few shareholders who are probably the directors or related to the directors. As regards the transfer of shares see **12.3.4**.

A minority holding in a private company may be acquired in a number of ways: it may be inherited; it may be bought from an existing shareholder; it may arise when a company is newly formed to undertake the starting of a business venture; or it may arise on the allotment of shares by a company taking over an existing company or undertaking.

A minority holding is, for the purpose of this chapter, any holding of shares or other securities which does not give the holder control of the company, and thus includes a holding of non-voting shares or debentures. Assuming that a company has shares of one class only of which each has one vote, a holding of less than 50 per cent is a minority holding. However, in some companies there are different classes of shares and shares of one class only, for example, might carry a vote, the others carrying no vote or giving the right to vote on certain specified matters only. In other companies there may be one class of shares carrying one vote each and another class of which the shares carry a hundred votes each, so that a holding, in nominal value, of more than half the company's issued capital does not necessarily carry control. Careful scrutiny of the company's capital structure is vital before making an investment in a private company.

12.3.2 Powers of the minority

At general meetings of a company, a vote is first taken by a show of hands (subject to anything in the articles of association), giving each member personally present one vote regardless of the size of his holding. At common law any one member may demand a poll, the votes then being counted, normally on the basis of one for each share held. The articles may include a requirement that a poll must be demanded by more than one member, but such a requirement is limited by s 373 of the Companies Act 1985 so that, except for certain purposes, an article is void if it requires the demand for a poll to be made by more than five members, or the holders of more than one-tenth of the voting rights, or the holders of more than one-tenth of the paid-up capital entitled to vote.

When a poll is held, each member has (in the absence of any contrary provision in the articles) one vote for each share held. Thus on a poll, one member holding 60 per cent of the issued shares will be able to outvote a dozen members holding the other 40 per cent between them.

An ordinary resolution requires a simple majority of members voting, so that a minority shareholder cannot, in the face of determined opposition, prevent its being passed. However, a special or extraordinary resolution, which is necessary for certain fundamental decisions, requires a majority of three-quarters of members voting, so that on a poll, where each share carries a vote, the holder of 40 per cent of the issued shares, although a minority shareholder, could block such a resolution. An extraordinary resolution is required for, among other things, winding up a company that cannot, by reason of its liabilities, continue in business, and the articles of the company may require such a resolution for various other purposes. A special resolution is necessary for, *inter alia*:

(1) the alteration of a company's objects (although, in that case, the holders of not less than 15 per cent of the issued share capital may apply to the court to have the alteration cancelled);
(2) the alteration of a company's articles;
(3) the change of a company's name (subject to the approval of the Department of Trade and Industry);
(4) a reduction of capital (subject to the approval of the court);
(5) the re-registration of a public company as private or a private company as public under the 1985 Act;
(6) the re-registration of an unlimited company as limited; and
(7) the winding up of a company voluntarily.

In addition to considering the effective powers of the majority, it must be remembered that the day to day running of the company's business is in the hands of the directors. As a last resort, majority shareholders can remove and appoint directors; minority shareholders cannot. In this connection it is important to note that most companies' articles of association preclude the payment of a dividend in excess of that recommended by the directors. If, therefore, the directors feel it is desirable for any reason to retain the profits, or the bulk of the profits, within the company rather than distribute them by way of dividend, the minority shareholder may find that he is not receiving a satisfactory return on his investment and, even with the assistance of the majority shareholders, there may be little he can effectively do about it.

Arising out of the matters discussed in the previous paragraph, it will be appreciated that the majority could deal with the affairs of a company in a way which might be to the detriment of the interest of the minority, particularly where the minority controls 25 per cent or less of the voting power. The law, however, provides protection for an oppressed minority in two ways. First, the minority may petition the court to wind-up the company on the grounds that it is just and equitable to do so. This is, in many cases, an unsatisfactory course to pursue since, at the end of the day, the assets will be sold at their break-up value, the goodwill will disappear and the minority will not have achieved its object, namely that the company should continue to operate but that its interests should be safeguarded. Secondly, the minority may petition the court for relief under s 459 of the Companies Act 1985.

Protection under the 1948 Act was provided where the court was of the opinion that the affairs of the company were being conducted in a manner oppressive to some part of the members (including the petitioner) and that to wind-up the company would unfairly prejudice that part of the members although the facts would justify winding-up on the grounds that to wind-up would be just and equitable. The court, on being so persuaded, could make any order which it thought fit. There is a considerable body of authority as to what constitutes oppression for this purpose.

Under s 459 of the Companies Act 1985, protection is afforded by the court if it is satisfied that the conduct of the company's affairs is 'unfairly prejudicial to the interests' of some part of the members. A petition may also be brought under this provision based on 'any actual or proposed act or omission' of the company. The meaning of 'unfairly prejudicial' is not defined and awaits judicial interpretation.

12.3.3 Liability for uncalled capital

The essential feature of a limited company is that the liability of its shareholders is limited to the capital they put in or agree to put in, and no further demands can be made on them by the company or its creditors except where shares are issued which are not fully paid. The holder of such shares may be called upon by the company to pay up the unpaid balance, and failure to pay on a call may result in forfeiture of the shares. Any holder of partly-paid shares must therefore always bear in mind that a contingent liability attaches to them. If the additional capital is required for development of the business, it will probably be all to the good. It sometimes happens though, that it is needed because the company is in difficulties and may amount to throwing good money after bad.

12.3.4 Transfer of shares

Difficulties may arise in connection with the disposal of a minority holding of shares in a private company. One of the hallmarks of a private company under the Companies Act 1948 was that it restricted transfers of its shares, and if the articles did not so provide, it was not a private company. The usual form, following reg 3 of Table A in Pt II of Sched 1 to the Companies Act 1948, provided that 'the directors may, in their absolute discretion and without assigning any reason therefore, decline to register any transfer of any share, whether or not it is a fully paid share.' It follows that, in such cases, the board must approve the proposed new shareholder and, where the articles are in the form set out above, the court will not inquire into the directors' reasons for refusing to register a transfer if none are given. Thus, whatever the value of the shares might be in terms of the assets and liabilities disclosed in the company's balance sheet, it may well be difficult to find a purchaser at anything approaching that value. The Companies Act 1948, s 28, which made restrictions on transfers essential for a private company, was repealed by the Companies Act 1980. There is nothing to prevent a private company from imposing such a restriction in its articles and in the case of any company whose articles already include it it will remain in force unless the articles are amended. The articles of any company in which it is proposed to invest should therefore be examined with this point in view. The new Table A (under the Companies Act 1985), which sets out a suggested format for the articles of association of a company, does not include any provisions relating to the refusal of directors to register a transfer of fully paid shares, but it is not unusual to see an express provision to the effect included in the articles of association of private companies.

Dealing with shares in a private company is often also restricted by a provision in the articles that a member wishing to dispose of his shares must first offer them to the other members at their fair value which is frequently determined in the absence of agreement between the intending seller and the directors, by the auditors, or an independent chartered accountant. The articles should therefore be examined with this in mind and also with a view to discovering whether, on death, a member's shares may pass to his personal representatives to be dealt with according to his will. In addition a minority shareholder who is an employee might be required under the articles of association to transfer his shares on ceasing to be employed by the company in question.

12.3.5 Loans

An investor may prefer to put money into a company by way of loan rather than by purchasing shares. A loan may be charged on all or any of the company's assets or its uncalled capital, or may be on a debenture, secured or unsecured. The nature of a debenture is difficult to define and Lindley J said in *British India Steam Navigation Co v IRC* (1881) 7 QBD 165, at p 172, '... what the correct meaning of "debenture" is I do not know. I do not find anywhere any precise definition of it'.

It is always necessary to proceed with caution when lending to a company. Its memorandum and articles should be inspected to ensure that the borrowing is intra vires, and the terms of any loan or debenture must be clearly set out and agreed. Independent professional advice is essential. In particular, where the lender is the settlor in relation to a settlement of which the trustees or a beneficiary are participators of the company, quite unexpected income tax liabilities may arise under s 677 of the Income and Corporation Taxes Act 1988 when the loan is repaid.

Money invested in a company by way of loan will normally entitle the lender to interest at a fixed rate. If the company fails he should not, if adequately secured, be out of pocket: if the company prospers he will receive his interest regularly, and in due course his loan will be repaid, but he will not share in the prosperity of the undertaking.

12.3.6 Taxation

Two applications of taxation must be borne in mind. First, when a dividend is received, a 'tax credit' is given equal in amount to the income tax at the basic rate which would be payable on the aggregate of the dividend and the tax credit. The company thereupon becomes liable to pay advance corporation tax on the dividend at a rate equal to the basic rate of income tax on that aggregate, such advance corporation tax ranking as a credit against the company's corporation tax liability. In addition, income tax may be payable at a higher rate depending upon the shareholder's total income. At the top rate the tax payable may be 40 per cent, leaving the investor with 60 per cent of his gross investment income—a considerable improvement on the position before 1979/80 when the top rate was 98 per cent.

Secondly, if and when shares are disposed of and a chargeable gain results, capital gains tax becomes payable. The provisions of the Finance Act 1988 include the change of the base date from 1965 to 1982, the reduction of the exempt amount to £5,000 and the unification of rates of tax on income and capital gains. A notional capital gain may arise where shares are given away or disposed of for consideration which is less than their full open-market value as though they had been sold for their full value but, generally, the gain arising could, before 15 March 1989 be carried forward and, provided the appropriate election was made, would not be taxed until the recipient would dispose of them. The Finance Act 1989 abolished this right to defer the payment of tax except in the cases of a gift of business assets, of property where the gift is subject to an immediate charge to inheritance tax and a few others.

A chargeable gain (or allowable loss) may arise on the disposal of a debt on a security. 'Security' is defined in the Capital Gains Tax Act 1979 as including loan stock and certain similar securities whether secured or unsecured. Accordingly, it is possible to have a debt on a security which is not secured (eg, an unsecured debenture) or a secured debt which is not a debt on a security (eg, a mortgage debt). There are judicial authorities on the meaning of a debt on a security too numerous to be discussed at length here. This is a matter on which legal advice should be sought.

Even where a debt does not fall within the category considered above, it may in certain circumstances entitle the lender to relief as a capital loss if it becomes irrecoverable. The conditions which render the loan a qualifying loan for this purpose are to be found in s 136 of the Capital Gains Tax Act 1979. These are as follows:

(1) the money lent must be used by the borrower wholly for the purposes of a trade carried on by him or for the setting up of a trade subsequently carried on by him;
(2) the borrower must be resident in the UK. The Act does not say at what point the borrower must be so resident and neither does it require the business to be carried on here; and
(3) the debt must not be a debt on a security. If it is it will fall within the provisions referred to previously.

Where an individual has subscribed for shares in a qualifying trading company and he incurs an allowable loss on disposing of the shares, he may claim relief from income tax instead of capital gains tax. This provision (to be found in s 574 of the Income and Corporation Taxes Act 1988 and generally known as the 'Venture Capital Scheme') applies to disposals on or after 6 April 1980. It must be noted that this relief applies only where the taxpayer has subscribed for the shares and not where he had bought them from another shareholder, unless that other is his or her spouse and acquired the shares by subscription. It applies only to ordinary share capital and stock and the company must be a 'qualifying trading company' in the terms of the definition provided by the section, that is to say:

(1) it must exist wholly or mainly for the purpose of carrying on a trade (other than dealing in shares, securities, land or commodity futures);
(2) it must be resident in the United Kingdom from its incorporation until the date on which the shares or stock are disposed of; and
(3) none of its shares or stock must have been quoted on a

recognised Stock Exchange at any time since 12 months before the date on which the shares or stock were issued.

The relief will be given if the loss results from a sale at arm's length for full consideration, a distribution on a winding-up or a claim that the value has become negligible giving rise to a deemed disposal. Partial claims are not allowed and if the loss exceeds income for the year of claim the excess may either be carried forward or set off against capital gains. Information may be obtained from the Small Firms Service of the Department of Trade and Industry.

Interest paid on a loan to an individual is eligible for tax relief only if the money borrowed is used for certain purposes. These include the acquisition of an interest in a close company or in a partnership. In the case of a close company it must be used for the purchase of ordinary shares in a trading or estate company or for the making of a loan to such a company to be used wholly and exclusively for the company's business. The individual will be entitled to the relief if: (1) he holds not less than 5 per cent of the company's ordinary share capital; or (2) he holds some part thereof, however small, and has in the period between the application of the loan and the payment of the interest been personally engaged in the conduct of the business in the case of a partnership, and 'worked for the greater part of his time in the actual management or conduct of the company', in the case of a company. During the same period he must not have recovered any capital from the company or partnership. For details of the complex provisions regarding this tax relief reference must be made to ss 360 and 362 of the Income and Corporation Taxes Act 1988.

12.3.7 Conclusion

It will be appreciated that many problems may arise in connection with company law and tax law. The latter in particular has become a matter of great complexity and specialist advice should always be taken. When all the legal hurdles are overcome, the sky's the limit, and if all goes well, the end result may be that the company 'goes public' or is taken over by a public company, leaving the shareholder with readily realisable shares in a company which may be or become a household word.

12.4 Private investment companies

The first part of this chapter is concerned primarily with trading companies, but much of what has been said applies equally to private investment companies. These are companies which do not carry on a trade but invest, usually either in real property or in stock, shares and similar securities, and receive rents, dividends and interest. The line between property investment and property dealing companies is a difficult one to draw and presents a problem which the courts have often been called upon to solve. Basically, the question is one of intention, but it is not always easy to decide how the available evidence (which may be scanty) should be interpreted. Some of the differences between dealing or trading companies on the one hand and investment companies on the other are dealt with below.

First, when a property is disposed of at a gain, the gain in the hands of a dealing company is part of its trading profit and is taxed at the appropriate rate of corporation tax. Where the disposal is made by an investment company, the gain may be a chargeable gain as defined for capital gains tax purposes and taxed as such. Secondly, an investment company is charged to corporation tax prima facie on the full amount of its income and must make a management expenses claim by virtue of which a deduction is allowed for the cost of management. Management expenses (nowhere defined in the legislation) are usually less than the expenses allowable against trading profits. Thirdly, an investment company, if it is a 'close investment-holding company', will be less favourably treated than a trading company as regards distributions. Under the Finance Act 1989 such a company will will be liable to corporation tax at 35 per cent and tax credits may be restricted in certain cases.

A further disadvantage which attaches to an investment company (or indeed to any company which makes chargeable gains) is that a double tax liability may arise on capital gains. On the sale of an asset by the company, tax becomes payable (as explained above) on the chargeable gain. That net gain increases the assets of the company and hence the value of the member's shares in it. On a disposal of those shares by him a further chargeable gain may arise.

A private investment company will have larger funds at its disposal than each individual shareholder and may thereby take advantage of opportunities not presented to the smaller investor. Furthermore, the minimum commission charged by a stockbroker may add disproportionately to the cost of investments of the smaller investor. Both these advantages, however, attach to any method by which small investors join together. So long as the basic agreement governing the project is carefully drawn up and fully understood by all those co-operating, a joint co-operative investment scheme may avoid the drawbacks of a private investment company while at the same time possessing many of the advantages. The taxation of unapproved investment companies (whether private or public) and their shareholders is discussed in Chapter 7, **7.7**.

12.5 Business Expansion Scheme

12.5.1 Introduction

The Business Start-up Scheme, introduced in the Finance Act 1981, was intended to encourage investment in new business activities by granting income tax relief on the amount invested. For an individual paying tax at the higher rates the benefit could be considerable. A major preoccupation of those designing the scheme was that it should not be used as a vehicle for tax avoidance, with the result that a perilous minefield awaited those who attempted to negotiate it without the most careful and expert guidance.

The scheme was intended to operate in relation to shares issued after 5 April 1981 and before 6 April 1984. In the event, it ceased to operate on 5 April 1983, having been replaced by the Business Expansion Scheme explained in some detail below.

The Business Expansion Scheme, introduced by Finance Act 1983 (where it is referred to as 'Relief for investment in corporate trades') took effect in relation to shares issued on or after 6 April 1983. As in the case of the earlier scheme, numerous and complex conditions must be complied with in relation to the individual, the company, the trade and the investment.

In contrast to the earlier Business Start-up Scheme, the present scheme is not restricted in its application to new trades and new companies. In order to assist advisers dealing with the matter, the provisions are dealt with below. Further information may be obtained from the Inland Revenue's leaflet, *The Business Expansion Scheme* (IR 51) and the current legislation should always be referred to or professional advice sought. Business Expansion Scheme legislation was published by the Inland Revenue in a booklet in 1989.

The relief is given by deducting from the investor's total income in the year of assessment in which the shares are issued, an amount equal to the amount subscribed for the shares. The maximum allowance is £40,000. Relief is not given for an investment of less than £500 unless made through an approved investment fund. From 1990–91 the £40,000 limit applies to husband and wife separately. In relation to investments made after 5 April 1987, provision is made for a carry back to the previous tax year of one-half of the relief due (up to a maximum of £5,000) on investments made during the first half of a tax year. Under SI 1990 No 862 the previous limit of £500,000 investment in any one company is increased to £750,000 from 1 May 1990. The higher limit of £5 million for investment in qualifying companies providing private rented housing or letting ships of charter remains.

It must be borne in mind that one of the conditions for the granting of this relief is that the company must, throughout the relevant period (see **12.5.4**), be unquoted. If, at the end of the five year period, the company is still unquoted the investor may find himself effectively locked in. Of some 500 companies funded under the scheme in 1983–84 and 1984–85 only about 20 have become quoted companies. If there is no quotation and the investor cannot find a purchaser for his shares he can realise his investment only if the company either disposes of its assets and winds up or sells its undertaking to a quoted company, so that its shareholders finish up with either quoted shares or cash. The directors may, however, be reluctant to accept the loss of directorships which would follow a winding-up and might well follow a take-over.

It must also be remembered that the Business Expansion Scheme was introduced to encourage the investment of risk capital and that that is exactly what such an investment is. Many new companies launched under the scheme have failed. Tax benefits may follow an investment under the scheme but there is no certainty that the investment will be successful. Sponsors of issues have constantly sought ways of making them more secure without taking them outside the ambit of the relief. Companies letting properties on assured tenancies were brought within the scheme to encourage the building of properties to let and a large proportion of scheme issues have since related to such companies. Companies in other commercial enterprises often have difficulty in producing a prospectus which is of much use to the prospective investor. Projections, by directors, of future profits should be read with caution. The cost of such professional reports as are required for a public flotation will often be prohibitive for new, small and possibly speculative enterprises.

12.5.2 Tax relief available

If all the conditions set out in **12.5.3** are complied with, a claim for relief may be made. It must be accompanied by a certificate from the company (authorised by the Inspector of Taxes) to the effect that it has, at all necessary times complied with the conditions set out in **12.5.4**. The claim may be made at any time after the company has carried on the qualifying trade or activity for four months and must be made not later than two years after the end of the year of assessment in which the shares were issued. If the four month period expires after the end of that year, it must be made within two years after the end of that period.

If a claim is allowed before the end of the qualifying period (which has different meanings for different purposes: see **12.5.3** and **12.5.4**) and any subsequent event results in a contravention of any of the conditions, the relief will be withdrawn. If the company fails to carry on the trade for four months by reason of a winding-up or dissolution for bona fide commercial reasons and not as part of a tax-saving scheme, the claim will not fail for that reason. Provision is made in the legislation requiring that information leading to a loss of relief must be sent to the Revenue.

12.5.3 Individuals eligible for relief

For an individual to be entitled to the relief under the Business Expansion Scheme he had originally to be resident and ordinarily resident in the United Kingdom throughout the year of assessment in which the shares were issued. This rule has been relaxed and it is sufficient if he is resident and ordinarily resident here at the time of issue (regardless of any change taking place during the year) or if he is a Crown employee serving overseas. He must not be 'connected with' the company at any time during the 'relevant period' (as defined at the end of this section).

The words 'connected with' are given a very wide meaning. An individual is connected with a company if:

(1) he or an associate (defined below) is an employee of the company or of its partner, or is himself its partner or is a paid director of the company or of a company which is in partnership with it;
(2) he possesses (directly or indirectly) or is entitled to acquire more than 30 per cent of the company's issued ordinary share capital, loan capital and issued share capital, voting rights or such rights as would entitle him to more than 30 per cent of the assets available to equity holders on a winding-up;
(3) he has power to secure that the affairs of the company are conducted in accordance with his wishes by means of the holding of shares or the possession of voting power of that or another company or by virtue of any power in the articles or other document regulating that or any other company; or

(4) he is a party to a reciprocal arrangement under which some other person subscribes for shares in a company with which the individual (or any other individual who is a party to the arrangement) is connected.

For the purposes of (1) above, 'associate' means:

(1) the husband or wife, parent or remoter forebear, child or remoter issue or any partner of the individual;
(2) a trustee of any settlement in relation to which the settlor is or was the individual or any of the persons mentioned in (1) (other than a partner), whether living or dead; or
(3) where the individual is interested in any shares or obligations of the company which are (with certain exceptions) subject to a trust or form part of a deceased's estate, any other person interested therein. It may, in this connection, be difficult to ascertain who is an associate and who is not.

For the purposes of eligible relief the 'relevant period' means the period beginning with the incorporation of the company and ending five years after the issue of the shares. If the company was incorporated more than two years before the date of issue, the relevant period begins two years before that date. It must be noted that for other purposes 'relevant period' has a different meaning: see below.

12.5.4 Qualifying companies

Two expressions used in connection with the qualification of a company require explanation.

(1) The 'relevant period'. This has different meanings in different contexts, one of which is set out in **12.5.3**. In relation to 'qualifying companies' and 'qualifying trades' it means the period of three years beginning with the issue of the shares or, if the company was not at the time of such issue carrying on a qualifying trade, the period of three years from the commencement of such a trade.
(2) A 'qualifying subsidiary'. This means a subsidiary company which is not less than 90 per cent owned and controlled by the parent company, no arrangements being in existence by virtue of which it could cease to be so owned and controlled. That condition must be satisfied until the end of the 'relevant period' unless there is an earlier winding-up or dissolution for bona fide commercial reasons which is not part of a tax-avoidance arrangement and on which the subsidiary's net assets are

distributed not more than three years after the commencement of the winding-up. The subsidiary must exist wholly or substantially to carry on qualifying activities or be a 'dormant' company ie, one which has no corporation tax profits and does not include the making of investments as part of its business.

The conditions to be complied with by the company are as follows:

(1) it must be incorporated in the United Kingdom;
(2) it must, throughout the 'relevant period' be an unquoted company resident in the UK and nowhere else. Dual residence is a disqualification;
(3) throughout the 'relevant period', the company must exist wholly or (in the words of the Act) 'substantially wholly' for the purpose of carrying on wholly or mainly in the UK one or more 'qualifying trades' (see **12.5.5**) or must carry on a business which consists wholly of either:
    (a) holding shares or securities of, or making loans to, one or more 'qualifying subsidiaries' (see (2) above); or
    (b) both (a) *and* the carrying on wholly or mainly in the UK or one or more 'qualifying trades'.
(4) the company's share capital must not, at any time in the 'relevant period' include any issued shares that are not fully paid up;
(5) the company must not, at any time in the relevant period, control (whether alone or with any connected person) another company or have a 51 per cent subsidiary or be controlled by another company (whether alone or with a connected person) or be a 51 per cent subsidiary nor must any arrangements be in existence at any time during the relevant period which could bring the company within any of the prohibited situations. An exception is made, however, for companies having subsidiaries which are themselves qualifying companies under (2) above.
(6) The company's interest in land must not exceed one-half of its total assets. The value of the company's land may increase or that of its other assets may fall (or both) and that relief may thus be lost. This restriction does not apply to 'assured tenancy scheme' companies (see **12.5.6**).

12.5.5 Qualifying trades

Some guidance has been given by the Revenue, in a Statement of Practice dated 12 September 1986, as to what, in their view, is meant by carrying on a trade 'wholly or mainly in the United Kingdom' referred to in point (3), above. Each case will be determined on its facts including the 'totality of the activities of the trade'. Thus, regard will be had to such factors as the location of capital assets, and the places where purchasing, manufacturing, selling and other things are done. The carrying on of some activities outside the United Kingdom will not disqualify the company if, in the words of the Revenue, 'over one-half of the aggregate of these activities takes place within the country'. The phrase 'over one-half' suggests, that some precise measurement must be possible. The Statement of Practice goes on to say that a company would not be excluded from relief solely because its output is exported, or its raw materials imported, or storage or marketing facilities exist overseas.

A 'qualifying trade' is one which does not to any substantial extent comprise:

(1) dealing in commodities, shares, securities, land or futures;
(2) dealing in goods otherwise than in an ordinary trade of wholesale or retail distribution;
(3) banking, insurance, moneylending, debt-factoring, hire-purchase financing or other financial activities;
(4) leasing, chartering ships, or hiring;
(5) receiving royalties or licence fees;
(6) providing legal or accountancy services;
(7) providing services of the nature of those set out in (1) to (6) for a trade carried on by any person who controls the trade carried on by the company; or
(8) oil extraction activities.

As to (5) above, a trade which consists to a substantial extent of the receiving of royalties or licence fees is not disqualified if the company carrying on the trade is engaged, throughout the relevant period in the production of films or in research and development and if all royalties and licence fees received by it in that period are in respect of films produced by it or of sound recordings or other products arising from such films or from research and development.

The trade must be carried on on a commercial basis and with a view to realising profits. It must have been carried on by the company for four months before the relief will be allowed and, if not carried on at the time of the issue, must be begun within two years thereafter.

An extension of the scheme was introduced in the Finance Act 1988 to cover companies providing rented housing under the new assured tenancy arrangements (see **12.5.6**).

12.5.6 Assured tenancy schemes

The Finance Act 1988 extended the Business Expansion Scheme to cover companies providing, maintaining and letting properties on assured tenancies under the Housing Act 1988. The relevant provisions apply to shares issued up to the end of 1993 only. In relation to such share issues some of the usual restrictions (eg, as to holdings of land and trades carried on by companies) do not apply. Such schemes have generated a good deal of interest but their success will depend on, among other things, the future of property prices. It must also be recognised that it may prove difficult for investors to realise their investment after five years, particularly if there is a sitting tenant. However, the ability to charge a market rent may make the property an attractive continuing investment and the existence of these schemes may stimulate the market for tenanted property.

A number of these schemes were launched as a series of close companies which offered the investor the additional incentive of tax relief on the interest on money borrowed to make the investment. Such relief was, under the Finance Act 1989, withdrawn in relation to business expansion. This, coupled with concern over the company's tax position as a consequence of the abolition of the apportionment rules has led to many of these schemes being withdrawn from the market.

12.5.7 Qualifying investments

For the investment to qualify for relief it must itself comply with a number of conditions:

(1) it must be made by the individual on his own behalf;
(2) the shares must be taken by subscription and not by purchase from an existing shareholder;
(3) the shares must be new ordinary shares which, throughout the five years from the date of issue, carry no present or future preferential rights to dividends, assets on a winding-up, or to redemption; and
(4) the shares must be issued for the purpose of raising money for a qualifying trade or activity carried on, or to be carried on, by the company.

Relief will not be given to any individual shareholder if at any time in the relevant period (as defined in **12.5.4**), the company in which he holds shares begins to carry on as its trade, or part of its trade, a trade which was previously carried on at any time in that period otherwise than by the company or any of its subsidiaries, or if it acquires all or most of the assets used for the purposes of a trade so carried on. This applies where the individual mentioned above is a person or one of a group of persons who:

(1) owned, at any time in the relevant period, more than a half share in the trade as previously carried on and owns at any such time more than a half share in the trade subsequently carried on by the company; or
(2) controlled another company previously carrying on the trade and controls, or has at any time in the relevant period controlled the company.

It does not apply to assured tenancy schemes.

Nor will relief be given to an individual where the company comes to acquire all the issued share capital of another company at any time during the relevant period and the individual (or a group of persons of which he is one) at any such time controlled both companies.

Although the investment, to qualify for relief, must be made by an individual, it may be made through an approved investment fund. Particulars regarding some of such funds are obtainable from the British Venture Capital Association.

12.5.8 Withdrawal of relief

If, within five years of the issue of shares in respect of which an individual has received relief, he sells all or any of them, the effect depends upon whether or not such sale is at arm's length. If it is, the relief is reduced by the amount of the consideration received. If it is not at arm's length, the whole of the relief is withdrawn.

Relief is also withdrawn if, during the relevant period defined in **12.5.3** the individual 'receives any value' from the company. The relief is reduced by the amount of the value received. In general terms, value is received when:

(1) the company redeems any capital held by the individual;
(2) the company repays a debt owed to him other than a debt which was incurred by the company;
(3) the company pays the individual for giving up his right to a debt;
(4) the company releases or waives a liability due by him or discharges his liability to a third party;
(5) the company makes a loan to him;
(6) the company provides him with any benefit or facility;

(7) the company transfers an asset to him for less than its market value or acquires one from him for more than that value;
(8) the company makes any payment to him other than by way of reasonable remuneration, interest, dividend or reimbursement of expenses or in discharge of an ordinary trade debt; or
(9) any person who is treated as connected with the company:
   (a) purchases any of its share capital belonging to the individual; or
   (b) makes any payment to him for giving up any right in relation to any of the company's share capital.

In either case the value received by the individual is deemed to be equal to the market value of the shares in question.

Relief may also be withdrawn if the company repays, redeems or repurchases any shares or makes a payment for the extinguishment of a right to any shares held by a member other than the claimant.

The comments set out above should be taken as a guide only. They do not cover every detail of the legislation but should help in identifying most of the difficulties to be faced in crossing this morass of regulations.

12.6 Dormant partnerships

12.6.1 Introduction

It is not unusual for a person commencing a trade to find himself short of capital. In such circumstances an investor who is persuaded of the potentiality of the trade may be prepared to put up the capital but not want to play any active part in the carrying on of the business. He will then be a 'dormant' or 'sleeping' partner. Since partners are generally entitled to take part in the running of the business, this arrangement must be the subject of a special agreement.

Unless the business name consists of the names of all the partners, it must comply with the provisions of the Business Names Act 1985. This Act governs names which may and may not be used for business purposes and how and where they must be disclosed. A register of such names was formerly maintained but was closed in February 1982.

12.6.2 Loan creditors

It is important to distinguish a dormant partner from a loan creditor. If the investor receives a fixed rate of interest on his investment he is probably not a partner at all. Under s 2 of the Partnership Act 1890 the receipt of a share of the profits is prima facie evidence of partnership, although the receipt of such a share or of interest at a rate varying with the profits does not of itself make the lender a partner. This apparent contradiction was explained by North J, in *Davis* v *Davis* [1894] 1 Ch 393, and it appears from his judgment that the Act means that all the relevant facts must be taken together, no special weight being attached to the sharing of profits. It is difficult to see how the Act could be intended to mean that, although, in fairness to North J, it is equally difficult to see that it could be intended to mean anything else either. In the majority of cases there will be (and there certainly should be) a written agreement making the position clear. If the agreement so declares and the name of the dormant partner is included in the name of the firm there will be little doubt of the existence of a partnership.

12.6.3 Rights and liabilities

Once it is established that the 'investor' (to use a neutral term) is a dormant partner and not merely a loan creditor, certain rights arise. For example, he will be entitled to inspect and take a copy of the firm's accounts and, in the absence of any agreement to the contrary, to investigate their contents.

A dormant partner is, generally, personally liable for the debts of the firm even if the creditors were unaware of his partnership at the time when the debts arose. This liability extends to the whole of the partner's personal fortune. Such an arrangement can therefore carry considerable personal risk, although this can be curtailed by the formation of a 'limited partnership'.

Under the Limited Partnerships Act 1907 it is possible for a partner to limit his liability to the amount contributed by him to the partnership at its inception, although there must always be at least one partner whose liability is unlimited. The limited partner may not receive any of his capital back so long as the partnership continues, and if any of it is returned to him, his liability up to the amount of his original contribution will remain. He is, of course, entitled to draw out his share of the firm's profits.

A limited partner must always be a dormant partner. Should he take any active part in the running of the business, the limitation of his liability is lost, and it will then extend to the whole of the partnership's debts and to the full extent of his personal assets.

The law relating to dormant partnerships is liberally sprinkled with traps for the unwary, and the law relating to limited partnerships is particularly unsatisfactory. No partnership of any sort should be entered into without taking legal advice, and although the law does not require a partnership agreement to be reduced to writing, it is always desirable that it should be. Whatever the relations may have been at the outset, it is only too easy for the partner entering too readily into informal arrangements to find the whole of his personal estate at risk in respect of liabilities which he played no part in incurring. It is when things start to go wrong that dissensions occur, and by then it may be too late to correct matters which ought to have been dealt with at the outset.

12.6.4 Taxation

A trading partnership, like any other trader, is normally assessed to tax on the basis of the profits of the trading year ending during the tax year prior to the year of assessment. For example, if the accounts are taken to 31 December, the profits for the year ended 31 December 1989 form the basis of the assessment for the tax year 1990/91. This general rule is subject to various complications relating to the opening years, the closing years, changes in partnership treated as a cessation, and losses. Having determined the amount of the assessment for, say 1990/91, that amount is apportioned among the partners in accordance with their profit-sharing arrangements for that year regardless of the way in which they actually shared the profit on which the assessment was based. It will be appreciated that this may lead to inequitable results.

Earned income is defined in s 833(4)(c) of the Income and Corporation Taxes Act 1988 as income which is 'derived by the individual from the carrying on or exercise by him of his trade . . ., in the case of a partnership, as a partner personally acting therein'. Any partnership income not falling within that definition is investment income. Since a dormant partner (whether with limited liability or not) does not, by definition, act personally in the business, it must follow that any income derived from the partnership will be investment income. This will be of significance in relation to retirement pension schemes.

12.7 Membership of Lloyd's

12.7.1 Introduction

Some 300 years ago Edward Lloyd opened a coffee-house in the City which proved to be a popular meeting place for men with an interest in shipping. In 1692 he moved to larger premises on the corner of Lombard Street and Abchurch Lane, where the financial quarter had become well-established, which soon became known as a centre where ship-owners could take insurance cover. With the increasing size of ships and value of cargoes the size of the risks grew and individual underwriters were obliged to join in syndicates, so creating the system which still functions today. Lloyd's itself, as in its coffee-house days, does no more than provide accommodation and facilities for the underwriters; it is not, and never has been, an insurer. Lloyd's was incorporated by Act of Parliament in 1871, and that and later Acts regulate the fundamental rules and authorise the making of by-laws by the members. An Act in 1911 authorised the underwriting of non-marine risks, regularising what had already become well-established practice.

Members of Lloyd's (called 'names') are grouped into syndicates and share in the syndicates' profits or losses. As regards losses, each member of a syndicate is liable only for his agreed share (unlike a partnership loss where each partner is jointly and separately liable for all losses) but that liability extends to the whole of his assets. Generally a name takes no part in managing the affairs of his syndicate. He is thus entirely in the hands of his Underwriting Agent (see **12.7.2**).

Income and gains received by names comprise:

(1) investment income and capital gains on deposits and reserve funds (see **12.7.2**);
(2) investment income and capital gains on premiums received and invested by the syndicate; and
(3) underwriting profits (if any).

It must not be forgotten that capital and underwriting losses may also arise.

Figures are produced three years in arrears. In 1981, 1982 and 1983 there were, overall, losses on underwriting although they were exceeded by total investment income. That trend has now been reversed and in 1984, 1985 and 1986 (the last year for which accounts have been finalised) there have been underwriting profits of, respectively, £138m, £190m and £144m.

There were heavy losses in 1980–82 and it is understood that members of one syndicate made losses averaging some £80,000. Since then the storm of October 1987 resulted in an insured loss estimated at three bn US dollars. In July 1988 the destruction of the Piper Alpha oil production platform and the tragic loss of life resulting from it also resulted in heavy claims. More recently the Lockerbie air crash emphasises the unpredictability of events and the importance of the protection of insurance generally and of Lloyd's in particular. It is estimated that Lloyd's share of the 1990 storm damage is likely to be over £1.5m.

In his report on the 1988 accounts the chairman of Lloyd's described the results for 1986 (the last to be closed) as the 'best ever' and commented that, although the 1987 prospects were encouraging, the next three years' results were likely to be less spectacular. Lloyd's, he said, was, like the rest of the insurance industry, still experiencing severe over-capacity in many areas.

The Lloyd's Act 1982 was a private Act of Parliament designed to assist Lloyd's to set up its own self-regulating system and severe penalites have been imposed in certain cases. Doubts have, however, been expressed as to the efficacy of self-regulation and it is felt in some quarters that Lloyd's should be statutorily controlled by legislation in line with that introduced to control other city institutions. The Trade and Industry Secretary has said that 'if the authorities at Lloyd's do not show a diligent and responsible exercise of the significant powers they already have . . . then I would have no hesitation in initiating legislative action by the government'. Special arrangements have been made to assist members of certain syndicates formerly managed by PCW which lost £73m in 1982 and £143m in 1983.

12.7.2 Application for membership

The aspiring member must satisfy Lloyd's that he is a proper person to join their number. His application form must be accompanied by a nomination form signed by one member as sponsor and by another to whom the applicant is personally known. The application form is posted in the Underwriting Room and the applicant will then be interviewed by a sub-committee. The sub-committee, whatever other questions it may ask, will always ask whether the applicant clearly understands that he will be trading with unlimited liability. The liability is not limited to the wealth shown (see below) nor to the amount of the deposit (see below). In the event of a substantial claim arising, the whole of the applicant's personal estate is at risk.

It is generally recommended that members should spread their risk among a number of syndicates. Membership of one syndicate only may mean a heavy financial loss in the event of a major disaster.

Business ventures (without participation in management)

At an early stage, and certainly before election, the applicant must investigate the syndicate or syndicates which he hopes to join. Assistance in the choice of syndicate may be obtained from a Names Underwriting Agent (not the same as a Managing Agent, although he may be so in practice). The policy for investing syndicate funds and the likely premium income will be explained by the syndicate's Underwriting Agent (see below) and the result of the last seven 'closed years' will be made available. A 'closed year' is one in respect of which the underwriting account has been closed by reinsuring any outstanding liabilities, usually at the end of the third year. The applicant should also enquire about the establishment of personal reserves, transfer to the Special Reserve Fund, and the form of accounts.

Applications for membership must be approved by the Committee, who apply a means test to the applicant's readily realisable assets which include Stock Exchange securities, life policies at their surrender values, reversionary interests and real property but not the applicant's principal residence. Gold (up to 30 per cent of the total), which must be held by an approved bank in the form of bullion or coins, is valued at 70 per cent of market value. Such things as shares in private companies, jewellery and antiques are not included. Where the applicant's wealth comprises items not readily realisable but is, in other respects satisfactory, the Committee may accept, in whole or in part, a guarantee or letter of credit from an approved bank, as collateral for which the principal residence may be included. The object of the means test is to ensure that as far as possible, funds will be available at short notice to meet a claim, however large it may be. A booklet entitled 'Membership: the Issues' is obtainable from Lloyd's and sets out all the information which an applicant should know. The previous figure of £100,000 of 'readily realisable assets' is increased, in 1990, to £250,000.

12.7.3 Conditions of membership

The Underwriting Agent is in complete control of the underwriting affairs of the underwriting members whose names appear in the syndicate lists. He maintains the accounts and records and deals with taxation, reserves, investments and other day to day matters as well as watching the statistics which give him a guide to current trends. It is also his duty to ensure that the rules laid down by the Committee of Lloyd's are complied with. Every underwriting member enters into an agreement with the agent which sets out the terms and conditions on which the agent acts, including his salary or fee and his rate of commission.

Every underwriting member is required to deposit with the Corporation of Lloyd's investments or cash which the Corporation holds as trustee. In general terms, the deposit has been 20 per cent of the gross premium underwriting limit for British residents and 28 per cent in other cases. This is now 30 per cent up to a gross maximum of £25,000 for all new members with interim arrangements for existing members until the beginning of 1992 when further increases are likely. For further details enquiries should be made from the deposits department at Lloyd's. The investing of the deposit may be delegated to the Underwriting Agent or may, within the Committee's rules, be dealt with by the member. The income arising on investments deposited remains the income of the member.

A member's premium limit is the maximum premium income which may be underwritten by him in any one year. It is allocated to the syndicate and is then divided among the members in proportions agreed in consultation with the agent. The limit may be increased or decreased according to the market value of the deposit and may be raised if additional amounts are deposited and evidence of sufficient means is produced. If the limit is exceeded the member will normally be required to increase his deposit.

An entrance fee is payable in cash on election and varies according to the category of membership. Entrance fees are not deductible from profits for tax purposes. An annual contribution to Lloyd's Central Fund is also required. The Fund was set up in 1926 for the protection of policyholders in the event of the inability of a member to meet his liabilities out of his syndicate's trust funds, his deposit, his reserves and his personal assets. The reserve is the amount which, under the Rules, has to be set aside each year to meet the estimated cost of winding-up the name's underwriting accounts.

12.7.4 Taxation

Special provisions apply to the taxation of the income of underwriters and are to be found in ss 450 to 457 of the Income and Corporation Taxes Act 1988. These should be carefully considered by the applicant with expert advice. Briefly their effect is as follows.

Underwriting profits are assessed on the basis of the profits of the underwriting year ending in the year of assessment and not on the normal basis of the previous year. Thus the profits of the underwriting year ending 31 December 1988 will be assessed for the fiscal year 1988/89 although they are not finally ascertained for three years thereafter. Underwriting profits are profits or gains arising from underwriting business or from assets forming part of a premium trust fund. A premium paid for reinsurance is deductible as an expense. Losses of an underwriting business are allowed against other income of the year of assessment in which they are incurred, or against that of the previous year if the underwriter was carrying on an underwriting business in that year. They cannot, however, be carried forward against general income of a later year but can be set against future underwriting profits.

Relief from income tax at the higher rate is given to underwriters on payments into reserve funds, such payments being limited to a sum which, after deduction of tax at the basic rate, does not exceed £7,000 or 50 per cent of underwriting profits for the underwriting year forming the basis period for the year of assessment, whichever is the less. If an underwriter incurs losses which necessitate payment out of the fund, such payments are liable to tax at the higher rate. Payments out of the fund are not generally so liable if they are made on death, but are if made on ceasing to be an underwriter. Payment into the fund is treated as an annual charge made under deduction of tax, and payment out as income received after deduction of tax. Changes were made in the administrative arrangements for taxing members of Lloyd's under the Finance Act 1988.

12.8 Investment in another's expertise

The first difficulty in making an investment of this kind lies in discovering the innovator whose expertise is to be given financial backing. The innovator seeking capital has many avenues open to him. He may consult the National Research Development Corporation, the Council for Small Industries in Rural Areas, Investors in Industry Group plc (formerly known as the Industrial and Commercial Finance Corporation) or the Small Business Capital Fund. Alternatively he may look for capital through his bank or a merchant bank, through local accountants, solicitors or insurance brokers, through the Rotary Club or the Round Table, through the local branch of the British Institute of Management or through the Small Firms Council of the Confederation of British Industry. The prospective investor can approach any of these agencies to inquire whether they know of any worthwhile ideas for which backing is sought.

Once the innovator has been located, the prospects of the venture must be carefully examined, not only by the investor's accountant but also by an expert in the technical field where appropriate. Inquiry should be made as to how much of his own capital the innovator is putting into the venture. If he has little he cannot be expected to put a lot in, but his intentions in this respect will indicate his real confidence in the venture. Plans should be carefully prepared and the amount required should be meticulously calculated, all contingencies being taken into account. The information required will include particulars of the product or process, with technical explanations and specifications of patents, if any. Its advantages over existing products or processes must be explained and the costs of development detailed, together with reasoned estimates of future sales. Mere hopes based on speculation will not do.

In general terms, an investor may back another's expertise by means of a private company, a partnership or a loan. A loan will probably be the least attractive method for two reasons. First, adequate security is unlikely to be available. Secondly, the income will be limited to interest at a fixed rate, thus denying the lender any participation in profits should the venture prove an outstanding success—the greatest attraction of this type of investment. As to private companies and partnerships, it will be necessary to determine the appropriate proportionate interests of the investor who is putting in capital and the expert who is putting in expertise. Both may be of equal importance: indeed both are essential, but 50:50 holdings can mean deadlock and are better avoided if possible. This immediately gives rise to a problem which needs professional advice and probably tough negotiating.

Some of the legal aspects of the arrangement (including any liability for taxation on profits or gains arising) have been dealt with in general terms earlier in this chapter. As has already been stressed, every case will present individual problems, and both commercial and professional advice should always be sought. Adequate financial and administrative control is essential for the investor, and he will usually be wise to insist on his own accountant auditing the books and his representative keeping a close eye on the running of the business.

12.9 Racehorses

12.9.1 Introduction

Investing in racehorses is not for the faint-hearted. The rules regulating racing in this country are made by the Jockey Club from whom detailed information may be obtained. Anyone proposing to invest in a racehorse is presumably already well-acquainted with the

Business ventures (without participation in management) 241

turf and will know something about horses. Investment may be either in horses in training or in stallions. (Investment in stud farms and training establishments is discussed in Chapter 11, **11.7.2**.)

The increase in the cost of buying and running a horse led to an expansion of syndicated ownership regulated (as to horses in training) by the Jockey Club 'rules of racing'. New syndicates are, however, no longer accepted by the Jockey Club and where a horse is owned jointly it must now be by way of a legally enforceable partnership of which each member is registered as an owner. The number of partners is restricted (as it was for syndicate members) to 12. The partnership agreement (which should be drawn up with legal advice) must be registered with the Jockey Club. All partners are jointly and severally liable for entrance fees, stakes, forfeits and jockey's fees. That is to say that any one of them may be held individually liable for the full amount and will then have to recover the due amounts from the other partners.

It is recommended by the Jockey Club that anyone proposing to become a part-owner by way of a partnership should contact them before taking any steps in the matter. The rules governing joint-ownership are complex and the Jockey Club would prefer to advise at the outset rather than unscramble an arrangement that contravenes the rules.

An interest in a racehorse may be bought through the medium of a limited company but it must be realised that the investor is then buying a share in the company and not a share in a horse. There are a number of public limited companies engaged in these activities.

12.9.2 Stallions

As well as investments in horses in training, investments may be made in syndicated stallions. In this case there are no rules of the sort set out in relation to horses in training—ad hoc arrangements are made in each case. A stallion may stand at stud until it is twenty years old, but the value of a nomination falls as it approaches that age. A stallion will give about 150 services each season, covering each mare three or four times. Stud fees at present range generally up to about 1,500 guineas, although that figure may be greatly exceeded in special cases.

In a typical syndicate there will be 40 shares, most of which will be held by shareholders with one share each. The agreement usually provides for a committee, including the major shareholder or shareholders, to be set up. The committee will be empowered to decide all matters relating to the management of the stallion and the affairs of the syndicate as agent for the shareholders, although its powers in relation to the disposal of the stallion are usually limited. Generally each shareholder is entitled to one nomination per share for the season. The maximum number of nominations for the season is fixed, and in so far as it exceeds the number available to shareholders, the excess may be sold and the proceeds set against expenses which are borne pro rata by the shareholders. The agreement usually provides that the committee must approve mares to be served by the stallion and that a barren mare must also be approved by a veterinary surgeon. A veterinary surgeon will examine any maiden mare before service. Restrictions are usually placed on the disposal of shares and nominations, but it may happen that during the season in question the shareholder has no mare suitable for nomination and in such a case the nomination will be sold.

12.9.3 Taxation

Income tax
It was held in *Benson* v *Counsell* (1942) 24 TC 178 that receipts from the sale of nominations were receipts of annual income chargeable to income tax under Case VI of Schedule D although they were not trading receipts within Case I. This decision was based on the fact that the taxpayer had not bought the rights to nomination that he sold: what he had bought was an interest in the horse. The sale of the rights merely realised the horse's reproductive faculties and it thus became an income-producing asset. In 1915 the Earl of Derby unsuccessfully contended that a stallion at stud was 'plant' for the purposes of capital allowances (see *Derby* (*Earl*) v *Aylmer* [1915] 3 KB 374).

Capital gains tax
The sale of a share in the horse, whether it is a horse in training or a stallion, does *not* give rise to a taxable gain, since s 127(1) of the Capital Gains Tax Act 1979 takes out of the charge to capital gains tax any gain accruing on the disposal of, or of an interest in, an asset which is tangible, movable property and a wasting asset. There is no doubt that a horse is tangible and movable, nor that it is a wasting asset (ie, one with a predictable life not exceeding 50 years).

12.10 Backing plays

It is possible that, somewhere, a playwright has just written a play that will take London by storm and play for years to packed houses. It is, on present showing, most unlikely. It is estimated that only one show in seven put on in the West End will be successful which suggests that somewhere along the line there is a failure to foresee what the public will and will not like. In the last year or so flops have included *Stop the World I Want to Get Off, Exclusive, Metropolis, Sherlock Holmes, Someone Like You, Look Look, Dean, Barnardo, Can-Can, Fire Angel, King, Top People, Y, Ziegfeld, Troubadour, Bus Stop* and *Bernadette*. Together they have lost millions.

This is not the place to consider the reasons for this failure rate but those tempted to put money into a play should realise that their chance of making anything out of it are slim. It is statistically more probable that money put in will be lost without tax relief. This is the ideal investment for those who enjoy losing money.

Those who put up the money for a theatrical production—the 'angels'—normally split the profits with the management: the angels usually take 60 per cent and the management 40 per cent, although the proportions are a matter for agreement. The agreement usually also provides for an 'overcall', ie, a liability on the part of the angels to put up additional capital should it prove necessary. Before the profits are divided between angels and management there has to be deducted such of the fees and expenses of management as may be specified in the agreement. The agreement should be carefully scrutinised by an adviser familiar with these matters to ensure that the angel is getting his fair share.

Anyone determined to risk this gamble against heavy odds should first become familiar with the track records of various producers. The eager investor should then attempt to force his money on one who seems successful. If a producer makes the approach, consider why his usual sources of finance are not available. There is no central exchange through which investments can be made although assistance may be obtained from the Society of West End Theatre. Whilst not arranging investments itself, the Society will give advice and maintains a list of prospective backers. Since the backer will normally have no opportunity even to read the play he is simply betting on the wisdom of the producer.

The cost of mounting a play will vary enormously. A large-scale musical can cost well over £1m to stage and with production and running costs at their present levels a show has to run for a considerable time before the production costs are covered and anything is paid out. If the production is successful the investor will receive an agreed share of the net profits which will, first, recoup the costs and, thereafter, constitute income for tax purposes.

As a variant of the traditional method of financing, advantage may be taken of the provisions of s 574 of the Income and Corporation Taxes Act 1988 which enables losses on unquoted shares in certain trading companies to be set off against a taxpayer's income. The resulting loss is thus, to some extent, cushioned by income tax relief.

12.11 Options on books

An investor with sufficient faith in a little-known author may back that faith by purchasing an option, exercisable usually for one year, to develop the book into a film or play. A little-known author is suggested as, in the case of a best-seller writer, the option is likely (if it is available at all) to be extremely expensive. It is, of course, much less expensive to buy such an option than it would be to buy the copyright outright.

Once the option is purchased it will become necessary to write or procure a script from the book and then to persuade a film company or theatrical producer to take it up. The time involved in these activities may necessitate the purchase of another year's option.

Would-be purchasers should consult a firm of literary agents for further advice. A list of agents is published in the *Writers and Artists Yearbook*.

12.12 Preview of the year ahead

The Chairman of Lloyd's has forecast that next year will be 'less spectacular' than this. Under the Members' Agent Pooling arrangement to be introduced in 1992, members will be able to spread their risk more easily. The majority of shows staged will probably flop. The majority of race horses will undoubtedly lose.

Sources of further information

Useful addresses

Registrar of Companies/
Registrar of Limited Partnerships
Companies Registration Office
Companies House

Crown Way
Cardiff
CF4 3UZ

Tel: (0222) 388588

Business ventures (without participation in management)

Lloyd's of London
Lime Street
London
EC3M 7DQ

Tel: (071) 623 7100

National Research Development
  Corporation
101 Newington Causeway
London
SE1 6BU

Tel: (071) 403 6666

Rural Development
  Commission
141 Castle Street
Salisbury
Wiltshire
SP1 3TP

Tel: (0722) 336255

Investors in Industry
  Group plc
91 Waterloo Road
London
SE1 8XP

Tel: (071) 928 3131

British Venture Capital
  Association
3 Cathennes Place
London
SW1E 6DX

Tel: (071) 233 5212

Development Capital Group
  Limited
44 Baker Street
London
W1M 1DH

Tel: (071) 935 2731

Department of Trade and
  Industry Small Firms Service
To obtain address of nearest
  centre, dial 100 and ask the
  operator for Freefone
  Enterprise.

British Institute of Management
Africa House
64–78 Kingsway
London
WC2B 6BL

Tel: (071) 405 3456

Confederation of British
  Industry
Centrepoint
103 New Oxford Street
London
WC1A 1DU

Tel: (071) 379 7400

Jockey Club
42 Portman Square
London
W1H 0EN

Tel: (071) 486 4921

Society of West End Theatre &
  West End Theatre Managers
  Ltd
Bedford Chambers
The Piazza
Covent Garden
London
WC2E 8HQ

Tel: (071) 836 9071

13 Life assurance

Vince Jerrard, LLB, ACII, Divisional Director, Allied Dunbar Assurance plc

13.1 Introduction

Life assurance contracts may be divided into three broad types, according to the nature of the primary benefits provided:

(1) life assurance policies (including single-premium bonds) pay out a lump sum on death or on the expiration of a specified period;
(2) purchased life annuities pay periodic sums as long as the annuitant is alive;
(3) pension contracts provide pensions and other benefits and are available through one's work or occupation.

Within each of these categories there are further subdivisions. Pension contracts are dealt with in Chapter 14.

13.2 Highlights of the previous year

13.2.1 Pensions and life assurance new business

1989 was another good year for the life assurance and pensions industry, following another year of strong growth in 1987 and 1988.

Regular premium life assurance business had a difficult year in some respects, in particular from lower mortgage-related endowment sales due to the depressed housing market (although levels of remortgage endowment business were high).

Lump sum investment business (single premium bonds) held its own but high interest rates and a continuing lack of confidence in stock markets meant that a good deal of business was in guaranteed income bonds.

The industry figures for the sales of new life assurance and personal pensions business in 1989 are set out in Tables 13.1 and 13.2 on pages 248 and 249.

Table 13.1 New individual life assurance business in the UK (including linked business, but excluding occupational pension and life schemes)

	Year ended 31 December					
	1984	1985	1986	1987	1988*	1989
	£ Millions	£ Millions	£ Millions	£ Millions	£ Millions	£ Millions
1. *New Annual Premiums*						
(a) Assurances and annuities	1,228 (−5%)	1,118 (−9%)	1,542 (+38%)	1,730 (+12%)	1,985 (+15%)	1,766 (−11%)
(b) Personal pensions	297 (+65%)	451 (+52%)	331 (−27%)	414 (+25%)	892 (+115%)	1,045 (+17%)
Total new annual premiums	1,525 (+3%)	1,569 (+3%)	1,873 (+19%)	2,141 (+14%)	2,877 (+34%)	2,811 (−2%)
2. *New Single Premiums*						
(a) Assurances and annuities	2,554 (+20%)	2,956 (+16%)	4,766 (+61%)	6,022 (+26%)	3,646 (−36%)	4,229 (+16%)
(b) Personal pensions	434 (+46%)	564 (+30%)	592 (+5%)	742 (+52%)	919 (+13%)	2,011 (+119%)
Total new single premiums	2,985 (+23%)	3,520 (+18%)	5,358 (+52%)	6,538 (+22%)	4,565 (−30%)	6,240 (+37%)

*estimate

Notes:
(1) Personal pensions are contracts available to the self-employed and those not in pensionable employment.
(2) The figures in brackets show the percentage increases of each year over those for the previous year.

Source: *Association of British Insurers—Life Assurance Business Statistics*

Table 13.2 New linked individual life assurance business (excluding occupational pension and life assurance schemes)

	Year ended 31 December					
	1984	1985	1986	1987	1988*	1989
	£ Millions	£ Millions	£ Millions	£ Millions	£ Millions	£ Millions
1. *New Annual Premiums*						
(a) Assurances and annuities	312 (+3%)	288 (−8%)	385 (+34%)	525 (+36%)	623 (+19%)	603 (−3%)
(b) Personal pensions	130 (+78%)	209 (+61%)	148 (−29%)	217 (+47%)	441 (+103%)	565 (+28%)
Total new annual premiums	442 (+18%)	497 (+12%)	533 (+7%)	742 (+39%)	1,064 (+43%)	1,168 (+10%)
2. *New Single Premiums*						
(a) Assurances and annuities	1,785 (+24%)	2,380 (+33%)	4,153 (+74%)	5,268 (+27%)	2,877 (−45%)	2,837 (−1%)
(b) Personal pensions	116 (+66%)	165 (+42%)	159 (−4%)	283 (78%)	280 (−1%)	863 (+208%)
Total new single premiums	1,901 (+26%)	2,545 (+34%)	4,312 (+89%)	5,551 (+29%)	3,157 (−43%)	3,700 (+17%)

*estimate

Notes:
(1) Personal pensions are contracts available to the self-employed and those not in pensionable employment.
(2) The figures in brackets show the percentage increases of each year over those for the previous year.

Source: *Association of British Insurers—Linked Life Assurance Business Statistics*

13.2.2 A new life office taxation regime

A very significant development concerned the review of life office taxation, announced in the Budget of 1989. The new regime was enacted in the Finance Act 1990.

In outline, and subject to certain transitional provisions, the rules: require separation of life new pensions business for tax purposes; reduce the tax rate on income and gains attributable to policyholder funds to 25 per cent; spread relief for companies acquisition expenses over seven years; levy tax charges on unrealised capital gains in unit trusts held by life funds and lay down a new formula for determining the part of a life company's profits attributable to shareholders and that attributable for its policyholders, for tax purposes.

Overall, the new rules will increase the tax charges on the life industry although performance in life funds should benefit from lower tax charges on policyholder income and gains. The policyholders will also benefit from the abolition of life assurance policy duty (stamp duty on life policies, calculated by reference to sums assured) with effect from 1 January 1990.

13.2.3 Policy taxation changes

During the year other topics were also discussed between the Inland Revenue and the life industry. One of these was the Revenue proposal for changes to the policy taxation regime. This was expected to be announced in the 1990 Budget, to take effect in 1991. Despite these expectations, no announcement was made and no changes are now anticipated in 1990. This is good news for the industry as the changes, as anticipated, are thought not to have been beneficial to policyholders.

13.3 Life assurance policies

13.3.1 Legal nature of life assurance policies

Life assurance policies are contracts between the individual policyholders and the life insurance company. The general principle underlying life assurance policies is that the insurance company is the collecting house of pooled risks and investments of policyholders and offers benefits directly to them based on personal contracts.

The life company maintains the underlying investment funds in its own right but, depending on the nature of the policy, undertakes to pay the policyholder either a specified sum, a sum which is increased periodically out of the profits of the company, or one which varies with the value of part of the underlying fund.

An important characteristic of the life assurance policy as an investment is that it does not produce an income, as such, but is essentially a medium- to long-term accumulator. The income and capital gains of the underlying funds accrue to and belong to the insurance company, but the benefit is passed on, to a greater or lesser extent, in the growth in value of the policy over and above the premiums paid by the policyholder. Many types of policy, however, allow regular or irregular encashment of part of the policy (withdrawal plans or encashment of bonuses) to serve as 'income', if required (but see 'Withdrawal plans and policy loans' at **13.3.4**).

13.3.2 Pre-conditions of life assurance policies

In order to take out a life assurance policy an *insurable interest* in the life to be assured must exist, ie, a pecuniary interest that would be adversely affected by the death of the life assured. At the time the policy is taken out the policyholder must have an insurable interest in the life assured commensurate with the sum assured. Individuals have an unlimited insurable interest in their own lives and those of their spouses.

Usually, where life assurance is taken out as an investment, the contract will be applied for and held by a person on his own life or that of his spouse, or on their joint lives, for his or her own personal benefit or for their joint benefit. Policies can, however, be the subject of gifts, in which case they would generally be written in trust for the benefit of the beneficiaries (see **13.3.7**). They can also be assigned, by way of gift, or for value, or as security for a debt (eg, as collateral security for a house mortgage or an overdraft).

13.3.3 Divisions and types of life assurance policies

Endowment, whole of life and term assurances
All life policies provide life cover—a sum or sums assured payable on death. Most policies, other than temporary assurances, generally also provide investment benefits—sums payable on surrender or maturity. Life policies may be divided into endowment, whole of life and term policies, depending on the emphasis that is placed on savings or on protection (life cover):

(1) An endowment policy, which has a high savings element, is one under which the benefits are payable at the end of a predeter-

mined period (the endowment period) or on death, if earlier.
(2) A whole of life policy is one under which the benefits are in general payable on death, whenever it occurs.
(3) A term policy is a temporary assurance, the sum assured being payable on death within a specified period only.

Both endowment policies and whole of life policies may be surrendered (ie, cashed in) prematurely for a cash lump sum, the size of which will depend on the nature of the contract. Term assurances generally do not have an investment element as far as the individual is concerned, and rarely have any surrender or cash-in value.

With profit, without profit and unit-linked policies
Within the endowment and whole of life categories, life policies can be of different types, depending on the way in which the sums payable by the company are determined:

(1) *With profit* contracts are policies under which a minimum sum is guaranteed to be paid by the life company, augmented from time to time by bonuses declared by the company according to its profits. These bonuses may be reversionary (bonuses added to the sum assured, either yearly or triennially) or terminal (bonuses declared at the end of the policy as an increment to the final payment). Reversionary bonuses may be simple or compound: simple bonuses are based only on the sum assured, while compound bonuses are based on the sum assured plus previous bonuses. Reversionary bonuses are usually expressed as a percentage of the sum assured or of the sum assured as increased by previous bonuses. Under a with profit endowment policy the individual will receive at maturity the minimum sum assured plus the bonuses, reversionary and terminal.
(2) *Without profit* contracts are policies under which the life company guarantees to pay an absolute sum and invests the premiums in such a way as to produce that sum, bearing any shortfall in the return or retaining any profit in excess of the guaranteed return.
(3) Under *unit-linked* policies the life company maintains a number of underlying funds, which are divided, for accounting purposes, into 'units'. The company undertakes to pay to the policyholder an amount equal to the greater of the guaranteed sum and the value of the units allocated to the policy. The underlying fund might consist of specific types of investment media (such as property, equities, unit trusts, investment trusts, government securities, local authority and bank loans or

deposits, or building society deposits) or the fund may consist of a combination of some or all of these ('managed' or 'mixed' funds). Out of every premium a proportion is allocated to the purchase of units which are credited to the policy. The movement in value of the underlying fund is directly reflected in the price of the units allocated to the policy and hence in the value of the policy benefits. Many types of policies give the policyholder himself the right to transfer his policy link from fund to fund at his option, by way of a simple procedure at low cost (eg, a policy that is linked to an equity fund may be switched so that it is, therefore, linked to fixed interest securities or bank deposits).

A life company generally has full investment freedom as to the type of investments it chooses, subject only to the investments being a suitable 'match' for its liabilities. In the case of unit-linked policies the Insurance Company Regulations only permit linkage to certain types of assets, such as those listed in the paragraph above.

If the contract is one under which a guaranteed minimum or guaranteed absolute amount is provided, the investor knows that he will get at least that sum. At the same time, in the case of with profit policies, he has the advantage of having the guaranteed minimum augmented from time to time by reversionary and terminal bonuses, or, in unit-linked contracts, augmented by the movement of the value of the underlying fund (capital growth plus reinvested income).

Regular premium and single premium policies
A further broad division of life policies (of all types) depends on how premiums are payable:

(1) regular premium policies (also known as annual premium policies) are those under which premiums are payable annually, half-yearly, quarterly or monthly, either throughout the duration of the policy or for a limited premium-paying period of time; and
(2) single premium policies are purchased by way of one single premium or lump sum.

Qualifying and non-qualifying policies
A brief introduction to qualifying and non-qualifying policies is given at **13.3.6**. The distinction between the two types of policy is important because they are treated differently for tax purposes.

13.3.4 Characteristics of regular premium policies

Investment and protection
All endowment and whole of life policies have an investment or savings element as well as a life insurance protection element. The extent to which the policy is slanted towards investment depends on the nature and duration of the policy and the relationship between the premiums payable, the age of the life assured and the extent of the life cover provided. In general, policies that have a low sum assured relative to the premiums payable over the policy life will have a high savings or investment element, and conversely, high sums assured relative to the premiums payable mean that the policy will be tilted more towards life assurance cover than towards investment. In considering life policies as investments, temporary or term assurances will be excluded, as these generally do not have a surrender value and benefits are payable only on death. They are usually taken out purely for life cover protection, to provide for one's family or to cover a prospective liability such as inheritance tax.

The type of policy that an individual should take out generally depends on his circumstances and objectives, weighing up not only the required degree of investment relative to protection but also the required degree of certainty of result relative to the potential for increased gain.

In general, the incidence of inflation and the conservatism of companies in guaranteeing a long-term return has meant that without profit policies have tended to provide a relatively poor rate of return compared with with profit and unit-linked policies.

A with profit policy gives the prospect of sharing in the company's investment performance where this exceeds that needed to meet the guarantee – but the need to satisfy the guarantee may still lead the company to a more conservative investment strategy.

With no guaranteed investment return a unit linked policy could be viewed as a little more risky but may also offer the prospect of better fund performance.

Withdrawal plans and policy loans
Until recently, a feature of many policies with a high investment content was the facility after a period of years to operate withdrawal plans, under which the premium was reduced to a nominal amount, eg, £1 pa and regular or irregular sums could be taken from the policy

by way of partial surrender to serve as an income, leaving the balance to accumulate. This withdrawal facility was challenged by the Revenue and withdrawn from qualifying policies issued on or after 25 February 1988. Policies issued before that date may continue as qualifying policies despite the presence of such an option. Substantially the same result may be achieved by taking out a series of smaller policies and cashing in individual policies from time to time while continuing the remainder and it may be possible to take withdrawals from a policy provided it has not suffered such a large premium reduction as was previously allowed. Many policies also give the policyholder the right to borrow from the insurance company at a beneficial rate of interest on the security of the policy.

13.3.5 Characteristics of single premium policies

In the main, the relevant single premium policies for investment purposes consist of single premium 'bonds'. These are whole of life assurance policies, purchased by way of a single premium, where the benefits are directly related to the values of underlying investment funds maintained by the life company—ie, they are unit-linked policies, such as property bonds, managed bonds, equity bonds, etc. There are also single premium endowment policies, but these are less significant.

The main investment characteristic of single premium unit-linked bonds is the high allocation of the premium to investment in the underlying fund, with relatively low life cover. Virtually the entire premium is allocated to 'units', save only for the initial management charges, resulting, in effect, in the direct investment of the premium in the chosen fund. Most companies offer a wide choice of unit funds for the bond linkage.

Subsequently, at no cost or for a small administrative charge, the policyholder may switch his investment to one or more of the other funds and is thereby entitled to select a fund which reflects his own view of market conditions. Switching does not amount to a realisation for tax purposes, which is an important investment advantage.

The income produced by the underlying fund is reinvested, net of tax and annual charges, in the fund. A bond, therefore, serves as an automatic income accumulator as well as giving the investor the benefit of the capital growth from the fund, less a deduction for the insurance company's tax on capital gains.

Withdrawal plans

Most unit-linked single premium bonds allow the investor the right to make regular or irregular withdrawals by way of partial surrender to serve as an income. The same result can be achieved by splitting the investment into a number of smaller policies and encashing individual policies in full from time to time. As these policies are not qualifying contracts they are not affected by the Revenue's attack on withdrawal plans referred to in **13.3.4**.

Ease of encashment

One of the most important characteristics of single premium bonds is the ease of encashment: there are few formalities other than production of the policy, a surrender form and proof of title. In the case of property bonds, some companies reserve the right, in exceptional circumstances, to defer encashment for a period so as to protect the general body of policyholders by avoiding forced sales of property.

13.3.6 Taxation of life assurance policies

Taxation of the life company

The Revenue's review of life company taxation, announced in the 1989 Budget, resulted in a statement by the Treasury in December 1989 and other changes announced in the 1990 Budget. Legislation is to be included in the Finance Act 1990 to give effect to these changes. In the main, they take effect from January 1990.

Proposals are less radical than some of those originally canvassed and build on the existing framework. The following is a brief outline of the new regime.

The life company's management expenses are deducted from the investment income and capital gains of the life fund and the net amount is subjected to tax in the life company's hands at a rate of 25 per cent in respect of the policyholders' share of profits and 35 per cent in respect of profits attributable to shareholders in the case of a proprietary company. However, the expenses associated with the acquisition of new business are (after a transitional period) to be spread over a period of seven years. Capital gains on disposals of gilt-edged securites are exempt from tax.

Where the policy takes the form of a single premium endowment, it provides the policyholder with a guaranteed investment return on his premium over the endowment period.

As life companies are generally able to defer realisations of assets for a long period, they usually pass on this benefit in the form of a lower rate of deduction for tax on capital gains from the funds. This is especially true of unit-linked policies.

Previously, deferring gains had also been achieved by investing life funds in units trusts. Much of the investment management could be achieved through the unit trust company selling its underlying assets, these being free of tax from capital gains. However, new rules (with transitional reliefs) have now been introduced to charge tax on unrealised gains in life company holdings of unit trusts. These new rules are likely to promote more direct investment by life company funds.

Taxation of the policyholder
Qualifying and non-qualifying policies—The income tax treatment of a life policy in the hands of the policyholder depends on whether the policy is a qualifying or a non-qualifying policy. A qualifying policy must be certified as such by the Inland Revenue and generally (although the rules do vary for different types of policy) is one where the premium-paying period is 10 years or more and where the premiums payable in any period of 12 months do not exceed more than twice the premiums payable in any other period of 12 months or $\frac{1}{8}$ of the premiums payable over ten years. In the case of a whole of life policy, the sum assured payable on death must not be less than 75 per cent of the premiums payable until age 75; and in the case of an endowment policy, the sum assured payable on death must not be less than 75 per cent of the premiums payable during the term of the policy, but this percentage is reduced by 2 per cent for each year by which the age of the life assured, at commencement, exceeds 55. Taxation of company-owned policies is considered later.

Qualifying policies
Tax relief on the premiums—In the case of a qualifying policy issued before 14 March 1984 the policyholder is eligible for tax relief on the premiums if the policy is written on his life or that of his spouse, if either of them pays the premiums, and if the person paying is resident in the UK for tax purposes. The current rate of tax relief on premiums paid is $12\frac{1}{2}$ per cent. If eligible, the premiums may generally be paid to the life company net of the tax relief and the company will obtain the difference from the Inland Revenue. Tax relief is allowed to the policyholder to the extent to which the total gross premiums paid by him in the year do not exceed £1,500 or, if greater, $\frac{1}{6}$ of his taxable income after deducting charges on income but before deducting personal reliefs. Tax relief will not be available if a person other than the life assured or his spouse (such as an assignee) pays the premiums.

No life assurance premium relief is available for policies issued in respect of contracts made after 13 March 1984. For these purposes a policy issued on or before 13 March 1984 is treated as being issued after that date if the benefits it secures are increased or its term extended (either by variation or by the exercise of an option built into the contract) after that date.

Policies intact—While the policies are intact there is no tax charge to the policyholder.

Tax-free proceeds if kept up for minimum period—If a qualifying endowment policy has been maintained for at least three-quarters of its term or ten years, whichever is the less, and has not been made paid-up within that period, the entire proceeds will be free of income tax in the hands of the policyholder. For a whole of life policy the appropriate period is ten years. If, however, a qualifying policy is surrendered or made paid-up within these periods, the profit ultimately made on realising the policy (whether by cashing in, death, maturity or assignment for value) will be potentially subject to the higher rate of tax as with non-qualifying policies (see below).

Capital gains tax—No chargeable gain arises on the disposal of either qualifying or non-qualifying policies (note that surrender and payment of the sum assured under the policy are treated as 'disposals' for these purposes) where the disposal is by the original beneficial owner or by an assignee who gave no consideration for the policy (eg, received the policy by way of gift), CGTA 1979, s 143.

On the other hand, if an assignee realises a profit on a policy (or an interest under it) that he, not being the original beneficial owner, acquired for value, it will be liable to capital gains tax in the same way as other chargeable assets.

A policy which is in the hands of a person who acquired it for value and who is not the original beneficial owner is outside the income tax legislation as it relates to life policies, unless it is a policy to which the 'second-hand bond' legislation applies. Such policies may give a potential liability to both income and capital gains tax although CGTA 1979, s 31 will prevent a double tax charge arising.

Person liable for the tax charge—see below.

Non-qualifying policies
Tax relief on the premiums—No life assurance premium relief is allowed in respect of premiums paid under non-qualifying policies whether issued before or after 14 March 1984.

Policies intact—While the policies are intact there is no tax charge to the policyholder.

Termination—On final termination of a non-qualifying policy, on death, cashing in, maturity, or sale, the only income tax charge, if any, is to higher rate income tax but not basic rate. To determine whether a charge arises, the gain—the excess of the cash surrender value over the premium paid—is divided by the number of years the policy has been held ('top slicing'). Any previous withdrawals are also taken into account. This slice is then added to the taxpayer's other income for the year (after reliefs and mortgage interest). If the slice, then treated as the upper part of the individual's income, puts him in the higher rate bracket, the average rate of tax on the slice at the higher rate less the basic rate is applied to the whole gain. If the slice does not attract the higher rate of tax, the gain is, similarly, free of tax.

Example—no income tax charge

A basic rate taxpayer whose income after personal reliefs is £1,000 below the higher rate threshold cashes in a single premium bond that he has held for eight years, for a total gain of £5,000. This gain is divided by eight to produce a 'slice' of £625. The slice, when added to his other income, still does not take him into the higher rate of tax. No tax is payable on the gain of £5,000.

Example—income tax on the gain

If the slice (£625 in the above example), treated as the upper part of the taxpayer's income, falls wholly in the higher rate band of 40 per cent, then the gain of £5,000 will be subject to income tax at the rate of 15 per cent (ie, £750) being the difference between the relevant higher rate (40 per cent) and the basic rate of 25 per cent.

It should be noted that it is only the income in the year of encashment that is relevant. If no chargeable events occur during other years, the individual's income, no matter how high in those years, is irrelevant. Thus, bonds or other non-qualifying policies can be realised tax-effectively in a year when the policyholder's other income is relatively low (eg, after retirement).

Note that, on death, the gain which may be liable to tax is calculated as the difference between the cash surrender value immediately before death and the premiums paid. In this way the 'mortality profit' from the policy is not taxed.

Withdrawals—Tax-free withdrawals or partial surrenders of up to 5 per cent per annum are permitted up to a total amount equal to the premium or premiums paid. Unused allowances are carried forward. If more than the 5 per cent annual allowance is taken a chargeable excess occurs. The excess becomes liable to the higher rate of tax (but is not liable to the basic rate) if, when added to the taxpayer's other income, it falls into the higher rate.

The 'top-slicing' procedure referred to above applies with some modifications: the first chargeable excess is divided by the number of years since commencement; subsequent excesses are divided by the number of years since the previous excess. The amounts withdrawn are taken into account in computing the gain or loss on final cashing in: the final gain or loss is equal to the cash surrender value, plus previous withdrawals, less the premium or premiums paid, less excesses previously brought into charge.

Example

If a bondholder who has taken withdrawals of six per cent per annum from a £5,000 bond for nine years cashes in the bond after ten years for £8,000, the final gain on cashing in is £8,000 + £2,700 (ie, $9 \times 6\% \times £5,000$) − £5,000 − £450 (ie, $9 \times 1\% \times £5,000$) = £5,250. The 'slice' is therefore £5,250 ÷ 10 = £525. This slice is added to his other income in the year of cashing in to determine if any tax liability exists on the slice and, if so, the rate of charge, after deducting the basic rate. The net rate of charge, if any, on the slice is then applied to the gain of £5,250.

Person liable—The person liable for the tax charge is the policyholder if the policy is held by him beneficially, or the individual for whose debt the policy is held as security. Thus, if a policy is assigned by a parent to his or her child by way of a gift and the latter encashes it after attaining majority, the liability, if any, is that of the child regardless of the donor's income and is determined by the child's income at the time of encashment.

Where a policy that is held in trust is cashed in, any chargeable gain is treated as income of the settlor and the tax is his liability, although the settlor can recover from the trustees any tax for which he is liable in this way. If a policy, previously held in trust, has been assigned to the beneficiary in execution of that trust and is subsequently encashed, any gain forms part of the beneficiary's income and is taxed accordingly.

13.3.7 Suitability of life assurance policies

Life assurance policies are different from the normal run of investments in that they are capital assets that do not produce income as such. All income and capital gains produced by the underlying fund of investments accrue to the life company, while the policyholder receives the benefit in the form of an increase in value of his policy: the net income and gains after tax are taken into account in the value of the units or bonus additions, as the case may be. For this reason life assurance policies are a very useful means of obtaining capital growth and accumulating income for medium- to long-term investment if immediate income is not required. This can be particularly important for higher rate tax payers and various types of trust.

Both regular premium and single premium policies (qualifying or non-qualifying) also have the advantage that while they are held intact, the policyholder has no administrative burdens or tax returns to render, as the income and gains are the responsibility of the company.

The medium- and long-term investor

Both single and regular premium policies are ideally suited to the medium- or longer-term investor seeking an institutionally managed investment. Life companies have considerable investment freedom and with profits policies reflect the results of investment across a wide spread of assets. Unit-linked policies offer a choice of property, equity, fixed interest, managed and many other types of unit funds, as well as the ability to switch investments between funds as market conditions change. Indeed, the keynote of most unit-linked policies these days is choice and flexibility to meet changing circumstances, so as to maximise the potential growth and protect the real value of the investment against inflation, particularly over the longer term; while with profit policies offer the relative stability of participation in the company's profits. For the individual who wants a direct link to a managed fund of commercial properties there are few investments comparable with a property bond, or a policy linked to a property fund, or a managed fund with a property content.

Qualifying policies issued pre-14 March 1984 have the added attraction of tax relief on the premiums—something not available to other comparable forms of investment—as well as freedom from tax on the proceeds if maintained for the required period. The ability of companies to defer realisations and thus make deductions for capital gains liabilities at a rate lower than the life company rate on chargeable gains is a continuing advantage. For these reasons, individuals, especially higher rate tax payers, may take out 'funding schemes', under which capital is transferred annually into a qualifying whole of life or endowment policy through a temporary annuity or the regular cashing in of, or withdrawals from, single premium bonds.

Beneficiaries

Life policies are suitable investments for individuals seeking personal investment benefits for themselves or their spouses, or for making gifts to beneficiaries. Since policies are automatic income accumulators, they represent useful investments as gifts for children or for children's own capital. As gifts of policies do not cause chargeable events, a higher rate taxpaying spouse can give a policy to a basic rate (or non-taxpaying) partner before encashment. In this way, any gain otherwise taxable may avoid being taxed by virtue of the new independent taxation regime introduced in April 1990 which no longer aggregates the investment income of married couples. Policies can also be taken out by trustees as investments of the trust, provided the power is given in the trust instrument to invest in non-income-producing property and provided an insurable interest exists, eg, a policy on the life of a beneficiary for the ultimate benefit of that beneficiary.

A donor wishing to take out a policy for the benefit of children or other beneficiaries can do so at the outset by completing a standard trust form produced by the life company, at the time of application. Trusts can range from very simple forms for the benefit of named beneficiaries absolutely (under the Married Women's Property Acts or corresponding legislation in Scotland and Northern Ireland, for spouse or children) to more elaborate forms, such as children's accumulation trusts and trusts where the settlor reserves a right to apply the benefits amongst a class of beneficiaries which may include the settlor himself (although to be efficient for inheritance tax purposes the settlor should be excluded from any personal benefit). Similarly, it is relatively simple to make a gift of an existing policy by assigning it to a beneficiary or to trustees for a beneficiary.

The tax considerations described in **13.3.6** should, of course, be taken into account, as well as the taxpayer's potential income and his tax position at the time of prospective encashment (as it is that time that is primarily relevant, not any time during the currency of the policy).

Companies

Companies have frequently found it useful to invest surplus funds in life policies, particularly where providing for a future liability or the replacement of an asset in the future. An insurable interest in the life of the assured must exist. In the past, the only tax consequence of such an investment has been that applicable to a close company in the case of a single premium bond or the premature encashment of a qualifying policy but the Finance Act 1989 contained new provisions so that, broadly speaking, that all policies owned by companies (and those assigned to secure a company debt or held on trusts created by a company) are treated, in effect, as non-qualifying policies and taxable to Schedule D, Case VI income.

The new rules apply to policies effected on or after 14 March 1989 and those altered after that date so as to increase the benefits secured or extend the term.

A measure of relief is given in cases where a qualifying endowment policy is used to secure a debt incurred by the company in purchasing land to be occupied by it for the purposes of its trade (or in constructing, extending or improving buildings occupied for that purpose). In such cases, and subject to certain conditions, only the excess policy proceeds over the amount of the debt will be taxable as a policy gain.

13.3.8 Charges

In the case of with profit and without profit policies, the company's charges are implicit in the premium rate for the sum assured. In the case of unit-linked policies, the company's charges consist of a proportion of each premium and charges inside the unit funds. For example, in the case of single premium bonds, typically an initial charge of 5 per cent of the premium is made. This is followed by annual charges of 0.75 per cent or 1.25 per cent of the value of the fund (although this does vary from company to company) deducted from the fund, either monthly or with the same frequency as the fund valuations. These charges cover the company's expenses, mortality costs and profit margins. Such annual charges can become quite significant where the policy has achieved a high value. For this reason a recent development in the unit-linked market has been the introduction of a policy charge which is designed to ensure that each policy contributes a fair amount to the company's expenses, irrespective of the size of the policy. In such cases any annual management charge deducted from the funds is reallocated to the policy.

Switching a unit-linked policy between funds can usually be done for a small administrative charge that is far lower than the equivalent cost of switching other investments.

13.3.9 Mechanics of life assurance policies

Life assurance policies are generally taken out through the intervention of an intermediary such as an insurance broker or salesman of the life assurance company, or a solicitor, accountant or estate agent acting as agent, or directly with the life company itself. The intermediary, although usually the agent of the policyholder, is generally paid a commission by the life company itself, although some insurance brokers charge the client fees (which are offset against their commission) for the work involved in preparing reports and undertaking financial planning for the client entailing the use of life assurance policies. The Financial Services Act has now introduced the concept of polarisation to the industry. This seeks to make clear to the consumer whether he is dealing with a representative of one company or a broker who will survey the market on his client's behalf.

13.3.10 Maintenance of life assurance policies

Policies can be held in the individual's own name (usually in the case of policies held for the individual's personal benefit) or by trustees. As long as the policy is not cashed in there are no tax returns and no paperwork. It is only where excessive tax relief is taken on qualifying premiums or gains arise on the happening of a chargeable event (eg, a single premium policy that is encashed or a qualifying policy encashed prematurely) that tax considerations arise. It is perhaps largely because of the ease of administration that many individuals with personal share portfolios take advantage of share exchange schemes introduced by life companies enabling them to exchange their shares for single premium bonds at reduced dealing costs.

Unit-linked policyholders may receive annual fund reports, though the level of useful information provided varies between companies. Because the investment performances of unit-linked single premium bonds are directly related to the underlying funds, as with any portfolio it is advisable to review the performance of the respective funds regularly with a view to switching between funds. This can be done with relative ease and at a low cost but for the majority of investors a carefully selected managed fund will satisfy the requirements in respect of a large proportion of their investment.

13.4 Purchased life annuities

13.4.1 Legal nature of purchased life annuities

There are two broad types of purchased life annuities:

(1) Immediate annuities are contracts under which, in consideration of a lump sum paid to the life company, the company undertakes to pay an annuity to the annuitant for life, or for some other term the rate of the annual annuity depending on the age and sex of the annuitant and on the yields prevailing for fixed interest investments at the time.
(2) Deferred annuities are similar to immediate annuities except that the annuity commences at a future date.

Both annuity contracts are direct contracts with the life company. Some annuity contracts provide for a guaranteed minimum number of payments; some allow the contract to be surrendered for a cash sum that takes into account the growth in the purchase consideration and any annuity payments that have already been made. Other types of annuity contract allow for a cash sum, representing the balance of the original purchase consideration, to be paid on death.

13.4.2 Pre-conditions of purchased life annuities

There are generally no pre-conditions to investment in purchased life annuities. The purchaser of the annuity will generally be the annuitant himself or someone else who wishes to provide for annual payments to the annuitant.

13.4.3 Characteristics of purchased life annuities

An annuity contract represents a fixed interest investment providing either regular annual payments for the life of the annuitant (lifetime annuities) or for a fixed period (temporary annuities). These payments represent a partial return of capital plus a rate of interest on the investment. In the case of deferred annuity contracts the initial purchase consideration is accumulated at a fixed rate of interest before the annuity commences. Frequently, deferred annuity contracts are purchased with the object of taking advantage of income accumulation before the annuity commencement date and of cashing in the contract before that time (these are commonly known as 'growth bonds'). In general the life company fixes the rate of the annuity in advance, although cash surrender values may be related to yields on government securities at the time of cashing in. The actual investment yield earned by the life company is irrelevant to the annuitant, as he enjoys a guaranteed benefit.

Sometimes two separate purchased annuity contracts are combined. A temporary immediate annuity for a limited period may be combined with a deferred lifetime annuity. This combination, known as a 'guaranteed income bond', has as its object the provision of a short-term 'income' in the form of the temporary annuity, with the cashing in of the deferred annuity before the annuity commencement date to provide the return of 'capital'. The contracts are so structured that the cash-in value of the deferred annuity generally equals the total purchase price of the two contracts. The tax consequences of this combination have to be closely watched, especially for higher rate taxpayers (see **13.4.4**). Another combination is that of an immediate lifetime annuity, to provide an income for life, and a deferred annuity that can be commenced at a later stage to augment the income or, if the additional income is not taken, to pay a lump sum on death.

13.4.4 Taxation of purchased life annuities

The life company

Annuities paid represent charges on the income from investments held by the life company for its general annuity business. To the extent, therefore, that the annuities paid equal or exceed the interest earned by the company, the interest does not bear tax, and can be passed on to the annuitants gross. The actual profits made by the life company on its general annuity business are currently taxed at 25 per cent in respect of income and gains attributable to policyholders and at 35 per cent in respect of those attributable to the company's shareholders.

The annuitant

Annuities paid are divided into capital content and income content, according to actuarial tables prescribed by the Inland Revenue. For example, if a man aged 70 purchased an annuity of £1,800 per annum payable half-yearly in arrear for a consideration of £10,000, £900 of the annuity might be regarded as capital with the balance of £900 being treated as income for tax purposes. In other words, every annuity is deemed to be partly a return of the original capital invested plus a yield or interest element. The interest element of each annuity payment received by the annuitant is treated as unearned income, although since the abolition of the investment income surcharge for individuals by Finance Act 1984 this is not currently a significant disadvantage.

Despite this treatment of payments as part capital and part income, the Revenue appear to regard annuities as substantially a right to income so that they cannot be transferred between spouses to take advantage of the new independent taxation regime introduced in April 1990.

Should an annuity contract be encashed or assigned for value, or any capital sum be paid on death, any profit made by the annuitant over and above the purchase price of the annuity, unlike single premium bonds, is subject to basic rate tax (as the company will not have paid tax on the income of its general annuity business) and also to higher rate tax in the same manner as single premium policies. In other words, the gain element is 'top-sliced' by the number of years the annuity contract has been in existence, and the resulting slice is added to the taxpayer's other income in the year of encashment in order to determine whether or not the higher rate of tax is applicable. The rate on the slice then applies to the entire gain. In calculating the amount of the gain the capital element of any annuities paid prior to encashment (but not the interest element) is included as part of the gain.

13.4.5 Suitability of purchased life annuities

Immediate life annuities are suitable for investors who wish to purchase a continuing income for the rest of their lives by way of a lump sum. Deferred annuities are a means of providing an income to start at a future date, or of accumulating a lump sum, taking advantage of the gross roll-up of income of the general annuity fund enjoyed in practice by the life company, with a view to encashment at a future time when other income may be sufficiently low to offset the tax disadvantages of encashment.

13.4.6 Mechanics of purchased life annuities

Like other life contracts annuities may be purchased through an intermediary or from a life company direct.

13.4.7 Maintenance of purchased life annuities

As far as immediate annuities are concerned, annual tax returns and tax payments are necessary in respect of the interest element of the annuities. In the case of deferred contracts, no maintenance is required while the annuity contract is intact and not paying an annuity, since the income is income of the life company and not the annuitant. On cashing-in, tax returns are necessary and tax may be payable.

13.5 Preview of the year ahead

It is likely that many companies will have to reprice the majority of their life contracts over the coming months, in order to restore profitability lost through the changes to life company taxation.

It remains to be seen whether the introduction of alternative savings media (eg, PEPs and, those recently, TESSAs) will make a real impact on savings through life assurance. TESSAs, being for only five years and not being asset-backed investments, may not prove to be a major threat, but it is quite possible that the industry will lobby for changes to the rules of life policies to enable more equal competition with the new tax-favoured savings (which are themselves an interesting move away from 'fiscal neutrality' which was a key plank of economic policy in this area in previous years).

13.6 Conclusion

Life policies remain a very simple way of making lump sum or regular investment, although they are best used for medium- to long-term savings.

They act as 'income accumulators' and the life company deals with all tax liabilities while the plan is maintained in force. Withdrawals can often be taken to provide the policyholder with a spendable 'income' and these too can often be taken very simply and with little paperwork. This makes policies easy to administer from the policyholder's viewpoint and they are attractive to many people as a result.

As a pooled investment, they offer a spread of risk normally unobtainable by individual investors, including exposure to the commercial property market. Inexpensive switching between the company's funds, the built-in life cover and the prospect of tax-free proceeds are also attractive benefits of investment through life policies.

The recent tax changes, which have increased liabilities on the industry have already led to contracts being repriced, but reduced tax rates applying to policyholder income and gains should provide some level of compensation for this.

Sources of further information

Useful addresses

Association of British Insurers
Aldermary House
10–15 Queen Street
London
EC4N 1TT

Tel: (071) 248 4477

National Association of
  Pension Funds
12–18 Grosvenor Gardens
London
SW1W 0DH

Tel: (071) 730 0585

Inland Revenue Public Enquiry
  Room
West Wing
Somerset House
Strand
London
WC2R 1LB

Tel: (071) 438 6420

Society of Pension Consultants
Ludgate House
Ludgate Circus
London
EC4A 2AB

Tel: (071) 353 1688/9

LAUTRO (Life Assurance and
  Unit Trusts Regulatory
  Organisation)
Centre Point
103 New Oxford Street
London
WC1A 1QH

Tel: (071) 379 0444

Occupational Pensions Board/
  Superannuation Funds Office
Lynwood Road
Thames Ditton
Surrey
KT7 0DP

Tel: (081) 398 4242

British Insurance and
  Investment Brokers
  Association
BIIBA House
14 Bevis Marks
London
EC3A 7NT

Tel: (071) 623 9043

Life Insurance Association
Citadel House
Station Approach
Chorleywood
Rickmansworth
Herts
WD3 5PF

Tel: (092 78) 5333

Pensions Management Institute
PMI House
124 Middlesex Street
London
E1 7HY

Tel: (071) 247 1452

14 Pension contracts

Vince Jerrard LLB, ACII, Divisional Director, Allied Dunbar Assurance plc

14.1 Introduction

Pension schemes in the UK can be divided, broadly, into three classifications; the State scheme, personal pension arrangements and occupational schemes. Recent years have seen far-reaching reform in all three areas as the government has tried to reduce the cost of the State scheme, increase flexibility and choice for the individual and permit institutions other than insurance companies to offer pension products.

Pensions schemes have many of the constituents of the perfect investment: tax relief on contributions, tax-free growth, the prospect of a tax-free lump sum (together with an annuity to provide ongoing income) and a wide choice of underlying investments in large pooled funds to spread the risk.

Not surprisingly, these benefits are carefully guarded by the appropriate authorities through a considerable number of rules and restrictions. This chapter summarises the main benefits and the conditions for their enjoyment.

14.2 Highlights of the previous year

Two of the key factors which have affected pensions business over the last twelve months were directly linked.

The first was the 5 April 1989 deadline for those effecting personal pensions to contract-out of SERPS, with the benefit of backdating to the tax year 1987/88; the second was the enormous strains suffered by life company administrations in the wake of the extremely high business volumes which resulted.

The 5 April deadline and the business resulting from a rush to beat the Finance Bill receiving its royal assent (to avoid new restrictions on the tax-free cash which could be obtained from a personal pension—see **14.7.2**) ensured a very good year for pensions business. However, the administration difficulties which resulted were a high price to pay and twelve months later some companies are still struggling to restore their normal standards of administrative support.

Another feature of the year was the stimulus provided to freestanding AVC (FSAVC) schemes by changes in the Finance Act 1989 to the rules concerning requirements for trustee questionnaires and rules which had previously prevented the client benefiting from any over-funding of the FSAVC (see **14.7.10**).

Ironically, perhaps the best news for pensions in the last year was the absence of any significant mention of the subject in the 1990 Budget. Although the absence of any new legislative deadlines will not help pensions production during the year, this respite is a most welcome aid to the continued recovery of companies' pension administrations.

14.3　The State pension scheme

The benefit the State provides to those in retirement falls into two main parts: the basic retirement pension and a supplementary earnings related pension (SERPS). Everyone is entitled to the basic retirement pension (payable at State retirement age; 65 for males, 60 for females), subject to payment of the necessary National Insurance contributions. For a married man whose earnings have been at the national average level throughout his working life, the State will provide a basic pension of approximately one-third of his final earnings level.

SERPS was introduced in April 1978 to provide an additional State pension based on earnings (within certain limits) rather than the flat benefit provided by the retirement pension. SERPS also provides a widow's benefit if a husband dies after retirement and also, in certain circumstances, if he dies before retirement. SERPS is funded by the higher rate National Insurance contributions payable by both employers and employees. The self-employed do not contribute towards, or benefit from, SERPS.

In recent years the State pension scheme has come under pressure by increases in life expectancy and larger numbers of retired people in the population. These concerns have lead the Government to reduce the benefits under SERPS so that only those reaching State pension age in the years 1998 and 1999 will receive the original maximum benefits.

Those reaching State retirement age in or after the year 2010 will receive a pension of only 20 per cent of their relevant earnings, instead of the 25 per cent originally intended, and the relevant earnings to be taken into account will be the average of lifetime earnings and not the best 20 years of earnings, as was the original rule for SERPS. A sliding scale will operate for those retiring in the years 2000 to 2009.

14.4 Contracting-in and contracting-out

Those who are participating in SERPS (ie, employees earning more than the lower threshold for standard rate NI contributions) are said to be 'contracted-in' to SERPS. Since SERPS was introduced it has been possible to opt-out of the scheme (referred to as 'contracting-out'), in which case NI contributions are reduced for both the employer and employee but with the loss of SERPS benefits.

Until 6 April 1988, this 'contracting-out' was only possible through an employer-sponsored occupational pension scheme which guaranteed to provide a broadly equivalent level of benefits to the SERPS benefits being lost. Since 6 April 1988, employers have been able to offer contracting-out on a 'money purchase' basis without having to provide the guarantee previously required. However, this change still left the decision whether to offer contracted-out status firmly in the employer's hands. Further changes which took effect on 1 July 1988 have now, for the first time, given the individual employee the right to contract-out of SERPS on an individual basis, without his employer's consent. The new plans which enable this are also money-purchase arrangements.

Contracting-out through the new money-purchase arrangements available for the first time in 1988, involves the payment of 'protected rights contributions' to the relevant pension contract. The contributions are identified separately from any other contributions paid and create a 'protected rights fund'; it is the 'protected rights benefits' paid out of this fund at retirement which replace the SERPS benefits lost through the decision to contract-out. The protected rights contributions are made up of the National Insurance rebate given in respect of those who contract-out, an 'incentive' payment made to those who are, broadly speaking, contracting-out for the first time and tax relief on the National Insurance rebate, where appropriate.

Contracting-out via a personal pension plan is an annual decision and the individual can contract back into SERPS for the purposes of future benefits.

In general, contracting-out will be of benefit to younger employees but may not match the likely SERPS entitlement for older people. For those contracting-out via a personal pension plan after 6 April 1990 the cut-off ages are approximately 50 (males) and 45 (females) if the 2 per cent incentive applies. In other cases the cut-off ages are approximately 47 and 42, respectively. Contracting-out is not always a simple decision and expert advice should be sought.

14.5 Types of pension contracts

There are two main types of pension contract in the context of life assurance investment:

(1) Personal pension plans for the self-employed and individuals who are not in pensionable employment take the form of deferred annuity contracts between the individual and the life company directly and are purchased by single or regular premiums.
(2) Occupational pension schemes take the form of contracts between the trustees of the scheme (set up by the employer) and the insurance company (in the case of an insured scheme) and provide benefits for employees as a group or on an individual earmarked basis. Controlling directors of director-controlled companies other than investment companies are also eligible for occupational pension schemes.

Since April 1988 individuals have been able to opt out of their occupational pension scheme and provide for their own benefit via a personal pension plan. Alternatively they will be able to top-up the pension provided by their occupational scheme by making Additional Voluntary Contributions to that scheme or by effecting a free standing AVC (FSAVC) plan with a pension provider of their choice.

14.6 Characteristics of pension contracts

As with life assurance policies there is a wide variety of types of investment. Companies offer without profit contracts with guaranteed specific benefits; with profit contracts with smaller guaranteed benefits but the right to participate in profits; and unit-linked contracts with a wide choice of unit funds and the ability to switch between funds to provide growth on top of any guaranteed benefits. It has become common in recent years for employers to split their pension investment between an insurance company and other investment media by what is known as a 'self-administered scheme'.

One of the attractions of such an arrangement is the facility of investing part of the pension fund in the employing company itself either by loans or equity investment (see **14.7.6**).

An attraction of all pension contracts is that the income and capital growth produced by the investment of the premiums accumulate on a gross basis, because pension funds are not generally subject to UK income tax or capital gains tax.

As the contracts provide essentially for retirement annuities and pensions, they cannot generally be surrendered for a cash consideration: benefits must take the form of pensions (part of which can be commuted on retirement) and life cover (including a return of the premiums with reasonable interest, which in the case of unit-linked contracts means the growth in value of the units). An important feature of many of these contracts is the 'open market option' at retirement, enabling the annuitant to use the accumulated fund built up for his pension to purchase an annuity or pension from any other company offering a higher rate. A recent development, designed to meet the drawback that funds invested in these contracts generally remain 'locked in' until retirement, is a facility offered by many insurers to give loans, on commercial terms, to companies taking out pension schemes or to individual members of these schemes (see **14.7.6**).

14.7 Eligibility, taxation, contribution limits and benefits

14.7.1 The life company

The income and gains attributable to the life company's pension liabilities are effectively free of UK tax, and it is thus able to pass on to its policyholders the entire gross increase in value of the assets and income, after deduction of its charges, without any deduction for UK tax.

14.7.2 Personal pension plans

Personal pension plans (PPPs) were introduced on 1 July 1988 and superseded Retirement Annuity Contracts (often called 's 226 contracts') which ceased to be available for new business after 30 June 1988.

Eligibility
You will be eligible to make contributions to one of these plans if you are in receipt of 'relevant earnings'. This means either earnings from

non-pensionable employments, or from businesses, professions, partnerships, etc. Generally you are not eligible if you belong to a pension scheme operated by your employers, but you are eligible if it provides only a sum assured payable on your death while in the employer's service. Controlling directors of investment companies are not eligible for any form of PPP in respect of earnings from such a company.

Tax relief on premiums and limits

If you have relevant earnings, and pay either single or annual premiums to a PPP within the limits mentioned below, you enjoy full tax relief on those premiums in the relevant years. However, an 'earnings cap' applies so that contributions to a PPP will only be possible in respect of earnings up to £64,800 (£60,000 when introduced in 1989/90) although it is proposed that the figure be increased in future years in line with the retail prices index.

Employees can pay premiums net of basic rate and any higher rate relief is claimed though the PAYE coding. The self-employed must make contributions gross and claim relief through their annual tax return. The annual limit for contributions to PPPs is 17.5 per cent of your 'net relevant earnings'. This means relevant earnings from your non-pensionable employment or business, etc, less certain deductions such as expenses, trading losses and capital allowances. The limits for older taxpayers (for years 1988/89, 1989/90 and 1990/91) are increased as follows:

Age at beginning of year of assessment	1988/89 %	1989/90 and 1990/91 %
36–45	17.5	20.0
46–50	17.5	25.0
51–55	20.0	30.0
56–60	22.5	35.0
61 and over	27.5	35.0

An amount not exceeding 5 per cent of your net relevant earnings can be used to provide a lump sum payable from the PPP in the event of your death before age 75. Premiums used to provide this life cover must be included as part of the contributions you are permitted to pay to your PPP.

Contributions may be paid to a PPP and a s 226 contract (see **14.7.4**) at the same time but the contribution limits apply to the 'aggregate' of contributions to the two plans (although the 'aggregation' is not always straightforward and paying contributions of both a PPP and a s 226 contract can restrict the overall contribution possible in some cases). Note that the increased contribution percentages which apply for tax years 1989/90 and 1990/91 do not apply to s 226 contracts (for which the 1988/89 figures shown above remain appropriate). Note also that the 'earnings cap' does not apply to s 226 contracts.

If your employer pays contributions to your PPP, these too must be taken as part of the maximum contribution which can be made to your plan. Employer's contributions are not treated as the employee's income. Protected rights contributions paid to your PPP to enable you to contract-out of SERPS can be paid in addition to the maximum permissible contribution calculated as the appropriate percentage of your net relevant earnings.

Years for which relief is granted
Generally, relief is given against net relevant earnings of the tax year in which the contributions are paid. However, you can elect to have any premium you pay treated for tax purposes as if it has been paid during the preceding tax year, or, if you had no relevant earnings in that year, for the premium to be relieved against earnings in the tax year before that; ie, there is a 'carry-back' period of one or two years.

To the extent that premiums paid in any year fall short of the permitted maximum of net relevant earnings, it is possible to carry forward the shortfall on unused relief for up to six years and use the shortfall (on a first-in first-out basis) to obtain relief against a premium paid in a subsequent year, to the extent that that premium exceeds the maximum percentage limit of net relevant earnings for the year in which it is paid.

Benefits payable and age at which they may be taken
The PPP scheme established by the pension provider can allow the individual to make more than one contract (or arrangement) under it. The advantages of this are that, as benefits from an arrangement can, generally, only be taken once if they are to include a cash lump sum, multiple arrangements can give the opportunity to take benefits in stages. This approach also maximised the cash lump sums which could be taken from plans effected prior to the 1989 Finance Bill receiving royal assent, as the maximum limits on the lump sums payable under such plans applied to each arrangement, not to the PPP as a whole (see below).

Your pension may start being paid at any age between 50 and 75. It is not necessary for you actually to retire before the annuity can commence. In certain occupations the Revenue allow an annuity to start earlier than the age of 50 (eg, jockeys, motor racing drivers, cricketers, etc).

Should your PPP incorporate a sum assured, on your premature death the lump sum would be paid and this can be arranged to be free of inheritance tax by writing it in trust where the PPP scheme itself is not set up under trust. The whole of any annuity payable either to you, your spouse or your dependants will be treated and taxed as income (and not, as is the case with purchased life annuities, partly as income and partly as a return of capital, see Chapter 13, **13.3.4**). However, the annuity will be treated as earned income to the extent to which contributions have been allowed for tax relief.

A lump sum may be taken from the PPP, between the ages of 50 and 75, up to a maximum of 25 per cent of the fund then being used to provide you with retirement benefits. For lump sum payments made before the passing of the Finance Act 1989, the lump sum was subject to an overriding limit of £150,000 per arrangement under the PPP. For payments made on or after that date, the lump sum cash limit will not apply. As the lump sum is calculated as a percentage of the fund accumulated and the contributions are now subject to the monetary ceiling on earnings, the Revenue no longer need this overriding limit to restrict the lump sum benefit.

If the contract so provides, you are permitted, instead of taking the annuity from the life company with whom you hold the contract, to utilise the fund built up for your annuity in order to purchase an annuity from any other company, thus obtaining the best terms then available ('open market option'). If your PPP is provided by an organisation which is not a life assurance company, your pension (and life assurance) must be provided by a life company.

14.7.3 Contracting-out via a PPP

Scheme certificates
If a PPP has an 'appropriate scheme certificate' from the Occupational Pensions Board it will be able to receive protected rights contributions (and may be funded by them entirely) and so enable the individual employee to contract-out of SERPS. A PPP which receives only protected rights contributions (a 'PPP(PRO)') can be effected by an employee who is a member of a contracted-in occupational scheme but wishes to contract-out on an individual basis.

Contributions
Protected rights contributions are made up of the National Insurance rebate, the incentive (where applicable) and tax relief on the rebate

(which grosses it up at the basic rate). The rebate is equal to the difference between the contracted-in and contracted-out National Insurance rates on the individual employee's band earnings (the earnings between the upper and lower earnings limits.) Both employer and employee continue to pay full National Insurance but the rebate is paid by the DSS to the individual's plan after the end of the relevant tax year.

The incentive is 2 per cent of band earnings and is payable for up to six tax years commencing 1987/88. Until 5 April 1989 a plan could be 'backdated' to receive the incentive and rebate for tax year 1987/88. Broadly speaking, the incentive is payable to those who contract-out for the first time and those who have been in contracted-out employment for less than two years.

The protected rights pension must commence between State pension age (65 males, 60 females) and the age of 75. It must increase at 3 per cent pa or the rate of the retail prices index, whichever is lower, and must not discriminate between males and females, married or single people in terms of the annuity rates offered. No lump sum benefit can be taken from the protected rights fund.

A protected rights pension must continue for the benefit of a widow/widower or dependant on the individual's death, at a rate not less than one-half of the individual's pension. On death before retirement age the protected rights fund can be paid to the deceased's estate or nominees but no life assurance sum assured can be included in the protected rights benefits.

14.7.4 Retirement annuity contracts (s 226 contracts)

No new s 226 contracts can be entered into after 30 June 1988 but contracts in existence by that date can continue much as before. Contributions can continue to be paid to such contracts and regular contributions can be increased in the future.

In many ways s 226 contracts were similar to the new PPPs but there are some key differences, eg no employer's contributions; contributions paid gross and the tax reclaimed; no facility for an employee to contract-out through a s 226 contract and no general entitlement to take benefits before the age of 60. One important way in which a s 226 contract could be more favourable than a PPP was in providing a cash commutation equal to three times the annual annuity payable after the cash had been taken. (Contracts entered into on or after 21 March 1987 are subject to a maximum cash lump sum of £150,000 per contract.) Neither the cap on earnings for contribution purposes nor the increased contribution percentages introduced in 1989/90 apply to s 226 contracts.

It should be noted that, although many s 226 contracts contain an open market option to allow the annuity to be purchased from a life company other than the one with whom the pension plan has been effected, exercising such an option after 30 June 1988 will have the effect of transferring the policy proceeds to a new PPP (unless the policyholder has a second s 226 contract already in existence with that other life company). Thus, in the absence of another s 226 contract, the benefits will be paid out of a PPP with the resulting less favourable calculation of the maximum cash lump sum compared to the s 226 contract.

14.7.5 Occupational schemes

These are schemes provided by an employer for the benefit of some or all of his employees but they are not available to directors of investment companies. To be effective, the scheme should be approved by the Superannuation Funds Office (SFO) which is a branch of the Inland Revenue.

'Approval' will prevent contributions paid by the employer being taxed in the employees' hands as a benefit in kind. 'Exempt approval' will give the additional benefits of the gross roll-up in the fund and tax relief for the employee in respect of regular contributions he makes to the scheme. Exempt approval will also mean that the employer's contributions will be deductible business expenses without relying on the normal rules for deductibility applying to Schedule D income. In most cases approval is given under the SFO's discretionary powers which are extremely wide-ranging.

Since 6 April 1988 it has not been possible for an employer to make membership of an occupational scheme (other than one providing death in service benefits only) compulsory. Employees are also able to opt out of their employer's scheme and so become eligible to effect their own PPP, independent of the employer. In general, leaving an occupational scheme is unlikely to be wise except where its benefits are extremely poor and expert advice should be sought if this is contemplated.

Contributions
The employer must make some contribution to the scheme although the employee may indirectly provide the necessary funds by agreeing

to a reduction in salary—'a salary sacrifice'. Contributions by the employer to an exempt approved scheme are deductible business expenses, although relief in respect of non-regular contributions may be deferred by being spread over a maximum of five years. The employee may make personal contributions of up to 15 per cent of his remuneration. Personal contributions attract tax relief at the highest rate paid by the individual.

Unlike PPPs there are no specific limits on the amount of contributions which may be made to an occupational scheme, instead (subject to the various 'income capping' rules referred to below) the controls operate on the level of benefits which is allowed. If a scheme becomes 'over-funded' (ie, where the scheme has more capital than is necessary to meet its prospective liabilities), payment of further contributions may be restricted or capital may have to be returned to the employer. If a refund is made to the employer it is taxable at a special rate of 40 per cent.

Benefits

Benefits are payable on retirement at a specified age not earlier than 60 (55 in the case of women) and not later than 70. Many schemes provide a pension of one-sixtieth of final remuneration for each year of service so that the maximum pension of two-thirds of final salary is reached after 40 years' service.

Finance (No 2) Act 1987 (now ICTA 1988, s 590 *et seq* and Sched 23) made significant changes in the permissible benefits and distinguish between those who were members of schemes prior to 17 March 1987 and those joining schemes on or after that day. In addition, the Finance Act 1989 imposed further restrictions on members of schemes set up on or after 14 March 1989 and new members joining pre-14 March 1989 schemes after 31 May 1989.

Pre-17 March 1987 members

An 'uplifted sixtieth' scale may be used to provide the maximum benefit after only ten years (taking into account benefits from previous employments). Final salary or final remuneration may be calculated in either of the ways permitted by the SFO:

(1) the remuneration in any of the five years preceding the normal retirement date (remuneration includes the average of fluctuation emoluments earned over at least three years ending with the year in question); or
(2) the highest average of total emoluments over any period of three consecutive years ending within ten years before the normal retirement date.

For those retiring after 16 March 1987 'final salary' excludes certain income and gains from shares, etc acquired through share option, share incentive or profit-sharing schemes. In addition, those with final salaries of over £100,000 pa will have to use definition (2) above, subject to transitional reliefs for those retiring before 6 April 1991. As an alternative they may use £100,000 as final salary for benefit purposes. For lump sums the maximum final salary figure is £100,000 (subject to increase by Treasury order).

The employee is often given the right to commute a part of his pension for a tax-free cash lump sum up to a maximum of $1\frac{1}{2}$ times final remuneration (three-eighths of final salary for a maximum of 40 years' service). An 'uplifted eightieths' scale may be used to provide the maximum lump sum after 20 years' service.

The scheme may provide a lump sum of up to four times final remuneration on the death of the employee in service, together with a refund of the employee's personal contributions. Such payments are usually made by the trustees of the scheme who have a discretion as to selection of the recipient, from a class of potential beneficiaries. Such payments are usually free of inheritance tax. Pensions may be paid for a spouse or dependant, of up to two-thirds of the maximum pension to which the deceased would have been entitled at the normal retirement date.

On death in retirement a pension may be provided for a spouse or dependant in the same way as for death in service.

Post-16 March 1987 members

The rules are broadly the same as those above but the 'uplifted sixtieths' scale can now provide maximum pension benefits only after 20 years' service. The 'uplifted eightieths' scale for lump sums can only be used in conjunction with the use of the uplifted sixtieths scale for the pension.

Post-13 March 1989 schemes, etc

The changes to the regimes outlined above are as follows:

(1) For schemes set up on or after 14 March 1989, and for members joining pre-14 March schemes after 31 May 1989, benefits may not be provided (and personal contributions cannot be made) in respect of any of the member's salary in excess of a specified amount. For 1989/90 this was £60,000 and for 1990/91 is £64,800. The figure is to be increased in line with the rise in the retail prices index.

(2) For these members the calculation of the maximum cash commutation is amended so that the lump sum can be 2.25 per cent the initial pension payable (ignoring commutation) or, if more advantageous, 3/80ths of the final salary for each year of service up to a maximum of 40 years. The overall limit of 1.5 × final salary for the lump sum payment remains.
(3) The maximum two-thirds of final salary which can be provided under an approved scheme may be provided on retirement between the ages of 50 and 70, subject to 20 years' service with the employer.

It is possible that members not caught by these rules would prefer to be subject to them eg, to enjoy a more favourable lump sum calculation. Such members may elect (with the scheme trustees' consent in the case of pre-17 March 1987 members) to become subject to these rules but they will then apply as a package, ie, it is not possible to elect to become subject to only some of them and not to others.

Company directors

In general, the same rules apply to 'controlling' directors as to any individual in an occupational pension scheme, however, because a director of a family company is in a rather different position from an ordinary employee, the Revenue have imposed some limitations on directors with at least 20 per cent control, eg, the measurement of final salary is more stringent than for non-controlling directors. Directors with 20 per cent control and members of families controlling more than 50 per cent of the company are not eligible to join a company's approved pension scheme if it is an investment company.

14.7.6 Loans and self-investment

A very important development in recent years has been the use of pensions in connection with loans made to the pension planholder or occupational scheme member. This helps to reduce one of the disadvantages of pension schemes, capital invested in the fund is 'locked-in' until retirement.

Typically, a lender who makes an interest-only loan to the individual might expect him to repay the capital out of any lump sum to which he is entitled from his pension. Such lump sums will not be assigned to the lender as security for the loan but, for example where the loan is for house purchase, the mortgage over the property, assigned life assurance protection and the existence of the pension cash entitlement will usually satisfy the lender's requirements.

It is important that the pension contracts remain independent of the loan arrangements and that effecting the pension does not guarantee the availability of the loan. The pension must not be taken out in order to obtain the loan as the pensions legislation requires the pension scheme to be solely for the purpose of obtaining retirement benefits.

Another approach to 'unlocking' some of the pension fund is for the fund to be invested, in part, in shares of the employer company, in making the loans to the company or in purchasing premises from which the company trades.

At present, loans are limited to 50 per cent of the fund and the other approaches, which are also subject to restrictions, are usually only available to self-administered schemes in which the trustees have wide powers of investment compared to 'insured schemes' where the investment is usually confined to a policy issued by the insurance company concerned.

Regulations which are anticipated to follow the passing of the Social Security Act 1990 are expected to impose tighter restrictions on the availability and amount of loans that can be made to the employer company, except where the scheme is a self-administered one and all the members are 20 per cent Directors of the employer company.

14.7.7 Contracting-out via an occupational scheme

As already mentioned, money-purchase schemes can now be used to contract-out of SERPS without the previous requirement of a guarantee attaching to the benefits which are, in effect, replacing SERPS.

A contracted-out money purchase (COMP) scheme will receive protected rights contributions by way of National Insurance rebate and incentive payment, where appropriate, as is the case with a PPP. However, a COMP will receive the National Insurance payments monthly direct from the employer and not as a lump sum, a year in arrears, as does a PPP. With a COMP, the Inland Revenue's limits on maximum benefits apply to the aggregate of the protected rights and non-protected rights benefits; a contracted-in occupational scheme member may obtain the maximum benefits from the occupational scheme, in addition to the protected rights benefits, from a PPP(PRO) effected to contract-out of SERPS.

In response to the recent European Court decision in *Barber* v *GRE*, with effect from 17 May 1990 the Social Security Act 1990 allows schemes to reduce the minimum age at which a COMP's protected rights can be taken by males. This was previously 65 but can now be as low as 60 (the age at which females can take such benefits).

14.7.8 Unapproved occupational schemes

These may be established by employers to provide benefits greater than those otherwise allowable. In this way, for example, benefits in excess of two-thirds of final salary can be provided and top-up pensions can be given to employees with short service or those who are subject to 'income capping'.

There are none of the special tax benefits normally received by pension schemes but employer contributions will obtain relief as normal business expenditure and lump sums can be paid free of tax from funded schemes.

14.7.9 Simplified occupational schemes

These are schemes which can be established using standard documentation provided by the Inland Revenue and the DSS. Created primarily for the new pension providers (banks, building societies and unit trust groups) they are easier to administer but are restricted in the benefits they can provide compared to 'full' occupational schemes.

14.7.10 Free-standing AVC schemes

Since October 1987 all occupational scheme members are entitled to top-up their pensions by making contributions to a separate pension scheme of their own. Such a 'Free-Standing' Additional Voluntary Contribution (FSAVC) scheme may not be commuted for a cash lump sum and must be aggregated with the occupational scheme to determine the maximum permitted benefits. The overriding limit on personal contributions, 15 per cent of salary (capped where appropriate) remains.

Although regulated by the occupational pension scheme tax legislation, FSAVC schemes also have similarities to PPPs in that they are individual arrangements independent of the individual's employer. They can also be used by a member of a contracted-in occupational scheme to receive protected rights contributions and so contract-out of SERPS in much the same way as a 'protected rights only' PPP (although, as PPPs can offer this facility few if any, FSAVCs offer contracting-out). The main differences are that: no tax relief is allowed on the employee's share of the National Insurance rebate paid to an FSAVC scheme; and that, if an occupational scheme member contracts-out of SERPS by means of an FSAVC scheme, the

Revenue's maximum benefits limits apply to the aggregate of the benefits from both schemes. An employee's contributions to such schemes may be paid net of tax relief at the basic rate.

The 1989 Finance Act introduced significant simplifications in the administration of these schemes so that the employer has no involvement in an employee joining a FSAVC if contributions to it do not exceed £2,400 pa. Even where the contributions exceed this sum the employer's involvement at outset is less than was formerly the case. These changes may result in more schemes becoming over-funded and over-provision is returned to the scheme member subject to a tax charge. This charge also applies to AVC schemes established in-house by employers.

14.8 Suitability

Personal pension plans, retirement annuity contracts and occupational pension schemes provide highly tax-efficient benefits. In consequence they are suitable for and extremely attractive as investments for those with earned income who wish to provide for personal cash and income during retirement and protection for their wives and families during their working lives. Because the premiums are deductible for tax purposes from earned income, the effective cost is relatively low, while the tax-free growth inside the pension fund enables substantial accumulation of funds for pension benefits. The emerging benefits, in the form of tax-free cash commutation or pensions, receive beneficial tax treatment.

14.9 Preview of the year ahead

In production terms, the industry faces an uphill task in 1990 to match the performance in 1989, quite apart from maintaining the pattern of growth which has been achieved in recent years.

The administration problems referred to previously may also not help as some agents and brokers will have turned their attention to other markets (eg, life assurance protection or investment) as a result of the service levels they received from pensions administrations in 1989.

The challenge to companies in the industry is to deal with their pensions backlogs and complete the necessary systems developments to provide better computer support for the new contracts, in order to restore the confidence of those agents who have previously specialised in this market.

Regulations expected to be made under the Social Security Act could be a significant factor in encouraging a shift from defined benefit schemes towards money purchase schemes and it is anticipated that the Act will also play a part in promoting self-administered schemes for small companies seeking to avoid expected restrictions on self-investment.

Also of considerable interest will be the practical consequences of the case of *Barber* v *GRE*, recently heard by the European Court, concerning equal treatment for men and women under pension schemes.

14.10 Conclusion

The tax-deductibility of premiums, tax-free growth and prospects of a tax-free lump sum make pensions an extremely attractive investment.

There are, of course, some restrictions (lack of access to the fund until a minimum age, ability to take only a proportion as a lump sum, limits on the investment permitted, etc) but these do not detract from the investment benefit of pensions where the pension is effected for the right reasons, ie, as long-term planning for retirement.

In the past, pensions have been something of a political football and subject to frequent change. However, during the last ten years of continuous Conservative government the rate of change has continued unabated (and has even accelerated in the last few years) and in consequence the industry is now looking for a period of stability during which it can consolidate and restore previous high levels of service.

Sources of further information

See end of Chapter 13.

15 Commodities

David Fuller, Chairman, Chart Analysis Ltd, Editor, Fuller Money

15.1 Introduction to the commodity markets

Commodity markets evolved from the basic functions of buying and selling commodities or produce. Although these markets are possibly the least understood of all the City institutions, historically they provided a broad base for virtually the entire range of financial functions associated with the City of London today.

The commodity markets fall broadly into groups which correspond with the successive phases of Britain's commercial history. With the colonial empire and early industrialisation came markets for coffee, cocoa and wool, while the nineteenth century brought with it a growing demand for lead, copper, zinc and rubber.

Modern commodity markets still bring together buyers and sellers. The main difference is that today they are more concerned with transactions in the rights to commodities than with transactions in the physical products. The markets also offer the producer and consumer the vital facility of what is effectively insurance against risk through the hedging system (see **15.3.2**).

The commodity markets of the UK are the most important in Europe and offer the widest trading facilities. They are as sophisticated and highly developed as any others in the world. Turnover in the London commodity markets, and indeed in commodity markets worldwide, has remained high in recent years despite the recession of the early 1980s. In the main British markets the value of the combined annual turnover is well in excess of that of the fixed interest and equity market.

The discussion in this chapter is largely confined to those commodities that can be bought and sold through or are regulated by the International Commodities Clearing House (ICCH), the London Metal Exchange (LME), the London Commodity Exchange (LCE) or other recognised commodity exchanges and London International Financial Futures Exchange (LIFFE).

15.2 Highlights of the previous year

The most significant factors affecting commodity markets in the last year were further, sustained growth in the industrialised countries, increased production of industrial commodities in particular, a generally steady dollar, high real interest rates and a gradual rise in the worldwide inflation rate.

Strong growth rates in continental Europe and the developed Asian countries more than offset the slower pace of economic activity in other industrialised countries. This kept demand firm for most commodities and petroleum in particular.

Consequently oil prices moved erratically higher throughout 1989, with the Dubai spot crude price surging to $19 a barrel in January, helped by cold weather in the USA and rumours about Soviet production difficulties. However, this proved unsustainable as OPEC production quickly expanded to exceed consumption, pushing the Dubai price back below $15.

Over the year base metal production finally caught up with demand and exceeded it, resulting in a surplus. Simultaneously, rising interest rates encouraged both metal producers and consumers to reduce inventories. These factors caused base metal prices to slump during the second half of 1989, resulting in some production cutbacks.

Concern over the stability of financial assets, higher oil prices and a downward lurch in the US dollar, caused precious metals to rally sharply in the final quarter of 1989. However, these influences proved temporary as stockmarkets steadied by year-end, oil fell and the dollar steadied against European currencies while rallying strongly against the yen. Precious metals fell back to their lows in early 1990.

More enduring trends were emerging for agricultural commodities over the last year. Prices for many food commodities had fallen to their lowest levels, at least in real (inflation adjusted) terms in 1989. These depressed levels proved unsustainable and most agricultural commodities had established overall upward trends by April 1990.

15.3 Nature and divisions of commodities

15.3.1 Softs and metals

The commodity markets can be divided into two categories: soft commodities and metals.

The term soft commodities loosely describes all the non-metallic commodities: cocoa, coffee, sugar, wool, rubber, grain, potatoes, oil etc. The London Commodity Exchange is responsible for matters affecting the London soft commmodity markets as a whole, including the provision of market floors and supporting services. Market rules, contract specifications and arbitration of disputes are dealt with by the market associations which exist for each soft commodity.

The LME is an important centre for trade in the main non-ferrous metals such as aluminium, copper, lead, nickel, silver, tin and zinc. Trading in the LME takes place on the 'ring' where full members have seats. Companies in the 'ring' represent producers, consumers, brokers and merchants. Non-ring members trade through full ring dealing members.

Clearing and settlement of contracts is handled by the International Commodities Clearing House (ICCH), membership of which guarantees the fulfilment of the contract to both buyer and seller thus avoiding the need to put up mutual funds. The ICCH's advanced computer systems for settlement and clearing are available both to soft commodity brokers and to ring and associate members of the LME.

15.3.2 Physicals and futures

Both the soft commodity and metals markets can be further broken down into 'physicals' and 'futures'. The physical markets offer the straightforward facility of buying and selling a commodity, and an agreement is reached in the expectation of delivery. In the futures markets, commodities are bought and sold for delivery at a future date, but there is often no expectation of delivery. The contract will generally be liquidated before maturity date, which means that the contract will be cancelled by a corresponding and opposite contract and a profit or loss realised.

By buying and selling in the futures markets against a physical position, the *trade hedger* is able to safeguard himself against the risk that the value of his unsold goods will depreciate through a fall in prices or, alternatively, against the risk that forward sales will show losses if the commodity price rises.

Example

A consumer company with 25 tonnes of copper not for immediate use hedges this position by selling short (ie, before purchasing) one three-month futures contract (25 tonnes) on the LME.

The *speculator* on the other hand enters the markets in the expectation of making profits. By taking an opposite view in the market to that of the hedger, he removes from the consumer and producer what is to them an unwanted element of risk while at the same time hoping to make a profit for himself.

Example

A speculator believes metals will rise in price and buys copper futures enabling the consumer (in the above example) to hedge in a more liquid market environment than would otherwise exist.

The fact that the volume of turnover in any commodity futures market is much in excess of actual production or consumption over a given period should not obscure the purpose of such markets, which is to provide a clearance mechanism for producers and consumers.

Investment in the physicals markets is best limited to the purchase and sale of cash metals (see **15.7.1**). Soft commodities are bulky, and the costs of warehousing, etc would be prohibitive to the pure investor. Further, soft commodities are perishable, which would add to the investor's risk should he take delivery.

Investment in the futures markets need not be so limited. The speculator, in most cases, does not contemplate ever taking possession of the commodity, and he is able to deal in softs as easily as in metals. The futures markets are available to him through private trading accounts.

15.3.3 Opportunities for investment

As well as investing directly in commodities, there are other avenues open to the investor. He may purchase options conferring the right to buy and/or sell commodites (see **15.7.4**), or he may place his capital in the hands of a fund manager to be invested in accordance with agreed objectives or at the discretion of the manager (see **15.7.3**).

15.4 Pre-conditions for commodities

There are opportunities for everyone in the commodity markets, if they have the time, the temperament and the capital. The scope for UK residents has greatly increased as a result of the Government's decision in 1979 to drop virtually all exchange control regulations.

This means that UK residents can buy gold bullion, which has a long tradition as an investment medium, or trade commodities on any of the overseas exchanges. These transactions can be handled effectively by any established UK commodity broker, who will have reciprocal business agreements with firms in New York, Chicago or other commodity centres.

15.5 Characteristics of commodities

It is their sophisticated structure and method of operation, together with frequent dealing opportunities, which make the soft commodity and metal markets an increasingly attractive trading proposition.

International markets—Every country has an interest in commodities, as a consumer even if not always as a producer, and the markets are thus truly international. Because of this, they usually have a high turnover and high liquidity. This, in turn, makes it possible in most cases to move funds in and out of the markets fairly quickly without unduly disrupting the price balance.

Low dealing costs—Another advantage of these highly liquid markets is that dealing costs, including commission and the spread between bid and offer prices, are extremely low and very competitive when compared with other forms of market. For example, the total commission for buying and selling a commodity rarely exceeds 0.5 per cent and in many instances is considerably less. No stamp duty is payable on commodity trading.

Frequent opportunities—All commodities, but particularly the softs, respond to their own supply and demand factors, which means that they do not all move in the same direction at the same time. Thus, there are always trading opportunities to be found across the entire range of commodity markets. However, the market movements do, of course, require close attention on the part of the investor, who is best advised to seek the guidance of an established broker.

Flexibility—Another advantage of the commodity markets is that they offer dealing flexibility. It is equally possible to go long or short ('bull' or 'bear' trading), which means that profits can be made both when prices are rising and when they are falling. The investor can also participate in commodity options trading.

Real assets—Finally, commodities are real assets, and therefore they will always have some value (albeit fluctuating). However, they do have an advantage over some other real assets in that they are immediately convertible into cash. Because commodities are real assets, over the long term they are a good potential hedge against inflation or currency uncertainty.

15.6 Taxation of commodities

15.6.1 Commodity transactions

UK residents now benefit from a change in the taxation of commodity/futures contracts which were previously assessed on the basis of Schedule D, Case VI, resulting in the treatment of gains as income, while losses were not able to be offset against profits from other investments. Profits from non-trading transactions on recognised dealing exchanges in commodity or financial futures or in traded options are now treated as capital gains, with losses which can be offset against other capital gains. There could, however, be a disadvantage in this, namely that if in previous years dealings in futures having given rise to losses treated as income losses under Case VI, those losses cannot be offset against capital gains arising under the new treatment.

15.6.2 Options

Similar considerations are likely to apply in the case of options, although the greater degree of risk perhaps increases the likelihood of the transactions falling within Case I, while correspondingly reducing the risk of their being within the charge to capital gains tax. Were the latter to apply, the wasting assets rules would have to be considered. If traded options fall within the Capital Gains Tax Act 1979, s 137(9), being options quoted on a recognised stock exchange or on a recognised futures exchange, the wasting asset rules which normally apply to assets with a predictable life not exceeding 50 years are excluded. Options now excepted from treatment as wasting assets are those quoted either on a recognised stock exchange or on the London International Financial Future Exchange (LIFFE) and include:

(1) traded options in company shares;
(2) traded options in assets other than shares, such as bonds, loan stock, Government securities, currency and gold;
(3) quoted option warrants to purchase or subscribe for securities other than shares; and
(4) quoted (nil-paid) provisional letters of allotment for securities other than shares.

15.6.3 Managed funds

Managed funds may be treated differently from the other forms of investment so far described. In the case of the private discretionary account, the investor's involvement is reduced, and this may arguably prevent the activity from being regarded as trading and establish that the transactions should be regarded as capital so as to be only within the charge to capital gains tax.

In the case of commodity unit trusts (which, for reasons explained earlier in this book, are based outside the UK), the acquisition and disposal of units until the end of 1983 were generally regarded as capital transactions, falling within the charge to capital gains tax, and gains and losses were treated as falling within the capital gains tax regime. As a result of legislation in 1984 (now incorporated in Chapter V and Schedule 7, Income and Corporation Taxes Act 1988), a gain made by a UK resident investor on the disposal after 1 January 1984 of any interest in certain offshore or overseas funds is taxed as income under Schedule D, Case VI. The funds that are affected (which include unit trusts with non-resident trustees) are those which do not distribute all their income throughout the period for which an investment is held and those from which the investor is entitled to more than a mere repayment of his original consideration. There are special provisions for treatment of gains where the interest was already held by the UK investor before 1 January 1984. It is possible for UK residents to trade commodities through a licensed financial betting shop, thus avoiding the 40 per cent capital gains tax on profits. However, it should be borne in mind that net losses from most trusts cannot be offset against profits made elsewhere.

15.6.4 Suitability of commodities

The world commodity markets offer many opportunities for investment at all levels. Commodities are not investments in the strict sense of the word, that is to say, they are not income-producing. However, with the inflation rates that have been seen over the last two decades, it is worth considering whether this is an outdated concept of investment. People now speak openly of investing in real assets as a hedge against inflation or currency uncertainty.

To consider which area of commodity involvement is most suitable the potential investor should consider the following questions:

(1) What percentage of his total portfolio is to be put into commodities?
(2) What sort of capital appreciation is he looking for (bearing in

mind that greater reward is seldom achieved without greater risk) and over what period? How might this compare with a capital investment in the stock market, gilts, property or works of art?
(3) Is he likely to want to realise his investment at short notice, or can the money be committed for long-term growth?
(4) Does he wish to be involved in the commodity markets on a day-to-day basis, or would he prefer to hand his capital over to a fund manager and give him discretion to handle it in accordance with the investor's requirements?

The spectrum of investment possibilities ranges from speculative, highly geared trading accounts for the investor who enjoys an element of risk in return for the possibility of high rewards, to the purchase of cash metals or investment in commodity unit trusts for the individual who desires a more conservative approach to the commodity markets and does not wish to involve himself on a day-to-day basis.

15.7 Methods of participation

Traditionally, the commodity markets have a high risk reputation. However, the truth of the matter is that investment opportunities run the entire gamut from conservative investment to pure speculation. The decision lies with the potential investor/speculator as to the level at which he wishes to participate.

15.7.1 Cash metals and metal trusts

Possibly the least speculative activity on the commodity markets is the purchase of physical metals. These are tangible assets which will always have a value (albeit fluctuating) and which are immediately convertible into cash.

Anyone from a private investor to a pension fund may purchase cash metals. Precious metals such as gold, silver or platinum can be stored at home or in the bank. In the case of the bulkier metals such as lead or copper, the investor can make use of the LME warehouses for storage. This costs around 1 per cent per annum including insurance.

Cash metals are most safely purchased when they are at or below the cost of world production, and then held for recovery. The metals are paid for in full at the time of purchase, so there are no further hidden financial commitments beyond insurance and storage costs. In addition, they represent a real asset which will always have a market value, so the risk involved in the purchase of cash metals is minimal.

Additionally, there are now physical metal trusts in such metals as gold, silver, aluminium and copper. These are of equal use to the small private investor who may wish to build a position gradually, or at the other extreme, the pension fund manager who wants an unleveraged and unmanaged position in metals, which can be bought or sold, or otherwise treated like any other security.

Anyone investing in cash metals should bear in mind two natural supply and demand equations, which cause cyclical price swings, albeit with a long-term upward bias during periods of inflation. First, high prices result in lower consumption of, or substitution of other commodities for, or increased production of the particular commodity, or possibly all three. Therefore, a strong price rise will inevitably lead to a period of lower prices. Secondly, and conversely, low prices result in increased consumption or lower production, or possibly both. Therefore, the longer prices remain below the average cost of world production, the greater the certainty that a price rise will eventually follow.

15.7.2 Cash and carry transactions

The cash and carry transaction is a risk-free way of trading in commodities for a guaranteed return on the money employed. Additionally, it will occasionally provide an opportunity to secure capital appreciation.

In essence, cash and carry transactions are very simple. They are confined to trading in metals, which are always quoted in terms of the cash price for that day and the price three months ahead, which is known as the forward price. Usually the forward price is higher than the cash price (exceptions occur when there is a shortage), and the difference between the two prices is known as the contango. Normally the contango reflects the costs incurred in holding a commodity for a three-month period. In other words, it reflects the interest on the money employed, together with the cost of storing and insuring the physical asset.

The main purpose of the cash and carry is to generate a guaranteed rate of return on the money employed. This is achieved by purchasing the physical metal and simultaneously selling an equivalent amount of metal three months forward. Six or nine month cash and carries can also be established. The transaction is normally completed when the physical metal is used to offset the forward sale on expiration of that contract. This releases the cash which can be re-employed in a similar transaction.

Occasionally during the life of a cash and carry a shortage of cash metal will occur. Usually due to production delays, this can squeeze the cash metal price until it trades at a premium to the futures position. Known as a backwardation, this development enables the holder of the cash and carry to establish a capital gain by selling his physical position and simultaneously buying back the forward contract.

15.7.3 Managed funds

Money can be invested in commodities and managed at any level of capital outlay from £1,000 upwards. Funds are an ideal medium for the investor who does not have the time, inclination or expertise to interpret the markets but who wishes to diversify his portfolio to include commodities. With prudent management, the risk/reward element can be harnessed and exploited to produce long-term growth. There are two categories of managed fund: the private discretionary fund and the public commodity unit trust.

The private discretionary fund
The private discretionary fund generally exists for the larger investor—the minimum capital outlay tending to be in the region of £25,000. The capital is placed in the hands of a fund manager, who is given total discretion to invest the money in accordance with general objectives decided upon between the manager and the investor. It is essential that comparatively large sums of money are made available for this type of investment if the manager is to have the flexibility to take advantage of new opportunities as they occur in the markets and, at the same time, to meet margin requirements.

Normally, the only cost to the investor—over and above his capital outlay—will be standard brokerage charges plus an incentive fee which is assessed on the performance of the fund. This fee generally averages about 10 per cent of the increase in value of the fund in an agreed accounting period.

The public commodity unit trust
The public commodity unit trust which speculates in futures and options or holds physical commodities rather than shares, did not exist prior to the 1970s. While these funds are still regarded as a fringe investment, interest has grown steadily as investors seek to diversify their portfolios.

Commodity unit trust managers operate in very much the same way as managers of private discretionary funds. The main differences are that there will be no prior consultation as to objectives—the aim is to seek steady capital appreciation while attempting to avoid violent swings in either direction—and that the investor will not be kept personally up to date on transactions, valuations, etc. Apart from, in some instances, a quarterly report to unit holders, the investor will get the bulk of his information from the unit prices quoted in the financial press.

Although the number of commodity funds currently available to the UK investor is not large, between them they offer considerable scope. They range in investment philosophy from those which exist simply to buy and hold a specific commodity to those which give their management flexibility to use all the investment techniques that the commodity markets can offer.

Flexibly managed unit trusts, which give the manager the greatest degree of mobility, are, arguably, more speculative, since their success is largely dependent on the skill and judgment of the manager. However, anyone who invests in a fund with a 'buy and hold' philosophy, come what may, is himself speculating on a rise in the price of the particular metal which is bound to fluctuate in price. Perhaps the best criterion for evaluating the commodity unit trust is past performance, even though this is obviously not a guarantee of future performance.

Authorised UK unit trusts (see Chapter 8) are only permitted to invest in 'securities' and so may not invest directly in commodities. Consequently, collective investment in commodities is arranged through the medium of 'unauthorised' unit trusts or 'open-ended' companies, which are established offshore so that their activities do not attract UK taxation. Offshore commodity funds designed to be attractive to UK investors are generally based in the Channel Islands or the Isle of Man and have their capital denominated in sterling. Most US dollar commodity funds established primarily for UK investors are based in Bermuda.

These *funds* may be taxed locally as 'dealers' in commodities generating trading profit (and not as 'investors' realising capital gains) but, so long as they do not trade or become resident in the UK for tax purposes, they will be taxed at the rates applicable where they are resident and, in the case of the Channel Islands and the Isle of Man, these rates are lower than the comparable rates prevailing in the UK. The Bermudan funds are not taxed locally. However, the UK *investor* will be subject to UK taxation in respect of his investment and so, as well as considering the taxation position of the offshore fund, he should be aware of the UK tax consequences of making or holding an investment in the fund.

The minimum initial investment in a commodity unit trust probably averages around £1,000. The only costs to the investor who purchases units are a buying and selling charge and a management fee, all of which are reflected in the bid and offer prices quoted for the units (see Chapter 8).

15.7.4 Options

An area of commodity speculation with limited liability is the purchase of options. The investor's maximum liability is established from the outset—no matter what happens to the market price of the underlying commodity, it cannot exceed the size of the premium paid—and he also has the opportunity to 'lock in' profits with corresponding and opposite trades on the futures markets before the life of the option expires. Additionally, the advent of traded options for many contracts, particularly in the US markets, enables the speculator to participate without ever buying or selling the underlying commodity. The traded options are issued in series and can be bought and sold through the broker at the prevailing price, prior to expiration.

Clearly, the availability of options varies with market conditions since there must be both buyers and sellers prepared to do business. Nevertheless, options business is done over a wide range of market conditions.

There are three types of commodity option: put options which confer on the buyer the right to sell a commodity; call options, which confer the right to buy; and double options, which confer the right both to buy and to sell.

The cost of the option is the premium which the investor pays. Obviously, the size of the premium is not constant and will vary according to price volatility on the markets, so that it is essential to adopt a flexible approach when assessing the cost. Generally, a premium approaching 10 per cent of the value of the underlying commodity will represent an attractive opportunity.

The holder of an option has the right to buy or sell a given commodity at a predetermined price at any point during the life of the option. This right will apply whatever the market price of the commodity happens to be. If market prices move higher, then the holder of a call option will exercise his right to buy at the predetermined striking price. If the price falls, he will allow his option to expire and his loss will be limited to the cost of the premium.

The traditional grantors of options are the trade (both consumers and producers), who use options as a method of raising cash. Other grantors of options are private institutions, some commodity brokers and the unit trust industry. In recent years, unit trusts have been enthusiastic buyers of options when premiums are low, and grantors of options when premiums are believed to be high.

The growth of traded options has been rapid in recent years. Issued at fixed intervals by the futures exchanges, they enable the client to establish a highly leveraged position with a limited liability. This can be extremely profitable if the purchase of the option is well timed: however, it is always a speculation. A mistimed option purchase can easily result in the complete loss of the capital involved as the option becomes worthless on expiration.

15.7.5 Private trading accounts

For anyone seeking a greater element of risk in the pursuit of considerable financial reward, the answer is to open a private trading account which will give access to the terminal (or futures) markets. This section deals with the private speculator rather than the consumer or producer who uses the futures markets for hedging (see **15.3.2**).

To trade on the futures markets, it is necessary to take a view on the likely price of a given commodity at a particular point in the future. Contracts taken out on the futures markets can be terminated at any point during the life of the contract. That is to say, they can be cancelled by a corresponding and opposite contract before delivery of the actual goods becomes due.

Because dealing is for forward delivery, only a proportion of the full value of the goods is required as payment. This proportion is normally around 10 per cent of the value of the underlying commodity (ie, £10,000 will buy £100,000 worth of commodities) and is known as the initial margin payment. However, should market prices move against the position, further monies will be required immediately to maintain the margin level.

It is this system of margin payments, generally known as the 'gearing' element, which has earned the commodity markets their high-risk reputation. By the same token, it also allows the speculator to decide precisely what level of risk he wishes to incur.

A speculator may decide to 'gear up' as high as 10:1 and allocate the whole of his available capital to initial margin payments. A 10 per cent move in commodity prices in the right direction will double his initial stake; a 10 per cent move in the wrong direction will eliminate it totally. A more prudent approach would be to lower the gearing element from 10:1 to, say, 3:1 (eg, £10,000 is used to buy £30,000 worth of commodities). Thus, by keeping a percentage of his liquid capital in hand the investor will have the flexibility to meet margin calls and will also be able to take advantage of new trading opportunities as they occur on the futures markets.

Numerical examples
10:1 gearing
  £10,000 purchases £100,000 of commodities.
  A 10 per cent rise or fall in value produces . . .
  a £10,000 profit or loss.

3:1 gearing
  £10,000 purchases £30,000 of commodities.
  A 10 per cent rise or fall in value produces . . .
  a £3,000 profit or loss.

1:1 gearing
  £10,000 purchases £10,000 of commodities.
  A 10 per cent rise or fall in value produces . . .
  a £1,000 profit or loss.

It will thus be seen that, although the risk in commodity trading can be high, the facility exists for the investor to regulate his risk/reward ratio through prudent use of the gearing element.

The only other cost involved in commodity trading is broker's commission (see **15.5**).

15.7.6 How to participate

Although there is a wide range of investment opportunities, the commodity markets are no place for the inexperienced operator. It is not sufficient merely to have access to the most accurate and up-to-date market information. The key to success lies in knowing how to interpret and use that information, and this knowledge is most likely to be found amongst commodity brokers who have had many years' experience in the professional trading of commodities.

The ICCH and the LME will supply lists of commodity brokers. Once these names are available there are several further points which should be considered and these are outlined below.

15.8 Preview of the year ahead

As 1990 commenced, the industrialised economies were facing the prospect of slower growth rates and/or the threat of recession, due primarily to high interest rates and excessive levels of debt. Eight years of sustained real growth and abundant liquidity were finally resulting in a revival of inflationary pressures. Meanwhile, German reunification and the fall in Japanese bond and stockmarkets were drying up the world's two main capital surplus pools, threatening a liquidity squeeze. The dollar was showing signs of renewed vulnerability, responding to the USA's debt problems.

Rising inflation, slower growth and capital dislocations are recipes for financial instability and volatility. This is bound to produce some choppy and perhaps even extreme moves among industrial commodities. While continued high interest rates should prevent a sustained advance for oil or base metals, for instance, production difficulties in the Soviet Union appear inevitable and there is also the prospect of political instability. Industrial commodity prices are likely to lurch in response to these dramatic and sometimes conflicting forces.

Precious metals may be similarly affected. They are not expensive relative to their historic and inflation-adjusted levels, and they are cheap compared to shares or collectibles. A weaker dollar will tend to support prices, but high interest rates are a strong negative factor. Additionally, there may be some central bank selling of gold bullion to acquire hard currencies. Precious metals may not see another sustained advance until global interest rates are clearly falling.

Foods are another matter as many multi-year bear markets have now ended. The fall of authoritarian governments from eastern Europe to South America will produce a shift in priorities from military hardware to consumer necessities, with food heading the list.

World consumption of sugar, cocoa and coffee is now rising. This trend appears certain to continue and will lift prices.

Stockpiles of grains and soya beans are not high but prices have been very depressed. This is now changing as producers, consumers and speculators buy in advance of the crucial US crop season. Any adverse weather conditions would result in explosive advances.

As this book has gone to press, Iraq has invaded Kuwait and the crude oil price has almost doubled. The effect of this on the world's economies is dramatic, and the likely course of events, always difficult to foresee in the Middle East, is unclear.

Sources of further information

Bibliography

Guide to World Commodity Markets, Edwards and Reidy, 6th edition, Kogan Page, 1989

Trading in Commodities; an Investors Chronicle Guide, Granger, 4th edition, Woodhead-Faulkner, 1983

Useful addresses

International Commodities
 Clearing House Ltd
Roman Wall House
1–2 Crutched Friars
London
EC3N 2AN

Tel: (071) 488 3200

The London Metal Exchange
4th Floor
Plantation House
Fenchurch Street
London
EC3M 3AP

Tel: (071) 626 3311

The London Fox
1 Commodity Quay
St Katherine's Dock
London
E1 9AX

Tel: (071) 481 2080

London International Financial
 Futures Exchange
The Royal Exchange
London
EC3V 3PJ

Tel: (071) 623 0444

16 Gold and other valuables

John Myers and Valerie Bennett of Solon Consultants

16.1 Introduction

16.1.1 A long-term hedge in precious metals

Three hundred years ago, a troy ounce of gold would pay for a fine man's suit of clothes; an Indian diamond of quality would have funded the purchase of a house in the City. Today, the same ounce of gold would give just about enough money to dress up like a putative merchant banker, and a Hatton Garden diamond might be eagerly snatched as a deposit on a flat in the Docklands. Fashions change, generations pass, but over the years such valuables have kept their appeal to investors. That helps to explain why some financial counsellors encourage their clients to put some of their savings into gold, or maybe platinum or silver—but rarely into diamonds, and no longer into ivory.

The abiding worth of precious metals and other valuables makes them potentially useful as a long-term hedge against political tumult or economic chaos. When inflation rises, when currencies look weak, when stock markets twitch, precious metals gain in attraction. Buyers hold them not out of greed but out of fear. The money they put into gold, for instance, is a long-term insurance premium they pay for protection against the collapse of economies, markets and currencies. Gold 'bugs' are convinced that the metal will retain, or even increase, its value during times of economic uncertainty.

J M Keynes may have dismissed the metal as 'a barbarous relic', but there are many who believe that 'something which has been a store of value for 5,000 years will not go out of fashion'. In their view, a holding of gold should counterbalance a severe downturn in portfolios of stocks and shares during a monetary or political crisis. Bullion (in the form of bars, wafers or coins) is largely immune to the effects of weather, moisture, oxidation or sea water, and to the corrosive effects of most acids and alkalis. Furthermore, as the prices of gold and platinum are usually expressed in US dollars, such metals can be a hedge against sharp falls in the value of other currencies, although they remain susceptible when foreign exchange falters. In the shorter term, the volatility of the metals markets provide some opportunities for speculative trading.

The case is strong enough for level-headed financial planners to recommend that some investors keep from 5 per cent to 10 per cent of their assets in these investments. In practice, when share prices weaken, more often than not gold strengthens. The opposite is often true as well. In principle, buying gold should help to even out the volatility of an investment portfolio. Nonetheless, prices of precious metals can oscillate in spectacular ways in a short time. They are not investments for the nervous or the vulnerable; and in times of relatively low inflation—the early 1980s, for example—shares, bonds and unit trusts substantially outperform gold or the other noble metals.

Silver and platinum have also become respectable vehicles for investment. Respectable but risky: most experts would suggest that gold should be more than half of a precious metals portfolio. Silver and platinum are used primarily as industrial materials, so there is at least a chance that their prices will fall during a recession. Platinum is also highly volatile, and its popularity largely depends on its present use in automotive catalytic converters. The unpredictability of precious metals prices does, of course, make them unsuitable investments for individuals with limited sums to invest, or for investors who require a flow of income from their savings.

16.1.2 Gold coins

Gold coins are another form of bullion investment. They are minted by the governments of many countries. Examples are the American Golden Eagle, the Soviet chervonetz, the Mexican peso, the Austrian corona and philharmonic (it has a fiddle on the obverse), the Luxembourg lion, the Australian nugget, the South African krugerrand, and others enjoying culturally redolent names. Mauritius has its dodo; France, its Napoleon; Britain, the Britannia; China, its panda; Canada, its maple leaf; Japan, its Hirohito and soon its Akihito (of which more anon). Many of these coins are legal tender, but generally their value is derived from their metal content.

The nugget was Australia's first major attempt to break into the bullion coin market. The Gold Corporation tested demand for the coins by issuing 15,000 proof sets in November, 1986. They sold out in three months, producing a profit of $6 million for the Corporation. It subsequently expanded production. The largest market for these coins was southeast Asia—mainly Hong Kong and Taiwan—followed by Europe and Japan. Demand in the US was lower, principally because of competition from north American coins and krugerrands. In Britain, the Royal Mint launched the Britannia during October 1987. The imposition of VAT at 15 per cent has, however, handicapped sales of the new coin.

16.1.3 Coins manufactured in other precious metals

The platinum Koala is stirring up new interest and visibility for Australia's ambitious bullion coin programme. The Koala is one of only a few platinum bullion coins currently on the market. The earliest seems to have been the platinum Noble, issued by the Isle of Man, minted originally in 1983. The Australian Gold Corporation selected platinum instead of silver because of the metal's rarity. Only about three million ounces of platinum are produced worldwide annually, compared to 40 million ounces of gold. The Koala image was used partly to position the coin toward the Japanese market, which accounts for 50 per cent of world demand for platinum. A day after the platinum coins were launched in Japan, 4,093 ounces of the platinum Koalas were sold at prices between $510–$520 an ounce, according to the Gold Corporation.

In parallel, the USSR is offering a set of four historical commemorative coins that feature two made of silver, one of platinum and one of palladium. The full set has been selling for about £500. The Russians, in urgent need of currency, are aggressively selling palladium coins to collectors and metals speculators. The Soviet government is marketing a bullion palladium coin, made of 99 per cent palladium and priced to sell at a premium of 20 per cent above the metal's daily spot market price. The coins, which bear a face value of 25 roubles, carry the image of a ballerina—the first of what the Soviets hope will be a long-lasting series of 'palladium ballerina' coins. Only 30,000 have been minted so far, dated 1989; and 3,000 are of proof quality. The plan is to produce an annual 'edition', with novel designs that show ballerinas in classical ballet positions. At the end of 1989, the first coins of the series were selling for about £100 each.

Knowledgeable dealers believe that the palladium coin serves as an important precedent, and that palladium could be the investment metal of the 1990s. Only three countries—the Soviet Union, South Africa and the United States—have enough palladium to mine the mineral commercially; it is primarily employed in electronic components. Other countries to issue coins manufactured from palladium are Bermuda, France, the Isle of Man and Tonga. All these coins were special-issue commemoratives. The Soviet coins are just one case of the increasing competitiveness with which foreign mints are seeking customers. Mexico, for instance, is offering the Mexico Rainbow Proof Coin Collection—a set of silver, gold and platinum coins. When they were launched, the first year's coins, bearing 1989 dates, were priced at £440.

16.1.4 Other valuables

Apart from precious metals, investors can also consider valuables such as gemstones—emeralds, sapphires, semi-precious stones and diamonds. The most significant of these investment markets is for diamonds, currently dominated by the Central Selling Organisation. This is the London-based marketing organisation of De Beers.

At the regular sales, the CSO's experts sort heaps of rough diamonds that represent about four-fifths of the world's annual production. De Beers chooses its 160 or so buying customers from thousands of applicants. Ten times a year, at the sales (called 'sights'), the favoured few are offered a selection of diamonds chosen by the organisation and placed in a simple container. The set can be bought as a whole, or not at all. The gems are then passed on to diamond cutters in the world's major centres: Antwerp, Tel Aviv, New York and Bombay.

About one in six of the diamonds mined ends up in rings or other jewellery, but these account for most of the diamond output's value. The remainder are put to industrial use. The market's performance therefore largely depends on the success of its promoters in stimulating demand. To this end, De Beers spends large sums on advertising and sales promotion—for example, in an effort to persuade more men to buy and wear diamonds as jewellery. One result had been to stimulate demand through retail jewellers, but the markups make it more difficult for the investor to achieve gains. The addition of VAT accentuates this problem.

Thus, over the decades, De Beers has succeeded in mass-marketing what was once an aristocratic luxury without greatly diminishing its value. Diamonds remain 'the gem of gems' even though millions own them. De Beers' aim is long-term stability and prosperity for the industry. In its view, price fluctuations would undermine confidence in the value of diamonds. So far, the strategy has succeeded. While markets for many other commodities have suffered successive seizures, rough diamond prices have held up since the organisation began publicising price changes in 1964.

16.1.5 Selected forms of investment in valuables

Another way to invest in gold is to purchase bullion bars or ingots. Some institutions have 'certificate programmes', through which a private investor can specify how much to invest (usually a minimum of £500 or £1,000), and the institution then puts all the orders together and makes an appropriate purchase at the going market rate. The institution then divides the purchase between all the investors, issuing certificates for each allocation. Delivery and storage can be subsequently arranged. Investors should ensure that the company that they are dealing with is trustworthy, that the purchase is made and stored in their individual names, and that proof of ownership is provided.

Parallel approaches to investing in gold and platinum continue to attract some attention, depending upon sentiment among investors. These include buying of mining shares, and speculating in futures or options, or the movements in indices related to the price of precious metals. To a degree these facilities enable investors to hedge their positions, and enthusiasm for them reflects the high volatility of the prices—a volatility between abject depression and euphoria, which is likely to be a continuing feature of the scene over the next year or more.

16.2 Highlights of the previous year

16.2.1 Hoarded gold

The world's central banks hold massive stocks of gold which, if released in any bulk onto the bullion market, would depress prices. Otherwise, hoarding for investment purposes occurs on a large scale outside Europe and North America. The major concentration is in the Far East, as a result of increasing affluence. Japan accounts for the bulk of these purchases, but bar hoarding also occurs in other countries such as Hong Kong, Indonesia, Singapore, South Korea and Taiwan. Gold in jewellery is also held privately in large quantities throughout Asia.

In 1989, bullion hoarders in these countries sustained their interest, and gold markets continued to display increasing sophistication, with rapid growth in the options markets. The development of these markets gave producers, industrial buyers of gold, and speculators a framework to maximise profit and limit risks. Options are highly leveraged forms of speculative investment—the premium paid is no more than a small proportion of the commodity's total value.

16.2.2 Gold in manufacture

Carat jewellery remains at the core of the gold business. Bullion purchases for these applications have remained strong internationally, although demand has tended to fall in countries experiencing high interest rates and pressures on consumer demand. Despite these problems, the sector accounted for about four-fifths of total fabrication.

In some parts of the world—Germany and Italy in particular—there has been a demand for high value jewellery created by skilled designers and craftsmen. This demand was not restricted to any one geographical region. On the other hand, changing fashion preferences resulted in a decline in demand for some jewellery lines, especially chain. In 1989, this was compensated for by improvements in demand for other lines, such as lightweight rings. In the meantime, gold for use in dental alloys is under threat from ceramics and silver/palladium alloys, which contain little or no gold. The trend may be offset by improved health care becoming more common in newly industrialising countries.

Table 16.1 Gold mine production 1989 (tonnes)

Country	1987	1988	1989
South Africa	607.0	621.0	608.3
United States	154.9	201.0	259.1
Australia	110.7	157.0	197.0
Canada	116.5	134.8	158.4
Brazil	83.8	100.2	96.9
Philippines	39.5	39.2	37.1
Colombia	32.5	33.4	30.7
Papua New Guinea	33.9	36.6	33.7
Chile	21.4	24.9	26.1
Venezuela	16.0	20.0	15.0
Other Africa	63.4	66.9	66.7
Other Latin America	48.8	52.5	59.9
Other Far East/Oceania, etc.	37.9	44.5	43.1
Europe	16.9	18.6	20.9
Total	1,383.2	1,550.6	1,652.9

Source: *Gold Fields Mineral Services Ltd*

As was brought out above, more countries are minting gold coins. Nevertheless, in the official coin sector, demand for bullion is waning. This decline seems unlikely to change, unless there is significantly higher inflation. In practice, for coins to be in great demand,

Table 16.2 Western gold fabrication 1989 (tonnes)

Region	1987	1988	1989
Europe	464	527	646
North America	292	252	248
Latin America	31	38	61
Middle East	216	227	265
Indian subcontinent	191	223	261
Far East	369	541	666
Africa	27	43	45
Australasia	16	14	15
Total	1,606	1,865	2,207

inflationary price rises would need to be combined with uncertainties about the main trading currencies and lower interest rates. Another prerequisite would be a deteriorating performance of other investments. Without such factors, gold coins are unlikely to be in massive demand in North America and Europe. In 1989, the risk of a substantial fall in the price of gold was only limited by the sustained level of demand in the Far East.

16.2.3 Diamonds

There are signs that the diamond business is losing some of its attractions. Sales have declined sharply, and the CSO is facing pressures from producers. They are looking for improved terms and the chance to sell more of their own stones. After rises of 19 per cent in 1987 and 35 per cent in 1988, rough diamond sales fell 2 per cent to $4.09bn in 1989, mainly because of weakening economic conditions, high interest rates and the past price increases.

The decline was sharpest in the latter half of 1989, when sales fell 24 per cent from the first six months. One effect has been to limit De Beers' scope for raising prices. In the first half of 1990, De Beers announced it was increasing prices by 5.5 per cent. The comparable figure in the previous year was 15.5 per cent.

16.3 Current developments

16.3.1 Gold internationally

In this century, gold has recorded five major price rises in world markets. Its history, of course, is as a coinage metal and a

Table 16.3 Supply and demand, gold, private sector (tonnes)

Sources and Applications	1984	1985	1986	1987	1988	1989
Non-Communist mine production	1167	1236	1296	1383	1551	1653
Net sales from the Communist Bloc	205	210	402	303	263	296
Supply of new gold	1372	1446	1698	1686	1814	1949
Scrap	291	304	474	407	328	304
Net supply of gold to the private sector	1747	1618	2027	2021	1857	2477
Absorbed by:						
Carat jewellery	1071	1146	1118	1160	1477	1811
Electronics	130	114	124	125	134	138
Dentistry	52	53	51	49	51	49
Other industrial	56	54	56	56	59	62
Medals and imitation coins (sales)*	44	14	12	16	19	19
Official coins (sales)*	131	105	327	200	126	127
Bar hoarding	332	306	214	258	459	516
In Europe and North America**	(68)	(175)	126	157	(468)	(246)

Totals may not add due to rounding.

Source: *Gold Fields Mineral Services Ltd*

* Any medals and coins manufactured but left unsold are excluded.
** Includes the net impact of gold loans and forward sales.

measurement of national wealth. In 1934, as part of America's 'new deal', the bullion price was upgraded and fixed in US dollar terms at $35 per ounce. This lasted for forty years until President Nixon severed gold's links with the dollar. On the open market, bullion reached $200 per ounce, principally as a consequence of petrodollar inflation and weak central banking strategies.

Between 1976 and 1980, the London gold price rose rapidly to $850 per ounce. It then fell back to $300 an ounce in mid-1982, only to rally again, reaching $500 per ounce in June 1983. Between then and 1987, the price oscillated between about $300 and $500 an ounce, although moving relatively little against the world's harder currencies. Since 1987, gold has fallen back once more. Its advocates expect another cyclical upswing of some duration before long.

According to Salomon Bros, the US brokerage firm, investments in gold over the past 10 years produced a compounded return of 9.6 per cent annually, somewhat above the retail price index but less than shares or fixed interest securities. One of the issues currently raising questions is the future of East-West relations. Some commentators predict that the Soviet Union soon will denominate the rouble in gold, as part of its effort to join the world economic system. The effect would be to stimulate demand for gold.

Other commentators, doubting that the Russians would link their rouble to gold, believe that Western central banks—in an effort to increase the Soviet Union's foreign exchange earnings and its ability to borrow—will support a higher gold price. The effect would be to add to the collateral value of the huge Soviet bullion reserves. On the other hand, if gold prices go up at a high rate, that might rekindle fears of inflation.

Conversely, there is the distinct possibility that the USSR's greater involvement with Western economies could be bearish for gold. The Soviet Union may have to sell some of its gold hoard to afford Western goods. Recently, there has been evidence to support this view. In any event, for many investors, the shares of some gold-mining companies, and unit trusts that invest in such shares, have tended to offer far better returns than bullion.

16.3.2 Japan's entry into the market

The global dimensions of precious metals markets mean that events on the other side of the world can be of vital importance to UK gold 'bugs'. Japan is a case in point. Investors there once shunned gold.

They are now shifting their opinions, largely as a result of deregulation and changing attitudes. When stock market prices wavered, many Japanese investors began looking for other places to invest their money. Gold prices fell close to the lowest level for a decade. This factor, together with reduced margin requirements, prompted retail investors and smaller firms to enter the precious-metals markets of the Tokyo Commodity Exchange. In November 1989, prices moved upwards. Gold and silver volumes surged 500 per cent.

In the Japanese retail market a similar trend emerged. Investors brought their cash straight from the securities firms to the offices of bullion merchants and other gold retailers. Gold accounts at banks and securities firms also drew fresh interest. Admittedly, the shift from equities into precious metals was minuscule. It was still sufficient to cause a resurgence of international gold prices at the time. Japanese money moved into precious metals, especially gold futures, at a surprising rate. The question is whether the volumes can be sustained. Tokyo is as yet a small market compared with Chicago, New York or London, but there are strong incentives for the players.

Japanese investors are learning about gold and other precious metals. Tokyo's institutions have also started to realise that commodities might have a role in elaborate hedging strategies. In addition, MITI (the powerful Japanese Ministry of International Trade and Industry) and the Ministry of Finance are promising to repeal regulations inhibiting trading in commodities.

Japan's gold imports already account for about 20 per cent of world gold production; and volumes are rising on Tokyo's gold futures market. Past figures indicate that gold investment in Japan has been rising since 1982. In that year, Japanese financial institutions started to sell gold bullion, gold coins and investment accounts. They also bought gold through trading companies to back up the sales. Since then, total demand for gold as an investment has risen from 78 tons to 202 tons in 1988 and now accounts for more than half of bullion purchases.

Conspicuous consumers have taken to wearing gold. As a result, demand for gold jewellery rose 20 per cent last year to 130 tons. In 1989 Japan was the world's largest importer of gold. The imports included about 13 tons of bullion coins, such as the Canadian maple leaf and the South African krugerrand.

Innovative schemes have helped stimulate this demand. Investors are offered monthly accumulation plans, mail order trading of bullion in exchange for jewellery, and buying plans that encourage investors to speculate on the direction in which the gold market is moving. If investors guess correctly, they share the profit with the financial institution; if they are wrong, they might still enjoy a return on their money.

For the financial institutions which hedge their positions gold accounts also offer an attractive return. Sanwa Bank, which has been one of the main movers, now ranks among Japan's top five gold retailers. Other leading banks such as Mitsubishi, Sumitomo, Fuji and Industrial Bank of Japan have also entered the market, partly with a view to setting up similar operations in London and other financial centres.

For the present, Tokyo still lags behind Hong Kong as a centre of precious metals trading in the Far East. The colony has market makers who can handle larger gold orders than the Japanese futures or inter-dealer markets can absorb. As Tokyo steadily develops more of a leading role in precious metals, its major bullion and trading houses will probably become far more aggressive on the London inter-dealer market during Far Eastern business hours.

16.3.3 Other precious metals

About 80 per cent of all platinum produced comes from mines in South Africa. The second largest producer is the Soviet Union, which may become an uncertain source of supply. Platinum stocks are estimated to account for no more than six to nine months of the world's annual demand. The rise in demand for platinum is expected to continue, fuelled by positive appraisals of the market's fundamentals.

Tokyo is a major force in platinum, importing between half and two-thirds of the free market economies' supply. The metal is imported for industry, investment and Japanese platinum-jewellery makers. They hold 90 per cent of the world's market in this form of trinket. Tokyo's annual platinum futures volume surpassed the New York Mercantile Exchange's in 1988, just four years after platinum futures were first offered in Japan.

16.4 Counterfeits and forgeries

16.4.1 Counterfeit coins

One of the problems of purchasing coins made from gold bullion or other precious metals is the risk of forgeries. In the 1970s, when inflation was soaring upwards, interest in UK sovereigns was so high that the Mint found itself unable to produce enough. As a result, there was an increase in the premium (the difference between the face value and the metal value). The coins began to sell at almost one and a half times their face value. The opportunity attracted middle eastern forgers. In practice, the vendors and buyers could easily detect the counterfeit coins.

A more recent case, affecting international gold bullion trading, was the Hirohito coin scandal. The incentive for a forger of a Hirohito coin is its gold content. Each is worth only half the ¥100,000 (about £400) which the Bank of Japan promises to pay the bearer. Counterfeiting allegations began to come to light when a large and respected coin dealer in Tokyo tried to cash 1,000 Hirohito coins, which seemed genuine. A Fuji Bank clerk in Tokyo became suspicious about the plastic containers protecting the metal.

The original Japanese coin venture formulated in 1986 required the Bank of Japan to issue millions of gold coins to celebrate the 60th anniversary of Hirohito's accession. Their manufacture called for 300 tonnes of gold, then worth almost £2bn, representing about one-quarter of all the gold mined that year. To appease the US trade regulators, the Bank of Japan imported the gold via New York, as refined precious metal classified as 'manufactured goods.' That helped partially to redress the trade imbalance.

The sales of the coins were also meant to absorb some of the cash in the hands of the Japanese, who enthusiastically bought the first 10 million Hirohito gold bullion coins—the first legal tender gold coins to be issued by Japan for almost 60 years. They paid ¥100,000 for each coin. Because the gold content was worth only about half the nominal value, the Bank of Japan made ¥600bn profit, worth £2bn at that time, mainly out of private Japanese investors. The coins could be redeemed—the Bank of Japan promised to pay ¥100,000 for each of them. Most investors had, however, bought them for sentimental reasons and probably would not cash in their coins—leaving the Bank comfortably in credit. Another unusual feature is the Hirohito coin which, unlike the American eagle, the Canadian maple leaf, the Australian nugget or the British Britannia, does not rise or fall with the market price of gold.

A forger can make tempting gains, if he can produce a plausible imitation of the Hirohito. This, the Japanese police claim, is what has been happening since early 1988. In Japan allegedly suspect coins have gone through the hands of local dealers. Others said to be involved in the transactions were reputable international bankers and numismatists, who have grounds for doubting the evidence of forgery.

In November 1989, the Bank of Japan announced that some of the 100 tonnes of gold left from the Hirohito issue would be used for another coin. It would celebrate the enthronement of the new Emperor Akihito. The original plan was to issue a coin very similar to the Hirohito, but each Akihito coin will contain 30 rather than 20 grams of gold. This amount will represent about ¥60,000 worth of gold in a coin that the Japanese plan to sell for ¥100,000. Forgers will be looking forward to another windfall.

The Akihito coins will be minted in a way which ought to make them harder to copy. At current gold prices, the new venture could mean an apparent loss for the Japanese authorities of £250m. On the other hand, if they dispose of the whole issue and few buyers redeem the coins, the Bank of Japan would still make a profit of perhaps £500m.

16.4.2 Gold mine frauds

Precious metals investing also has been beset with fraud. The chief problem lately is with promoters selling interests in gold mines that are nearly worthless or non-existent. As a case in point, telephone salesmen may call offering gold not yet mined. They say they will sell it for £100 under the going price.

Such frauds are an international problem. One US commentator believes that there are 'probably 30 to 40 gold mining scams going on now in the United States'. He cautions investors to be distrustful of salesmen who offer interests in gold mines. They promise gold for perhaps half the market price; the explanation is usually that the mine owner has a special process or patented techniques for extracting the metal.

16.5 Opportunities and costs

16.5.1 Suitability

Who should buy gold, in what form should it be purchased and how much should one invest in the metal? 'It depends on the investor,' says one dealer. 'Every portfolio should have at least 10 per cent in gold. A person who has little money to invest and is conservative should concentrate on gilts. If you are more aggressive, you could have up to 50 per cent in gold.' For many investors who wish to hold gold, coins make sense, because they are easier to sell than bullion. Alternatively, investors can buy precious metals in bars or wafers, which may, for an extra price, have decorative stampings. A 100-ounce gold bar is about the size of a brick. Wafers are sold in various weights, down to a few ounces, although premiums tend to be higher on smaller unit weights. Gold coins, bars or wafers could be stored in a safe-deposit box or home safe.

Some banks offer gold purchase programmes, and may be willing to finance these purchases. If you buy on credit, the bank will want to keep the gold in its vault, and charge you for storage. But there is a problem with valuables. To follow the recommended practice in the alternative investment markets, investors are advised to purchase the best. The difficulty is that the best is becoming scarce and very expensive, in many classes of alternative investments. Diamonds are no exception. One of the consequences is interest in other gemstones, such as sapphires, which are almost as durable as diamonds, and for which a grading system has been developed jointly by a Sri Lanka government agency and the Gemological Institute of America Gemological Laboratories. The established grading certificate is an important supporting document when buying or selling diamonds or sapphires. Other gemstones, for example, emeralds, are less attractive because they are still being mined in large quantities.

16.5.2 Recovering gold from wrecks

Recovering gold bullion and coins, and other precious metals and valuables from undersea troves has also attracted attention in recent years. The costs can often be considerable, and there are risks to the health of the divers. Nonetheless, treasure has been retrieved from wrecks in substantial quantities. As a result, the backers of these ventures have recovered gold, thousands of coins, and scores of bars of a type virtually unseen in more than a century.

16.5.3 Costs of ownership

Some investors are put off by, among other things, the transaction costs, storage expenses and lack of dividends associated with precious metals investments. Investors should remember that, unlike bank deposits and securities, gold does not pay interest or dividends. Its value depends on changes in the general market for bullion. Storage and insurance costs can erode profits from investments in gold bars or coins.

16.5.4 Advisers

Even for investors who have good reasons for investing in precious metals, financial advisers offer words of caution. Anyone who buys gold or another precious metal, or gemstones, should use a bank, a specialist trading house or a reputable dealer. In any event, it is important for the investor to make sure he or she can obtain possession of the asset when it is needed. In times of great financial crisis, it is as well to remember that banks may be closed.

In Britain, gold coins can still be bought direct from certain members of the London gold market or, more commonly today, through dealers, precious metal brokers, investment consultants, some banks and jewellers. Gold sovereigns and half sovereigns are still being sold in quantity, and the products of other countries' mints can also be purchased. It should be noted that there are advantages in buying coins in popular demand. The premiums charged (ie, the difference between the price of the coin and the value of the bullion it contains) tend to be higher for coins that sell in low quantities.

16.6 Taxation

16.6.1 Tax planning

The income, capital gains, capital transfer and inheritance tax considerations reviewed in the chapter on arts and antiques are generally relevant to valuables. The same advice applies on careful tax planning.

16.6.2 VAT

Until 1982 purchase of bullion coins did not attract VAT if the coins were still legal in their country of issue. Following the Exchange Control (Gold Coins) Exemption Order 1979 and the Value Added Tax (Finance) Order 1982, there are now two main ways for UK private investors to buy gold bullion coins. One is to pay the VAT, which would make it more difficult to realise a gain from the transaction. The other is to buy the coins overseas and store them there.

Other approaches may be promoted in advertisements or through direct mail circulars—they should be carefully evaluated and treated with the utmost caution. It should be noted that, in the UK, where bullion coins are subsequently sold back by VAT registered traders (who buy and sell gold coins by way of business), the dealer who makes the purchase should now pay the VAT on the transaction directly to HM Customs & Excise.

Buyers and sellers of gold bullion, gold coins and gold scrap should also study VAT leaflet no 701/21/87. It describes the VAT liability in respect of transactions in, or arising from, gold or gold coins under the VAT Act 1983. The statute describes a voluntary accounting scheme introduced on 1 November 1983 to combat VAT frauds involving smuggled gold (which is liable to forfeiture under the Customs & Excise Management Act 1979). Under the scheme a VAT-registered trader selling gold to authorised dealers receives payment only for the price of the gold, given the undertaking to make direct payment of the tax.

The forfeiture provisions of the Customs & Excise Management Act apply, even if the smuggled gold is found in the possession of an innocent purchaser. It is, therefore, in the best interest of buyers to satisfy themselves that the gold has been properly imported before agreeing to complete a purchase. The questions to ask are: Where has the gold come from? Has it been imported? Has VAT been paid on it? Why is it being sold? How is it delivered? Is a quick settlement demanded? Is the seller new to the gold market? Does he regularly supply large quantities? What references can he offer? Such basic checks are clearly advisable in view of the growing number of frauds.

VAT regulations also apply to silver and platinum. As in the gold and silver markets, zero-rating for VAT applies only to transactions between wholesale traders. In the past, zero-rating was not necessary as transfers of metal among traders in London were relatively unimportant. The rapid rise in demand for platinum, together with the uncertainties about the political future of South Africa (the dominant supplier), has increased the need for rapid, inter-trader movements of metal.

16.7 Preview of the year ahead

16.7.1 Limiting factors

Gold, silver and platinum as valuables are likely to be in continuing demand among many of the market's 'bugs', partly because holders of investment diamonds (another possible haven for those worried about economic and political trends) have shown poor returns in recent years. Owners have discovered that their assets can be difficult to trade, and they have found it necessary to hold their diamonds in bank vaults (for example, in the Channel Islands) so as to avoid VAT liability when importing the gemstones into the UK.

16.7.2 Market fundamentals

One of the key factors in 1990–1992 will be jewellery sales worldwide. Volumes in this market are largely a function of the gold price in terms of currencies. In many places, the price of gold has fallen by as much as 30 per cent over the last five years. The main factor has been the decline of the dollar against the yen and major European currencies. In early 1985, a year in which gold fell to $300 an ounce, the dollar was at a high level—¥270, DMs 3.5, and close to parity with sterling. In early 1985, an ounce of gold would have cost a West German about DMs 1,025, at the end of 1989, he could have bought that same ounce of gold for about DMs 735. A British investor who would have paid about £275 in early 1985, would have paid slightly more than £250 at the end of 1989. The Japanese counterpart would have laid out approximately ¥80,000 in 1985, against ¥6,000 in late 1989.

In some countries, people buy jewellery for its gold content—usually necklaces or other items of 18–22 carats with a minimum of decoration. The products are bought by weight and serve as a storehouse of value. The large volumes of purchases from the Middle East and Far East include jewellery in such forms.

16.7.3 Behind the rusting curtain

One more final element in the price equations for gold and other precious metals is the political sea change occurring in Eastern bloc countries. Traditionally, the USSR has been a major seller of gold, to raise hard currency. There is a confusion of opinion among analysts, as indicated above. Some now believe that Soviet sales of gold will decline. There is an increasing demand for the metal among Russians that generates a higher margin of profit from the pent-up demand. In many major cities throughout the USSR, the longest queues are at stores where gold items are sold.

The Soviet government may also put more gold into reserve, to provide backing for either bonds or the rouble. If perestroika is to have any chance of working, the Russian authorities will need a stable currency that is internationally convertible. At present, the rouble is neither stable nor convertible, so there is a prospect that the USSR will employ their gold as collateral. If 200 metric tons of Russian production is held back each year—about 6.4m ounces—£1.2bn to £1.8bn in gold would be kept off the market, pushing up the bullion price.

Eastern bloc uncertainties are leading people to buy gold in Europe. Individuals who are thinking of coming West cannot move their assets out in currency. The markets and the black markets for gold have gained momentum. In many Eastern bloc countries, there are expectations of currency controls. People there are beginning to hoard gold and are making preparations to transport their wealth.

16.8 Conclusion

The end result of all these pressures could be to keep the price of gold moving up and stabilising, perhaps at $450–$475 per ounce. Other precious metals might move in harmony. For the holders of the physical commodity itself—either in the form of coins or bullion—that would represent a hefty gain on a substance that is in itself a store of value and a traditional hedge against inflation and uncertainty.

Other options are gold mutual funds, which hold mining equities and some bullion, and direct investment in the mining stocks themselves. The equities in major league mining operations tend to outperform gold itself because of the profit leverage they enjoy. These days, with many mining companies of all kinds concentrating on low-cost production, the differentials can be striking. But forecasts in these markets are notoriously fallible: it was the cynic who defined prophecy as 'selling one's credibility for future delivery!'

Sources of further information

See Chapter 18.

17 Art and antiques

John Myers and Valerie Bennett of Solon Consultants

17.1 Introduction

17.1.1 A form of alternative investment

The promoters of 'alternative investments' confidently advocate tangible assets as sound purchases for 'financially secure and intelligent buyers'. The assets they have in mind include works of artistic or historical significance—that is, items which are 'museum-worthy by any standards' or 'culturally significant', and which appeal to collectors. Small investors are generally recommended by advocates of alternative investments to allocate roughly 10 per cent of their investment capital (excluding the equity value of their main residence) to the acquisition of 'traded artifacts' ie, possessions such as works of art and antiques, which will, it is hoped, protect investors against inflation and currency fluctuations in the future.

On occasion, larger institutional investors and corporate bodies are also advised to accumulate Old Masters and rare antiques to complement their investments in securities and real estate. The apologists argue that these investors can afford to ride out slumps lasting up to a quarter of a century, if the eventual return is sufficient. At present, one of the advantages of such investments for certain institutions, such as pension funds, can be freedom from tax on their gains. On the other hand, art and antiques cost money to insure, preserve and store. Capital appreciation has to be substantial to make up for the loss of income and the tax relief advantage.

Nonetheless, art objects are increasingly seen as investments, the value of which rise and fall as new assessments are made of their aesthetic, historic or functional value. Other factors stimulating the evolution of this sector have been the marketability of art and the success of the auction houses in improving the liquidity of art as an investment. Buyers are also influenced in their choices by critics, art historians, exhibitions, and even by the track record of each field.

In general, the alternative investment is recommended by its promoters as an asset for the buyer to retain over a prolonged period to allow the value to mature. Speculative trading in works of art and antiques is frowned upon as too risky. There is, it is said, too much uncertainty in the rewards to justify gambling on the chance of making a perfectly-timed purchase and sale; it is difficult for even the expert to identify the under-valued piece which is certain to come into fashionable demand at some time in the future.

17.1.2 The dividends

The advocates of the alternative investment argue for including fine art and antiques in private or funds' portfolios as long-term investments on grounds which are, essentially, those of the economist: while the number of buyers in the markets is tending to go up, the supply is static or declining. On the one hand, the volume of 'discoveries' or 'retrievals of lost works' is restricted. On the other, valued items do disappear through fires, thefts and other calamities; and, perhaps more significantly, there has been, until just recently, a steady drain from the market of works acquired for permanent retention by museums and institutional collectors. The features of the alternative investment market which should therefore attract buyers who are looking for assets of permanent value are a growing demand, a diminishing supply and a general upward movement in prices.

The cosmopolitan origins of buyers who attend major sales might seem to indicate that this argument has gained wide acceptance. There is an international demand for authentic items of quality. Apparently these buyers have been persuaded that works of art and rare antiques are safe assets to acquire with spare capital, or revenue which might otherwise be subject to tax—even though they bring their owners no income. Yet, many would deny an investment motivation. To them such motives degrade the purity of artistic endeavour; they are aesthetes who are seeking a cultural dividend, the delights of living with rare, historically important, satisfying works which give pleasure to their owners. Similarly, large institutions are buying works of art to improve their employees' working environments. Investment is then a secondary motive.

17.2 Highlights of the previous year

17.2.1 Structure of the market

In the 1980s, spectacular prices have been paid for works of art. Many people outside the art world—and some inside—consider £20m, or more, an absurd sum to pay for a painting. They fail to take account of the edifice of values that provide a logical basis and grounds for such prices. The Art Sales Index shows that 256 paintings went under the hammer in 1989 for more than £1m. Of the 79 artists in question, Monet made it 34 times; Picasso, 30 and Renoir 23. Many more artists broke this barrier, though they are hardly household names—Derain, Giambologna, Hassam, Noland and Zoffany, to name a few.

Markets for art and antiques have developed considerably in recent years, especially over the last two decades. Their growth has been prompted by both negative and positive considerations. In the early years of this period, investors were choosing to buy these tangible assets because of failures of stock markets and interest-bearing securities to protect their capital against inflation. It is worth noting that immediately after the October 1987 Stock Market crash, record sales occurred in the auction houses, reflected in record prices. Sotheby's, for example, sold van Gogh's *Irises* for £30m, at the time, the highest price ever paid for a work of art.

With the greater spread of higher disposable incomes and an increase in leisure, a demand has emerged for assets which have a worth and an interest beyond their monetary cost. Social changes have also made an impact: for example, dealers and auctioneers report that young, wealthy buyers have been entering the market for works of fine art—paintings, prints, ceramics, engravings and sculptures. Antiques markets have also experienced a comparable rise in demand. Nowadays, important sales are attracting bidders who are constantly setting new record prices for old furniture, oriental carpets, rare books and manuscripts, antique jewellery, worked silver, arms and militaria, and other pieces of artistic and historic value.

17.2.2 Record prices

In May 1990 new records were set: an enthusiast paid £45m for Vincent van Gogh's *Portrait of Dr Gachet* and £43m for Pierre Auguste Renoir's *Au Moulin de la Galette*, easily shattering the record set in 1987 for van Gogh's *Irises*. The purchases made the headlines, but two of five major sales in May 1990 fell below the auction houses' low estimates, and about a third of the works failed to sell in three of these highly publicised auctions. While the five big evening sales sct 50 artists' records, highly valued works by Clyfford Still and Willem de Kooning failed to attract buyers. Despite these problems, the two tables below show the spectacular results achieved by auction houses, especially in the past two seasons.

Table 17.1 'Big ticket' auctions

Date of auction	Sales price £m	Sold	Unsold	Average price £
9 November 1988	20	86	4	230,000
10 November 1988	36	76	6	475,000
11 November 1988	44	56	23	785,000
15 November 1988	31	48	15	645,000
2 May 1989	31	103	7	300,000
3 May 1989	18	60	6	300,000
9 May 1989	113	67	10	1,700,000
10 May 1989	34	86	7	400,000
7 November 1989	34	93	8	365,000
8 November 1989	54	68	6	800,000
14 November 1989	128	68	29	1,900,000
15 November 1989	148	70	4	2,100,000
7 May 1990	22	51	26	430,000
8 May 1990	31	55	32	565,000
15 May 1990	148	57	24	2,600,000
17 May 1990	157	70	12	2,250,000

17.2.3 Buyers with cash to spend

In recent years, inherent risks in all the investment markets have been brought forcefully to the attention of investors. They have been made acutely aware of the markets' dependence on developments and events which affect international confidence and economic prosperity. However, in 1989 (as for several years) many alternative investment markets have recorded continued growth, as the strength of Japanese and European interest stimulated demand.

Thus the auction houses and dealers in Western Europe and North America who specialise in works of art and antiques have seen some shifts in this demand over the past two to three years. High interest rates attracted away funds which a number of investors might otherwise have used to buy valuable chattels. Then, uncertainties about future prospects prompted many individuals to save rather than spend. In 1989, however, the number of buyers at auction remained high and the global spread of these buyers underlined the international nature of the alternative investment market.

The auctioneers and dealers found that there were collectors and buyers with larger amounts of cash to spend and—although supply also remained high as vendors were attracted into the market—as in earlier cycles, the rise in demand proved to be the governing factor. Prices continued to rise, particularly in those sectors of the market which attracted fashionable interest. Impressionist paintings are

Table 17.2 Top prices paid for paintings at auction

Date sold	Price £m	Artist	Painting
15 May 1990	45	van Gogh	Portrait of Dr Gachet
17 May 1990	43	Renoir	Au Moulin de la Galette
11 November 1987	30	van Gogh	Irises
30 November 1989	27	Picasso	Les Noches de Pierrette
9 May 1989	26	Picasso	Yo Picasso
15 November 1989	22	Picasso	Au Lapin Agile
30 March 1987	22	van Gogh	Sunflowers
28 November 1988	21	Picasso	Acrobat and Young Harlequin
31 May 1989	19	Pontormo	Duke Cosimo d'Medici
15 November 1989	15	Picasso	The Mirror
14 November 1988	14	Picasso	Maternity
28 June 1988	14	Monet	Dans la Prairie
9 May 1989	13	Gaugin	Mata Mua
8 November 1989	11	de Kooning	Interchange
29 June 1987	11	van Gogh	The Trinquetaille Bridge
15 November 1989	10	Picasso	Mère et Enfant

currently one of the most popular forms of art. A spectacular growth in their value occurred over the 1988/89 and 1989/90 seasons. This growth was reflected in the record-breaking sales. In other words, some alternative investments have once more shown gains in value in real terms.

English furniture also produced the highest prices yet seen in this market. At Christie's, £1.1m was paid for a rococo commode extraordinaire by John Channon; at Sotheby's £550,000 was paid for a carved commode in the style of Chippendale. These were masterpieces; the Channon commode was made for Fonthill Splendens in Wiltshire, the house of Alderman William Beckford.

In 1989 and 1990 the art market, spearheaded by the major auction rooms, explored ways of exploiting neglected areas and attracting new collectors. Picture sales devoted to themes such as flowers, dogs, cats or marine subjects became well established; and there were successful auctions devoted to bird pictures.

17.2.4 Leveraged purchases and guarantees

There are about 500 people alive today who might pay more than £10 million for a work of art. For them, the main attractions are the market's performance and the opportunities to 'collateralise' art—a development that seems to have a bright future. After several years of rapid escalation, the auction scene cooled amid controversy over Sotheby's leveraged sale of *Irises* to the Australian entrepreneur, Alan Bond. The arrangement led to charges that auction prices were being artificially inflated. Bond later sold the painting to the J Paul Getty Museum for an undisclosed sum, after he failed to pay off his £16m loan from Sotheby's. The rate of interest on such loans can be as much as 4 per cent above prime.

The loan system tends to inflate prices whether the borrower wins the painting or not: like a roulette player with chips on house credit, he will bid it up. Pre-financing by the auction house artificially creates a floor, while a dealer who states a price sets a ceiling. If the borrower then defaults, the lender recovers the painting, writes off the unpaid part of the loan against tax, and can resell the work at its new inflated price.

The auction practice that attracted the most criticism in 1989 and 1990 goes to the heart of the nature of auctions themselves and the ethics of the trade. Auction houses have been giving guarantees to the seller of a work of art and loans to the buyer. If a collector has a work of art that an auctioneer wants to sell, the latter can issue a 'guarantee' that the collector will get say, £3m from the sale. If the work does not make £3m, the collector still receives the payment, but the work remains with the auction house for later sale. Guarantees are a strong inducement to sellers, but clearly risky for the auction house.

Most top private dealers dislike the system of guarantees and loans. They argue that it creats a conflict of interest. One dealer is on record with the comment: 'If the auction house has a financial involvement with both seller and buyer, its status as an agent is compromised. Lending to the buyer is like margin trading on the stock market. It creates inflation. It causes instability.' The advocates defend the policy as 'right, proper and indeed inevitable'. They claim that guarantees are given 'very sparingly'.

17.2.5 Consumer protection

In the United States, there has been a battle between the auctioneers and consumer affairs. For more than a year a team of officials pored over leading auctioneers' records, identifying such exotic-sounding practices as 'bidding off the chandelier' (announcing fictitious bids to drive up the price) and 'buying in' (leaving a work unsold because it does not reach the seller's reserve price). Stiffer rules are pending in the US, including those governing loans. The current consumer affairs code says that 'if an auctioneer makes loans or advances money to consignors and/or prospective purchasers, this fact must be conspicuously disclosed in the auctioneer's catalog'. These developments are likely to have repercussions in Britain and other parts of Europe.

According to a US official, the team found 'gross irregularities' in art auction houses. Chandelier bidding amounted to 'an industry practice, both above and below the reserve.' (A chandelier bid above the reserve violates present rules.) The spokesman was also concerned about the practices of not announcing buy-ins and of keeping reserves secret. The auction houses contended that, if bidders knew the reserve, it would chill the market. Art dealers, lobbying the agency, maintained that the reserve should be disclosed and that bidding should start at it.

Dealing in art, from a gallery or an auction house, is not a profession. There are representative bodies that attempt to set standards and to control their members practices. Nevertheless, art dealing has the characteristics of a trade. The case is being argued for regulation, for setting up an independent regulator—an art-industry Securities and Exchange Commission. The auction houses and dealers have doubts about the concepts; others think the idea may have some merit.

17.3 Current developments

17.3.1 Cosmopolitan buyers

Some buyers around the world have been persuaded by plausible arguments that alternative investments can act as a form of insurance against a fall in currency values. As a result, many of the markets for art and antiques have become more international: since the 1970s, North American, Continental European and Middle and Far Eastern investors have begun to frequent salerooms in greater numbers.

In recent years, London's traditional dominance as the centre for art and antiques sales has been challenged, in particular by New York, Geneva, Frankfurt and Paris, which nowadays are attracting important specialised sales. In some alternative investment markets—furniture is one example—the strength of American demand had meant that market prices have been set mainly in New York. With the weakening dollar, it is doubtful whether America's influence on the market can continue at such a level. Generally, the mobility of alternative investments, combined with the wider geographical spread of dealers and auctions, should mean that prices tend to be maintained in real terms and are somewhat less vulnerable to the ravages of inflation and volatile exchange rates.

17.3.2 Museum sales and purchases

The inflated market is also eroding one of the main functions of museums: the retrospective. Over the past two decades, museums have brought together many definitive exhibitions, produced at the highest pitch of scholarship and curatorial skill. Examples often quoted in the art world are exhibitions of late and early Cézanne, Picasso, Manet, van Gogh, Monet, Degas, Watteau, Velazquez, Poussin, up to the Museum of Modern Art's 1990 show of Picasso's and Braque's Cubist years.

To raise funds for these exhibitions and fresh purchases, some museums have been selling work from their permanent collections. Thus the Museum of Modern Art recently sold and exchanged seven paintings to purchase van Gogh's *Portrait of the Postmaster Roulin*. The initiative may encourage museum trustees to think of their permanent collections as an impermanent one, a stock portfolio that can be traded at will. According to one commentator, 'It's enough to warm the heart of any free marketeer: the privatisation of art'.

17.3.3 Auctioneers' strategies

Another trend which has gained momentum affects the large auction houses, with Sotheby's and Christie's acting as pioneers. One analyst recently pointed out that since Sotheby's became centred in New York, it has changed its business to the extent that lending and other investment services generate about a tenth of Sotheby's gross income. The auction houses are also providing more services directly to the public.

In the past, auction houses sold mainly to dealers, who put on their markup and then sold to their clients. Art lovers tended to be shy of going to auctions; the business of reserves, attributions, codes and bids seemed mysterious, and alarming. Make an impromptu gesture and the unwary might have bought a Picasso, it was feared. The auctioneers laid more emphasis on the investment value of art, and they deployed capable people to explain the significance of the terminology and the practices. Thus, they helped to reassure a new breed of art investors.

17.4 Purchasing art and antiques

17.4.1 Quality and provenance

The consensus of expert opinion is that the buyer should be concerned with the features which establish a work as one of quality. The condition of a painting, for example, is an important factor, as is its provenance, that is, its origins and history. An investor who acquires a work (which he plans to hold for some years before disposing of it, possibly in an overseas market) will want to make sure in advance that its ownership, authenticity and quality are established beyond reasonable dispute, and that it is marketable.

When negotiating to buy an asset, the investor will therefore need to go further in his investigations than would be necessary merely to check that the vendor has a good title to the piece. The research carried out into the history and previous ownership of the work should also indicate clearly the probability that it is a genuine item. A bill of sale which includes a full dossier of the purchase will be helpful both for the purposes of an inventory of assets and an eventual disposal. Preferably, the dossier will be endorsed by valuers of repute who will be in a position at some time in the future to verify the statements made.

These precautions are advisable for several reasons. Basically, they provide the buyer with evidence that the vendor has a good title to the piece. Equally, the research is important because there are frauds and forgeries in the alternative investment market, as well as reproductions and restorations which can be difficult to distinguish from the genuine article. Occasionally, the forgery may turn out to have a high value in its own right, but on the whole the investor will need to take due care that the authenticity of the work has been verified. It is also important to bear in mind that certificates may be counterfeited.

17.4.2 Fakes and forgeries

Dealers and auction houses take steps to reduce the risk of forgery and mistaken identity. Some offer the buyer a five-year guarantee against forgery. Because the largest houses trade in volume and compete intensively for material, they can sometimes be an unwitting conduit for fakes, particularly in ill-documented but now increasingly expensive areas of art. In sectors of the market where fakes are relatively common, some will inevitably turn up at auction; and where the rewards can be measured in millions of dollars, fakes will breed.

One growth area for forgery has been the work of the Russian avant-garde—Rodchenko, Popova, Larionov, Lissitsky, Malevich. As a result of perestroika, works by these artists are coming on the market in some quantity. Prices are moving up, and authentication is difficult. Some scholars believe that one recent sale included two outright fakes ascribed to Liubov Popova and one dubious picture, badly restored. According to reports, doubts about the authenticity of these works were voiced to the auction house, but its staff disagreed and the sale went ahead.

17.4.3 Choosing an adviser

When making a purchase, it usually helpful to have details in a dossier about the artist to whom the piece is ascribed. In the art market, for instance, it is common to use the names of artists to denote works 'in the style of' a particular painter, or paintings by unidentified members of a school associated with a famous artist. Therefore, not all paintings listed in an auction catalogue under the name 'Manet' will be by that painter; and it is important for buyers to appreciate the esoteric distinctions employed by the specialists in auction houses to indicate the provenance of a work. Ideally, those chosen to advise should have a wide knowledge of the field. Thus, a specialist offering guidance on the purchase of works of art should also be able to direct its installation, placement and maintenance.

He or she should have a background in art history, curatorial experience, an intimate knowledge of the art market, and up-to-date familiarity with trends in prices and values. In addition, care should be taken to check that the adviser has a good understanding of handling, shipping, conservation, restoration, insurance and security. Curators of art galleries and museums will sometimes indicate formally which dealers specialise in particular areas.

17.4.4 Exporting art

There are further precautions which the intending buyer of art or antiques should keep in mind. Suppose, for instance, that the plan is to send an item out of this country; authorisation may be needed. Among artifacts more than 50 years old, paintings valued at over £30,000, other antiques worth over £20,000, and arms and armour worth over £5,000 will require an open general export licence before they are removed from the UK. For photographs, the age limit is 60 years and the minimum value, £400. A specific export licence, as opposed to an open general export licence, will be needed when sending historic manuscripts, documents and archives of any value out of the country.

In practice, licence applications have to be accompanied by a black-and-white photographic copy of the item; and the decision whether or not to permit export will be influenced by independent advice. Where the item is regarded as part of the national heritage the issue of a licence may be delayed or refused on the advice of experts in the field. The procedures may include reference to the Office of Arts and Libraries' Reviewing Committee on the Export of Works of Art. It bases its decisions on the answers to three main questions:

(1) Is the object so closely connected with the country's history and national life that its departure would be a misfortune?
(2) Is it of outstanding significance for the study of some particular branch of art, learning or history?
(3) Is it of outstanding aesthetic importance?

In the past many licence applications have been made; few have been rejected. For example, in one recent year, 6,550 applications were made for export licences with a total value of £963m: only 24 failed to receive approval, subject to an offer to purchase at a specified price being made by a public collection in the UK within a reasonable time.

It is prudent to bear the requirement in mind when deciding to acquire a work of art or an antique of exceptional interest. When these items come onto the open market some foreign buyers may be deterred by the inconvenience and delays of up to seven months in the review procedure, and by the inherent risk that their offer will merely represent the buying-in price for a domestic museum. The absence of such foreign buyers could mean lower bids and less attractive gains when the time comes to dispose of the item.

17.4.5 National heritage bodies

The National Gallery

The National Museums of Scotland

The Ulster Museum

The National Trust for Places of Historic Interest or Natural Beauty

The Historic Buildings and Monuments Commission for England

The Trustees of the National Heritage Memorial Fund

The Historic Churches Preservation Trust

Any local authority (including National Park authorities)

Any university or university college in the UK

Any museum or art gallery in the UK which exists wholly or mainly for the purpose of preserving for the public benefit a collection of scientific, historic or artistic interest and which is maintained by a local authority or university in the UK

The British Museum

The National Museum of Wales

The National Art Collections Fund

The National Trust for Scotland for Places of Historic Interest or Natural Beauty

The Friends of the National Libraries

The Nature Conservancy Council

Any government department (including the National Debt Commissioners)

Any library the main function of which is to serve the needs of teaching and research at a university in the UK

Any other similar national institution which exists wholly or mainly for that purpose and which is approved for the purpose by the Commissioners of the Inland Revenue

17.5 Characteristics

17.5.1 Prospects of capital appreciation

Can alternative investments be justifed by private investors or by trustees and fund managers with powers to buy fine art or antiques? Essentially the question is whether the capital appreciation over a period of say, ten years, twenty-five years or even longer, will warrant the temporary diversion of funds and the expenditure incurred in holding the asset.

Frequent reports in the press of record-breaking prices paid for pieces at auction may seem to support the case for alternative investment. In 1989, some ten-year and twenty-year investments paid handsome dividends. The increasing number of investments which have provided significant capital appreciation short-term, also represents an interesting trend, that helps to endorse the advocates' case for buying arts and antiques.

Their counsel to both private and institutional investors is to buy the best examples that can be afforded and to take expert advice from a reputable dealer or appraiser. They suggest that an artist's early work will, in general, be less valuable than later, more mature, examples.

Reasonably enough, they also point out that prices can fall, as happened with Georgian silver after a boom in the 1960s, with nineteenth century fine art in the mid-1970s, and with many categories of art and antiques in the early 1980s.

17.5.2 Art as investment

A further characteristic of the alternative investment market is its appeal to investors who are nervous about the future. Some of the assets described are low in weight, small in size, and high in value: they are portable, concealable and readily negotiable in markets around the world. Those who fear political, economic, social or tax repression in their own countries tend to regard alternative investments as a means of safeguarding their wealth.

There are occasions when works of art and antiques do seem to meet demanding investment criteria. As a case in point, the Antique Collectors Club has reported that the value of furniture bought through dealers or at auctions has been rising. According to their figures, prices paid for these antiques between the end of the 1960s and the late 1980s rose by more than twice the Financial Times 500 Share Index, (after adding 4 per cent per annum for dividends). Even taking dealing cost into account the rise in values has been appreciable.

On the other hand, there is anecdotal evidence to make enthusiastic bidders at auctions cautious. According to one press report, a battle tableau by Ernest Meissonier, a much-favoured painter of a century ago, sold in London in 1892 for £20,700; again in 1913 for £6,300; and again in 1964 for £4,340. Lazare reports that John Singer Sargent's oil sketch *San Virgilio* sold for £7,350 in 1925 and just £105 in 1952. A scholarly study of London art auction transactions between 1652 and 1961 found that the average work appreciated just half a per cent a year—a poor return in anyone's passbook.

To set against these warning illustrations, there are some promising examples of the gains to be made. Paintings by the Scottish Colourists—S J Peploe, J D Fergusson, Frances Cadell and Leslie Hunter—have shown an average annual appreciation rate of 19 per cent from 1975. Similarly, Renoir's *Tête du Femme* was sold for £1.35m in 1987 and exchanged hands again in 1988 for £1.98m (an appreciation of 47 per cent in one year).

17.5.3 Costs of ownership

Typically, rates of return are only attractive if the owner is prepared to put a value on the pleasure of holding such works of art in his home or at his place of work. The investment may also be justified if the money used for the acquisitions would have been taxed at a high rate. Conversely, some items could have been a poor investment for the buyer, after taking into account outlays to meet insurance premiums, dealers' or auctioneers' commissions, any liability to capital taxation, the interest foregone, and security and maintenance costs.

The lack of income flows, means that the buyer of alternative investments is dependent on capital appreciation; yet he has to deduct the following costs from any gains he may achieve:

(1) costs of acquisition and disposal, including premiums and dealers' commissions;
(2) holding costs (insurance, storage, etc);
(3) valuation fees incurred;
(4) Revenue and possible tax benefits foregone by tying up capital in the asset;
(5) the value of time spent learning about the market and, increasingly, the advice of market experts or consultants;
(6) capital gains tax payable on realisation of the asset, or inheritance tax payable on its transfer.

Substantial gains are necessary to justify such an investment; or, alternatively, the investor has to be convinced that the assets he acquires can be relied upon to sustain their worth in times when traditional investments fail.

17.5.4 Malbin collection

An instructive example of one collector's approach came to light at the Sotheby's sale in May 1990 of collages by Enrico Prampolini, a little-known Italian artist. They commanded up to eight times the auction house's high estimates. The works formed part of the Malbin collection of modern art. Another piece sold from this collection was a Ferdinand Leger of 1913, *La Femme au Fauteuil*. Sotheby's believed a buyer would pay £6m to £7m. A Swiss buyer actually paid £4.5m.

This short-fall was exceptional. The Malbin collection totalled £40.4m, just below Sotheby's upper band estimate of £40.6m, and sold all but two of the 93 lots offered. Sophisticated collectors eagerly vied for Cubist, Dadaist, Expressionist, Surrealist and, most significantly, Italian Futurist works that had not been on the market for years. They carried the cachet of the late Lydia Winston Malbin, a perspicacious collector (aged 91 on her death in October 1989), who was the daughter of the Detroit architect, Albert Kahn.

Art and antiques 337

17.5.5 Independent sources of information

An independent source of information on the prices of paintings is the Art Sales Index. This lists the results of auctions for about 60,000 items each year which were sold for £150 or more. Using this source, an analysis has been made of transactions of a representative selection of 20th century modern masters. The analysis shows a compound rate of appreciation in excess of 14 per cent per annum since 1971. Such rates of growth make it easier to argue the case for the allocation of funds to alternative investments.

The growth of interest which has already taken place has prompted the development of improved sources of information on available media, prices and the advantages and limitations of particular types of investment. There are already computerised databases providing information to help determine sound investments. 'Artquest' provided by the Art Sales Index, holds details on paintings, drawings and sculptures which have been sold at public auction around the world. The gradual evolution of a more or less formal infrastructure of information sources in the alternative sector of the investment market will add to the understanding of which areas have potential growth and prospects.

Another guide to the way art pieces are moving is Sotheby's Art Index, re-launched late in 1981 and now based on a mass of information which is used to determine trends in the value of various categories of objects. The information is published *inter alia* in Sotheby's *Art Market Bulletin*.

These sources and others tend to show that the average annual appreciation over the past 40 years has tended to outstrip the rate of inflation, although there has been considerable volatility from sale to sale.

17.6 Taxation

17.6.1 Tax planning

It is equally prudent for the investor to plan so that he can properly avoid situations in which unnecessary tax liabilities could be incurred. For instance, if the investor eventually wishes to contend that isolated purchases are for the purpose of building up assets as long-term investments, then it may be prudent—indeed mandatory—to record the acquisition of chargeable assets in his tax returns. This step would help to support a claim that capital gains rather than income tax should be the basis for calculating any future liabilities when, despite the parity of the rates of tax, there are advantages in doing so for the individual taxpayer.

The private investor also may be faced with claims by the Inland Revenue that purchases and sales of alternative investments are adventures in the nature of a trade. This would lead to an income tax liability if the investor is held to be carrying on the trade on his own account, or to a corporation tax liability if he has set up a company for the purpose.

17.6.2 Capital gains

Alternative investments are subject to the general law on capital gains tax, although there are special exemptions. In broad terms the amount of the chargeable gain is the difference between the cost of the asset and the sale proceeds, less an adjustment for the inflationary element of the gain accruing since March 1982. For any asset held on 31 March 1982, there is the opportunity to base the cost of acquisition at its market value at that date. There is however no charge on unrealised gains on assets held by an individual at his death.

Special considerations apply in the case of works of art and other alternative investments. Thus, a gain accruing on the disposal of an asset which does not exceed £3,000 is generally exempt from capital gains tax with marginal relief (see Capital Gains Tax Act 1979, s 128). In this connection the exemption on articles which provide a gain of not more than £3,000 (for instance, individual pieces of antique silver) would become particularly relevant.

There are also exemptions in relation to individual objects of artistic, historic or scientific interest (and collections of such objects) which are accepted by the tax authorities as forming 'an integral and major part of the cultural life of this country'. These are often referred to as 'national heritage property'. Under the 'douceur' arrangements (referred to below), gifts of such alternative investments to national heritage bodies (and gifts of alternative investments to charities) are not charged to capital gains tax. In the case of sales, the notional capital gains tax liability will be one of the factors relevant in calculating the sale price that can be negotiated. There is a similar exemption applying to gifts of qualifying heritage property made for the public benefit.

Where national heritage property (accepted as such by The Commissioners of the Inland Revenue) is transferred by way of gift from one individual to another, or where such property is transferred into or out of settlement, the transfer will be treated for capital gains tax purposes as giving rise neither to a gain nor to a loss, provided that appropriate undertakings are given with regard to location, preservation and access. This means that any gain is carried forward to be charged at such time as the donee disposes of the property in a manner which does not qualify for conditional exemption.

17.6.3 Capital transfer

Capital transfer tax was introduced in the 1975 Finance Act. It applies to lifetime transfers of value made after 26 March 1974 and before 18 March 1986. Inheritance tax applies after 19 March 1986. Lifetime transfers are cumulated over seven years and tax is not charged unless transfers exceed a total of £118,000. Lifetime transfers are then charged at half the rate applicable to transfers made on, or within three years, of death. This tax is not charged on transfers between spouses domiciled in the UK, or on the first £3,000 of lifetime transfers which a person makes in any one tax year.

Specifically, the objects eligible for exemption are 'any pictures, prints, books, manuscripts, works of art, scientific collections or other things not yielding income which appear to the Commissioners of the Inland Revenue to be of national, scientific, historic or artistic interest'. If a claim for such exemption is accepted, the effect is to postpone capital transfer tax liability 'while the articles remain in the family', although rising values could make it imprudent to delay payment in this way.

The system can be illustrated by the example of a man who inherits a picture of national heritage quality from his mother, where he is able and willing to give undertakings about preservation and access. 'Reasonable access' to the public will normally mean that the room in which the object is displayed is open to the public for a reasonable number of days a year, or that the object is loaned on a long-term basis for public display—in both cases with appropriate publicity. No such tax would then be payable on the picture as part of his mother's estate.

If the investor decides to part with the picture, his liability to pay the tax will depend on the method of disposal he chooses. No capital transfer tax is payable if he gives the picture away to an individual or organisation prepared to renew the undertakings on maintenance and public access. In a similar way, he will avoid this capital taxation if he gives the work to a national heritage body.

Suppose, instead, he sells the picture by private treaty to a national heritage body. In these circumstances the value of the tax exemption is shared between the vendor and the purchasing body under an administrative arrangement known as 'douceur', which is approved by the Commissioners of the Inland Revenue. Under such arrangements the vendor and purchaser would negotiate the market value of the object and then deduct the tax which would have been payable, if the object was sold for that price on the open market. The vendor would receive the net sum together with a proportion of the notional tax (approximately 25 per cent for objects, subject to negotiation), and the purchasing body would get the benefit of the balance of the notional tax by paying less than the estimated market price.

The investor may also offer the picture to the government in satisfaction of some other tax liability on some other transfer. The standard of objects which can be accepted is very much higher than that applicable for conditional exemption. To qualify, objects have to satisfy a test of 'pre-eminence' either in the context of a national, local authority or university collection. The amount of the tax which will be payable will be calculated on the same basis as for a private treaty sale to a national heritage body, except that douceur is fixed at 25 per cent for objects.

If, on the other hand, the owner of the picture sells it on the open market, or gives it to someone who does not renew the undertaking on maintenance, preservation and access, then full capital transfer tax will be payable. The amount due will be the capital transfer tax which was not charged on the picture when he inherited it, but calculated on the sale price and not on the value at the date of inheritance. (If the picture has increased in value, capital gains tax will be payable on that gain in value and the amount of that tax will be deducted from the sale price for the capital transfer tax calculations although not statutorily binding.) If the picture is given to someone who does not renew the undertaking, then the Commissioners of the Inland Revenue's view is that capital transfer tax would also be payable on the gift of the picture, with the proviso that 'one lot of tax can be set off against the other'.

It should also be noted that three months' notice is now required from owners of objects exempted after 1 September 1982 who intend to sell on the open market. Notice in writing must be given to the Museums and Galleries Commission, 7 St James Square, London SW1 4IU. If the work of art is sold without giving this notice, problems can arise at a later stage if an export licence is sought, as the government has powers to withhold an export licence indefinitely where the requisite notice has not been given correctly.

In 1985, the Inland Revenue announced a concession relating to capital transfer tax on foreign-owned works of art. Where a work of art, normally kept overseas, becomes liable to capital transfer tax on the owner's death solely because it is physically situated in the UK at the relevant date, the liability will be waived—by concession—if the work is brought into the UK solely for public exhibition, cleaning or restoration. This concession also extends to works of art held by a discretionary trust.

More generally, the key to bringing capital transfer tax assessments on alternative investments down to a fair level is professional valuation by an appraiser in close touch with current market trends. Valuers normally charge on a scale basis and are liable professionally for their appraisals. A typical rate is 1.5 per cent on the first £10,000, 1 per cent on the next £40,000 and 0.5 per cent thereafter. It is, however, possible to negotiate valuation fees and some appraisers may be prepared to waive some or all of their fee entitlement if a work is sold through their firm within a reasonable period.

The professionals concerned with alternative investments also recommend owners to plan in advance for future capital transfer tax liabilities. They have in mind making full use of the annual exemptions in respect of gifts. Where the lifetime transfer takes the form of an alternative investment, the valuation will be carried out at that time.

17.6.4 Inheritance tax

Inheritance tax replaced capital transfer tax with effect from 18 March 1986. It was introduced in the 1986 Finance Act and applies to gratuitous transfers by individuals. The major difference between capital transfer tax and inheritance tax is the treatment of lifetime transfers. Outright transfers between individuals are exempt if the transferor lives on for seven years. Gifts made within seven years of death are charged at death rates, but the charge is tapered where the gift occurs more than three years before death.

The charge on death is retained within inheritance tax and most of the exemptions and relief available under capital transfer tax, including transfers between spouses domiciled in the UK. Trust related transfers remain subject to the full range of charges, at the time the transfers are made. The cumulation period for all chargeable transfers has been reduced to seven years and the threshold below which tax is not chargeable is £118,000. A flat rate of 40 per cent will now replace the former four-rate system.

Estate duty applies to property inherited before 13 March 1975. This may still be relevant to the sale of objects which have been previously exempted from estate duty. Estate duty will not be charged if exempted objects are sold by private treaty to a national heritage body or have again been transferred on a death and have been conditionally exempt on that occasion. Special rules apply when property which has previously been exempted is sold after 6 April 1976. The way in which this property is taxed, depends on what had happened since the original exemption was granted—either capital transfer tax or inheritance tax or estate duty only be payable. This is a complex issue and is dealt with fully in Appendix III (page 46) of *Capital Taxations and the National Heritage*. See bibliography at the end of Chapter 18.

17.6.5 VAT

HM Treasury has produced The Value Added Tax (Works of Art etc) Order 1983 (SI No 809) which exempts from VAT disposals of works of art and other objects (including manuscripts, prints and scientific objects), which are of national, scientific, historic or artistic interest, or which have an historical association with a particular building. To qualify for exemption, these heritage objects have to be disposed of by private individuals in the course of business either as private treaty sales or gifts to one of the approved list of public galleries and similar institutions or in settlement of tax debts under the 'douceur' arrangements. This change is also now incorporated in the Value Added Tax Act 1983, Schedule 6.

On 1 January 1986 a new harmonised system of customs duty and temporary importation reliefs came into effect under the Value Added Tax (Temporarily Imported Goods) Relief Order 1986 (SI No 1989). The relevant HM Customs & Excise Notices are 361 and 712. The latter is a new information 'package' about the VAT second-hand scheme for works of art, antiques and collectors' pieces (mainly for dealers in fine art and antiques who are VAT-registered). The new regulations apply to works of art brought in primarily for exhibition but later sold. VAT leaflet 701/36/86 also contains guidance on the insurance of second-hand goods such as works of art.

17.6.6 Stamp duty

Stamp duty will normally be payable only when the transfer is of interest in an alternative investment, and not when it is the work itself which is being transferred, since chattels are transferable by delivery and no document is required to effect a transfer of the interest.

17.7 Mechanics

17.7.1 Suitability

Research on individuals' investment preferences indicates that works of fine art and antiques only begin to figure to a significant extent in the portfolios of the wealthy. Initially, investors concentrate on property, building society investments, insurances, unit trusts or investment bonds, and possibly equity investments or gilts or National Savings certificates.

Thus the more esoteric investments tend to be bought when extra capital is available. Neither individuals nor pension funds have so far engaged in the purchase of alternative investments as a routine policy, although British Rail Pension Fund was, at one time, an exception; the Fund invested approximately £40m in about 2,000 works of art, but its trustees and managers subsequently decided not to make any more purchases in this market.

In November 1988 the BR Pension Fund disposed of 31 museum-worthy pieces of silver for £2m having paid £400,000 for them ten years ago. In 1989, the Fund sold paintings and sculptures, including works by Manet, Renoir, Monet, Picasso, van Gogh and Cézanne. Altogether the items put on sale realised £38.5m, leaving the pensioners with more than £30m after paying all expenses and commissions. A spokeman for the Fund commented, 'Generally, it was much better than we had a right to expect. It means a cash return of about 20 per cent per annum, and a real return (after inflation) of 12 per cent per annum.'

In general, pension fund investment managers see a problem in the marketability of such assets. It is not easy to convert alternative investments into cash at short notice without sustaining losses. In addition, pension fund trustees and investment advisers are cautious about committing themselves to a line of action which might be criticised in the future.

Trustees and investment advisers say that it is difficult to obtain accurate valuations on a regular basis and, even when valuers can supply a reliable service, there are few reliable and independent indices bases on which to compare their portfolio's performance, as with equities. There is also a lurking suspicion that funds should not be invested in areas which are regarded as unsuitable for investors who need income, and which cannot readily be converted into cash.

On the other hand, the infrastructure for making alternative investments is gradually being established; and in the course of the next few years there may be improvements in the information sources and the indices available to investors and trustees. The improvement of the information facilities and the build up of reputable sources of impartial market intelligence will help to make alternative investments more respectable—both for individuals and for investment managers with responsibilities for closed funds such as small self-administered pension schemes.

17.7.2 Sources of information

For the moment the sources of information and intelligence are diverse and scattered. There are, in each of the areas of alternative investment, several specialist journals and often societies or clubs exist which give the collector access to specialist knowledge. Auctioneers produce useful catalogues which highlight pieces coming onto the market; and those interested can find out about the prices paid at these sales.

The specialist journals and some of the directories produced by associations of dealers and auctioneers identify the areas in which particular firms are knowledgeable. The dealers will usually charge high commissions to cover their costs of holding expensive assets for periods, which can sometimes be prolonged, before a buyer emerges. Auction sales are, on the whole, a source of more competitively priced items, although many of the leading London firms now charge a commission to both vendors and buyers.

It is, however, becoming more difficult for the private collector to keep pace with developments in his chosen fields of alternative investment. Although London remains an important centre of trading activity in art and antiques, many important sales are nowadays being held outside the UK, which has become a net exporter of such pieces. In earlier times, collectors could rely on a steady flow of fine works.

17.7.3 Advisers

In recent years the established London firms have been experiencing parallel competition in specialised fields from provincial dealers and auctioneers. Consequently, to keep abreast of news and intelligence on alternative investments today, requires a complex web of contacts and information sources. In this context, it is important to locate one or two of the specialists among the dealers and in the auction houses who can be relied upon to assist the enthusiast.

To a degree, investors seeking advice on specific pieces can depend upon appropriate museums or art galleries, where curators are normally willing to give an opinion on the quality and authenticity of a work. Curators are also likely to be familiar with the market, or dealers who specialise in a sector, although they are usually reluctant to be seen to recommend a particular firm. Curators will not normally give opinions on market values.

Leading auctioneers are more willing to express a view on the price a piece might command if offered for sale and specialist dealers will also have an opinion on the value of an item in their field of expertise. Such valuations are important if the investor plans to make a sale; they will help him to arrive at a sensible reserve figure.

Dealers and auctioneers are generally keen to offer help, in particular to itemise and appraise assets. At the outset, the valuers will advise on insurance cover and the security of precious items, pending sale. They will then prepare a full inventory of the chattels, identify those which are of value and make arrangements for the disposal of the residue. Any gifts or bequests will also be valued for inheritance tax purposes; and recommendations will be made on the handling of any works which have national or historic interest. The experienced auctioneer or dealer will also advise on how best to sell items for disposal. Given that the market for art and antiques has become international, it is important to choose with care a time and a place when specialist collectors are likely to be at a sale.

The valuer will charge a fee, and the auctioneer or dealer will be thinking of a commission on sales. Before confirming instructions for an inventory and appraisal, it is advisable to discuss the eventual consignment contract for an estate which may include important pieces. Some firms in the art and antiques market will refund part of their valuation fee if any of the items they appraise are sold through their auction or dealing rooms within a year or so of the appraisal. There may also be opportunities to negotiate lower commission rates on sales. Within the trade, auctioneers and dealers are often prepared to cut their selling commission from 10 per cent to 6 per cent, and there is certainly scope for reductions in standard rates when the estate is large and valuable.

A further point to bear in mind when negotiating commission rates is the possibility that an item at auction may not reach the reserve price suggested by the valuer. In some instances, the auctioneer may be willing to make no charge to the vendor, or levy a reduced commission, if a lot fails to sell at the reserve which the firm has recommended. Auctioneering and dealing in art and antiques are highly competitive businesses and many firms are willing to consider special terms when an estate contains a number of worthwhile items.

For buyers who use the services of dealers there are often the attractions of 'buy-back' offers. These usually have many caveats attached to them. The dealer may undertake to buy back his valuation at the time of the re-purchase; or he may only be willing to commit himself to buying back at the original price paid by the investor. Almost no dealer is willing to purchase at the original price plus inflation since the date of the transaction; and, if any do make such an offer, the buyer might well consider it prudent to make such checks as he can that the firm is likely to be still in business at a future date when a re-sale might be contemplated.

The professionals who advise on alternative investment can also help when it comes to reviewing a portfolio. To offer sound advice, they should be in close touch with the market trends, so that they can recommend optimum times for the disposal of pieces which have reached a current peak in value. Equally, they should be well placed to identify pieces coming onto the market which would make a collection more representative and therefore more valuable in terms of the chosen theme.

17.7.4 Commercial galleries

New collectors may not necessarily understand the more recondite points of aesthetics when collecting art, but they are often keenly aware of the financial implications. They are also conscious of the social benefits of being a part of the collecting 'realm', and the prestige of owning museum-calibre works. In this context, one American dealer offers a useful checklist for those entering the art market for the first time:

'Use the expertise of dealer-owned galleries which represent the artists they exhibit. Ask for biographical materials on the artists. Seek advice from individuals in the art industry.

'Let the dealer know which artists you are interested in, so you can be notified of exhibits or new works. This way you'll get first-hand, fresh information and will likely be placed on a special list for private preview showings.

'Galleries don't always display everything they have either. Ask gallery owners to show you their "backrooms" and remember to ask questions. Galleries often present themselves as quiet enclaves, but staff ought to be knowledgeable and helpful.

'Dealers seldom give what is called a "collector discount" to occasional buyers. In major centres, it's not uncommon for dealers to discount up to 10 per cent. That's because most works are marked up substantially to take price negotiations into account.

'Whenever possible, view a one-person exhibition to see several pieces of an artist's work. This will help you see the depth of an artist's vision and quality of work.

'If you see a piece that strikes you, go for it. If you need a companion's approval or review by a trusted adviser, most dealers will hold it for you for 24 hours. This will give you right of first refusal—and time to think.'

Commercial galleries normally put on three kinds of exhibition: one-person shows, theme shows, and exhibitions from stock. Galleries tend to show from stock at the quieter times of year. From the standpoint of the exhibitor, the one-person or theme show is the best way to achieve the preferred effect: they allow the gallery to suggest the cultural significance of an artist's work. A few galleries can put on first-class exhibitions from stock because their backroom holdings are strong. They are able to mount exhibitions of acknowledged masters, or works that can reasonably be described as 'museum-quality'.

Some of the galleries and dealers are promoting art and antiques as alternative investments, because they believe there are worthwhile opportunities to plan and manage portfolios. They contend that the investor can specialise in one or two categories of investment but still spread the risks by diversifying the selection within these categories. In addition, they suggest that it is possible to use market intelligence and research to time purchases and sales to maximum advantage and to build up interest among potential bidders.

17.8 Maintenance

17.8.1 Safeguarding the investment

The prime consideration in the mind of the investor who buys works of fine art or antiques ought to be security. Theft, accidental damage, fires, floods and other catastrophes remove many works from the market each year, usually forever.

The immediate conclusion is that a purchase should be held safely. For economic reasons, a bank vault may be considered when items are not continuously on display. Even when the items are bulky, the cost of hiring vault space will be far lower than the valuation and subsequent insurance premiums for pieces held in less secure places. In other cases, the collector's pieces should be insured against all risks, and the items in a collection should be revalued at five-yearly intervals, or more frequently, to ensure that the insurance cover is adequate.

17.8.2 Insurance

Brokers and insurance companies who carry out these valuations with the aid of expert dealers or auctioneers will at the same time advise on means which will ensure that a collection can be protected by cost-effective outlays on security measures—cost-effective in the sense that they bring more than compensating savings in premiums. The valuers will, in particular cases, photograph pieces in a collection to provide a record in case of damage or theft.

A point to note is that the London head offices of insurers charge travelling and subsistence expenses, so it is usually sensible to contact the nearest regional office. However, if the item is a particularly specialised work of art, it may be advisable to consult fine art brokers. They may advise that it is unnecessary to insure well-known items against theft, giving substantial savings in premiums, on the grounds that any subsequent disposal by the thief in the art market would lead to his capture. By and large burglars usually avoid stealing such items, unless they already have a buyer or can realise the value of precious metal or gemstones from which an antique is made.

A collector may also wish to put his art or antiques on show. This can present problems. As values shoot up, it can be difficult to insure valuable exhibits. When the Metropolitan Museum of Art's show 'van Gogh at Arles' was being planned in the early 1980s, it was assigned a global value for insurance of about £1bn. Today it would be £5bn, and the show could never be done. In the wake of the May 1990 sales, every van Gogh owner wants to believe his painting is worth £50m and will not let it off the wall if insured for less. Even then, the problem is compounded by enthusiastic dealers or auctioneers: when consulted on insurance values, they may be tempted to set the maximum imaginable price on a painting to maintain the image of its market value and tempt the owner to sell.

17.8.3 Security

One of the security measures which is often overlooked is to preserve confidentiality when buying an alternative investment. News of purchases attracts those inclined to steal—a problem also faced by owners who have to allow access to the public to gain the tax exemptions referred to earlier.

In addition to tighter security, it is important with some works of art and antiques to consider the 'ambient' conditions in which a piece is to be displayed. Adverse lighting can, for instance, cause a valuable watercolour to fade, and many items of antique furniture need a suitably humidified atmosphere to survive without deterioration.

Normally, specialists in the field will advise on the best methods of preserving the qualities of a piece. They are also a useful source of information on firms which carry out restoration and repair work to appropriate standards, and on removal firms which have a good record of handling delicate and valuable pieces with due care.

17.9 Preview of the year ahead
17.9.1 The May 1990 sales

A 13-day series of auctions of Impressionist, modern and contemporary art ended in New York on Saturday 19 May 1990 with sales soaring beyond £400m. As was widely reported at the time, the auctions featured record prices for major van Gogh and Renoir works. The results confirmed that the best works of art can still command spectacular prices. Major works, like the van Gogh or the Renoir, reach extraordinary prices. The results showed that asset price inflation is far from dead. There remains a keen desire for truly important and highly decorative paintings.

On balance, it seems that the art market is very solid. It is robust, but probably could not continue its recent trajectory. A levelling-off period is seen as welcome and healthy. The market is correcting to a more realistic level, after the frenzied buying of the past few years. To be specific, the contemporary market seems due for a stronger correction or retrenchment than the better established Impressionist and modern art market. In line with this view, the auctions provided the latest evidence of a scaling back in the contemporary art market from the astronomical expectations of the last couple of years.

The sales also gave evidence that buyers are displaying greater selectivity. 'Selectivity' means that buyers will pay almost any price for a work they really want. On the other hand, they are no longer willing to bid for every poor quality painting that goes into the showrooms or on the block. In the May sales, bids tended to divide equally between those well over high estimate and those well under low estimate. In short, the 'rich' and the 'poor' were separating.

17.9.2 Japanese interest

Another important market force demonstrated its significance in the May 1990 sales. For some time the Japanese with their strong currency have been a force in the market at the big auctions; it was the department store, Mitsukoshi, which bought Picasso's *Acrobat et Jeune Arlequin* for £20.9m, a record price for a 20th century work of art. In Sotheby's and Christie's New York sales in mid-May 1990 both the Renoir and the van Gogh became the property of a Japanese businessman, Ryoei Saito, owner and honorary chairman of the Daishowa Paper Manufacturing Company. At 74, he is one of the wealthiest men in Japan. He borrowed against his company's land holdings to finance his purchases. His stated plan is to put the paintings in store for up to ten years ('for security reasons') before displaying them at the Shizuoka Prefectorial Art regional museum 100 miles west of Tokyo.

The sales supplied proof that the Japanese are the most powerful players in the art market today. Underpinning the strength of the market shown by these results are two important factors. One is the continuing vigour of Japanese demand. At the Impressionist and Post-Impressionist sales they played a major role, and account for a third of the activity in the auction room. Americans and Europeans represent the other two thirds. Leading dealers report similar experience.

Japanese collectors have bought five of the 11 most expensive paintings ever sold. Art experts attribute their strong presence to the wealth in Japan. Also, Japan has a tradition going back to the 1930s of collecting Impressionist art. Van Gogh was an artist who was an unabashed admirer of Japanese art and woodblock prints. Impressionists' notions of composition—like the flattened perspective—and colour come directly from Japan.

Japanese perception of art as an investment is expected to continue. The market's rise last year outpaced the Nikkei's 20 per cent growth. No one doubts that Japan now has the economic power to indulge its affinities. Japan imported ¥116 bn in art in 1987, ¥180 bn in 1988, and ¥280 bn in 1989—mostly from France. Many collectors in

Japan, especially corporations making the big purchases, view art as a sensible investment to add to their portfolios of stocks, bonds and properties.

They tend to buy big names largely for investment—and on a massive scale. Part of the reason has been the beneficial relationship of the yen to the dollar. The Japanese also can get unlimited credit at low interest rates from their financing sources at home. At the Sotheby's sales in May 1990, 19 works went to American buyers, 16 to European and 23 to Japanese. They dominated the Sotheby's sale of Impressionists and post-Impressionists, and paid almost £100m in an auction that totalled £155m, a record for any art sale. At Christie's on 15 May 1990 Japanese bidders came away with 25 of the 57 works sold, paying £85m in a sale that brought £145m.

In the May 1990 sales there was no abatement of the influx of Japanese investment in the art market. This is, to a degree, flight money—an escape from uncertain stock and real estate markets. There is volatility in the yen and vulnerability in the Japanese real estate market. The Japanese regard art as an intrinsically valuable financial instrument, and buyers from Japan are becoming active at all price levels.

17.9.3 Chinese interest

Another important trend affects Chinese art. For several years auctions of Chinese art have been dominated by Far Eastern buyers. According to some commentators, Hong Kong collections are being discreetly transported to London, Vancouver, and Los Angeles. When 1997 arrives, their owners can step aboard a plane, taking with them no more than hand luggage.

The Japanese have been early and discerning buyers. Until recently, they bought in the Far Eastern market through local dealers, although Sotheby's began holding sales in Hong Kong as long ago as 1973. Uncertainty over the future of the territories has sparked demand in the art market; small, delicate Ming vases now look a deal safer than the island's property.

Some sectors of the Chinese art market have increased more in value than the Impressionists. When Paul Bernat's collection was sold at Sotheby's Hong Kong, the top ten pieces went to Far Eastern buyers. A pair of Imperial ruby ground cups made £210,000—they had cost Bernat £42—with two other cups in 1946.

17.9.4 The desire to invest

The art world is experiencing revolutionary change, with 'record prices for works' big money investors and more buyers. There is also an increase in the movement of art from one buyer to the next. In the past, master works might change hands every 40 years or so. Today, it is not unusual for works to be bought and sold every five to seven years. Art is proving a sound investment because works are appreciating at record rates.

At some point, the rate at which prices rise will slow down. In the meantime, the market has become more international, with sales taking place in many locations other than New York and London. It also seems that the art market is beginning to react independently of other markets. In other words, the structure of the market has been radically changed.

17.10 Conclusion

The idea of art as investment was once thought rather sordid. Now it is widely accepted that collectors can take both pleasure and gain from a work of art—two forms of appreciation. It also seems that art will seep out of America toward Japan and Europe; and that a new era will come in which art management specialists take on responsibility for high-value portfolios. These values may be boosted still further by museums in Japan. One observer has identified 50 prefectorial, corporate, private, and municipal museums that could provide new homes for western art.

The genuine love of art is being complemented by an interest in art as an investment. This interest has caused some specialists to query whether the market will have a top limit. Bruno Frey and Angel Serna, in *Art & Antiques*, have examined the case of Yo Picasso. It was bought in 1981 for £5.83m and sold in 1989 for $47.85m—a 'real net rate of return' (after commissions, insurance costs, inflation and so forth) of 19 per cent a year. They calculated that the new owner, to break even five years ahead, would need to secure a bid of $81m, plus outgoings. And what will happen five years later?

Sources of further information

See Chapter 18.

18 Collectibles

John Myers and Valerie Bennett of Solon Consultants

18.1 Introduction

18.1.1 Collectibles as alternative investments

The fashionable urge to collect seems to extend to an ever-widening range of items with memorable, nostalgic or merely eccentric qualities—classic postage stamps, old cars, numismatic coins, Oriental carpets, banknotes, scrips, medals, vintage wines and spirits, musical instruments, playing cards, objets de vertu, bric à brac, scientific instruments, cars, and many other artifacts, including printed ephemera from bygone times. The enthusiasm for collecting such items stimulated the formation of various bodies, one of which was the Ephemera Society. It was set up in 1975 and has since built up a membership of more than 1,800 worldwide, who benefit from a lively range of activities and publications.

Despite this evidence of enthusiasm, many investors remain wary of collectibles. Caution is, of course, sensible when considering esoteric investment media, but several factors have lately made them more appealing. Many players on the stock markets have become acutely aware that equities are highly volatile. Every crash, or rumour of a crash, sends shareholders on a hunt to spread their risks.

Collectibles, which include many possibilities, seem comparatively safe refuges for spare capital. They seem unlikely to lose a quarter of their value in a single day's trading. In a period of threatening inflation, collectibles could offer a hedge against escalating prices. For many people, they warrant a small proportion of an investment portfolio.

An understanding of the field can best be illustrated by the examples in this chapter drawn from a wide range of collectable media. This review does not repeat information contained in the previous chapter on arts and antiques, and on gold and other valuables.

Collectibles do, however, have one factor in common with arts, antiques and valuables. That is, to attract those from all over the world with private wealth. Many people have astonishing sums of money with which to make worthwhile purchases. They are using their cash or borrowing power to diversify their assets, in the manner of new Renaissance merchant princes. Quality of life is their target, and they assess quality in terms of civilised styles of living. They seek a breadth of culture, and a wider consciousness of the finer experiences of life.

These nonchalant aficionados of the good life collect primarily from such motives, rather than merely speculating on the chances of a high gain. At the same time, there is an investment motivation. The buyer of an alternative investment compares an opportunity to buy a collectible with the risks involved with stocks and shares. After a substantial fall in the equity markets, he or she may see an art deco ornament or a rare musical instrument as more likely to hold its value.

A case in point was a Venini glass vase which, in the 1960s, sold through a run-of-the-mill department store at no more than £20. At a recent Geneva sale a bidder paid 176,000 Swiss francs (£70,000) for it. The glass had original qualities. Successive valuations of the few remaining examples of the piece to be offered for sale had proved inaccurate. At first, the bidder who paid £500 for one such Venini in 1978 could not find a buyer to take it off his hands at a profit. He was wise to wait: at an auction in 1984, the same vase fetched £25,000—over twelve times the auctioneer's estimate—equivalent to an annual compound rate of return of 92 per cent. In 1987, another Venini vase attracted a successful bid of £52,000. The pre-sale estimate was less than half that amount. The latest £70,000 figure was also double the auction house's estimate.

A recent Geneva sale of 20th century collectibles produced a similar result. French and Japanese dealers bid strongly for a delicately carved glass table lamp. The lamp, originally produced commercially by Daum and Louis Majorelle, and less than a hundred years old, was bought by a Japanese dealer for 1.58 million Swiss francs (£675,000). The seller had bought it about 20 years ago for less than £5,000, a compound annual rate of appreciation equal to approximately 30 per cent.

18.1.2 Collectible cars as a case in point

Classic cars offer another set of promising case studies. Some vehicles serve as 'benchmarks' for the trade. Their prices set the tone of the market. Examples include the Jaguar XK-120, and the T Series MG. American dealers cite early Corvettes and the Ford Mustang. The cosmopolitan enthusiast is keen on the V-12 Ferrari.

Well-known high quality marques of today—from BMW, Porsche and Mercedes—are also likely to prove a sound insurance against inflation, but they do require a large initial outlay. Maybe not all purchases of vintage and veteran models will be justified in monetary terms. Nonetheless, even if cars fail to appreciate as fast as hoped, their fortunate owners can perhaps gain an enjoyment dividend by driving them—subject to the laws of the land.

18.1.3 Numismatic coins as a further case

Rare coins have recently been treated almost on a par with the holding shares and bonds, and some stockbrokers (especially in the US) have recommended them to their clients as a substitute for stock market investments. The market for coins has been greatly enhanced by a wider acceptance of a grading system. Agreed methods of categorising coins according to their quality helps to structure the market for collectors and investors.

Knowledgeable players would like coins to become respectable as the basis for investment funds they are setting up. A typical scheme requires an initial tranche of capital—say £50m—to fund dealing in collectible coins. The essence of the plan is to acquire enough coins which will appreciate over a short enough period to generate worthwhile returns for the investor. A key question is how to calculate 'worthwhile'. Some coins will gain in value, others will lose. Whatever happens, the fund has to meet its overheads, which will include regular valuation of its portfolio. One analyst estimates that sets of coins will need to appreciate, on average, by more than 40 per cent to give investors a 20 per cent return. In the case of one such fund, the promoter's filings with the US Securities and Exchange Commission claim that similar types of investment company have previously achieved returns of this figure or more.

The promise of success is echoed in fresh price records at coin auctions. A Wall Street investment fund recently paid £600,000 for an 1804 United States silver dollar—a new record for a coin sold at an auction. The coin was one of only 15 known examples. The previous record price paid for a coin was for an American doubloon, dating from 1793, sold in 1979 for £250,000.

18.2 Highlights of the previous year

18.2.1 Auctions of collectibles

Similar examples of the eminently collectible appeared in a range of auction markets during 1989 and 1990. The disposal of several important book collections culminated in 1989 with the sale by Sotheby's of the first four folios of Shakespeare's works for £3.3m. The same auction house sold Audobon's *Birds of America* for £2.4m. The high prices underpin the structure of the market. Phenomenal prices abound, and prices have risen overall. Yet, ordinary buyers willing to hunt can still find collectable books at low prices.

A curious auction last year led to the sale of an unusual collectible, an Egyptian sarcophagus. It weighed three tons, and was said to date from the Old Kingdom period (2,686–2181 BC). The artifact had been in the back garden of a terraced house in north London. It fetched £46,000 at an auction of antique garden ornaments held in Cheshire by Phillips, against an estimate of £10,000–£20,000.

Photographs by Robert Mapplethorpe sold for record prices after his death last year. A shot taken in 1979 of two men clad in leather, *Larry and Bobby Kissing*, sold for a record £10,600. It outstripped the previous record for a Mapplethorpe photograph, when Sotheby's, New York, sold *Calla Lily* for £10,000.

The 1989–1990 season reverberated with records. In yet another market, silver pieces auctioned in London accumulated successful bids of £2.86m, with less than 8 per cent of the lots remaining unsold. A pair of Queen Anne wine coolers made in about 1710 by David Willaume hit the high point of the sale when they sold for £770,000, over twice the auction house's upper estimate. The wine coolers were part of an interesting group of silver objects stored in Glyn Mills Bank, Lombard Street, since 1831. The silver had lain neglected in a strong box for more than a century.

18.2.2 Auctions of automobiles and automobilia

A sale by Sotheby's in May 1990 produced a new record figure for a car sale. The automobiles and automobilia auction held in Florida attracted some of the best known collectors in the world. It made £12.52m.

The top price was £1.71m paid for a 1907 Rolls-Royce Silver Ghost Tourer, bought by a London dealer. The price was higher than the previous record for any Rolls Royce sold at auction—$2.09m in 1985 for the psychedelic car once owned by John Lennon. Other less prestigious cars have also sold for high prices during the last year. A 1966 Cobra 427, for example, sold for £160,000—a four-fold rise in value in eight years, representing a compound annual growth rate of 19 per cent. A 1959 Cadillac Eldorado sold for £40,000, a six-fold rise in five years, equivalent to 43 per cent a year compound.

In some instances prices fluctuate wildly over short periods—a May 1990 sale by Christie's in Monaco realised £8m, but only 23 per cent of the total value of cars offered was sold. The top attraction, a 1957 Ferrari 315S, expected to reach £6m in bidding, failed to sell. On the other hand, Sotheby's sold a rare Ferrari GTO a few days before in Monaco for £6.8m, topping the previous highest price paid for a classic car—the £5.5m paid for a 1931 Bugatti Royale in 1987.

Inhibiting some buyers are the national laws that prevent even fine examples of vintage or veteran cars from being driven by the proud owners. In some countries, it is illegal to drive such classic vehicles without fitting seat belts or pollution control devices—actions which would, of course, reduce the car's value.

18.2.3 Scope for creative imagination and knowledge

Last year also saw a new departure in the market for collectibles—chips off the Berlin Wall. Distributors and department stores in some countries have been keen to stock these as collectible items, priced at only $10.

Some 50 tons of material have been bought by a St Louis entrepreneur. His company acquired pieces of wall from 'a source friendly with officials in East and West Berlin'. The concrete blocks are being delivered to a warehouse in America, to be cut down and hammered apart into pieces weighing about two ounces each. Each will be accompanied with a certificate of authenticity. The ambitious intent is to chip 750,000 pieces out of its current tonnage.

Another group of entrepreneurs specialise in kitsch, or mementoes, or bric-à-brac. The souvenirs of today can be the alternative investments of tomorrow, or so the retailers argue. To today's purchaser souvenirs can be as garish as seaside postcards, and as uncouth as water-filled, shake-up, domed paper weights that snow on the Houses of Parliament. They can be as trendy as silk-screen impressions of Kew Gardens, as it was, in an autumnal breeze; or as modish as pewter replicas of Anne Hathaway's cottage kitchenware. Prices vary as much as quality, but it is certain that anyone can take a piece of London, Stratford or York home for less than $20.

The shops along the roads leading to almost any green park or attraction in central London on summer Saturdays or Sundays—and often on weekdays too—are packed with dozens of tourists and visitors to the capital, grabbing trinkets. They are buying small silver-plated spoons embedded with coats of arms, reproductions of the Magna Carta for a few shillings or pounds, or colourful postcards in five-packs. The junk of today becomes the jewel of tomorrow.

18.3 Current developments

18.3.1 Classic stamps

Prices of classic stamps escalated in the 1970s. Buyers were encouraged—some experts believe overly encouraged—to buy stamps as a hedge against inflation. Prices peaked and fell sharply in 1980, and some stamps have never again reached their over-inflated values. For fine examples of philatelic quality, the market is regaining its momentum. In the intervening period, the structure of the market has changed. Auction houses have come into the market to a greater extent, and prices have been bolstered by bids from Far Eastern collectors. Values of rare stamps are now rising at an annual rate of 15 per cent, and the specialists expect the market to remain firm in the early 1990s.

Some of the most valuable stamps turn out to be fakes. One dealer recalls a purchase of a forgery of an 1847 original—one of the first stamps issued in the United States. 'It was beautiful. The stamp wasn't done by a run-of-the-mill artist. It was produced by Speratti, a master forger. There have been volumes written on his work. People collect them and pay high prices for them.' Other forgeries among collectibles are in much less demand.

18.3.2 Rare books

Books have been collected since the times of monasteries and chain libraries. The collectors and their reasons have, of course, changed. From the Renaissance to the French Revolution books were mainly collected and used for what was in them rather than their appearance. By the time Jane Austen's novels were gaining shelf space, the nouveau riche began to see books as artifacts which granted status to their owners. Among some buyers, the appearance began to transcend the content.

The market is segmented. One sector is the 'first edition market'—a very specialised field. With some works, a book's value may depend as much on the presence and quality of its dust jacket, as the rest of its make-up. Experts cite as an instance the first printing of Scott Fitzgerald's *The Great Gatsby*. Without a dust jacket it might fetch between £30 and £250, depending on its condition. With its dust jacket, it could bring £3,000. The specialists know that some copies of the 1925 novel have a typographical error on the back of the dust jacket: a lower-case 'j' in the name Jay Gatsby. It seems that the error was initially corrected by hand, with the capital 'J' superimposed on the lower-case letter. A second, later dust jacket was printed without the error.

Inscriptions in books by the author or a famous owner, or a relation, or an influential friend of the author can also enhance values, maybe by a factor of five or even ten. The advice to collectors of rare books could easily be restated in many other fields of alternative investment: 'Buy the best of what you like. Rely on your own instinct, but work closely with knowledgeable dealers. Develop a collector's eye by looking at a large number of books. Browse in specialist shops. Search out auctions, fairs and even car boot sales.'

18.3.3 Syndicated buying of numismatic coins

Trends in American markets for numismatic coins may also point to the future of collectibles as alternative investments. In the US, coin traders have sought to create their own version of the modern stock market. The American Numismatic Exchange enables coin dealers to deal over a computer network. Through the same network, investors buy and sell as they wish. They do not have to wait for auctions and sales.

The advocates of this bourse claim that it has helped to stabilise a volatile market. The long term aim of the Exchange is to trade in coins of known and certified quality. They are seeking to securitise the collectible. If it develops as it might, the Exchange could trade in coin futures and coin options. Equally, it could extend its remit into other alternative investments where similar items matching a specified standard are traded. The Venini vases might become the Exchange's equivalent of a blue-chip investment.

Moves toward securitisation are intended to help investors. Critics of the scheme argue that coins are not equities and that the market in them bears little resemblance to share markets. In reality, coins are 'limited-edition art objects', so values tend to be set on a subjective basis. Another concern is that trading in such an exchange is largely unregulated. Dealers who oppose the concept suggest that coins lack the qualities of a liquid asset. Although it is sometimes possible to sell a coin in a day, an investor might often be delayed by weeks or, occasionally, months for the right price for a rare and valuable coin.

There are several implications of a trade mart in collectibles, such as numismatic coins. Certification and valuation would be in greater demand. Syndicates and funds could be set up to trade in certificates backed by physical assets, hedged on the Exchange. An information infrastructure could follow, as the traders and investors seek better intelligence on the fundamentals and technical performance of particular assets. Far fetched? Possibly, but informal coffee house trading years ago in the City led to the great commodity, insurance and shipping markets of today. At the time, it seemed an equally unlikely proposition.

18.4 Purchasing collectibles

18.4.1 Strategies

Collectors need to plan their strategies. Do they intend to become expert collectors, who gain thrill and pleasure out of the artifacts in which they invest? Or will they instead rely upon dealers to feed their hobbies or their alternative investment portfolios? If the latter, the player should realise that they will miss out on the social ambience of the market—the real enthusiasts will be in the know, as the dealers are.

18.4.2 Collectibles in general

In recent years, activity in the market for collectibles has increased, just as it has in the markets for art and antiques and for valuables such as gold and jewellery. Two factors help to account for the popularity of these alternative investments: changes in exchange rates, and uncertainties about the future. A further significant factor is the entry of players from countries not before on the scene.

As in markets for other alternative investments, the entrants come from the Far East, particularly from Japan and Hong Kong—both countries which are coming to have doubts about their futures, one for social, the other for political reasons. The players from these countries are taking advantage of the 'globalisation' of alternative investment markets. Improved communications, both telematic and physical, have helped to create an alternative investment village peopled by cosmopolitans.

The rapid, sometimes sensational growth; the record prices being featured in reports of sales; the apparent robustness of demand—they all tend to obscure one critical fact about all investment markets, actual and alternative. They are cyclical. As new groups of collectors emerge, they push up prices. As their demand is absorbed into the markets' infrastructures, growth rates tend to tail off, and both buyers and sellers become more selective.

Some markets are naturally cosmopolitan, some are limited by national or cultural appeal, some are restricted in their development by language. An example which crosses the boundaries of all three is the market for rare books and manuscripts. It offers many opportunities for many people. Incunabula appeal to those who value antiquity in their collectibles. A thematic set of works by a famous author may appeal to a collector who is able to read and enjoy them. An historic set of works about a great event in a nation's development may attract those with a personal interest in the subject. There are opportunities for collectors who want to pay no more than £100 for a book or a manuscript, and opportunities for enthusiasts who may be willing to bid a four, five or six figure sum.

Collectible cars

Classic cars have a more limited appeal, but remain cosmopolitan. A Porsche 959, a Ferrari F40 super car, or the Bugatti Royale may attract bidders from almost any part of the developed world. Their chances of gain can be considerable. In no more than 15 years, the value of a Bugatti Royale went up from £90,000 to £6m. The appreciation equates to a compound annual rate of 32 per cent.

The price furnace is being stoked to some extent partly by wealthy, middle-aged enthusiasts, nostalgic for the showy cars of their youth. Although this is a current fad, this market motivator could be the first to weaken. The people who collected cars from the 1920s and 1930s three decades ago are no longer buying, and others are finding that the limousines and open-tops of the era often handle like trucks when driven. As the present generation of buyers falls out of the market, demand for the vehicles popular with them is likely to decline in the same way.

The other main market firemen are the foreign buyers, whose more powerful currencies make goods bought abroad a bargain. Luxury-car lovers have helped too: faced with a £35,000 tag for a new import, many opt for what one commentator recently described as 'a chromosaurus from the 1950s' at no more than £18,000.

The most promising area in the classic car market seems to be vehicles with highly-charged engines, sports cars, and 'anything with fins from the Fifties'. The highly-charged cars include those with V8, V10, V12, V16 or larger engines. The classics for sports car lovers are old Ferraris, Jaguar XKs, Maseratis and MGs.

Intending purchasers are recommended to buy through a private transaction after placing a classified advertisement in a car magazine, or from an enthusiast who belongs to a specialist automobile club. Some experts believe that, when buying cars, auctions can be particularly hazardous. They argue that there may be little opportunity to inspect the car, and they suggest that an iron will is needed to avoid being swept away by the bidding excitement.

Another simple recommendation is not to buy a car unseen. It is advice that applies equally to many other alternative investments. Skilled salesmen may give 'cast-iron assurances that there will never be another chance to buy a car like this again, and urge the investor to send money without delay.' As a cynical commentator put it—'Two weeks later, you will find a pile of rust on your doorstep. The chance of a lifetime comes along about once a week.'

Buyers of a classic car are also encouraged to drive it. Unless it is a museum-quality machine, an ageing vehicle could benefit by being fired up to full running temperature on a regular basis. If it costs too much to insure the car for the road, the buyer is advised to change the oil periodically, to jack up the car to protect the suspension, and take other steps, such as dehumidifying the garage, to prevent deterioration.

Collectible wines

Some French wines, for example, fine vintages of Latour, have recorded an average annual appreciation of more than 20 per cent in the past 15 years. As with other alternative investment markets, it is the Japanese who are helping to sustain prices. According to one connoisseur, they are buying 'every case of Chateau Petrus they can'. It is costly: a case of the 1970 vintage is valued at £3,000. The 1954 season's product is valued at £6,000 a case.

Some specialists believe that wines can be restored. In one cited instance, in 1967 a buyer paid £425 for a double magnum of 1865 Chateau Lafite in 1967. Fourteen years later he took the bottle back to the chateau to have the bottles topped up and new corks inserted. Sold at auction after a few months, it reached £12,000 per double magnum—that is, 25 per cent a year compound. The same connoisseur believes its value in mid-1990 would be about £48,500.

18.5 Taxation

18.5.1 Tax planning

If purchases can be justified as requirements of a business—for instance, acquisitions of furniture or wall decorations for an office—investors paying high rates of tax may obtain benefits. They may be able to offset the costs of acquisitions as legitimate business expenses, but with a corresponding liability on disposal. If, on the other hand, the chattels which form the alternative investment portfolio are not regarded as income-producing, the owners will not normally be able to secure income tax relief in relation to insurance premiums or maintenance expenses.

18.5.2 Sets of collectibles

The investor may want to avoid acquiring 'a set of similar or complementary things' rather than a number of separate items which do not constitute a single set. The definition may affect future tax liabilities if the value of the set would exceed capital tax thresholds whereas the individual items would be exempt. Thus the Inland Revenue is of the opinion that a collection of postage stamps per se constitute a single set, although, in their view, the stamps of one definitive or commemorative issue would not necessarily do so.

One of the issues in the field is whether the acquisition of a set or sets of collectibles is a mere hobby or a pukka investment. Implicit in the question is whether expenses will be deductible. On balance, if the collector is in it strictly for investment and capital gains, and keeps accurate records, including purchase dates, prices, provenance, current values, then it may be possible to make a case for deducting certain expenses—insurance, relevant publications, even travel to sales and auctions. In the great majority of cases, however, the collector will be trying to create legal and tax history—in itself an expensive hobby.

When a collection is sold at auction, or after exhibition at a dealer's shop, the authorities may also be interested in the gains secured. Anyone who has purchased collectibles 'under the table', without a clean provenance, the tax assumption may find that the cost basis is zero. The gain would, therefore, be 100 per cent. The advantages of documented evidence is clear. If the authorities also take the view that efforts were being made to evade payment of tax, the legal penalties can be stiff, even if the action was naive.

18.6 Suitability and mechanics

18.6.1 Risks

An abundance of snares awaits the buyer. Markets may be thin. Collectibles can be difficult to sell quickly, and meanwhile they pay no interest. Instead they can soak up considerable amounts in insurance, storage, and maintenance. Repair and restoration can also be expensive. It might cost £60,000 to renovate a Ferrari; and only the reckless would drive it along the road. The car has a hand-formed aluminium body. If a passer-by leans against the fender it can easily dent.

Despite such costs and risks, enthusiasts may still pay massive sums for a rare vehicle. Recently, a 1936 Mercedes-Benz 500K Roadster, one of the most stunning automobiles ever built, was sold at auction for £1.6m. It was not in first-class condition. According to one report, rats had eaten through the upholstery. A butcher had left it sitting in his shed, unused, for more than 30 years. Originality means a great deal with great cars.

18.6.2 Precautions

Independent advisers who specialize in collectibles recommend that an investor should carefully check a dealer's reputation, before deciding to employ his services. They suggest that enquiries should be pursued to find out how long the dealer has been in business, and to what professional organisations he belongs.

In practice, it is also prudent to make sure that the collector fully understands what is being offered and promised. By way of illustration with coins, questions might be asked about the grade of the coin, and the backing for any guarantees. Does the dealer guarantee to buy back an investment? If so, at what prices, and on what terms. Are there, for instance, any deductions affecting buy-back warranties? Is a service charge levied?

With collectibles of any value, it may be worth seeking a second opinion on the quality and provenance of the artifact, before confirming a decision to buy. Familiarity with sales and the publications in the field will also reveal whether an asking price is in line with the market, or well above it.

18.7 Preview of the year ahead

The ideal alternative investment is, by definition, extraordinary. Suppose an artifact can be said certainly to be the only or the best of its kind in the world. Its value could be considerable. One specialist believes that leading politicians' papers are 'hot items', in investment terms. Another advocates books illustrated with coloured engravings. A third feels that Oriental rugs offer worthwhile prospects. He cited as an example a five-sided Turkoman camel trappings with an ivory background. These central Asian rugs go on the side of a camel during a wedding procession. A small one would be worth £25,000–£30,000.

18.8 Conclusion

In this field of alternative investments, the vital step is to decide whether to be an investor or a collector, or both. Those who take the trouble to understand a particular market well, and be a player, can gain the knowledge to be a specialist collector. In practice, only a limited number of people have the enthusiasm, dedication and resources to pursue the opportunities on a systematic basis. As was indicated above, any of these markets for collectibles is also a social network. The participants derive much pleasure from being involved in this network. Keeping in touch with fellow devotees is rewarding in the interchanges and in the exchanges.

The investor will quickly learn that he or she spends much time learning about the subtle connotations of hallmarks on metalware, manufacturers' symbols on ceramics, makers' names on antique clocks, the marks of well-known furniture craftsmen and many thousands of other characteristics which influence the attribution of collectors' pieces. Those for whom time is scarce will quickly recognise that they need the services of a specialist. The real collectors develop a burning fervour and could scarcely stop, even if they wanted to, or were forced to by circumstances. In essence, to be a mere investor is to miss out on the social rewards, and to enjoy only vicarious or second-hand advantages. But then collectibles are second-hand!

Sources of further information

Bibliography

Art as Investment 1984, The Economist Intelligence Unit (071 493 6711)

Sotheby's Art Market Bulletin (bi-monthly), Sotheby's (071 493 8080)

Antique Dealer & Collectors Guide (monthly), IPC Magazines Ltd

Art Sales Index (22nd edition), Art Sales Index Limited (0932 856 426)

The Guide to the Antique Shops of Britain, compiled by Rosemary Ferguson and Carole Adams, Antique Collectors Club (0394 385501)

Guide Emer (bi-annual European guide) available from Mr G Gillingham, 62 Menelik Road, London NW2 3RH (071 435 5644)

Capital Taxation and the National Heritage, The Board of the Inland Revenue, London 1986, (amended 1988)

The Ephemerist (quarterly), Ephemera Society (071 387 7723)

Inheritance Tax—A Practical Guide, B Stillerman, Kogan Page Ltd, 1989 (071 278 0433)

Inheritance Tax and How to Avoid It, Towry Law, (0753 868244)

Works of Art: A Basic Guide to Capital Taxation and the National Heritage, Office of Arts and Libraries, 1982 (071 270 5846)

Works of Art in Situ: Guidelines on In Situ Offers in Lieu of Capital Taxation, Office of Arts and Libraries, 1984 (071 270 5846)

Works of Art Private Treaty Sales: Guidelines from the Office of Arts and Libraries, Office of Arts and Libraries, 1986 (071 270 5846)

Useful addresses

Antiquarian Booksellers
　Association
Suite 2
26 Charing Cross Road
London
WC2H 0DG

Tel: (071) 379 3041

Arts Council of Great Britain
105 Piccadilly
London
W1V 0AU

Tel: (071) 629 9495

British Antique Dealers
　Association
20 Rutland Gate
London
SW7 1BD

Tel: (071) 589 4128

Ephemera Society
12 Fitzroy Square
London
W1P 5HQ

Tel: (071) 387 7723

Incorporated Society of Valuers
 and Auctioneers
3 Cadogan Gate
London
SW1X 0AS

Tel: (071) 235 2282

International Association of
 Professional Numismatists
11 Adelphi Terrace
London
WC2N 6BJ

London and Provincial Antique
 Dealers Association
535 Kings Road
London
SW10 0SZ

Tel: (071) 823 3511

Oriental Ceramic Society
31b Torrington Square
London
WC1E 7JL

Tel: (071) 636 7985

Royal Academy of Arts
Burlington House
Piccadilly
London
W1V 0DS

Tel: (071) 439 7438

Royal Fine Art Commission
7 St James Square
London
SW1X 4JV

Tel: (071) 839 6537

Society of Antiquaries of
 London
Burlington House
Piccadilly
London
W1V 0HS

Tel: (071) 734 0193

Wine and Spirit Association of
 Great Britain (Inc)
Five Kings House
Upper Thames Street
London
EC4V 3BH

Tel: (071) 248 5377

Index

Agricultural land—
  Agricultural Mortgage Corporation, 200
  borrowing, 200
  disadvantages, 201
  finance, 200-1
  generally, 186-7, 189
  highlights of previous year, 189-91
  linked investments—
    accommodation land, 205
    farm shops, 204
    garden centres, 204
    grazing sales, 205
    mineral-bearing land, 203-4
    restored excavated land, 204
    sporting rights—
      fishing, 206
      generally, 206, 207
      shooting, 207
      stalking, 207
  management, 189
  mortgages, 200
  preview of year ahead, 208
  security, 200-1
  stud farms, 209-10
  tenanted land—
    costs, 197
    death of tenant, 199, 200
    generally, 196-7
    management, 200
    opportunities, 198
    rents, 197, 199-200
    Scotland, 199, 200
    taxation, 197-8
    terms, 198-9
    valuation, 197
  vacant possession—
    advantages, 193-5
    Agriculture Improvement Scheme, 195
    generally, 191
    government policy, influence, 195
    grants, 195

Agricultural land—*contd*
  intensive livestock farming, 196
  management, 196
  premium, 197
  quality grading, 191
  rates, 196
  returns, 191-2
  taxation, 192-5
  values, 191
  see also Real property
Art and antiques—
  advisers—
    art galleries, 345
    auctioneers, 345
    choosing, 332
    commission, 345-6
    dealers, 345
    fees, 345
    museums, 345
    review, 346
    specialists, 344-5
    valuations, 345
  allocation of capital to, 323
  alternative investment, as, 323-4
  auctions—
    guarantees, 328
    loan system, 328
    services of auction houses, 330
  benefits, 324
  buy-back offers, 346
  characteristics—
    appeal as investment, 335
    capital appreciation, 334-5
    costs of ownership, 335-6
  checklist for first purchase, 346-7
  commercial galleries, 347
  confidentiality, 349
  corporate bodies, 323
  developments, current—
    auctioneers' strategies, 330
    cosmopolitan buyers, 329-30
    museum sales and purchases, 330
    prices, 329-30

Art and antiques—*contd*
  generally, 352
  highlights of previous year—
    buyers in cash, 326–7
    consumer protection, 328–9
    leveraged purchases and
      guarantees, 327–8
    market's structure, 324–5
    record prices, 325–6, 327
  information, sources, 337, 344
  institutional investors, 323
  maintenance—
    insurance, 348
    preservation, 349
    safeguarding investment, 347–8
    security, 349
  Malbin collection, sale, 336
  marketability, 343
  National heritage bodies, 333–4
  preview of year ahead—
    Chinese interest, 351
    desire to invest, 352
    Japanese interest, 350–1
    May 1990 sales, 349–50
  purchasing—
    adviser, choosing, 332
    authenticity, 331
    exporting, 332–3
    forgeries, 331–2
    guarantees, 331
    provenance, 331, 332
    quality, 331
  regulation of art dealing, 329
  suitability, 343–4
  taxation—
    capital—
      gains, 338–9
      transfer, 339–41
    douceur arrangements, 340
    estate duty, 342
    inheritance tax, 341–2
    planning, 337–8
    recording acquisition, 337–8
    stamp duty, 342–3
    VAT, 342
  trustees, 343–4

Background—
  aim, 1
  exchange control, 1–2, 20
  investment—
    adviser, 2–3, 22
    capital value, 5–6
    collective, 4
    income yield, 5–6
    inflation, hedging against, 6

Background—*contd*
  nature, 5–7
  overseas, exchange rates, 7
  policy—
    advice of specialists, 8
    balance, 7–8
    benefits, generally, 11
    borrowing, 11–12
    capital gains tax considerations,
      9–10
    commissions, 10
    diversification, 7, 8
    expenses, 10
    future, investing for, 10–11
    gearing, 11–12
    influences on, 1
    methods of investment, 11
    overseas investments, 8
    prices, buying and selling, 10
    taxation factors, 8–10
  protection, statutory, 4–5
  time factor, 6–7
  ways of arranging and holding, 5
  investor—
    categorisation, 4
    motivation, 3–4
    overseas—
      exchange control, 1–2, 20
      restrictions, 22
      taxation—
        capital gains tax, 21
        domicile, 21
        generally, 20
        income tax, 22
        inheritance tax, 21
        residence, 20
    personal factors, 4
    protection, *see* Protection of
      investor
    review, need for, 22
    trustees—
      advice, expert, 19
      authorised investments, 19
      diversification, 18
      generally, 18
      liability, provision for, 20
      powers of investment, express,
        19
      suitability of investments, 18,
        19–20
    types, 3–4
    UK—
      categorisation, 12–13
      medium-wealthy, 14–15
      small investor, 15–16
      trustees, 18–20

Background—*contd*
  wealthy, 13–14
  widows, 16–18
Business ventures—
  addresses, 244–5
  books, options on, 244
  Business Expansion Scheme—
    assured tenancy schemes, 230, 231
    generally, 214, 224–5
    individuals—
      connected with company, 226–7
      eligibility, 226–7
      qualifying—
        companies, 227–8
        investments, 230–1
        subsidiary, 227–8
        trades, 228–9
    quotation of companies, 225
    security, 225
    tax relief—
      availability, 225–6
      withdrawal, 226, 231–2
  Business Start-up Scheme, 214, 224
  dormant partnerships—
    advice, 234
    agreement, 232, 233, 234
    generally, 232
    income, 234
    liabilities, 233
    limited partnerships, 233–4
    loan creditors distinguished, 232–3
    rights, 233
    taxation, 234
  expertise, investment in another's, 239–40
  generally, 213–14
  highlights of previous year, 215
  Lloyd's membership—
    annual contribution, 238
    application, 236–7
    background, 234–5
    choice of syndicate, 237
    conditions, 237–8
    deposit, 238
    entrance fee, 238
    means test, 237
    organisation, 235
    premium limit, 238
    regulation, 236
    results, 235–6
    risk, spreading, 236
    taxation, 238–9
    Underwriting Agent, 237, 238
  plays, backing, 242–4
  preview of year ahead, 244
  private companies—

Business ventures—*contd*
  capital requirements, 215
  investment companies, 222–4
  meaning, 215
  minority holdings—
    acquisition, 216
    capital losses, 221
    dividends, 220
    liability for uncalled capital, 218
    loans, 219–20, 221, 222
    meaning, 216
    petition for—
      relief, 218
    winding-up, 217–18
    powers of minority, 216–18
    shares' transfer, 218–19, 220–1
    taxation, 220–2
  Venture Capital Scheme, 221–2
  professional advice, need, 213, 214
  racehorses—
    generally, 240–1
    ownership, 241
    stallions, 241–2
    taxation, 242
  taxation, 214

Collectibles—
  addresses, 366–7
  bibliography, 365–6
  cars—
    auctions, 356–7
    generally, 354–5
    purchasing, 361–2
  developments, current—
    classic stamps, 358
    numismatic coins, syndicated buying, 359–60
    rare books, 358–9
  Ephemera Society, 353
  generally, 353–4, 365
  highlights of previous year—
    auctions, 355–7
    creative imagination, 357–8
    numismatic coins, 355, 359–60; *see also* Gold and valuables, coins
  precautions, 364
  preview of year ahead, 364–5
  purchasing—
    cars, 361–2
    generally, 360–1
    strategies, 360
    wines, 362
  risks, 364
  taxation—
    planning, 363
    sets of collectibles, 363

Commercial property—
    capitalisation rate, 178
    generally, 177
    hi technology, 186
    industrial—
        factories, 185
        institutional criteria, 185–6
        location, 185
        warehouses, 185
        yields, 186
    investors, types, 177–8
    leases, 179
    leisure facilities, 187
    offices, 184–5
    purchases, 178–9
    rent—
        growth, 179–82
        reviews, 179
        yields, 179–82
    reverse yield gap, 178
    shops—
        generally, 182–3
        out of town, 182, 183
        ownership, 182–3
        prime, 183
        secondary, 183
        tertiary, 183
    types, 178
    valuation, 178
    see also Real property
Commodities—
    addresses, 304
    background, 289
    bibliography, 304
    characteristics, 293–4
    costs, 293
    division, 290–1
    flexibility, 293
    futures, 291–2
    highlights of previous year, 290
    investment opportunities, 292
    markets, 289
    metals, 291
    participation—
        backwardation, 298
        cash and carry transactions, 297–8
        cash metals, 296, 297
        contango, 297
        gearing, 301–2
        generally, 296
        managed funds—
            generally, 298
            private discretionary fund, 298
            public commodity unit trust, 298–300

Commodities—*contd*
    metal trusts, 297
    method, 302–3
    options, 300–1
    private trading accounts, 301–2
    physicals, 291, 292
    pre-conditions, 292–3
    preview of year ahead, 303–4
    soft, 290–1
    speculators, 292
    suitability, 295–6
    taxation—
        managed funds, 295
        options, 294
        transactions, 294
    turnover, 289

Finance Act 1990—
    businesses, 26
    capital gains tax, 23
    charities, 26
    composite rate tax (CRT), 24–5, 27
    implications, 27
    importance, 23
    income tax, 23
    inheritance tax, 24
    investments, 24–6
    savings, 24–6
    stamp duty, 24
    tax exempt special savings account (TESSA), 24, 27
    VAT, 24

Gold and valuables—
    advisers, 318–19
    background, 305
    coins—
        buying, 319
        counterfeit, 315–17
        gold, 306–7
        other metals, 307–8
        palladium, 307
        platinum, 307
        VAT, 319–20
    developments, current—
        gold internationally, 311–13
        Japan's entry into market, 313–15
        precious metals, 315
    diamonds, 308, 318
    gemstones, 308, 318
    generally, 322
    gold—
        bullion bars, 309
        coins, 306–7
        commodity market purchase, 296
        costs of ownership, 318

Gold and valuables—*contd*
  hedge, use as, 305–6
  internationally, 311–13
  mines, fraudulent sales of interests, 317
  recovery from wrecks, 318
  smuggled, 320
  suitability for investment, 317–18
  trusts, 297
  VAT, 319–20
  hedge, long-term, 305–6
  highlights of previous year—
    diamonds, 311
    gold—
      hoarded, 309
      in manufacture, 310–11
    mining shares, 309
    platinum as investment, 306
  preview of year ahead—
    limiting factors, 320
    market fundamentals, 320–1
    political changes in Europe, 321
  prices, 306, 322
  silver as investment, 306
  suitability, 318
  taxation—
    planning, 319
    VAT, 319–20

Investment trusts—
  acquisition, 130
  annual general meeting, 131
  borrowing, 125–6
  characteristics—
    capital gains, 121–2
    currency management, 122–3
    distinctive, 118
    flexibility, 118, 121
    gearing, 125–6
    income, 121–2
    overseas investment, 122–3
    risk spread, 120–1
    stock market price, 123–5
    underlying net asset value, 123–5
  constitution, 119, 120
  costs, 130, 131
  disadvantages, 118–19
  discounts, 123–4
  generally, 117, 132
  highlights of previous year, 118–19
  historical background, 117–18
  information, 120, 130
  legal nature, 119–20
  maintenance, 131
  mechanics, 130
  offshore funds, 150–1

Investment trusts—*contd*
  operation, 130
  overseas, 150–1
  pre-conditions, 120
  preview of year ahead, 131–2
  realisation of investments, 123
  split-level, 122
  suitability, 129–30
  take-overs, 124
  taxation—
    advance corporation tax, 128
    approval of trusts, 127
    withholding, 127
    approved trusts—
      capital gains, 127–8
      income, 128
      meaning, 127
    concessions, 118
    unapproved trusts, 118, 128–9
  unitisation, 123–4, 129

Life assurance—
  addresses, 268–9
  advantages, 268
  generally, 268
  highlights of previous year—
    life office taxation, 250
    new business, 247–9
    policy taxation, 250
  pension contracts, *see* Pension contracts
  policies—
    assignment, 251
    characteristics—
      regular premium policies, 254–5
      single premium policies, 255–6
    charges, 263
    commission, 264
    divisions, 251–2, 253
    encashment, 251, 256
    gifts, 251, 262
    legal nature, 250–1
    maintenance, 264
    mechanics, 264
    pre-conditions, 251
    security for loan, 255
    suitability—
      beneficiaries, 262
      companies, 262–3
      generally, 261
      investors, 261–2
    taxation—
      life company, 256–7
      non-qualifying policies, 257, 258–60
      policyholder, 257–60

374 Index

Life assurance—*contd*
    qualifying policies, 257–8, 260
    types, 252–3
    withdrawal, 254–5, 256
    preview of year ahead, 267–8
    purchased life annuities—
        characteristics, 265–6
        growth bonds, 265
        guaranteed income bonds, 265–6
        legal nature, 264–5
        maintenance, 267
        mechanics, 267
        pre-conditions, 265
        suitability, 267
        taxation—
            annuitant, 266–7
            life company, 266
    types, 247
Listed investments—
    addresses, 103–4
    bibliography, 102–3
    company fixed interest securities—
        characteristics, 86–7
        convertible stocks, 86–7
        debenture stocks, 84–5
        floating charges, 84–5
        generally, 56
        legal nature, 84–6
        loan stocks, 85
        mechanics, 88
        pre-conditions, 86
        preference shares, 85–6, 88
        safe custody, 88
        suitability, 88
        taxation, 87–8
        yields, 86
    generally, 57, 101–2
    graphs, 60–2
    highlights of previous year, 58–9
    legislation, 102
    ordinary shares, *see* Ordinary shares
    personal equity plans, 94–5
    preview of year ahead, 100–1
    public sector—
        British government stocks—
            accrued income scheme, 79
            benefits, 77
            characteristics, 76–9
            classification, 76–7
            index-linked, 78
            interest, 76
            legal nature, 75
            mechanics, 80–2
            new stocks, purchase, 81–2
            overseas holders, 79
            pre-conditions, 75–6

Listed investments—*contd*
            prices, 77–8, 79
            redemption, 76–7
            safe custody, 82
            suitability, 80
            taxation, 79–80
            timing of transactions, 78
            yield, 77
        Eurobonds, 84
        generally, 56, 83–4
        gilt-edged securities, *see* British government stocks
        local authority negotiable bonds, 82–3
        Stock Exchange, *see* Stock Exchange
    types of security, comparing—
        convenience of dealing, 64
        cost of dealing, 64
        generally, 62–3
        rate of return, 63
        security against default, 63
        tax advantages, 63–4

Minerals, 203–4

Offshore funds, 150–1
Ordinary shares—
    bearer, 89
    characteristics, 90
    dividends, 90, 91, 93–4
    generally, 56
    indexation relief, 92
    information requirements, 89–90
    legal nature, 88–90
    maintenance, 93–4
    mechanics, 93
    offers from companies—
        capitalisation issues, 99
        generally, 97
        maintenance, 100
        placing with clawback, 99
        provisional allotment letter, 99
        rights issues, 98–9
        sale offers, 97–8
        take-over offers, 99–100
    options, 95–6
    partly paid, 89
    pre-conditions, 90
    prices, 90
    rights of holders, 89
    safe custody, 93
    Stock Exchange listed, 89
    suitability, 92–3
    taxation, 90–2
    warrants, 95, 96

Index

Pension contracts—
addresses, 268–9
characteristics, 274–5
classification, 271
contracted-out money purchase (COMP) schemes, 284–5
contracting-in, 273
contracting-out—
of occupational pension schemes, 274
of SERPS, 273–4, 284
via occupational scheme, 284–5
via PPP, 278–9
free-standing additional voluntary contribution (FSAVC) schemes, 285–6
generally, 271, 287
highlights of previous year, 271–2
loans, 275, 283–4
occupational schemes—
approval, 280
benefits, 281–3
company directors, 283
contributions, 280–1
exempt approval, 280
opting out, 280
over-funding, 281
simplified, 285
taxation, 280
unapproved, 285
open market option, 275
personal pension plans—
benefits, 277–8
eligibility, 275–6
introduction, 275
tax relief, 276–7
preview of year ahead, 286–7
retirement annuity (s 226) contracts, 275, 279–80
self-administered schemes, 274–5, 284
self-investment, 284
SERPS, 272–4
State pension scheme, 272–3
suitability, 286
taxation—
generally, 275
life company, 275
types, 274
Protection of investor—
addresses, 37–8
aim, 29
background, 29
client money, 35
complaints, procedure, 35–6
framework—
authorisation, 30–1

Protection of investor—*contd*
criteria for authorisation, 31
exemptions, 31
generally, 30, 37
representative, appointed, 31
future developments, 37
intervention powers, 36
overseas aspects, 36–7
polarisation rule, 34–5
principles, 32–3
rules and regulations—
advertising, 34
breach, 36
compensation, 35
complaints, 35
conduct of business, 34
customer agreements, 35
generally, 31, 34
seeking business, 34–5
self-regulation, 29

Real property—
addresses, 210–12
camping sites, 210
caravan sites, 210
costs—
acquisition, 165–7
agents, 168
disposal, 168–9
management, 168
professional advisers, 167, 169
Scotland, 166
golf courses, 208
horse training establishments, 210
investment, as, 156–7
legal position—
generally, 157
landlord and tenant legislation, 158
protection of community, 158–9
Scotland, 157
mansion houses, 208–9
meaning, 155
mobile home parks, 210
needs, 155–6
ownership, 155
pleasure gardens, 208
rates, 159
riding schools, 208
Scotland, 155
taxation—
capital taxes, 159–63
generally, 159
poll-tax, 159
revenue taxes, 163–5
specialist advice, 159
types, 157

376 Index

Real property—*contd*
  wild life parks, 208
  see also Agricultural land;
    Commercial property; Residential
    property; Woodlands
Residential property—
  flats—
    blocks, 174-5
    let, 172-4
    management, 174
    rent, 172-3, 174
    security of tenure, 172-4
    yields, 174
  generally, 175
  highlights of previous year, 170
  homes—
    abroad, 172
    factors, 171
    holiday, 171-2
    insurance, 171
    personal, 170-1
  let houses, 172-4
  preview of year ahead, 175
  time sharing, 172
  see also Real property

Stock Exchange—
  brokers, 67, 73-4
  capitalisation issue, 72
  commission, 67, 73
  constitution, 64
  dealings—
    bearer shares, 72
    Big Bang, effect, 67
    certificate, 72
    contract note, 69-70, 72
      example, 71
    method, 67-71
    price, 69
    SEPON, 70
    settlement date, 70
    stamp duty, 73
    TALISMAN, 70, 72
    time, 69
    transfer form, 70
  dividends—
    mandate form, 72
    payment, arrangements, 72
  indices, 74
  information, sources, 74-5
  jobbers, 67
  licensed dealers in securities, 73
  market-makers, 67, 73
  markets—
    new issue, 65
    primary, 65

Stock Exchange—*contd*
  secondary, 65
  trading, 65
  overseas securities, 66-7
  regulatory role, 64-5
  rights issue, 72
  Rule 535.2, 66
  Securities and Investments Board's
    powers, 64, 73
  Securities Association, 64-5
  TAURUS, 73
  Third Market, 65-6
  TOPIC service, 69
  Unlisted Securities Market, 65-6

Tax benefit investments—
  appropriateness of investment, 105
  enterprise zone property trusts—
    generally, 114-15
    planning, later, 115
  friendly society investments, 113
  generally, 105-6, 115-16
  insurance policies, 113; *and see* Life
    assurance
  National savings—
    certificates—
      generally, 107-8
      practical aspects, 108
      review, 108
    index-linked certificates—
      comparison with TESSAs, 110
      generally, 110, 116
    yearly plan, 108-10
  pension policies, 114; *and see* Pension
    contracts
  personal equity plans (PEPs), 111-13,
    115-16
  premium bonds, 111
  school fees provision, 107
  TESSAs, 106-7, 115
Trusts, *see* Investment trusts *and* Unit
  trusts

Unit trusts—
  acquisition, 146-7
  addresses, 153
  approval of unitholders, 138
  authorisation, 134
  back to back loans, 142
  bibliography, 152-3
  borrowing, 126, 138
  characteristics—
    convenience, 140
    generally, 139-40
    marketability, 141
    professional management, 140

Unit trusts—*contd*
  risk, spread, 140
  simplicity, 140
  charges, 147–8
  dealings with units, 137
  deed, 134, 136–7, 138
  exempt, 149
  gearing, 126, 138, 142
  generally, 133
  highlights of previous year, 135–6
  historical background, 133–4
  income distributions, 140
  investments, 139
  legal nature, 136–8
  legislation, 152
  maintenance, 147–8
  meaning, 133
  mechanics, 146–7
  offshore funds, 150–1
  overseas—
    trusts, 142, 150–1
    unitholders, 139
  pre-conditions, 138–9
  preview of year ahead, 149–50
  pricing of units—
    forward, 136
    historic, 136
    information, 136
    quoted prices, 137
  property trusts—
    authorised, 152
    unauthorised, 151–2
  public commodity unit trusts, 298–300
  regulation, 133, 134
  reports, 148
  suitability, 146
  taxation—
    authorised unit trusts, 143–5
    disadvantages, 148–9
    generally, 142–3
    shareholders, authorised unit trusts, 145–6
  termination, 138
  types, 141–2
  UCITS Directive, 133, 144, 145
  unauthorised—
    property trusts—
      generally, 151
      suitability, 151–2

Unit trusts—*contd*
    trusts, 148–9
  unitisation of investment trusts, 123–4, 129
  valuation formula, 137
Unlisted investments—
  building society accounts, 50–1
  certificates of tax deposit, 52
  commercial banks, 48–9
  comparing types—
    convenience of dealing, 54
    cost of dealing, 54
    disadvantages, realising investment, 54
    generally, 53
    rate of return, 54
    realisation, ability, 54
    security against default, 53
    tax advantages, 54
  highlights of previous year, 39, 42
  local authority mortgage bonds, 48
  maintenance, 55
  National Girobank deposit accounts, 49–50
  National savings—
    bank accounts, 42–3
    capital bonds, 46
    certificates, 43–4
    income bonds, 45
    index-linked certificates, 44–5
    yearly plan, 46
  premium savings bonds, 47–8
  preview of 1991, 55
  rates of return—
    generally, 39
    table, 40–1
  tax exempt special savings accounts (TESSAs), 24, 27, 51–2, 55
  Treasury bills, 52–3
  types, 39

Woodlands—
  Farm Woodland Scheme, 202
  generally, 186–7
  grants, planting, 202
  prices, 203
  taxation, 202–3
    relief, 202
  Woodland Grant Scheme, 202
  see also Real property

Other titles in the Allied Dunbar Library

- Allied Dunbar Business Tax and Law Guide — WI Sinclair & John McMullen

- Allied Dunbar Capital Taxes and Estate Planning Guide — WI Sinclair & PD Silke

- Allied Dunbar Expatriate Tax and Investment Guide — Nigel Eastaway and Jonathan Miller

- Allied Dunbar Pensions Guide — Tony Reardon

- Allied Dunbar Retirement Planning Guide — Barry Bean, Tony Foreman & Dr Beric Wright

- Allied Dunbar Tax Guide — WI Sinclair

All of these titles in the Allied Dunbar Library are available from leading bookshops

For more information please contact: Longman Law, Tax and Finance, 21–27 Lamb's Conduit St, LONDON WC1N 3NJ Tel: (071) 242 2548

Other titles in the Allied Dunbar Library

Allied Dunbar Money Guides

- Buying Your Home — Richard Newell
- Financial Care for Your Elderly Relatives — Beverly Chandler
- Financial Planning for the Over 50s — Robert Leach
- Insurance: Are you Covered? — Mihir Bose
- Investing in Shares — Hugh Pym & Nick Kochan
- Leaving Your Money Wisely — Tony Foreman
- Making Your Job Work — David Williams
- Managing Your Finances — Helen Pridham
- Planning School and College Fees — Danby Block & Amanda Pardoe
- Planning Your Pension — Tony Reardon
- Tax and Finance for Women — Helen Pridham
- Tax for the Self-Employed — David Williams
- Your Home in France — Henry Dyson
- Your Home in Italy — Flavia Maxwell
- Your Home in Portugal — Rosemary de Rougemont
- Your Home in Spain — Per Svensson

All of these titles in the Allied Dunbar Library are available from leading bookshops

For more information please contact: Longman Law, Tax and Finance, 21–27 Lamb's Conduit St, LONDON WC1N 3NJ Tel: (071) 242 2548